INNER TRADITIONS
ROCHESTER, VERMONT

VOICES OF THE FIRST DAY

BY ROBERT LAWLOR

AWAKENING IN THE ABORIGINAL DREAMTIME

Inner Traditions International, Ltd.
One Park Street
Rochester, Vermont 05767

LIBRARY OF CONGRESS CATALOGING-IN-PUBLICATION DATA

Lawlor, Robert.
Voices of the first day : awakening in the Aboriginal dreamtime /
Robert Lawlor.
p. cm.
Includes bibliographical references and index.
ISBN 0-89281-355-5
1. Australian aborigines—Philosophy. 2. Mythology, Australian aboriginal.
3. Australian aborigines—Social life and customs. I. Title.
GN666.L38 1991
299'.92—dc20   91-26253
                                                                                    CIP

Printed and bound in the United States.

10   9   8   7   6   5   4   3   2

Distributed to the book trade in the United States by
American International Distribution Corporation (AIDC)

Distributed to the book trade in Canada by
Book Center, Inc., Montreal, Quebec

Distributed to the book trade in Australia by
E. J. Dwyer (Australia) Pty. Ltd., Sydney

DEDICATION

*To the ancient and the living spirit of the Aboriginal people
and to Joanna Lambert, whose love and deep respect for the
Australian countryside, its creatures, and its indigenous people
served as a constant guide.*

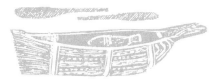

Proceeds from the sale of this book will be given to the Doonooch Aboriginal Healing Centre and to the South Australian Earth Sanctuaries Pty Ltd.

The Doonooch (native owl) Aboriginal Healing Centre, founded by Aboriginal activists Bobby and Darren McLeod, assists Aborigines to free themselves from alcohol, drug, and tobacco addiction by employing tribal healing methods and by teaching the beauty and truth of Aboriginal culture and identity. Alcohol abuse now threatens the existence of the Aboriginal people, as it does many indigenous populations throughout the world. Commenting on this world problem, Bobby McLeod has said, "The state or territory which the Aborigines must regain is the health of their minds and bodies." With that restored, their culture and its powerful relationship to their land can be reborn. The Doonooch Healing Centre is developing close ties to similar efforts by Native Americans in the United States and Canada.

The South Australian Earth Sanctuaries were founded by Dr. John Walmsley and Ms. Proo Geddes, who have worked tirelessly and independently to provide a home for Australia's endangered species.

TABLE OF CONTENTS

PREFACE
xiii

INTRODUCTION
EARTH DREAMING
1

PART ONE
IN THE BEGINNING WAS THE DREAMING

CHAPTER 1
IMAGES OF OUR ORIGINS
Darwin Meets the Dreamtime
Listening to the Seed Language
From Molecules to Redreaming Our Origins
The Archaeology of an Australian Genesis
From the Ladder into the Dreaming
14

CHAPTER 2
TIME AND SPACE IN THE DREAMING
Dreamspace
35

CHAPTER 3
DREAMING AND CREATION
How the Sun Was Made
World Creation Myths and the Dreaming
44

CHAPTER 4
COLONIZATION AND THE DESTRUCTION OF THE DREAMING
Hero/Destroyer: The Two Faces of Power
The Dreaming Dies in the West
The Sword, the Plough, or the Dreaming
51

CHAPTER 5
REVELATION, PARADISE, AND FALL: THE MYTH OF THE GOLDEN AGE
The Southern Cross
The Riddle of the Tasmanian Aborigines
68

CHAPTER 6
EARTH DYING, EARTH REBORN
Earth's Body
The Magnetic Earth
Life, Mind, and Magnetism
Blood and Iron: The Dreaming of the Magnetic Cosmos
Ecstatic Ritual: A Tuning to the Earth
88

CHAPTER 7
IN THE WOMB OF THE RAINBOW SERPENT
THE SERPENT OF THE SOUTH: POTENTIZING, GIVING, MANIFESTING
SONGLINES AND THE BLOOD OF CULTURE
THE SERPENT OF THE NORTH: ACTUALIZING, RECEIVING, INSPIRING
THE FORGOTTEN CYCLE OF THE POSITIVE NORTH
EARTH AND SERPENT REAWAKEN
113

CHAPTER 8
SEED DREAMING
RECOGNIZING THE SHADOW
CULTURE: THE SOURCE OF DIVISION AND CHANGE
CULTURE AND THE CYCLE
IN DARKNESS THE DREAM DISCOVERS ITS SOURCE
135

PART TWO
LIVING THE DREAMING

INTRODUCTION
154

CHAPTER 9
COMING INTO BEING
BIRTH AND THE SPIRIT OF THE UNBORN
SPIRIT CHILD, SPERM CHILD
CHILDHOOD—THE LUST FOR EMBODIMENT
FREEDOM OF BODILY FUNCTIONS
FREEING THE EMOTIONS
THE FREEDOM OF CHILDHOOD SEXUALITY
FREEDOM TRANSFORMING
156

CHAPTER 10
THE CYCLES OF INITIATION
RITES OF TRANSITION
MASCULINE ENERGY AND THE THREE REALMS OF THE DREAMING
MALE INITIATIONS
THE SEIZURE • THE JOURNEY • RETURN TO HOMELAND •
THE CIRCUMCISION • THE SECLUSION • THE SECOND RETURNING • THE BETROTHAL
ADVANCED INITIATIONS
SUBINCISION • THE INITIATIC WOUND
WOMEN'S ROLE IN MALE INITIATIONS
FEMALE INITIATIONS
THE TRICKSTER AND THE GIRL
INITIATION AND SALVATION
178

CHAPTER 11
ABORIGINAL SEXUALITY
THE SOCIAL FACE OF LOVE
OLDER HUSBANDS, YOUNGER WIVES—OLDER WIVES, YOUNGER HUSBANDS
THE PERSONAL FACE OF LOVE
THE RITUAL FACE OF LOVE
209

CHAPTER 12
DREAMTIME AND THE SENSE OF BEING
THE ORIGINS OF INDIVIDUALITY
SELF AND EARTH—*NGURRA*
SELF IN MOVEMENT
232

CHAPTER 13
THE ABORIGINAL KINSHIP SYSTEM
KINSHIP AND SOCIAL ORDER
KINSHIP AND EMOTION
COMPASSION—THE EMOTIONAL GROUND OF BEING
MODESTY, RESPECT, AND EMBARRASSMENT
SORROW, GRIEF, AND REVENGE
KINSHIP AND RECIPROCITY
CONFLICT AND KINSHIP
INDIVIDUAL DISPUTES • DISPUTES AMONG TRIBES
242

CHAPTER 14
DREAM, EARTH, AND IDENTITY
THE ONTOLOGY OF THE DREAMTIME
THE DREAMING AND THE TANGIBLE, NOTHING MORE
MIND AND LANDSCAPE
261

PART THREE
TOTEMISM AND ANIMISM

CHAPTER 15
TOTEM AND SOCIETY
GOOLA-WILLEEL, THE TOPKNOT PIGEON
BEHOLDING—NOT POSSESSING
278

CHAPTER 16
TOTEM AND IMAGE
IMAGE AND INTIMACY
IMAGE AND SOCIETY
TRANSFORMATION AND THE SACRED IMAGE
IMAGE AND INTEGRATION
IMAGE AND RENEWAL
285

CHAPTER 17
HUNTER-GATHERERS AND TOTEMISM
CHICKEN HAWK SUCCEEDS IN STEALING FIRE
KINSHIP WITH THE SPIRIT OF NATURE
MEN AND WOMEN IN THE QUEST FOR FOOD
EARTH, SPIRIT, AND NOURISHMENT
300

CHAPTER 18
TOTEM AND MIND
The Frog Heralds
From Fixation to the Unbounded
Perception, Language, and Totem
313

CHAPTER 19
TOTEM AND ANIMISM
Blood and Spirit in Heredity
The Psychic Energy of Blood
Descent from Totem Ancestors
328

PART FOUR
DEATH AND THE INITIATIONS OF HIGH DEGREE

INTRODUCTION
341

CHAPTER 20
DEATH—EXPANDING INTO THE DREAMING
Death—Unnatural yet Inevitable
Death and the Divine Marriage
Passage into Death's Dreaming
Death and Sorcery
342

CHAPTER 21
DEATH—THE PREPARED JOURNEY
Death and Meditation
358

CHAPTER 22
WISE WOMEN AND MEN OF HIGH DEGREE
The Black Swans
Sleeping in a Fire
Crystals and Initiations of High Degree
The Dreaming Body
Steps into the Dreaming
365

CHAPTER 23
PRESERVING THE SEED
386

ENDNOTES
392

BIBLIOGRAPHY
399

INDEX
407

NOTE ON THE ILLUSTRATIONS

Many of the photographs, shown here for the first time from the Baldwin Spencer Photographic Collection of the Museum of Victoria Council, Melbourne, are among the earliest ever made of the Aboriginal people. They were taken at the turn of the century by anthropologist and adventurer Baldwin Spencer during his travels to the remote regions of Central and Northern Australia. At this time much of the Aboriginal culture was intact, therefore these photos provide an authentic glimpse into the oldest known human society.

Other important photographs were provided by the Museum of Natural History in New York and by the Australian Consulate General in New York. In addition, artist's drawings have been made that are based on some of the finest early photographs from collections around the world.

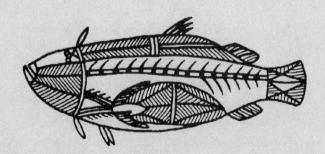

ACKNOWLEDGMENTS

I would like to thank Brian Syron, whose creative achievements in theater, film, and teaching draw equally from the genius of his Aboriginal blood and from his inspiring gifts of expression in the tradition of Western art. Mr. Syron's work always contains an essence of the modern Aboriginal psyche—its humor, resilience, creative intensity, joyousness, and anger. These qualities in his personality and work have contributed immeasurably to the awakening of contemporary Aboriginal art. With a pioneer spirit he initiated the first Aboriginal playwrights' conference, which led to the organization of the Aboriginal National Theatre Trust. I owe my introduction to Aboriginal Australia to Brian.

Special thanks go to Bobby and Darren McLeod, who with their wonderful kin Bell McLeod, Uncle Bul, Auntie Ruth, and others allowed me to record our gatherings and long conversations and provided me with an intimate view of the Aboriginal world. Bobby, a poet, musician, and a teacher of self-healing, gave generously of his time and teaching so that I might begin to develop a vision and an understanding of the Dreamtime.

It is certainly not uncommon for an author to have a sense of gratitude to his publisher, but in this case special thanks are more than appropriate. The dynamism, enthusiasm, and understanding provided by Ehud Sperling made the realization of this work possible, as did his numerous direct contributions to the text as editor. His company, Inner Traditions International, has throughout the years maintained a courageous, innovative, and nonsectarian approach to the publishing of esoteric and spiritual material. Exploring beyond "New Age" trends, Ehud Sperling has brought out important in-depth studies of ancient esoteric symbolism, music, and geometry, as well as ground-breaking works on the role of sexuality and social order in the spiritual development of human consciousness. I am indebted, not only as a writer and translator but also as a reader and researcher, to Inner Traditions' important contribution in these fields.

I am very grateful to many institutes and individuals for providing the photographs for this book. They include the Museum of Victoria Council in Melbourne, Australia, and its helpful staff, especially Mary Lakic, who gave endless time and assistance while we sorted through nearly 3,000 photographs of the Baldwin Spencer Collection; the Museum of Natural History in New York; Peter Carrigan of the Australian Consulate General in New York; Anthony Wallace of Sydney, Aboriginal art consultant; and Jonathan Cohen for the use of his rare edition of the journal of Captain Cook's travels.

Howard Rower and Kate Flynn, of the Australia Gallery in New York, require special thanks not only for providing artwork but also for their generosity with information and the use of Aboriginal artifacts from the gallery's fine collection.

Special thanks are given to Terence Shewring for his remarkable four paintings showing the emergence of humanity from the countryside.

Ray Rue, artist and illustrator, must also be acknowledged for his sensitive and accurate renderings of Aborigines in their traditional settings.

I would like to thank Jimmy Everett, Roselie Graham, and Roberta Sykes, who from the point of view of the Aboriginal community provided encouragement and insight. My thanks go also to the Tiwi Land Council of Bathurst Island for having us as guests and allowing us to experience firsthand some of the culture and the depth and warmth of the Aboriginal people. Others have been generous in directing me toward relevant material; I particularly thank Josh Mailman for pointing out the importance of the synesthesia experience in ecstatic ritual; Stephen Larsen, PhD, for his discussions with me on shamanism; Dr. Robert Becker for his innovative research in human physiology; and Dr. Richard Moore for reviewing and clarifying issues concerning Darwinism. I am particularly indebted to the published works of numerous anthropologists, especially Ronald and Catherine Berndt, Robert Tonkinson, and Fred Meyers.

Finally, I extend my appreciation to Ehud Sperling, Cornelia Bland Wright, Leslie Colket, and Joan Kocsis for their formidable editing skills; to Jeanie Levitan and Bonnie Atwater for their joyful, skillful and dedicated work in creating the final book mechanicals; and to Joanna Lambert, my companion in spirit and in love, who discussed with me every idea and whose hand touched each page. Without her constant assistance this project would have remained an unmanifested dream.

PREFACE

As a child, I would go to the Metropolitan Museum of Art in New York and marvel at the grandeur of the art in the Egyptian corridors. How had this civilization reached such heights? What lay behind the smiling faces of its people? Their apparent beauty and happiness reached into my childish heart, and their image and my identity were one. I was called to the archaic.

I reached manhood in the 1960s. As my hair grew down my back, all around me I saw visions of a time past—a time of the incarnation of the gods, when Shiva and Dionysus danced and the world moved to their beat. In the midst of war, injustice, and subjugation, science and government dreamed of a perfect world. I went to sleep and found myself in an underground home, somewhere in the far north, where men and women of culture and science had gathered. This was a dream of endings—of a time when the grand cycle of human development falls to the earth and our great mother takes us once again into her belly and digests us, as she digests all her creations.

When I awoke, I started publishing books and searching for that inner tradition that reached back, while still dreaming of a renewal of human society. I was struck by the contrast between our world and the golden ages of humanity. Yes, there are today extraordinary experiences, great teachers, esoteric traditions, religions, and philosophies. But where is the human society that embodies its culture and lives its teaching fully, exposing itself to the total range of human experience? Something has been lost.

Who are we? Where have we come from? Where are we going to? Most of us can, and probably have, asked these questions. As I traveled back to the great cultures and teachings of the past through my publishing work—exploring those questions—I kept wondering about our origins. What came before history, writing, the secret teachings, and the metaphors of science?

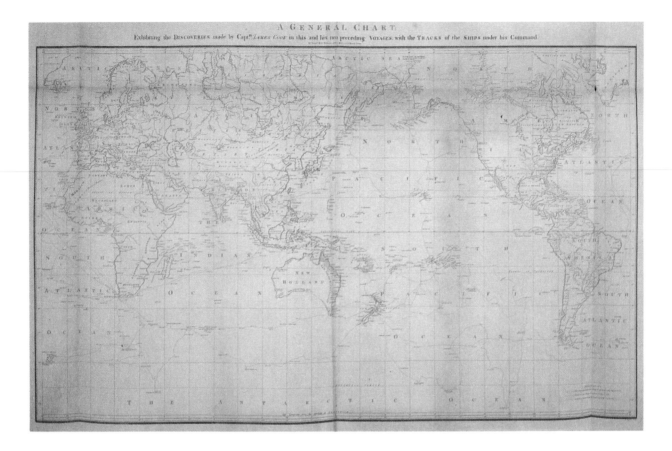

A GENERAL CHART Exhibiting the Discoveries made by Capt. James Cook in this and his two preceding Voyages, with the Tracks of the Ships under his Command.

Figure 2
Map of the voyage of Captain Cook.

Figure 3 →
Bush Tucker. The Aborigines perceive the landscape and its fertility as interconnected fields of concentric, subtle, energy emanations.

These two images expose the dreams of two vastly different and contrasting peoples. We can see Captain Cook in the age of discovery, exploration, and colonialism. Just 200 years ago, men traveled on ships of wood and hemp and named the world after themselves and their homelands. They would endeavor to make every place just like every other place.

Yet the captain's map is now outdated and no longer meaningful with its "New Holland" and "Negroland." Its inaccuracies make it useless to the modern navigator.

For the hunter-gatherers, "Bush Tucker" maps the food sources and paths that have nourished their people for more than 100,000 years. I look at it and wonder at the modern imagery, its language of patterns emerging out of fields of energy, speaking directly to the psychology, science, and spirit of today.

The inner traditions at the core of culture point to our higher qualities. They offer a door to the path of initiation, where all the potentialities of body and mind are to be realized. These traditions claim an ancestry in the earliest memories of humankind. The world's great religions and philosophies speak of a time before the fall of

xiv

humanity, a time and a place in which the earth and its life were one. How far back can we travel?

No, this is not the story of an ideal, perfect paradise: a place with only pleasure and no suffering or hardship. That story is reserved for a people uncomfortable with the human experience, a disembodied humanity no longer able to be wild, free, and naked, except for a moment—secret, hidden, and separate from each other. Can the full range of human experience find release? A frightening thought in our era of speed and destruction—so frightening that the dream of a rebirth of human society and all the living creation is lost, only a memory.

We did not invent, discover, improve, or evolve the human experience. Born, each and every one of us, into the natural world, we know no other place. Yet we dream. The Dreaming has no religious, racial, or cultural boundaries, no governments or social castes. The stage is set, images appear, senses cross. Worlds turn into worlds; subject and object are one. The transformations of the dreamtime are as original and unusual as the creation that appears when we open our eyes. Perception and dreamtime are the two worlds of all Aboriginal people. Can we dream of a future, a new direction or age, without an experience of our origin and destination?

I put my pen down and walk into the garden. Because I grew up in the city, this garden is my first. What colors and forms, every one unique and original! I am thrilled by my contact with other species. They enliven my imagination. I look up into the forest, the wilderness of wild animals and plants. Listen—can we hear their voices? Can you reach back in your blood and feel our common ancestors stamping their feet on the earth, see them lit by the glow of a fire? It is very late. Exhausted, you fall asleep. Embraced by your kin, you feel the spirit of the oldest living culture on earth move. You wake and start to dream again.

Ehud C. Sperling
Publisher

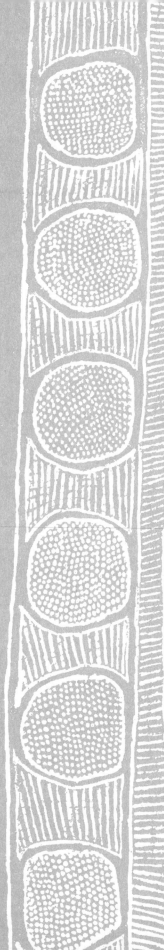

VOICES OF THE FIRST DAY

AWAKENING IN THE ABORIGINAL DREAMTIME

INTRODUCTION

EARTH DREAMING

THE EARTH HOLDS an infinite profusion of seeds. Seeds contain forms and worlds yet to germinate; the roots, leaves, and flowers of the entire plant are invisibly enclosed in the seed. Paradoxically, the unborn potential of future life is fused, within a seed, to primordial patterns that were laid down in the very beginning. The seed's capacity to engender new life seems to derive from the imprint of patterns carried through the ages.

This image of the earth with its seeds is comparable to Carl Jung's description of humanity's collective unconscious: both hold the entire heritage of primal patterns that are continually reborn through nature's seasons. Like seeds, myths, ideas, and images are dispersed throughout the world on the winds of thought, the waters of emotion, and the fires of passion.

The Australian Aborigines speak of *jiva* or *guruwari*, a "seed power" deposited in the earth. In the Aboriginal world view, every meaningful activity, event, or life process that occurs at a particular place leaves behind a vibrational residue in the earth, as plants leave an image of themselves as seeds. The shape of the land—its mountains, rocks, riverbeds, and waterholes—and its unseen vibrations echo the events that brought that place into creation. Everything in the natural world is a symbolic footprint of the metaphysical beings whose actions created our world. As with a seed, the potency of an earthly location is wedded to the memory of its origin. The Aborigines called this potency the "Dreaming" of a place, and this Dreaming constitutes the sacredness of the earth. Only in extraordinary states of consciousness can one be aware of, or attuned to, the inner dreaming of the earth.

I first witnessed the Aborigines' keen sensitivity to the "earth's dreaming" while walking with my Aboriginal friend Brian. We were in a graveyard on a desolate, windswept island in the Bass Strait, one of a group of islands that may once have formed a land bridge connecting the island of Tasmania to the southeastern tip of Australia. Admired for its

← *Figure 4*
Simpson's Gap, MacDonnell Ranges, Central Australia, 1895.

1

pristine beauty, this island is also remembered as the place where the last Tasmanian tribal people were brought by their colonial captors and confined to a mission. Within a matter of years the remnants of this proud and ancient culture perished.

That day as Brian and I walked, the black, weather-stained granite gravestones seemed to reach through the radiant green pasture grass like the infirmed fingers of an ancient giant, buried alive. My friend suddenly became noticeably perturbed and began pacing among the gravestones like a person searching for something. He began muttering, "They are not here. The old people are not here . . . I can feel that . . . I know that."

Disappointed because I had anticipated that he would be very moved by this place, I explained that all the records verify that many of the last surviving tribal Tasmanians were buried here. My explanation slipped unheeded through the ashen, granulated darkness into which Brian disappeared as he returned to the car.

That evening during dinner, Brian for the first time spoke openly to me about his life—about growing up in urban white Australia with Aboriginal blood. The emotions in his resonant voice rose and fell as the humming intonations of a gale-force wind cascaded down the mountains to the east and buffeted the side of the house.

Brian spoke of his Aboriginal grandmother, to whom he had been sent in times of family hardship. "She caught me with her gaze so that I never could forget my Aboriginal heritage. She seemed to sense even when I was a child that I might try to disown the past. I can remember in my earliest boyhood her strong black hands on my shoulders. Looking straight into my eyes, she would say, 'The white men say terrible things about the Aborigines only because we are not farmers, builders, merchants, and soldiers. The Aborigines are something else—they are dancers, hunters, wanderers, and mystics, and because of that they call us ignorant and lazy. Someday, Brian, you will see the beauty and power of our people.'"

It was many years before Brian allowed himself to experience that beauty. After a period of living outside Australia, he returned to his country a successful theater director and actor, and made a journey with a friend to the outback of Australia.

While he was driving through a scorching hot desert region, his binoculars picked up a lonely figure standing like an apparition on a rocky outcrop. "It was the first time I had actually seen a tribal person. He was standing on one leg, with the other folded and the sole of that foot pressing against the inside of his thigh. He was holding a spear in one hand, his other hand firmly cupping his scrotum. His folded knee was leaning on a hollow wooden spearthrower. His front hairline had been plucked clean so as to display a high forehead gleaming like a polished black granite stone, and his hair was pulled back tightly and bound with

Figure 6
Procession of Tiwi men through the forest during a yam ceremony on Melville Island, Northern Australia, 1912.

a woven diadem. The tight, curly black beard with the strong, heavy brow line framed an unyielding and stolid visage. Although he was elderly, his body was light and perfectly proportioned. Wrapped low around his hips was a belt woven from thousands of fine black threads; from it hung the lifeless bodies of several speared goannas. His oiled body had a soft, matte veneer of desert dust, increasing the sense that his nakedness had only recently been transformed from the earth itself."

Brian seemed to be gazing over a great distance as he spoke. "We stopped the Land Rover, and I stared at him for a long time. His body remained motionless, as if his spine were connecting the earth to the sky. As the Aborigines say, he was beholding his country, seeing all the stories of the Dreaming from these sacred places." Brian rose from the table and began putting on his coat and hat as if we had been planning to go for a walk. "After seeing that tribal person I knew I could never hide or be ashamed of my Aboriginality. From that time onward all my work, all that I had learned, all my energy would go toward revealing the beauty and power of my culture."

We walked out into a splendid night, the air glistening with impartial clarity. There was no moon; everything was illuminated by starlight. The Milky Way bridged the entire sky. Its spaciousness liberated our spirits, while the incalculable number of stars humbled us. As we walked, Brian suddenly became very agitated. "They are here," he said. "They are here." "Who?" I asked. "The old people—I feel them . . . they are here." Brian's hand on my shoulder confirmed the intensity of his feeling. Before I could speak further he had turned and been transformed into a silver shadow hurrying back to the glow of the house.

Years later, after having investigated more deeply the Aboriginal culture and its history on this island, I learned that indeed most, if not all, of the Aborigines said to be buried at the official historical graveyard had been exhumed in the early decades of this century. Grave robbers could fetch a good price for Aboriginal skeletal parts by selling them to museums or curiosity markets, which carved ashtrays or other knicknacks from the bones of these ancient "cave men." It became a fashion among some Australians to have tobacco pouches made from the scrotums of dead Aborigines. This ought to have been considered shocking behavior for good Christian colonialists, but such atrocities were justified by learned scholars from the British Royal Academy of Science who, using Darwinian concepts, depicted the Aborigines as the freakish remains of a bygone phase of evolution, likely candidates for the "missing link" between monkeys and early humans.

Later, I also found out that the exact place where Brian and I had stood on that star-filled night was the location the imprisoned Tasmanians had sought for their Sunday outings. This hillside was the only place where

FIGURE 7
The meditative stance of the Aboriginal hunter. Every distinct sitting and standing body posture has a specific name in Aboriginal languages that is often related to an animal—a practice reminiscent of Eastern yoga traditions.

they could view, in the distance, the azure silhouette of the mountains
of their Tasmanian homeland. An old island farmer told me that the
black folk loved this spot; they would perform lamenting ceremonies
here in which they wailed and cried, attempting to send their spirits back
to their beloved countryside in Tasmania.

In this way I discovered Brian's sensitivities to the memories and
potencies of earthly places. In the years that followed, through my continued involvement with Aboriginal people and culture, I encountered
echoes of an intelligence and a way of being in the world that is in utter
contrast to our present ways. The Aborigines have no concept or word
for the two things that most torment modern man: the passage of time
and the accumulation of possessions. I encountered language forms whose
unusual structure and rich vocabulary opened new worlds of perception
and comprehension. I began to uncover the imprint of a culture in which
every aspect of the natural world contained, like a seed, the spirit of its
original creators, a vision in which land and spirituality are inseparable.
I came in contact with initiatic rituals and ceremonies whose essence
holds the origins of esoteric, yogic, magical, and shamanic traditions. I
got to know a culture whose Dreaming, or Dreamtime, revelation directed the people to turn their backs on everything that we consider the
basis of civilization. The Aborigines did not clear and tear up the earth
for agriculture. They did not enslave animals and subjugate plant species
for systematic exploitation and slaughter. They did not build homes that

cut them off from a natural adaptation to the wonders and ever-changing fluctuations of nature. They did not wrap themselves in clothing to subdue their vitality and sexuality and falsify their identity. All of these practices by which we have altered and desecrated our environment and isolated our own lives are, for the Aborigines, the earth's Dreaming turned into a nightmare.

The Australian Aborigines, and indeed indigenous tribal peoples all over the world, believe that the spirit of their consciousness and way of life exists like a seed buried in the earth. The waves of European colonialism that destroyed the civilizations of North America, South America, and Australia began a five-hundred-year dormancy period of the "archaic consciousness." Its potencies disappeared into the earth.

There is an interim between the end of a seed's dormancy and the moment when the seedling bursts into the light. Swallowed in the darkness of the earth's womb, the reawakening seed begins to absorb water and gradually rehydrate each of its cells, one by one. Moistened by the blood and sorrow of our degenerating age, the seed swells, cracking the surface above as it splits apart. The swelling of the seed of archaic awareness became evident in the developed world during the 1960s, when the moral and philosophical fabric of our social structure cracked. The tender first shoots of this seedling are soon to appear. The innovative forms resulting from the inspirations, aspirations, and experiments of a new age remain covered with the subsoil of a monolithic civilization engrossed in its own destruction. The split seed may require more time to establish its developing roots before it can burst into the light. As the roots grow, the plumule, or tender head of unborn foliage, is curled downward in the

FIGURE 9
Aranda welcoming dance: entrance of the strangers, Alice Springs, Central Australia, 1901. The older men of the clan form a ritual dancing party to greet visitors who have come to settle old disputes.

fetal postion, while the bent stem forms a loop. The neck of the stem pushes its way upward through the soil, pulling up the all-important plumule behind it. Similarly, the forms and qualities of the new consciousness are yet fragile, incomplete, or shrouded in uncertainty and darkness. Archaic consciousness—the seed of our human origins—nonetheless continues to press for reemergence within the ground beneath us. The seed, like the sun, is a universal symbol of growth, death, dormancy, and inevitable rebirth. A contemporary Aboriginal poet has expressed this idea in a poem.

MY PEOPLE

A race of people who rose with the sun,
As strong as the sun they had laws,
Traditions coexisting with nature.
The cycle of the sun is likened to the life of man;
The snake is said to bite when the sun is at its most powerful
    zenith.
The snake has already bitten,
When the snake bites the sun,
The clan, the man, the sun,
Must sink cooling to its inevitable settings,
Yet, it is said, the sun will rise again.

ALBERT BARUNG

This book is an invitation to leave behind the most basic assumptions of our civilization along with its destructive arrogance and false sense of superiority. It is an invitation to enter, as in a dream, a lost memory of our race as well as a fresh imagining of the earth's cycles of death and rebirth.

Dreams, deep collective memories, and imaginings are more potent than religious faith or scientific theories in lifting us above the catastrophic ending that confronts us all. A recollection of our origins—a remembrance of a sense of reality in its pure and primary form—is essential if we are to understand our present circumstance and imagine the possibilities of our collective destiny.

Ten thousand years ago all of humanity lived as hunter-gatherers, as do a few tribes of Australian Aborigines today. The earth's undisturbed natural fertility provided for and nourished all. Earth was indeed the paradisiac garden alluded to in so many world mythologies. At that time, it is estimated, there were not more than 10 million people on the entire earth. Now there are some 6 billion people, many of whom are impoverished, starving, or at war. Many others are crowded into huge polluted cities, trapped in an industrial system that, like a parasite, is destroying the earth upon which it depends. Today, only one thousandth of one

FIGURE 10
The tribal elders maintain a vital physicality and participate in ceremonies and the rigors of hunting and gathering throughout their entire life.

percent of humans are hunter-gatherers. We know that Western civilization is based on the ancient cultures of Greece and Egypt, but our ancestral roots extend far beyond; the so-called primitive tribal world is the common ancestry of us all. This entire way of life, its cultures, its languages, its knowledge, its technologies, have been all but exterminated, and this genocide forms a horrific tributary feeding the sea of blood on which our civilization floats.

The environmental disruptions, the ever-increasing list of species extinctions—all are evidence to those who are willing to see that this past 10,000-year phase of development does not mark great evolutionary progress but a terminal crisis in the life cycle of the planet. It is time to imagine beyond endings.

Our reference and spiritual guide for this imagining will be the oldest known human culture, that of the Australian Aborigines. Traditional archaeological evidence holds that Aboriginal culture has existed in Australia for 60,000 years, but more recent evidence indicates that the period is more like 120,000 to 150,000 years. The Aborigines' rituals, beliefs, and cosmology may represent the deepest collective memory of our race.

As with all of life, the growth of humanity and culture begins with a germinating seed and returns to seed at the completion of the cycle. Life reborn from the death or dormancy of the seed never duplicates exactly a past formation; rather, it grows in the paradox of ever new possibilities held within an unchanging essence. It is a centrifugation into the mystery of that which is the same yet different, unchanging yet novel. The dance begins when the seed sheds its shell. The breaking of the encasement is a symbol of throwing off the accumulated encrustation of the previous cycle to reveal anew its essence. The Aboriginal culture symbolizes the eternal seed of human cycles.

This exploration of Aboriginal traditions is neither an emotional plea nor a rational proposal to return to their hunter-gatherer way of life. It is a re-visioning intended to nourish a dream of the seed and to fortify our imaginations for a renewed sense of the dignity and mystery of human life. As the poet T. S. Eliot wrote,

> We shall not cease from exploration
> And the end of all our exploring
> Will be to arrive where we started
> And know the place for the first time.

I invite the reader on a journey to the most distant memory of our race—the Dreamtime of the Australian Aborigines. My preparation for guiding this journey consists of many years studying the thought forms of ancient civilizations, particularly the ancient Egyptians, and absorb-

9

FIGURE 11
Flinders Island, off the coast of Tasmania.

ing myself in their mathematical methods of problem solving. I lived for six years in South India in open-walled grass huts without electricity, running water, or motorized vehicles. I worked barefoot in the fields each day with Dravidian village people whose language and way of life has remained virtually unchanged for the last four thousand years.

Each of my life's researches has carried me further back into the life and mind of the archaic. After I left India, a land blanketed with layers of history and burdened with overpopulation, I was drawn to the open, austere emptiness of Australia. While living in Australia I gradually became involved with members of the most ancient of all cultures, the Australian Aborigines. I began by listening carefully to every morsel of information my Aboriginal friends offered about their culture and their contacts with tribal people. In preparing to write this book, I decided not to pursue field work with any one particular tribal group but rather to seek out Aborigines who were involved in a renaissance of the universal aspects of their culture. In addition, I selected from the sizable body of published anthropologic works some of the more prominent research on early, precontact tribal life (that is, before contact with the West).

The traditional customs and rituals I describe may or may not be fully practiced among tribal people in Australia today. I refer to them in the present tense, however, since I believe they are part of an eternal tradition. In my attempt to show the meaning this tradition holds for our times, I may have made errors of interpretation. However, I have in all cases followed the guidance of my unwavering respect for and belief in the Aboriginal people.

Perhaps my most important qualification as guide is my having lived for 10 years on a beautiful island off the coast of Tasmania, considered by the Aborigines to be a sacred abode of their deceased ancestors. I have attempted to listen to the spirit imbued in the dark green mountains; the mist-combed, granite pinnacles; and the long, pure, beige, open beaches. I have listened to the howling anguish of its windstorms and the massive calm of its sparkling coves and bays; to the wild song of eagles, swans, hawks, cockatoos, dolphins, wallabies, and wombats who live in the bush and burrows, the seas and trees of this time-lost land. It is within this listening above all that I have felt connected to the most ancient, enduring, and nature-integrated culture of human history.

I invite you, then, to travel with me to a world, to the Dreaming, where one can still hear the voices of the first day.

"Wandjina"

PART ONE

IN THE BEGINNING

WAS

THE DREAMING

CHAPTER 1

IMAGES OF OUR ORIGINS

DARWIN MEETS THE
DREAMTIME

THE AUSTRALIAN ABORIGINAL culture is founded entirely on the remembrance of the origin of life. According to some recent evidence, their story of creation, along with the world view it fostered, has survived for perhaps 150,000 years. The Aborigines refer to the forces and powers that created the world as their Creative Ancestors. For them, our beautiful world could have been created perfect only in accordance with the power, wisdom, and intentions of these original ancestral beings. During the world-creating epoch called the Dreaming, the Ancestors moved across a barren, undifferentiated field in a manner similar to that of the Aboriginal people wandering across their vast countryside. The Ancestors traveled, hunted, made camp, fought, and loved, and in so doing they shaped a featureless field into a topographical landscape. Before their travels, they would sleep

They say we have been here for 60,000 years, but it is much longer. We have been here since the time before time began. We have come directly out of the Dreamtime of the Creative Ancestors. We have lived and kept the earth as it was on the First Day.

*ABORIGINAL
TRIBAL ELDER*

FIGURE 13
The thorny devil is one of Australia's many rare and unusual reptiles which commonly figure in the Dreamtime stories.

and dream the adventures and episodes of the following day. In this manner, moving from dreams to actions, the Ancestors made the ants, the grasshoppers, the emus, the crows, the parrots, the wallabies, the kangaroos, the lizards, the snakes, and all the foods and plants. They made all the natural elements, the sun, the moon, and the stars. They made humans, tribes, and clans. All these things were created by the Ancestors simultaneously, and each could transform into any of the others. A plant could become an animal, an animal a landform, a landform a man or woman. An Ancestor could be both human and animal. Back and forth the transformations occurred as the adventures of the Dreamtime stories required. Everything was created from the same source—the dreamings and doings of the great Ancestors. All stages, phases, and cycles were present at once in the Dreamtime. As the world took shape and was filled with the species and varieties of the ancestral transformations, the Ancestors wearied and retired into the earth, the sky, the clouds, and the creatures, to reverberate like a potency within all they had created.

These journeys are preserved in the stories, ceremonies, symbols, and patterns of living that have been assiduously maintained by the Aborigines for millennia. For Aboriginal tribespeople every aspect of daily life reflects the stories of creation associated with a place where the Aborigi-

FIGURE 14
Kangaroos, large marsupials, are unique to Australia.

15

FIGURE 15
The Aborigines place the
highest value on keeping the
earth in its original purity and
potency.

nes traveled and made camp. Every day is lived in remembrance of the day when a place and its creatures first came into being. Aboriginal culture and society thus share the identity of the forms, principles, and activities by which the natural world was created.

Although stories and symbols may vary slightly from one group to another, these Dreaming stories are common to all Aboriginal people across the vast continent of Australia. In these stories the Ancestors took innovative action and unprecedented risks, discovering as they went along customs, techniques, and behaviors that either helped to bring joy and order or precipitated pain, destruction, and disease. The lessons of life implicit in the stories were distilled into what the Aborigines called the Dreamtime Law and were reflected in the utter simplicity of the Aboriginal way of life.

All creatures—from stars to humans to insects—share in the consciousness of the primary creative force, and each, in its own way, mirrors a form of that consciousness. In this sense the Dreamtime stories perpetuate a unified world view. This unity compelled the Aborigines to respect and adore the earth as if it were a book imprinted with the mystery of the original creation. The goal of life was to preserve the earth, as much as possible, in its initial purity. The subjugation and domestication of plants and animals and all other manipulation and exploitation of the natural world—the basis of Western civilization and "progress"—were antithetical to the sense of a common consciousness and origin shared by every creature and equally with the creators. To exploit this integrated world was to do the same to oneself.

The Dreamtime stories extended a universal and psychic consciousness not only to every living creature but also to the earth and the primary elements, forces, and principles. Each component of creation acts out of dreams, desires, attractions, and repulsions, just as we humans do. Therefore, the entrance into the larger world of space, time, and universal energies and fields was the same as the entrance into the inner world of consciousness and dreaming. The exploration of the vast universe and a knowledge of the meaning of creation was experienced through an internal and external knowledge of self.

Every land formation and creature, by its very shape and behavior, implied a hidden meaning; the form of a thing was itself an imprint of the metaphysical or ancestral consciousness that created it, as well as the universal energies that brought about its material manifestation. These aspects of the Dreamtime creation myth imply a world in which the metaphysical and physical are held in symbolic integration. One cannot consider the visible and invisible worlds separately. The Aboriginal languages that emerged from this world view are rich in a metaphoric flow integrating physical, psychological, and spiritual levels of experience.

17

Like any creation myth, the Dreamtime stories cannot be proved. The value of any creation myth is determined by its effect on people, the image they hold of themselves, and their place in the universe. For perhaps 150,000 years, the Dreamtime mythology sustained a culture that lived in harmony with nature and was full of vigor, vitality, and joyousness.

Darwin's theory of evolution—the creation story accepted for the last 150 years by Western civilization—is also only a story. While Darwin and his proponents claimed to have "proved" his theory, it cannot be scientifically tested. Nevertheless, Darwinism grew into an unquestioned scientific and academic orthodoxy. It has become the paradigm, or lens, through which all thinking about human origins is assessed. The edifices of modern life sciences are built on a belief in this story.

Evolution is defined as developing or causing to develop gradually. In biology it refers to undergoing slow changes in a process of growth. For Darwinians, the process of growth extends to the evolution or gradual growth of species from simpler or earlier forms. Darwin's theory of evolution, based on the principle of natural selection, postulates that species regularly overpopulate, resulting in a continual struggle for survival in which the victors are the strongest species or members of a species with characteristics most adaptable to their environment. Individuals choose mates with characteristics that make them highly likely to survive. Weaker or less adaptable individuals or species—the majority of contestants—die out.

Applied to human evolution, this theory implies that *Homo sapiens'* superior characteristics triumphed over those of the lower primates. Darwin's theory projects a world view based on competition and conflict in which nature is a hostile force that must be kept at bay. It also can be used to justify exploitation of the earth and all other creatures to satisfy human requirements.

Basic to the Darwinian creation myth is what has been called the ladder mentality; this image has infected all aspects of our view of the world. The "ladder" symbolizes a climb through gradual stages: from the simple to the complex, from instinct to intelligence, from nonliving to living, from less conscious to more conscious, from inorganic elements to plants to animals to humans, from disorder to order to self-organization. In each case the world is pinned to a ladder of progressive development. In scientific thought, the straight climb up the ladder of evolution has been dropped recently in favor of different pathways: loops, punctuated equilibrium, nonlinearity. However, the idea of the ladder is retained in the concept of an overall movement from one determined state or quality (i.e., simple) toward another determined state (i.e., complex). In its social application, for all intents and purposes, white males are placed at the top of the ladder and all the rest—other races, women, children, plants, and animals—take up the rungs below. All are there to support the institutions, structures, and theories of those at the exalted pinnacle.[1]

This ladder is repeated in all Western cultural structures. Traditional state religions have one God-man at the top, toward whom we must morally and spiritually strive (in the Middle Ages Christ was pictured with the natural world as his footstool). Contemporary humanistic philosophy shows human beings elevated above any other creature. The same ladder is visible in the structure of military, government, and economic systems; the hero or "star" orientation of Western popular culture and art; the educational grading system; and a science of theories and "truths" that rise to overthrow the ignorance of the past. The ladder image is there, stimulating the drive for competition, perfection, and transcendence.

In the nineteenth century, Darwin built his explanation of the origin of species on ideas that had cast their shadow, centuries before, over Western thought. Among these "stories" were those of Francis Bacon, the seventeenth-century magistrate and philosopher who proposed that it was man's God-given right to subdue, control, and exploit the natural world and every living creature. Bacon dismissed the entire language of mythology and established reason as the basis of true religion. Bacon's vision earned him the title of the "father of modern rationalistic science." His work directly inspired the founding of the Royal Society of London, which began what biologist and philosopher Rupert Sheldrake calls "the priesthood of science." Following Bacon, René Descartes, the seventeenth-century philosopher and mathematician, converted the ideal of a mathematically perfect universe (contemplated by Kepler and Copernicus) into a universal machine that ran according to mathematical laws of matter and motion. Descartes applied this mechanical way of thinking to plants, animals, language—even his own body. For Descartes, the human mind and thinking process rose above the blind mechanics of the natural world to stand supreme as that which defined human existence. Isaac Newton extended the mechanical story to the very essence of matter, which was seen as an innate, spiritless, atomized structure, controlled by the same strict mechanical laws that moved the heavenly bodies.[2] As in Darwinian evolution, each of these stories features man, with a single aspect of his particular form of intelligence, astride the ladder with all the rest of nature beneath him.

These stories were made possible by attitudes that can be traced back to the puritanical oppression of early Christianity. In its efforts to con-

trol people through repression and guilt, the Christian church divorced the spiritual realm from the physical, debased human sexuality, and looked with loathing on all the drives and vital functions that humans share with the natural world. The medieval church etched its myth of a fallen creation into the European imagination through four centuries of inquisitions, witch hunts, tortures, and executions in which six to eight million people, mostly women and children, were put to death. Darwin voiced this same shadow of a sinful and fallen world in his theory of evolution:

> What a book a devil's chaplain might write on the clumsy, wasteful, blundering, low and horribly cruel works of nature.[3]

Although they appear to be philosophical adversaries, Western Christianity and scientific Darwinism have both supported the expansion of the Industrial Revolution, with its unbridled exploitation of the environment for the material benefit of mankind. Darwinian biology affirms this exploitation by ignoring the intelligence, beauty, and purposefulness of nature and replacing it with chemical and mechanical explanations. This reductionism lends an artificial supremacy to the methods and mentality of industry. The theory of evolution is a product of Western civilization and provides a rationale for humanity's self-appointed position in the universal order. Darwinism, in one form or another, has been used to justify nineteenth-century political, social, and economic systems, such as industrial capitalism, as well as the colonial expansion of European civilizations that began centuries earlier. Social Darwinism, the theory according to which economic and social success depends on the ability to adapt and compete (and the "losers" deserve what they get), is an application of the ladder structure inherent in Darwin's original theories.

Many contemporary Darwinian biologists attempt to wash their hands of the glaring simplicities and often horrific side effects of social Darwinist thinking, but it is not possible to deny the larger issue: myths concerning the origins of humanity and creation reverberate throughout the cultures that adapt them. Ironically, social Darwinism theorizes a vision that the Aboriginal Dreamtime realized long ago, that the laws and principles from which the natural world arose should be the same as those that generate human culture and society. Unfortunately, the popular Darwinian view of biological evolution, with its "survival of the fittest" assumptions, provides such a distorted view of nature that the systems based on this image, such as capitalism and its socialistic variations, have hurried us toward planetary destruction.

Since the late nineteenth century, Darwinian theory has changed. It now incorporates new information in genetics, fossil studies, and other fields, but its basic premise of humankind representing the pinnacle of evolution and its image of a progressing universe have remained in place. Cracks are beginning to appear in the edifice of Darwinian evolution; dimly, through these cracks, one can glimpse a return to the Dreamtime story of creation.

The entire question of evolution revolves around the perennial contemplation of the seed. All of life passes on information about itself from one generation to another through codes or patterns carried by seeds. Modern Darwinian biology supposes that this transmission takes place entirely through the genetic material (DNA) contained in our reproductive cells. The story of genetic evolution is a drama in which the forces of perpetuity, order, and continuity confront the forces of innovation, disorder, and change. The genetic molecules zealously protect unchanging chemical patterns that encode a specific combination of characteristics for each species. These species and types tend to persist through their code, or seed, but they also appear to adapt gradually to environmental changes and perhaps to evolve into new varieties and species. Although the process of change is considered to be so gradual that it eludes our ordinary time-bound perception, the evolutionary process must be all-pervasive if billions of life forms (from viruses to plants to humans) have all emerged out of a single genetic code.[4] The evolution of entirely new forms and species to evolve from a single code implies something more than permutations and recombinations of the existing pattern. The question as to how change, innovation, and species emerge is conventionally explained in terms of random genetic mutations followed by natural selection, but this theory of evolution is "more a dogmatic assertion than an established scientific fact."[5]

There are many questions, even mysteries, concerning the concept of the genetic code or primal seed. If each specific seed code holds *in potential* the characteristics of a particular plant or animal, then wouldn't it follow that the original code must hold *in potential* all characteristics of all species? A seed or code must be, by definition, a seed or code of *something*. For what are the original 64 combinations of nucleic acids a code? In other words, who or what is the parent of the primal seed? The 4,000-year-old Chinese book of transmutations, known as the *I Ching*, has been analyzed by several mathematicians in a way that exactly parallels the combinatory possibilities of the genetic code.[6] The *I Ching*, however, is not a code for the biological possibilities of amino acids but rather for combinations of psychological, ethical, and spiritual states of consciousness. It appears that the essence of this code is a language that speaks on many different levels of experience simultaneously.

In considering genetic transmission as a language, the DNA code could be compared to the grammar of the language—a universal stem that metamorphoses endlessly into spoken and written creations. The scribes and monks who for centuries copied manuscripts with devout fidelity, or the printing presses that replaced them, can be seen as manifesting the power of replication inherent in the seed cell. Poets, we can imagine, mutate language, giving birth to unanticipated characteristics and images. Natural selection acts like an editor, systematically selecting and rejecting from an indiscriminate flow of poetic innovations. In the creation story of Darwinism, the editor is utilitarian, selecting characteristics for survival rather than beauty; the poet is visionless because all mutations result only from random occurrences. For the Aborigines the earth holds the genetic code. Earth's topography, together with the energy emanating from its varied landscape, is a primary edition of the code of life. It is through the earth itself that the language of the primal seed speaks across time.

Darwin himself knew nothing of the language of genes or mutations. He believed that genetic change could occur through learning, behavior, and excesses or deficiencies in the utilization of body parts. He thought, for example, that ostriches had lost the power of flight through disuse of their wings and acquired longer, thicker legs as a result of increased use over successive generations.[7]

The followers of Darwin, known as neo-Darwinians, rejected the idea that acquired adaptations tend to become hereditary and, in the spirit of Descartes, pushed the idea of biological evolution farther in the direction of a mechanistic theory.

> According to neo-Darwinians, organisms just pass on the genes they themselves have inherited, and the only changes that occur in the genes are random *mutations*. There can be no inheritance of acquired characteristics because there is no genetic mechanism by which such characteristics can be passed on.[8]

The strength of the neo-Darwinian theory is based on the idea that the mechanisms for gradual change in the evolution of species are known and understood. Even though a mechanical approach to evolution, based on mutation theory and the genetic survival of adapted traits through natural selection, is still widely preached in schools and textbooks, in scientific circles it is being seriously questioned.

Voices that dissent from neo-Darwinian orthodoxy have been growing louder over the past decade or more. Biologists Augros and Stacui, in their recent book *The New Biology*, present the views of a number of biologists who see the origin of humanity and the development of the natural world as unencumbered by the elements of nineteenth-century thought that shaped Darwinism. According to them, the most recent field studies of animals in undisturbed natural habitats discredit a theory of natural selection based on a continual struggle for survival. Animals do not tend to overpopulate, and cooperation is common among members of the same species and even among members of different species. Peaceful coexistence, not endless competition and survival, is seen as the prevailing mode of the natural world.[9]

Findings in the fossil record over the last hundred years also contradict Darwin's theory that species and subspecies have arisen gradually over long periods of time. There is no evidence of the gradual appearance of one species out of another, such as *Homo sapiens* evolving from other primates, nor of the existence of intermediate types between recognizable species. The fossil record should be teeming with intermediate species; but, as paleontologist David Raup asserts,

> Different species usually appear and disappear from the fossil record without showing the transition that Darwin postulated. New species typically appear suddenly in fossil records and persist alongside what the Darwinian theory considers to be their progenitor for millions and millions of years. There is no gradual change of one to another and no replacement of one by the other.[10]

This type of observation, drawn from fossil records and animal behavior in the wild, makes it increasingly difficult to assume that natural selection functions in the way it was originally described or that it functions at all in the development and emergence of new species.[11]

FROM MOLECULES TO REDREAMING OUR ORIGINS

Although many aspects of natural selection and gradual evolution are being seriously reconsidered by some research biologists, the theory and the associated image of humans evolving from monkeys have become ingrained in the public imagination and have reshaped humanity's dream of itself.

Neo-Darwinian theory states that naturally induced, random muta-

tions in the DNA code caused by radiation, chemical reagents, or recombinant irregularities can gradually accumulate and, in combination with natural selection, account for the branching off of one species from another or the emergence of new species.[12] Recent scientific research on artificially induced mutations calls into question such assumptions. For example, Augros and Stanciu report the following:

> Since the early part of this century, in continuous genetic experiments, fruit flies, subjected to X-rays and other treatments to increase their mutation rate up to 150 times the normal, have been bred for thousands of generations and closely monitored. These experiments have produced offspring with fringed wings, vestigial wings, no wings at all, and other variations, but all were clearly fruit flies. No beetles, no mantids, no butterflies. Not even a new species of fly.[13]

There is no evidence that random mutations can produce new species or that complex organs can develop as a result of mutation and selection. The eye, for example, could emerge only as a result of thousands of simultaneous mutations—a mathematical impossibility. Nor has it been explained how organisms could develop new behavior patterns to adjust positively to genetic changes. Mathematicians have protested that only one in 20 million mutations can be expected to be positive. Generating new species through natural selection by means of mutated genes seems about as probable, in the words of astronomer Fred Hoyle, "as a tornado sweeping through a junkyard assembling a Boeing 707."[14]

Observations of this sort discredit the idea that genetic mutations play a *positive* role in the origin of species or the branching off of one species from another. Genetic mutation has, however, become the basis of a molecular theory of evolution. In brief, molecular evolutionary theory states that the greater the accumulation of mutations, the older the species. Therefore the presence of fewer mutations implies a more recent species because there has been less time for differences to accumulate. However, differences in accumulated mutations have been used in this theory to postulate when one species branched off from its predecessor or species of common origin. According to the theory prior to molecular evidence, humans, chimpanzees, and gorillas are supposed to have branched off from a common origin about 20 million years ago. However, they differ by a mere one percent of accumulated mutations. According to molecular biologist Cherfas, "By comparison with other species, a genetic difference of this amount ought to correspond to a separation of man and the African apes from a common stock less than 5 million years ago."[15]

Scientific information is often presented in such an authoritarian manner that we forget that the data have value that is independent of the theory they are supposed to support. Since there is little or no evidence for the branching of one species from another—considering the lack of fossil records of intermediate species and the improbability of positive DNA mutations—it is plausible to reject the neo-Darwinian theory that DNA mutations contribute to the branching off of species from a common ancestor while accepting that the accumulation of mutations may be used as a time clock for the age of the species. The use of this time clock supports the theory that the Australian Aborigines were the first *Homo sapiens* on the planet.

Based on the initial examination of the DNA evidence, evolutionary biologists believe that 40,000 years ago all the racial types branched off from the African Negro, who emerged directly from *Homo erectus* 100,000 years ago, and so on back to the African primates (see Figure 17). This theory is supported by skeletal evidence from Africa and affirms the much publicized and widely accepted theory of African genesis.[16]

Using more accurate methods of examining in-cell DNA mutations, recent molecular research has challenged the African genesis theory in favor of an Australian one. Mitochondria, the tiny organelles in each cell responsible for manufacturing energy-rich compounds, have yielded a surprising clue to the mystery of our origin (see Figure 18). Instead of the double strand of DNA found in the cell, the tiny mitochondria contain a single circular strand of DNA that is inherited asexually; in other words, it is contributed by the mother's side only. Because of this, the DNA of the mitochondria is not subject to shuffling and recombination, and, therefore, the accumulated mutations are clear and develop much faster.

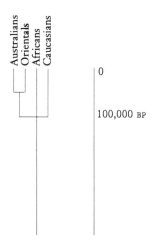

FIGURE 17
The family tree of Homo sapiens *provided by nuclear DNA accumulated mutations, showing the human races originating from Africans about 100,000 years ago and diverging about 40,000 years ago.*

FIGURE 18
A living cell with a mitochondrion shown in detail.

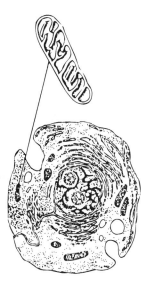

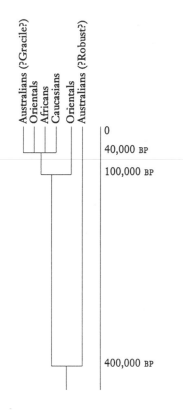

FIGURE 19
Mitochondrial DNA puts the origin of Homo sapiens *much further back and indicates that the Australian Aborigines arose 400,000 years ago from two distinct lineages, far earlier than any other racial type. (Based on R. Cann's sample of 112 humans, including twelve Australian Aborigines, all from Western Australia, after Gribbon and Sherfas, 1982.)*

The study of mitochondrial DNA has revealed a surprising pattern among four of the five major groupings of *Homo sapiens:* Negroid, Caucasian, Australian, and Mongoloid (see Figure 19). The Australian racial group has a much higher number of mutations than any other racial group, which suggests that the Australians split off from the common ancestor about 400,000 years ago. By the same theory, the Mongoloids originated about 100,000 years ago, and the Negroid and Caucasian groups about 40,000 years ago.

This dates the origin of the Australians as almost concurrent with the emergence of *Homo sapiens* from the previous *Homo erectus.* To quote evolutionary geneticist Allan Wilson, "It seems too far out to admit, but while *Homo erectus* was muddling along in the rest of the world, a few *erectus* had got to Australia and did something dramatically different—not even with stone tools—but it is there that *Homo sapiens* emerged and evolved."[17] According to this view, *Homo sapiens* would have evolved free from competition out of a small band of *Homo erectus* 400,000 years ago in Australia.

Why then did the African genesis theory achieve such prominence? As in all scientific speculation, bias played a role: before people began to look in Africa, there was not a great deal of evidence for an African origin.

> People looked in East Africa for the origins of humanity mainly because there were thick, easily dated layers of sedimentary rock. Australia is a terrible place for archaeology because there is no sedimentary rock and almost no volcanic activity so there are no well-dated layers in which you can look for fossils. Also the Australian Aborigines were not a culture very much interested in stone tools or weapons. The fact is that East Africa became the focus of attention mainly because it is a relatively easy place for archaeologists to work, not because it really holds the key to the emergence of modern man.[18]

The all-too-predictable reason conventional archaeologists give for denying human origin in Australia is that the apelike ancestors from whom we are supposed to have evolved did not exist in Australia. In other words, their blind faith in a crumbling paradigm has taken precedence over the explorative use of new and changing data.[19]

Aboriginal creation myths completely reject the idea of *Homo sapiens* or any other species branching out in Darwinian fashion from another animal species. The chronological implication of the molecular evidence supports the Aboriginal view of creation, placing the origin of humanity in Australia. A tribal elder, in conversation with an Aboriginal friend of mine, also supported this point of view. My friend asked the old man, "The scientists and learned white men have been saying we have been here on this land for more than 60,000 years, is that right?" The old man answered, "It is much longer than that. We have been here since the time before time began. We have come directly out of the Dreamtime of the Creative Ancestors. . . . All other peoples of the world came from us. People who farm the land or make buildings and keep animals—these people do not belong to the spirit of this land and must go out from here because those things are against the Law of this land."

The existing theories on the Aborigines' appearance in Australia are conflicting and unconvincing. The most common one is that the Aborigines arrived in boats from Asia or New Guinea. The boats produced by the Aborigines at the time of European contact were not capable of this ocean journey, though, even considering the lower sea levels that existed during the Ice Age.[20] Added to the recent findings regarding molecular mutations, such flaws and inconsistencies in conventional theory encourage us to explore other sources of evidence—namely, those that show the Aboriginal culture reaching back to the beginning of human consciousness and emerging out of the Dreaming.

FIGURE 20
The ceremonies of the Aborigines call us back to the primal origins of creation.

Old Melanesia, c. 20,000 B.C.

— Configuration of "Old Melanesia"
— Late Pleistocene shorelines
— Contemporary shorelines
• Significant archeological sites

FIGURE 21
During the ice ages Australia formed a continuous land mass with the islands of New Guinea and the tip of Southeast Asia.

THE ARCHAEOLOGY OF AN AUSTRALIAN GENESIS

Archaeologists have recently acknowledged the importance of cultures that rely solely on wooden tools and technology. These cultures leave no documented evidence of their existence. Once widespread in equatorial and southern subequatorial regions of the world, they are now considered the "invisible counterplayers" to the easily documented stone and iron cultures of the north.

Cultures built on wood-based technologies, of which the Tasmanian Aborigines are the purest example, are considered by archaeologist Leo Frobenius to be a second kind of culture, "as distinct from the Northern cultures as the plant world is from the animal world." Although historical documentation is rare, Frobenius believes that these original cultures from the south had a profound influence on the historical development of humankind. The carving of stone sculptures and tools, for example, was undoubtedly realized and established in the southern wood-based cultures before its sudden appearance in paleolithic Europe or neolithic Egypt.

A land configuration called old Melanesia, composed of present-day Australia and the islands of Indonesia and believed to have existed before 20,000 B.C., is thought to be one of the places of origin of wood-based cultures.

The remains of the oldest *Homo sapiens sapiens* have been found in three regions: old Melanesia, northeast Africa, and northern Iraq. There has been great debate over which of these regions might have been the "garden of Eden" from which modern *Homo sapiens sapiens* emerged. The dating of burial sites in these regions ranges from 30,000 to 50,000 or 60,000 years, but because of controversy over dating techniques the age question is still open.

Archaeological work in Australia is in its infancy, yet already evidence for an Australian origin is beginning to strengthen. Opinion is tending toward the belief that the oldest skeletons representing modern *Homo sapiens sapiens* come from the Australian and Indonesian finds. Carleton Coon, considered a leading expert on racial origins, believes the Australian and Indonesian finds are of the Tasmanian type of Aborigine, that is, from the southernmost location in Australia.[21]

In the late 1970s, in the tablelands of South Australia at a site called Lake George, archaeologist Gurdip Singh made a 72-meter core drilling into the sediments at the bottom of the lake. This drilling provides the longest continuous record of vegetation and fire history in Australia, covering a period of 350,000 years. The sequence shows that 120,000 years ago a sudden increase in the amount of burning occurred, which

Singh argues could only have been caused by Aboriginal fire sticks, used in hunting to ignite fire-sensitive bush and drive out game.[22] Another piece of evidence is a fragment of human bone, too old to date with carbon, found in the central Australian desert in 1987. Analyzed with a new radioactive uranium residue dating process, it appears to be close to 150,000 years old.[23]

Shred by shred, evidence is accumulating to support the claims that have long been maintained by Aboriginal tribal elders: culture arose and spread from southern regions, such as old Melanesia and Australia, where the oldest human remains have been found and where the oldest traditions have been preserved. Archaeological evidence shows that these wood-based cultures maintained their wood technology, while the northern centers of origin, especially Iraq, moved on rapidly to stone and metal technologies. Frobenius speculates that the wood-based cultures of southern origin (Melanesia, Australia, and Africa) at one time extended much further north and then retreated in response to climatic change.[24] For some reason inexplicable in terms of conventional theory, "Australia, as though a museum of human origins, retained all the arts

FIGURE 22
Kunmanara, a Pintupi Aborigine, removing a wood slab to make into a spearthrower. The wooden tools of the Aborigines are as strong, primary, and vital as the people who create them.

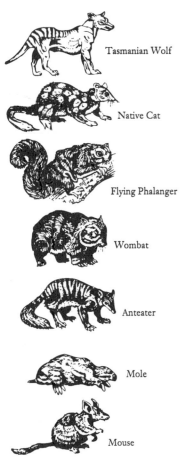

Tasmanian Wolf

Native Cat

Flying Phalanger

Wombat

Anteater

Mole

Mouse

FIGURE 23
Marsupials, which carry their young in frontal pouches, predate the appearance of placenta-bearing mammals by millions of years. For each of these species of placenta-bearing mammals there exists, in Australia, a marsupial prototype, strikingly similar in body structure and behavior to its more recent counterpart on other continents of the world.

and ways of the 'fathers' and 'grandfathers,' preserving an epi-paleolithic hunting age to the present day."[25] Perhaps wood-based cultures did not "evolve" because their revelations, or Dreamtime laws, prevented them from doing so.

Other factors also support an Australian origin of humanity: Australia is the oldest geological land mass and has the oldest animal species. Australian marsupials predate all other mammal forms by at least 125 to 120 million years. Each marsupial species is a prototype for a later placental species, for example, the Australian wombat is the prototype for the European groundhog, and the Tasmanian tiger is the prototype for the North American wolf. It is as if the marsupials served as archetypes for subsequent species. The Australian marsupial possum is a species that has remained unchanged for 65 million years. It is interesting that all the Australian marsupials, such as the kangaroo, were preceded by a giant form of each of these species. These giant marsupials disappeared from Australia only 15,000 years ago.[26]

What seems to be true for the development of animals may also apply to human development. The Australian Aborigines seem to be a predecessor or prototype in that they exhibit, throughout their populations, distinctive characteristics of all the other four major races.[27] Aboriginal skin color ranges from very dark to light brown, and facial features range from negroid to caucasian and sometimes mongoloid. Some dark-skinned Aborigines have light green eyes and blondish hair. It is as if the Aborigines are the quintessence of the primary fourfold division of the races. Carleton Coon has proposed that the peoples of the world can be divided into five originally geographic groups: the Negroid (Congoloid) race, with a complexion ranging from black to mahogany, everted lips, broad nose, and kinky hair; the Caucasian race, with a typically fair complexion and heavy beard and body hair; the Mongoloid race, with light yellow to coppery brown skin, straight black hair, and usually a heavy upper-eyelid fold; the Capoid race (originally of northern Africa, now considered virtually extinct), with reddish-yellow complexion; and the Australoid race, which exhibits many of the typical characteristics of the above four. The Mongoloid races are believed to have spread into North and South America, becoming ruddier in complexion, and so they are sometimes considered a recurrence of the apricot-skinned Capoid race. The skeletal evidence from the regions of the earth associated with each of the five races indicates that racial differences extend back to the earliest *Homo sapiens.* The oldest bones of Cro-Magnon man in Europe are not from some generalized human type, they are definitely Caucasian. The same is true in Africa, where the oldest recognizable humans are Negroid; China, where they are Mongoloid; and Australia, where they are decidedly Australoid.[28]

The four races—black, white, yellow, and red—correspond to the fourfold archetypal division of creation found in many indigenous cultures. Native Americans relate the four colors of their corn, white, yellow, black, and red, to the four orientations of north, east, south, and west and to the four races of men. Their entire cosmology is ordered by this color division. The same archetypal pattern, based on the four colors and four directions, is found in the Sanskrit cultures of India. This cosmological division also existed in ancient Egypt and continued in the esoteric philosophies of alchemy and astrology. The ancient Taoist philosophies of China and Japan order the entire universe around the same colors. And the Aborigines divide their universe according to the colors of the four earth pigments: red ochre, yellow ochre, white pipe clay, and black carbonic soils. Material science reveals the same fourfold pattern: the four elements basic to all organic substance—nitrogen, hydrogen, carbon, and oxygen; the four universal fields of force—electromagnetism, gravity, and the two nuclear fields; the four types of rock that make up the earth's body—igneous, sedimentary, conglomerate, and metamorphic; and the four major tissues of the body—nerve, bone, blood, and the layered tissue (skin, fat, muscle).[29]

It may seem to be coincidence that modern astronomers have designated the four major phases in the life cycles of stars as black holes, red giants, white dwarfs, and yellow suns. However, their respective qualities are related to and consistent with other symbologies of the four colors. Black, red, white, and yellow can be considered a signature for a fourfold relationship of universal qualities. This fourfold pattern of metamorphosis occurs on every level of manifestation—spatial, stellar, energetic, plant, animal, and human. In the oldest form of African tribal dance, each step is repeated four times because "To be in this world is to be four in spirit and in body, like the four winds and the four legs of

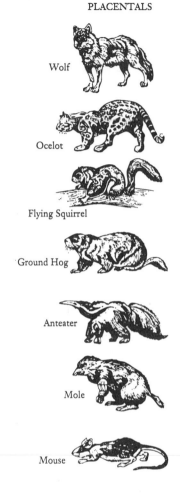

Wolf

Ocelot

Flying Squirrel

Ground Hog

Anteater

Mole

Mouse

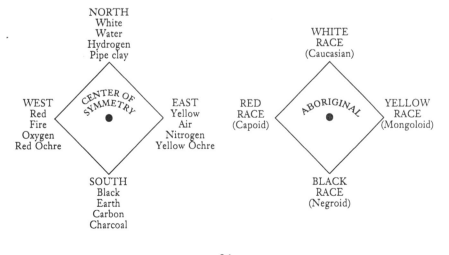

NORTH
White
Water
Hydrogen
Pipe clay

CENTER OF SYMMETRY

WEST
Red
Fire
Oxygen
Red Ochre

EAST
Yellow
Air
Nitrogen
Yellow Ochre

SOUTH
Black
Earth
Carbon
Charcoal

WHITE RACE
(Caucasian)

ABORIGINAL

RED RACE
(Capoid)

YELLOW RACE
(Mongoloid)

BLACK RACE
(Negroid)

← *FIGURE 24*
Many indigenous and ancient cosmologies divide the natural world into a fourfold symmetrical order following the south, east, north, and west orientations. These divisions include earth, air, water, and fire, or black, yellow, white, and red. The center of symmetry of the fourfold division of the races can be considered the Australian Aborigines.

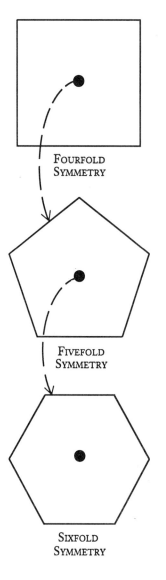

FOURFOLD
SYMMETRY

FIVEFOLD
SYMMETRY

SIXFOLD
SYMMETRY

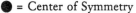 = Center of Symmetry

FIGURE 25
In a symmetrical figure, such as a square, the center of symmetry constitutes a fifth element and can be considered the potential or "seed" for the next order of symmetry—in this case, the pentagon.

the animals." Fourfoldness is one of the archetypal patterns through which the foundations of the natural world are generated. Entering into these primary symmetries—or what the Aborigines call dreaming patterns—in dance, music, image, and thought allows one's being to join in the interrelatedness of seemingly separate phenomena. These types of thought patterns are prevalent in many indigenous cultures and help explain why the further back one goes in history and prehistory, the richer the languages are in metaphor and the greater the utilization of geometry in art and design.[30]

The archetypal process of metamorphosis in matter and language can be explained geometrically if we refer to the above image of the four races with the center of the square considered the quintessence. This fifth component, the invisible center, is the potential within the square for the appearance of the next form, the pentagon. At the center of the pentagon is the inner potential to manifest the hexagon. The square, pentagon, and hexagon may be seen as a sequence or related to each other in any number of less obvious ways, but they are all held within each other in a relationship of potential to actualization, of seed to fruit.

Similarly, the four phases of stars are all present in the heavenly expanse at once. The conceptual mind sees a sequence between them, but to an open perception there is no sequence, only the ever-present unity with all its potentials luminously present.

This last image suggests a way of conceiving our origins and the origins of creation that integrates levels of human experience, as does the ancient Greek idea of archetypes.

The grammatical structure of language, the primary codes in genetics, and the primary symmetries in geometry are sets of fundamental patterns which act as formative forces comparable to the great Ancestors of the Aborigines. These patterned activities manifest all their possible variations and transformations. Evolution seen in this way is better termed an "unfolding"; in Sanskrit, *lila*, a cosmic play—or as the Australian Aborigines say, an Ancestral Dreaming.

FROM THE LADDER INTO THE DREAMING

Some research biologists now admit that they no longer believe that random mutation and natural selection can account for the great complexity and variety of life forms. Many others have backed away from the previous story of man directly "ascending" from monkeys or apes with evasive comments such as, "Really, man and monkeys, as with all of life, are considered to be related to one another."[31] Indigenous people have always understood the basic relatedness of all things, without the imposition of evolution. As a Maori woman stated, "White men may have evolved from monkeys—but we did not! We have come from the Universal creative spirits."[32]

With such significant alterations afoot in scientific thought, there is no doubt that the bits of molecular and archaeological evidence I present here will soon be, or already have been, argued, disproved, or displaced by other bits of information. New information will always appear to replace the old, because nature has far more depth and complexity than we have powers to observe or record it. Scientific theories based solely on information will always proliferate and conflict, because bits of information are like individual dance steps: they can be organized into any number of dances or paradigms. The value of presenting this particular slice of molecular and archaeological research lies in shattering some conventional assumptions and momentarily opening up the possibility for viewing our origins in the light of our most ancient ancestry. The Dreamtime creation myths of the Aborigines guided them to see the physical world as a language, as a metamorphosis of invisible spiritual, psychological, and ethical realms. In this way, the Aboriginal involvement with the physical world includes and resonates with all other aspects of human experience. I believe we must educate ourselves to use observations of the natural world in a similar, more integrated and expansive manner.

Scientific methodologies reflect a misunderstanding of the universal nature and influence of language. Rational empirical scientism is banal in its attempts at utter concreteness. Its methods of investigating and structuring reality make little use of metaphor or symbol, of analogy or simile; it compartmentalizes, isolates, and fragments reality. Despite the advances in relativity and quantum theory, scientists still expect to view a world in which things are exactly as they appear to be, discrete and unperturbed by the subjective depths of the mind from which our very perceptions and rational intellect emerge.

In contrast, Aboriginal languages, initiatic lifestyle, and thought processes have an extraordinary capacity for integrating the products of the conscious and unconscious minds as well as maintaining sensitivity to a living and conscious natural world. The aspects of modern scientific philosophy (relativity and quantum theory, cybernetics and whole systems) that have begun to recognize the interdependence of mental and physical phenomena are reserved for an educated elite who can master the required formulas and concepts. Unfortunately, the rest of us are vaguely educated in the analytical and fragmenting thought processes of the past. Members of the scientific priesthood may have the time to explore and shift from Newtonian to quantum physics or from classical biology to self-organizing systems; an advanced biological researcher may discard the neo-Darwinian concepts of mutation and natural selection in favor of even more abstract mechanical concepts such as gene duplication, exon shuffling, and the transposition of genetic sequences.[33] Meanwhile, the old thought patterns and linguistic practices, along with the social, political, military, economic, and medical institutions based on Aristotle, Descartes, and Newton go rolling along. Furthermore, the same scientific priesthood, for a price, continues to supply those institutions with the knowledge and technological equipment by which they sustain their power.

All of these institutions and thought processes converge in a single world view that not only separates our external world from our inner world but also refuses to acknowledge in practice the feeling, intelligence, and internal consciousness in any aspect of creation except human beings. This world view enables us to guiltlessly accept our civilization's constant onslaught on the rest of creation. Each year in the United States alone, six billion helpless domestic animals are marched to the slaughterhouses as if they were empty, feelingless things. Every eight seconds an acre of forest is destroyed along with its living inhabitants,[34] as if the life and consciousness of these creatures were of less value than the piles of lumber used for our wasteful consumption. Any form of wildlife, insect, or organism that threatens grain or tomato crops is systematically destroyed to ensure that we, at the pinnacle of evolution, are well fed. It is also very clear precisely who occupies that pinnacle. This year, it is predicted, 60 million people will starve to death; very few of them will be from white-dominated Western industrial nations.[35]

We can hope to free our minds from the church of scientific and human progressivism by seeking an understanding of a culture that has proved its capacity to integrate the entirety of human experience harmoniously within the natural and metaphysical worlds. The traditional Aboriginal culture is the prime extant example of that sort of culture.

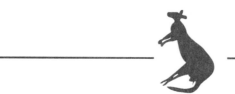

CHAPTER 2

TIME AND SPACE IN THE DREAMING

A very old man, the last member of his tribe to possess the skill of fracturing quartz into cutting tools, is teaching some younger Aboriginal men this art. The small flakes of quartz used for cutters and scrapers are the only supplements to an otherwise wood-based technology. He takes the younger men many miles into the bush to a place where he knows the earth "prepares" stones for this purpose. He points out the features of the land, which has been visited by his tribal ancestors for generations to collect stone for tools. A soft breeze in the leaves of the tall gum trees relieves the heat of the midday sun. The old man squats, traditional sorrow or mourning scars on his chest, one leg drawn underneath him. With his deep-set eyes shut he passes his weathered black hand, in a sensuously fluid motion, over boulder after boulder. To each stone he mumbles a phrase: "This one is pregnant, but she is not ready yet," "This one will be very good in its time." Finally he finds a stone that he picks up and holds in both hands; with a knowing smile, he says, "The flint lives inside this stone like a dream inside your mind. Its essence has been prepared inside the stone since the Dreamtime . . . now it is ready to be born!"

← *FIGURE 26*
The most ancient craft of splitting stone cutters and scrapers from quartz boulders.

FIGURE 27
An Aboriginal quartz scraper.

TIME AND SPACE
IN THE DREAMING

Quick, sharp blows with another stone shatter the boulder, and the desired implement appears out of the rock. The young Aboriginal men watch the old man intently as he removes the newborn tool from the dark womb of its parental rock and holds it up with noticeable satisfaction. In most cases there is no need to chisel or shape these pieces of stone; they are "born" perfect and are almost identical to the 13,000-year-old cutting tools that archaeologists have found.[1]

T HIS STORY SHOWS some of the fundamental values and sensibilities of Aboriginal culture. The old man touches each stone to see if it contains a potency that has predestined it to become a tool and lifelong companion. In the language of the Walbiri, a major Western Desert tribe, the word for this innate potential of a thing is *guruwari*—literally translated as "totem design." *Guruwari* refers to the invisible seed or life-creating energy that the Creative Ancestors deposited in the land and in all forms of nature.[2]

The great ancestral beings were vast, unbounded, intangible, vibratory bodies, similar to fields of energy. They created by drawing vibratory energy out of themselves and stabilizing this energy and by specifying, or naming—the inner name is the potency of the form or creature. The comparable image is the creation of sounds, words, or songs from the vibration of breath. Aborigines refer to the Dreamtime creation as the world being "sung" into existence.[3]

Human creations also first exist as subjective energetic states of consciousness: dreams, intuitions, and thoughts that move, like a pendulum, toward objectification in the external world. Once consciousness has participated in an external creation or activity, it swings back from an objective reality to a subjective state. This return, which we call memory, forms the residual base of all existence.

The Dreamtime process of creation resembles the simple act of baking bread. First there is an internal desire, a hunger, a need for a delicious morsel existing in a purely energetic state of mind. The desire comes before the bread, just as the dream of the flint is present in the stone before its emergence in the world. Conscious activity then gathers the ingredients in the physical world that correspond to those in the dream. By combining and working the ingredients, the dream of the bread clothes itself in body. As the bread is eaten, the dream is devoured; it becomes internal and invisible again. The dream of the bread has been digested into a memory.

Aborigines believe that ancestral spirits created the earth and human-kind in a similar manner, through a sequential swing between an internal dream and a physical objectification.

> In their view, the ancestor first dreams his objectifications while sleeping in the camp. In effect, he visualizes his travels—the country, the songs, and everything he makes—inside his head before they are externalized. Objectifications are conceived as external projections of an interior vision: they come from the inner self of the ancestry into the outer world.[4]

Because Indo-European language dictates that we express all our thoughts in past, present, or future tense, we have the notion that time is an abstract backdrop moving in one direction, like the hands of a clock, from past to future. None of the hundreds of Aboriginal languages contain a word for time, nor do the Aborigines have a concept of time. As with creation, the Aborigines conceive the passage of time and history not as a movement from past to future but as a passage from a subjective state to an objective expression. The first step in entering into the Aboriginal world is to abandon the conventional abstraction of time and replace it with the movement of consciousness from dream to reality as a model that describes the universal activity of creation.

The ritual dances and songs that the Aborigines perform every day celebrate the movement from subjective to objective that created the world. This perception guides every aspect of daily life. Even today, an Aborigine stays awake at night before a hunt, watching his sleeping dogs.

FIGURE 28
A Ngatatjara woman preparing spinifex gum. This sticky resin, the only adhesive used by the Aborigines, serves many purposes, including fastening prepared pieces of stone to their predominantly wood-based implements.

TIME AND SPACE
IN THE DREAMING

CONCEPTUAL	Subjective	→	Objectification	→	Subjective
BIOLOGICAL	Seed	→	Growth to Fruition	→	Seed
PSYCHOLOGICAL	Internal Dream	→	Externalization	→	Internal Memory
ENERGETIC	Potential	→	Actual or Kenetic	→	Potential
PHYSICAL	Vibration or Field Activity	→	Formation	→	Vibration or Field Activity
SPIRITUAL	The Unborn	→	The Living	→	The Dead

FIGURE 29
The plant is the Dream of the seed. A movement from subjective to objective to subjective in conceptual processes has counterparts on many levels of existence.

The dog that jerks and growls while dreaming signals to the observant Aborigine that this animal has dreamed of capturing the prey. The dog will be chosen as his hunting companion on the following day.[5] In some Aboriginal tribes the first thing a person does upon awakening is to wander alone into the bush or along the seashore and create a song based on the dreams of the previous night. The animals and birds, the Aborigines believe, hear the dream being sung and recognize that the singer is in touch with the inner world, and therefore they assist him or her in daily hunting and gathering.

Dreaming is extended to every facet of creation. Natural light, when absorbed in the chlorophyll of green leaves, begins the miraculous transformation of energy into tissue. Through digestion and assimilation, this initial transformation of light in the plant kingdom becomes the basis for all subsequent manifestations of conscious life. Only the spectrum of natural daylight can generate this succession of transformations. The Aborigines would say that the grasses and leaves, as well as the flesh that feeds on them, preexist within the "dream of light." Their creation myth acknowledges the intrinsic creative power of light: "All living things are borne in the womb of the great rainbow serpent."

Whether it be sunlight, gravity, rocks, or trees, every distinguishable energy, form, or substance has both an objective and a subjective expression, or, as the Aborigines say, "Each has its own Dreaming." The Western world denies an internal or subjective consciousness to all things and creatures except humans. The rest of nature, we believe, has no dreaming and consequently we feel justified in cutting down trees, gouging the earth, and killing and enslaving animals as if they were all empty

FIGURE 30 →
The Serpent is one of the most profound mythic images.

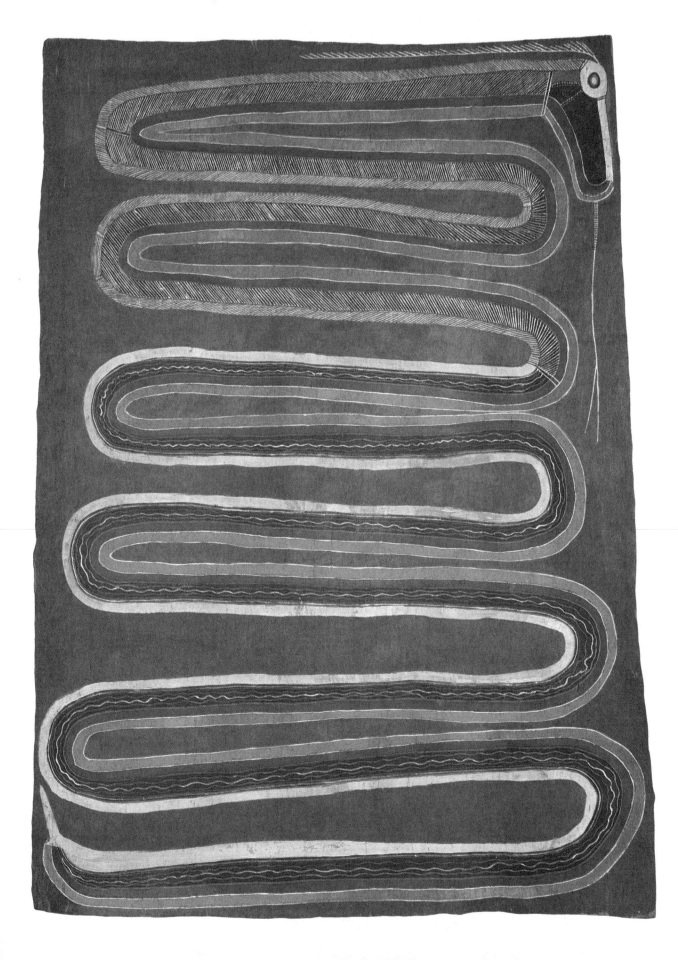

forms. In denying the universe an internal life we imprison our own awareness, so that we live in only the shallow surface of our world. Science used to view the internal in the same rational, material way as it did the external. Recently, though, theoretical physicists have described the subatomic world as if it were a vast thought process or mind. This new approach may increase our sensitivity to the consciousness in all things.

An Aboriginal elder commented, "Unless whiteman learns to enter the dreaming of the countryside, the plants, and animals before he uses or eats them, he will become sick and insane and destroy himself."

I once visited a huge standing rock formation at sunset, in a glowing red canyon outside Sedona, Arizona, with a man of the Cherokee tribe, Willy Whitefeather. When we arrived he sat down directly facing the stones and played a lilting melody on his flute. Later, he said that stones have silicone crystals inside them, through which they listen! "They are like lonely old people, standing and waiting to be sung to. Our people have always sung songs of admiration to the qualities of strength, beauty,

and endurance that stones bring into the world. . . . They are tired and lonely now because the white world has become so blind and selfish. They live in a hollow, unsung world."[6]

Both the Aboriginal and the Native American perceptions can guide us toward a way of being in which our inner vision and outer projection are woven into the natural world in a constant interchange with the dreams and forms of all of earth's creatures.

DREAMSPACE

Space, in our conventional awareness, is basically felt as distance, the empty interval separating objects. Our notion of space depends on our notion of time, which is necessary to measure distance. Hence most of the words we use to describe space, such as long and short, are also used to describe time.

Aborigines do not perceive space as distance. Space for them is consciousness, and, like consciousness, space is divided into two modes. The perceptible, tangible entities in space are like the conscious mind, and the invisible space between things corresponds to the unconscious mind. The term *unconscious* is misleading: the unconscious mind is always conscious; it is a continuum of dreaming. In Western culture, the presence and activity of the unconscious is obvious only during sleep and dreams. For the Aborigines, the unconscious mind is continuous and ever-present, permeating all levels of existence, just as space invisibly fills everything from galaxies to the interior of the atom. The conscious mind is like the things of this world: appearing and disappearing, alternating between wakefulness and sleep, between life and death.

The visible actuality of a form exists simultaneously with its invisible potential, just as the conscious perception exists simultaneously with the flow of the unconscious. Similarly, the potential of the seed and the actuality of the plant appear to follow one another in sequence, as day follows night. From the perspective of the Dreaming, though, day and night exist simultaneously as the opposite sides of a spinning sphere. The Aborigines refer to the inseparable relationship between the actual and the potential, the conscious and the unconscious, as the light and dark faces of the moon—both are always present. In a similar manner, the genetic code might appear to be evolving in sequence from simple to complex, but the simple, primary cells and patterns are present on earth at the same time as the complex forms, varieties, and combinations. The apparent all-pervasiveness of the sequential pattern results from our elevation of and total reliance on the functions of the conscious mind.

← *FIGURE 31*
Aboriginal paintings in Carnarvon National Park, western Queensland, are considered some of the finest and most colorful in Australia still in their natural state. The splattering of pigment, outlining a hand or implement, creates an inversion between the negative (background) space, which appears as a positive activated surface, and the object, which then becomes an empty silhouette. This sort of inversion is basic to the Aboriginal view of reality. As in the cosmologies of modern physics, the Aborigines conceive that space (as well as all that occurs or appears in space) has no physical existence independent of the activity of the perceiving mind. Therefore space must be primarily considered and described as an aspect of consciousness.

Everything that has a spatial existence results from a relationship between the Dreaming and the perceivable world, between the conscious and unconscious aspects of mind. To the Aborigines, the rainbow symbolizes the edge of the unconscious; it is the Dreaming, where the invisible potentials begin to become visible. Birds, who wing their way through empty space, are the messengers of the unconscious, and flashes of lightning are violent discharges of energy from the depths of the unconscious.

To define consciousness as a field of activity with the potential to create unlimited forms, comparisons, analogies, and meanings is to approach the space perception of the Dreamtime. All spatial relationships in the Dreamtime are primarily symbolic. Meaning and information are not transported across distances and time, they are an integral part of consciousness expressing itself as spatial order and arrangement. For this reason, if an Aboriginal child inadvertently kicks a stone or twig, he or she is instructed by a tribal elder to replace it exactly as it was. To the Aborigines, the spatial landscape is a perfect symbolic description of the psychic content of humans and of the ancestral forces that created the world. To disturb the earth in any way is to obscure the meaning and history of humanity and reality. Knowledge is shared through resonance in space and time. Meaning, not space and time, connects all things.

The logic of space is the logic of a dream. An Aboriginal woman recently interviewed on television said, "With your vision you see me sitting on a rock, but I am sitting on the body of my ancestor. The earth, his body, and my body are identical."[7] The logic of dreams does not prevent our being from flowing into the being of other creatures, so that we live in their form and in their awareness. In dreams, other creatures enter and inhabit us. Every character in a dream is fabricated from the stuff of consciousness. In dreams, subject and object interpenetrate.

There is no external space separate from the internal. There are no objects or events—be they stars, spaceships, or molecules—separate from the feelings, desires, projections, activities, and images of consciousness. All are children born from the relationship between the conscious and the unconscious. Once we have been deluded by imbalanced modes of perception or misconstructed language into believing that space is separate from consciousness and time is other than the rhythmic swing between the subjective and the objective, then we have lost sight of the reality of creation.

The phenomenal world is considered the dream of the ancestral beings. Neither the dream nor the phenomenal world is considered an illusion; rather, together they constitute reality. Toward the end of his life, the visionary biologist Gregory Bateson intuited the existence of the Dreamtime.

The individual mind is imminent but not only in the body. It is imminent also in pathways and messages outside the body, and there is a larger mind of which the individual mind is only a sub-system. This larger mind is comparable to God and is perhaps what some people mean by God, but it is still imminent in the total interconnected social systems and planetary ecology."[8]

At this juncture in human history, it is imperative that we recover a sense of the deep logic that underlies the Aboriginal language, rituals, and way of life.

CHAPTER 3

DREAMING AND CREATION

*The seed of the Spirits
blind and huge desire
From which the tree of
the cosmos was conceived
And spread its magic
arms through a dream
of space
Immense realities took on
a shape*
SRI AUROBINDO

HOW THE SUN WAS MADE

For a long time there was no sun, only a moon and stars. That was before there were men on the earth, only birds and beasts, all of which were many sizes larger than they are now.

One day Dinewan the emu and Brolga the native companion were on a large plain near the Murrumbidgee. There they were, quarreling and fighting. Brolga, in her rage, rushed to the nest of Dinewan and seized from it one of the huge eggs, which she threw with all her force up to the sky. There it broke on a heap of firewood, which burst into flame as the yellow yolk spilled all over it, and lit up the world below to the astonishment of every creature on it. They had been used to the semidarkness and were dazzled by such brightness.

A good spirit who lived in the sky saw how bright and beautiful the earth looked when lit up by this blaze. He thought it would be a good thing to make a fire every day, and from that time he has done so. All night he and his attendant spirits collect wood and heap it up. When the heap is nearly big enough they send out the morning star to warn those on earth that the fire will soon be lit.

The spirits, however, found this warning was not sufficient, for those who slept saw it not. Then the spirits thought someone should make some noise at dawn to herald the coming of the sun and waken the sleepers. But for a long time they could not decide to whom should be given this office.

At last one evening they heard the laughter of Goo-goor-gaga, the laughing jackass, ringing through the air.

"That is the noise we want," they said.

Then they told Goo-goor-gaga that, as the morning star faded and the day dawned, he was every morning to laugh his loudest, that his laughter might awaken all sleepers before sunrise. If he would not agree to do this, then no more would they light the sun-fire, but let the earth be ever in twilight again.

But Goo-goor-gaga saved the light for the world.

He agreed to laugh his loudest at every dawn of day, and so he has done *ever since, making the air ring with his loud cackling, "Goo goor gaga, goo goor gaga, goo goor gaga."*

When the spirits first light the fire it does not throw out much heat. But by the middle of the day, when the whole heap of firewood is in a blaze, the heat is fierce. After that it begins to die gradually away until, at sunset, only red embers are left. They quickly die out, except a few the spirits cover up with clouds and save to light the heap of wood they get ready for the next day.

Children are not allowed to imitate the laughter of Goo-goor-gaga, lest he should hear them and cease his morning cry.

If children do laugh as he does, an extra tooth grows above their eye-tooth, so that they carry a mark of their mockery in punishment for it. Well the good spirits know that if ever a time comes when the Goo-goor-gagas cease laughing to herald the sun, then no more dawns will be seen in the land, and darkness will reign once more.[1]

WHAT HAS HAPPENED to the powers of perception and language that allowed the integration of our inner and outer experience? What has become of the vision of the physical world as manifestation of the invisible? What has obliterated the image of a whole and unified creation from the mind of humanity? Is the eternal Dreaming still present, hidden beneath the facts, theories, and fantasies of our present awareness?

The Aborigines speak of the beginning as a creative epoch when world-shaping influences pervaded the universe, before its material formation. Every culture possesses creation myths, and all creation myths—from the Aboriginal Dreamtime to the story of Genesis to the Big Bang theory—postulate an energetic phase prior to the appearance of matter and life. In essence all the stories are similar. Vast fields of turbulent energy interact through the spinning furnaces of galaxies and stars and eventually form stable elements. These elements are then combined into the substance of life under the earth's geological and climatic pressures.

In the Dreamtime creation, the Ancestors' travels, skirmishes, hunts, assaults, and lovemaking scored the earth's surface, leaving their imprints in the earth's topography. In our scientific view, the earth evolved through a phase in which powerful geological and climatic forces shaped the earth's surface, raising mountains, creating oceans, carving riverbeds, and forming rocks and deserts. The major difference is that our cosmology acknowledges only physical forces and the Aborigines attribute consciousness to the creative forces and everything in creation.

Disguised in the language of astrophysics and geology is the essence of the Dreamtime creation; it has slipped beneath the horizon of our conscious thought, like a seed yet to germinate. The active fields in the Dreamtime creation myth are fields of consciousness. The kinetic and psychic energies of the fields are symbolized by the ancestors' ability to alternate between animal apparitions and pure spiritual powers.

The Dreamtime epoch concluded with the achievement of three fundamental conditions that made possible the embodiment of conscious life: the earth's unique topography, speciated life forms, and patterns for social relationships.[2] These three can be regarded as the sacred trinity of

FIGURE 33
Kangaroo Dreaming. Before and during the physical appearance of an animal species, the Aborigines image an energetic field, which is regarded as the spirit or Dreaming of that species.

Aboriginal spirituality. With this task completed, the Ancestors transferred their vibratory potency into the hills, creeks, lakes, and trees and then departed, diving into the earth and rising into the sky. The stage was now set for the physical emergence of the tribes, the plants, and the animals. From then on, the entire cosmos is continually revitalized by the primal potency flowing between the great Ancestors of creation: the unconscious and the conscious, earth and heaven, the All-Mother and the All-Father.

WORLD CREATION MYTHS
AND THE DREAMING

The divine marriage between the great Ancestral couple is also found in the creation myths of Egypt, India, Mesopotamia, China, Central America, and other places. In all these myths the creation is brought about through a great cosmic copulation—the "divine marriage," or *hieros gamos*.[3] The image of the primal couple, the All-Mother (Waramururungundju) and All-Father (Baiame), suggests the Aboriginal belief that they can experience the vast creative process through ecstatic dance and sexuality. They, and all the world, share in the currents of life emanating from this cosmic union.

In myths, new life results from any impassioned act, whether the passion is lust or anger. The story of how the sun was made begins with the fight between Dinewan the emu and his consort Brolga. When Brolga throws the egg, the level shifts to the metaphysical interaction between earth and sky. The image of this metaphysical union is symbolized in the biological world by the proportionally vast egg as it absorbs one sperm and is enveloped by a swarming multitude. Absorption and reemergence is the rhythm of the dance of universal copulation. It is a pattern that permeates all of existence: the fundamental particle emerges, dissolves, and reemerges from the quantum field; the awakened state rhythmically dissolves and reemerges from sleep and dream; the static rises and falls back into the ecstatic.

As the copulation continues, as the Dreaming unfolds, the mighty acts of the great Ancestors—their pains and joys, successes and failures, blindness and revelations—sculpt the earth. These acts accumulate and are retained as a memory, as a world-shaping code. The seed energies that the Ancestors spill sustain the earthly life to follow. In the story of the sun's origin, the yolk of the egg explodes in space, to merge with a fire that illuminates the earth. The earth, then, is the love- and battle-strewn trysting ground of the Ancestors, undulated and saturated with blood and semen from the virginal, wild, ecstatic union of the boundless uni-

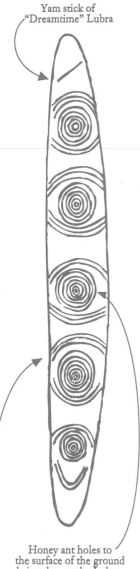

Yam stick of "Dreamtime" Lubra

Honey ant holes to the surface of the ground being dug out by Lubras with their yam sticks

"Dreamtime" Lubras sitting at the ant holes and digging the ants out with their yam sticks

FIGURE 34
These carvings belong to the honey ant totem clan of the Wailbri Tribe of the western desert. They depict a Dreamtime story revealing the locality where the honey ants disappeared into the earth in Lubra country after completing their mythic travels.

versal Dreaming with the name-giving power of the the seed (which defines innumerable variations: the *one* opens itself up to the *all*).

The intercourse of Geb and Nut in the Egyptian creation myth and that of Shiva and Paravati in the Indian myth reflect the theme of the much earlier Dreamtime creation. Absent from the Egyptian and Indian versions is the image of the creation story written like a book in the earth's topography. Although there are residues of this idea in many myths, such as the Indian concept of the earth as body of the goddess, the vision of the sacred earth as a ledger of cosmology is unique to the Australian Aborigines. Unique also is the fidelity to these unwritten stories with which the Aborigines conduct their lives. The legends are sung and danced daily. Each Dreamtime story is designated and remembered by the place where it occurs. Each series of stories, therefore, define a path across the countryside that connects localities and the mythic episodes associated with them. These Dreaming tracks, or *songlines*, stretch in all directions, criss-crossing the entire continent of Australia. No local band, hunting group, or dialect unit "owns" a complete mythic line: each group "owns" only a section of these journeying pathways, making the "songlines" a network of communication and cultural exchange among people separated by great distances.

The mythic stories guide all the nomadic movements of the Aborigines. The connections between myths may or may not be concurrent with the fertility cycles in various regions. The Aborigines nonetheless primarily follow the mythic songlines in their hunting and gathering, they do not pursue a particular flock, herd, or seasonal growth. Their adherence to a mythic dimension rather than a practical knowledge of hunting or the seasons demonstrates their faith in the sacred relationship of the cycles and rhythms of nature, in accordance with the story of the earth's metaphysical creation. For them, as for perhaps no other culture, the earth is the center of the intelligence of creation; a symbol and memory of the primordial Dreaming; a receptacle of all seeds cosmic, metaphysical, and biological; the nurturer of all life, both visible and invisible. By listening to the songs and energies of the earth the Aborigines hear the voices of the universal Dreaming.

In the Aboriginal myth, the theme of reciprocity between the creation and the Dreamtime Ancestors is heightened. Humanity and all the world dreams, and through these dreams continually receive the potencies of the Ancestors. With equal constancy humanity returns the power to them in daily life, in song, in ritual and dance. Our tangible world is nothing other than the Dreaming of the Ancestors. Reciprocally, our desires, dreams, and inner activities of mind are the embodied life of the Ancestors. In other words, the interiority of the gods is our external reality, while the interiority of humanity and earthly life is the objective existence of the gods. The Ancestors and we, their earthly creation, exist inseparably and appear as the interiority and exteriority of each other. We are dreaming within a Dreaming.

The internal-external reciprocity between humans and the creative forces of nature was explained to me by an Aboriginal friend while walking through the business district of Sydney. He said, "With your mentality, these tall buildings are the result of the dreams and plans of architects, engineers, and builders. But the Aborigine also sees that the stones and bricks themselves have an inner potential—a dreaming to become a structure." As much as the builders dreamed and projected the building, so too did the stones dream and project the minds, hands, and activities of the builders. The essence of stone—calcium, iron, carbon, and other minerals—is present in the bones, nerves, and tissues of the builders. Why is it not possible, then, that the essence of consciousness is inside the stone? The buildings are ugly and alienating because, through our wilfullness, our dream and the dream of the stone have been diverted from remembering the great Dream of the Ancestors.[4]

Human dreams, human creations, take place within a Great Dream that is already complete. Humankind must remain cognizant and respectful of the Great Dream of the world, so that all our works, ways, and energies reflect the heartbeat of the Ancestral Creators. This, in essence, is the Dreamtime Law: maintaining sensitivity to an invisible, metaphysical prototype, physically sensed and symbolically read in the topography of the land. The subtle energy and symbolic forms of the landscape provide organizational norms and precedences that people must maintain for there to be harmony in the world. The role of dreaming in the creation lifts the concept out of the personalized, subjective box of modern psychology and gives it universal importance. Our dreams can be a peek into the expanding circle of the dreams of the creative world that reach back to the Dreamtime. The subjective states of all beings—animals, plants, matter, energy, stars, the moon, and humans—converge in the Dreamtime. The Aborigines believe that when we hold in balance within ourselves the two worlds of space and consciousness, we do not need to fantasize or construct any other worlds. This implies that we cannot hope to integrate ourselves and our society into the consciousness and ecology of the earth until we have deeply integrated these two worlds in our own daily existence.

The Dreamtime is as permanent and unchanging as the earth itself. Innovation and change for the Aborigines occurs as a result of developing their capacity to discover and reenact the eternal elements of the Dreaming. In their cosmology, this discovery replaces our idea of evolution. Consciousness expands by increasing exchange between its two domains. Aboriginal life reflects the ideal that the hunter-gatherer way

Underground tunnels of the Honey ants

Yunajadi—a food of the Honey ants

Holes to the Surface of the Ground

Track followed by the "Dreamtime" Honey ants when traveling from Mt. Doreen to Yulumu, the hill where they disappeared that is now their Totem Center

of life affords a highly refined sense perception, great physical strength, and purity of cultural, environmental, and intellectual order. It is this way of life that enables humans to live simultaneously in the Dreaming and in the embodied world.

Sleep is but one entrance into the Dreaming. The Aborigine's education begins in developing awareness during sleep and during the hypnotic state. Becoming increasingly lucid in sleep—to the point of being able to act consciously in the dream world and to bring symbolic messages received while asleep into the awakened world—is the beginning of the initiation process for every tribal person. The Aboriginal tradition maintains that the extraordinary reality of the Dreamtime can only be experienced through extraordinary states of consciousness. The capacity to move back and forth between the two worlds with clarity and agility is developed through a series of initiations that lead the participant through deep trance states, both hypnotic and ecstatic. In this way, they learn to integrate the mystery of the supersensory world of nature into everyday life.

CHAPTER 4

COLONIZATION AND THE DESTRUCTION OF THE DREAMING

There is a Dreamtime story that goes way back. It tells about the wise men or tribal doctors of old. They used to be able to see into their special crystals. They could see pictures of the past, pictures of what is happening far away, right now, and pictures of the future. Some of the future pictures fill the old fellas with dread. They saw a time when the color of the blackfellas, like the stones, seems to grow paler and paler, until only the white faces of the spirits of the dead could be seen all over Australia. Aborigines associate white skin with the dead, as we all turn white as skeletons after death. When the white men first came to Australia, the blackfellas thought they were spirits of the dead people coming back to their old country and so they welcomed them. The Dreamtime Law says, the living must make ceremonies and help the spirits of the dead find their way up to the sky where the dead spirits live. The ceremonies failed to carry the white-faced people to the realm of death, but the white man sure brought the realm of death to earth.[1]

FIVE HUNDRED YEARS AGO, European colonization of North and South America and Australia began, and so initiated the final death blow to the archaic consciousness founded in the Dreaming. The archaic world perception, its customs, initiations, and languages, had held the invisible realms as an essential part of every moment of daily life. This world view finally sank into an ocean of blood, as an estimated 60 million hunter-gatherers and other indigenous people perished. The conquest of the "new world," which we glorify as heroism/adventurism and progress, was a massive crescendo of plunder, massacre, enslavement, and dispossession that had its origins in the advent of agriculture 10,000 years ago.

FIGURE 35 ➜
Some Aboriginal tribes remained undiscovered in the desert well into the twentieth century. The confrontation of these two worlds represents the greatest possible contrast in human cultures. The first time a tribal elder of the Tiwi people from Bathurst Island saw an automobile, he keeled over and died of fright, believing it to be an ugly demon. Certainly the automobile has been a demon of destruction to the earthly environment.

Hero/Destroyer: The
Two Faces of Power

History reveals that the invasion of one culture by another occurs in two basic forms. When an invading people conquers another culture with similar fundamental structures, the existing culture is not destroyed. The conquerors are usually able to maintain their dominance by setting up institutions within the existing structures. Some taxes and goods are commandeered for the benefit of the conquerers, and the fundamental way of life is permitted to continue. The aggressors often refrain from disrupting the social fabric and the customs and lives of the people. This enabled the power hold of the Roman Empire in the Middle East, the Egyptian control over Nubia, and the Greek take-over in ancient Egypt. In fact, the Greeks even adopted the customs and religion of the conquered Egyptians.[2] This type of invasion, referred to as military or political imperialism, developed as an accepted, if undesirable, way of life among city-based agricultural settlements.

The other type of invasion, called colonization, is marked by a sweeping away of the entire way of life of the invaded peoples. The economic base is plundered and destroyed, sacred sites are obliterated, and the native people deported or exterminated *en masse*. Colonization usually occurs when there are deep cultural, spiritual, and socioeconomic differences between the invaders and the indigenous peoples. It is often heralded as the transformation of a backward, primitive culture into the image of the more advanced conquering society. The Assyrian and Babylonian cultures, whose economies were based on irrigated agriculture, are typical of early colonialists: they destroyed the surrounding nomads' way of life and established their own system in its place.

Historically, the most extreme cultural contrast has been that between hunting-gathering and agricultural, city-based societies. These two societies radically conflict on every level of existence from the spiritual to the physical. The confrontation of these two cultural forms has often meant the genocide of the hunter-gatherers. Often, these acts of mass destruction are glorified as colonial heroism, as in the case of the decimation of the Native American and Australian Aboriginal cultures. "The famous American historian, Francis Parkman, wrote of the American Indian: 'He will not learn the arts of civilization, and he and his forest must perish together.'"[3]

Colonizing invaders came not as conquerors but as replacements for an older social order that was either completely transformed or annihilated. Because hunter-gatherers do not disfigure and exploit the natural environment or lay claim to the land in the manner of the conquerors, they have been denied the rights of conquered nations as well as the basic rights of human beings. Cultures that colonize have a fundamentally different view of the world from those that do not. To the Aborigines, the violation of the sacred relationship between human groups and their place of origin represents a spiritually degenerate condition that has disrupted the fundamental harmony on which creation is based.

Most prehistorians now agree that the so-called primitive hunter-gatherer lifestyle did not include the activity of warfare as we know it. Conflict between hunter-gatherer groups is carried out as a ceremonial play of hostilities, a form of ritual theater in which there is little injury or damage. Warfare arose with civilization, and civilization arose with agriculture. Historian W. Newcomb writes, "In a very real sense true warfare may be viewed as one of the more important consequences of the agricultural revolution."[4]

This recently revised view of warfare in primitive culture has cast doubt on the validity of applying Darwinian natural selection to our understanding of the growth and movement of prehistoric populations. (It also calls into question the Darwinian model for the emergence of *Homo sapiens* from earlier intermediate species.) The model of the stronger, intellectually superior culture invading, destroying, and replacing a weaker or less-evolved culture appears to be applicable only to agriculturally based civilizations. It is meaningless as a dynamic for hunting and gathering populations, since the acquisition of land and the subjugation and destruction of surrounding tribes is unknown to them.

Alongside the frightful, ever-mounting list of biological extinctions is the even starker evidence of major cultural extinctions that began with the advent of agriculture. The disappearance of indigenous hunting and gathering peoples constitutes a horrific, almost unacknowledged, genocide in human history.

THE DREAMING DIES IN THE WEST

The history of Judeo-Christian civilization is associated with the colonialist pattern of expansion. In each stage of the growth of this multifaceted culture, the expansion barbarously eradicated what existed before. When the Hebrews (nomadic tribes who herded livestock) went into Canaan to claim their promised land, they destroyed the ancient Canaanites, Philistines, and other tribal or simple agrarian settlements. The Canaanites, judging from their rituals, were typical hunter-gatherers. The history of the Jews, as recorded in the Old Testament, is one of

conflict with their indigenous hunter-gatherer predecessors and conquest of and merging with simple sedentary agricultural centers. The structure of Judaism reflects these profound transformations.

An agricultural and livestock-based society such as that of the Jews requires hierarchy and centralization. Unlike archaic hunter-gatherer societies, where each person independently obtains his or her needs from nature, agriculture creates a system of interdependencies. One sector of the society must constantly attend to food cultivation, while others occupy themselves in the storage and dispersal of seasonal crops. Others must build the structures required by permanent settlement and the accumulation and storage of goods. Eventually, a military sector develops to defend and control the fixed boundaries, and an administration is required to oversee the entire system. Since rain and predictable weather patterns are necessary for crop growth, agricultural religion focuses on the heavens and weather. They elevate to highest status a god of thunder and rainstorms, such as Zeus, combined with a god of time and periodic order, such as Chronos. Judaism's singular composite sky god, named Yahweh, ascended and subsumed all the gods and goddesses associated with earthly places and creatures.

The rise of a single deity marks an important shift in the history of religion. The living Mother Earth, which had provided all, was no longer worshipped but plowed and controlled. The places where her nourishing energy and substance flow to the surface, the places of animal, plant, and human fertility, could no longer be considered sacred. The multitude of local gods and goddesses had to be ignored in favor of propitiating the one heavenly God. The Jewish kings cut down the vibrant sacred groves, desecrated the spirit-filled deep caves, grottos, and waterholes, and used the energy-charged hills and mounds as building sites. To ensure that their God was transcendent and universal they forbid any image of deities, especially god-animal images. They smashed the bronze serpent and forbade the exhibition of the golden calf, which was associated with ecstatic sexual rites. Instead of living in small hunting bands or villages, people were rounded up to form cities whose center was a hilltop temple. Religious worship was allowed only within the confines of architecture.[5] The king and the God, the palace and the temple—each reinforced the power that the others held in subjugating the people. Fed by the regular food source, populations expanded rapidly, filling the needs of productivity, defense, and expansion. Some of the sacred sites were allowed to remain, but where archaic hunting and gathering people had danced ecstatically in order to enter the spirit of the animal and plant species, the new religion began human and animal sacrifice to propitiate the all-powerful God.

> The rule of power and the destruction of the innocent marked the
> entry of the Hebrews into the Promised Land. When the He-
> brews went into Canaan, to claim the land God had promised
> them, they slew those whom they found there and counted it not
> among their sins. God says this to Moses about Og, the king of
> Bashan: "I have delivered him unto thy hand, and all his people
> and his land. . . . So they smote him and his sons, and all his people
> until there was none left alive: and they possessed his land.[6]

With the spread of agriculture came not only warfare and colonization
but also architecture, cities, monotheistic religion, and the accumulation
of wealth and possessions. Lost was the worship of the earth as the
source of creative spiritual energy.

Rupert Sheldrake, in *The Rebirth of Nature*, describes the succession of
historic epochs that emerged from the important developments in
Hebrew culture. The Hebrew tradition was one of the most important
influences on the foundation of Western civilization. I follow Sheldrake's
progression and add my own interpretations in my analysis of these
developments.

The Christian era is really a growth or extension of Judaism, being a
branch that had become inflamed with a form of Eastern Gnostic asceticism. The Christianizing of old Europe, with its many pockets of neolithic
earth-mother religions, required the same brutal practices as the Hebrew colonization of Canaan. The regions in the far reaches of the
Roman Empire were populated by small nomadic bands or tiny agricultural villages. They were polytheistic, earth-oriented, and decentralized.
The polytheistic Roman Empire, while extracting tribute from these
lands, also tolerated their indigenous culture. The roots of the archaic
in old Europe were deep and relatively undisturbed. To extend and
strengthen the Roman church's dominance over the pre-Christian influences, Christianity employed methods that were later echoed in the
techniques used in the European conquest of the New World.

The Hebrew conquest of their Promised Land differs in important
ways from the Christianization of Europe. While annihilating the old
ways, the Jews also absorbed important aspects of the previous cultures,
including kinship loyalties and deep familial respect; food taboos, in
respect for the sacramental nature of eating; a rigorous respect and
perpetuation of tradition; wailing and other emotionally releasing rituals; and circumcision and the ideal of male initiation.

The Roman church also assimilated much from the earlier polytheistic cultures—in order to draw them under the umbrella of the mother
church. It respected some of the sacred places only to the extent of
building its churches on them. Early Christians adopted and rein-

terpreted—to the point of disfigurement—many of the ancient myths and symbols of the pre-Christian world. They transformed some of the older rites and seasonal holidays without acknowledging their origins. In unobtrusive ways, the seed of the archaic consciousness did survive in the esotericism of both Christianity and Judaism, but the sacred sense of a living earth was never tolerated, and the strong matriarchal traditions were subsumed under a patriarchal system. The inquisitions and witch hunts of the Roman church were an onslaught not only against heresy and female-based religious rites but also against the practices associated with sacred sites and the particular earth energies surrounding them.

In melding Middle Eastern monotheism and forms absorbed from the pagan or neolithic worlds, the doctrine of the Roman church became muddled with inconsistencies, superstitions, and corruption. This led to the next phase of growth from the stem of the Hebrew tradition, the Protestant Reformation. The Reformation tried to rid Christianity of all its pagan residues, especially any hint of nature worship and reverence for sacred places.

> The Protestants were trying to bring about an irreversible change in attitude, eradicating the traditional idea that spiritual power pervades the natural world, and is particularly present in sacred places and in spiritually charged material objects. They wanted to purify religion, and this purification involved the disenchantment of the world. All traces of magic, holiness and spiritual power were to be removed from the realm of nature. . . . The Protestant iconoclasts had a different goal: not the substitution of one kind of sacred place for another, but the abolition of all sacred places.[7]

From the Protestant Reformation and the Italian Renaissance sprang the third branch of the Judeo-Christian continuum, the growth of the scientific revolution. The work of Francis Bacon and the ensuing development of the "scientific priesthood" rested on the foundation of the new ambitions and the riches gleaned by colonialism in the New World. Scientism flourished, and its view that knowledge gave humans power over all of creation was gaining ground.

Rooted in Middle Eastern agricultural imperialism, fertilized by the blood of colonialistic destruction, and armed with unprecedented technological power and material wealth, the European-American empire is finally uprooting the last remnants of native cultures. The Western world leaves no place on earth for the archaic world to survive. The "corporate extension" of the British Empire continues to mine and graze to death the homeland of the Australian Aborigines. In concert, the destruction of the rain forests in Brazil, Indonesia, and Malaysia marks the end of the last hiding place of the Dreaming. With the death of the dreaming, we are witnessing the dying of the earth.

The purely economic values of twentieth-century capitalism follow the same pattern as the religious colonialism that preceded it. Capitalist models of consumption and productiveness permeate and transform everything they touch, leaving behind only remnants of the original values of the culture.

Soviet socialistic imperialism has also sought, with sword in hand, to impose its own standards on the culture of the people its empire encloses. Chinese socialism has been ruthless in its attempts to destroy Tibet, one of the last great sanctuaries of mystical culture. Such economic colonization may be considered the newest branch on the tree of the religion of agriculture and industrialism.

This brief history of Western civilization bears out the Aboriginal concept of the passage of time as movement from subjective to objective. What we view as the historic era is a process of gradual externalization of the seed powers of the Ancestors latent in creation. Archaic cultures were based in the vision of the collective and universal unconscious. The activities and religion of agriculture began the externalization of human attention, which turned toward the physical manipulation of the material world. As consciousness moved from inner subjective toward outer objective, manufacturing of material forms and energies has increased. These externalized powers are, in essence, the spirit potential inherent in humanity and the entire natural world. The conventional scientific mentality is the extreme expression of a concrete externalized mode of perception and thought. We can only hope that its absolute domination means that the pendulum must be about to start a return toward the internal sense of existence.

The Sword, the Plough,
or the Dreaming

The lack of any form of agriculture in Aboriginal Australia is now fully recognized as the result of a conscious choice. It is not, as Darwinian experts previously claimed, due to "primitivism," racial deficiencies, or the result of environmental hardship. Rather, it was an active choice of Aboriginal culture to adhere to their ancient Dreamtime Law. The Dreamtime stories are the longest continuous religious belief documented anywhere in the world.[8] In all the thousands of stories, hunting and gathering is the only form of food procurement mentioned. The adventurous joy of hunting and foraging, free and naked in the open air of primal forests, makes other possibilities unthinkable for a healthy,

59

FIGURE 36

The Aborigines live so in tune with nature that they utilize the most painless methods for killing their game. As one tribal Aborigine stated, "There is no danger in hunting because the snakes and crocodiles are our kin and speak the same language as we do."

sensual, and spiritual people. As anthropologist Leslie White suggests, "Hunting and gathering society was unquestionably the most satisfying social environment man has ever lived in."[9]

Paleopathologists who study the skeletons of ancient hunter-gatherers say they tend to be stronger and more robust and show fewer signs of degenerate diseases than those of later agriculturalists.[10] The very real necessities of agriculture—the tedious repetition and endless chores of crop cultivation; the necessity of laboring on and defending denuded, exhausted plots of land from weather damage, insects, and wildlife; the bondage to one particular locality and one measured domicile—were responsible for the separation of human activity into the duality of work and play. In all hunting and gathering societies there was no real differentiation between the two. As physiologist Jared Diamond argues, "Agriculture is the worst mistake in the history of the human race."[11]

It was not a naive choice of the Aborigines to abide by their Dreamtime Law and reject agriculture; archaeological evidence indicates that the Aborigines had all the proadaptations for initiating agriculture and domesticating animals. There is evidence that they made contact with cultivators from New Guinea 7,000 or 8,000 years ago but never adopted their methods. And although at that time they were also exposed to the use of bows and arrows and earthenware vessels, they did not deviate from the purity of their technology and the Dreaming.

The Aborigines gathered the seeds from wild grasses and trees and had a complex system for processing grains, including winnowing and seed grinding, that dates back more than 40,000 years. There appears to be no explanation for why these cereal gatherers did not become cereal cultivators other than deliberate choice.[12] The choice was dictated by the plan of life laid down by the Ancestors. This culture also refused to adopt clothing, even though they had an abundance of skins and used refined weaving techniques. They refused architecture, even though they made complex structures for ritual purposes. They refused writing, even though they were accomplished artists and makers of signs, with an exquisite capacity for abstraction and symbolic representation. The Aborigines chose to transmit information from generation to generation through example and through shared experience in stories, art, songs, and ceremonies, again in conformity with the ancient Law.

Any custom, ritual, social behavior, or form of technology that was not mentioned in the Dreamtime stories was not included in the Aboriginal way of life. Written language, clothing, and domestic architecture are, like agricultural practices, nowhere to be found in the vast oral literature of the Dreamtime. These stories guide the Aborigines toward a relationship with the external world that is entirely mythic and metaphysical rather than physically exploitative and manipulative. In the words of archaeologist Rhys Jones:

> Instead of putting their surplus energy into getting more food out of the landscape, Aborigines expended it on religious and artistic development in a huge release of intellectual effort. For them, there was the religious and artistic imperative. In that sense, Aborigines, supported by their technology and skills, were able to float above the harsh vagaries, the great stresses thrust upon them by an ever-changing continent.[13]

The fully sensual lifestyle of the Aborigines, their deeply spiritual communication with the earth, and their unshakable belief in their Ancestral Laws created an Aboriginal psychology that was disinterested in acquiring and possessing material things. Their lack of desire for anything outside their own simple tools continually baffled early explorers.

> In botanising today on the other side of the river we accidentally found the greatest part of the gifts and clothes which we had given to the Aborigines left all in a heap together, doubtless as lumber not worth carriage.[14]

Westerners assume that agriculture, writing, clothing, and architecture comprise the very definition of civilization and the unquestioned pinnacle of human progress. Yet all the evidence of environmental destruction, constant warfare, starvation, and moral and social decline is asking us to overturn our ingrained assumptions and view our so-called technical advances as representations of a cycle of degeneration. Here is a summary of what a brief exposure to our civilization has brought to archaic, indigenous peoples all over the world.

1. Wholesale enslavement, displacement, and dispossession of peoples, and near cultural genocide.

2. The destruction of abundant natural food sources that provided a balanced, healthy diet and their replacement by agriculture, which drains the fertility of the earth while insufficiently feeding large numbers of malnourished dependent populations.

3. The replacement of a society in which each individual was respected and cared for by a competitive, unsupportive social system in which only the strong survive.

4. The written word and forms of language that propagate deep misconceptions as to the nature of reality, allowing for falsification, illusion, and empty abstractions, has replaced a rich oral tradition that promotes an expansion of memory and high levels of subtlety of expression and perception.

5. The displacement of a rich, intensely spiritual metaphysical world view, which integrated the metaphysical and the physical and which imbued all stages and forms of life with the mystery and dignity of the original creation, by a code of hypocritical morals, arbitrary symbols, and childish miracles, manipulated and twisted to hold the subjective masses in a consensual delusion.

It is difficult enough to look at what our civilization has inflicted on the archaic world, but it may be even more difficult to admit the frightening ambush we have laid for ourselves, our race, and our planet.

In a brief period of 10,000 years, "civilization" has brought humanity and the planet to the brink of destruction. Agriculture has developed into a widespread, mechanized rape of the environment. Deforestation, soil salinization, and land erosion and degradation are among its many side effects.

Because trees trap and re-evaporate so much moisture, deforestation for agriculture significantly affects the amount of rainfall. Further deforestation in the Amazon could have dramatic affects

FIGURE 37
Wooden bowls used by Nyatunyatjara Aborigines. The large one, for carrying food and water, is called Ngunma. The smaller one, used for digging, is called Wira. Wooden bowls like these, together with a dilly bag of twine, are the only containers utilized by the Aborigines. Earthenware was not developed, nor were methods of food preservation, as the Aborigines relish eating freshly gathered foods.

FIGURE 38
*Kaititja woman grinding seed
in the women's camp,
Northern Territory, 1901.
The Aborigines developed all
the methods of grain
cultivation but chose to remain
gatherers of seeds rather than
planters.*

on rainfall throughout the entire world. In Africa, deforestation may be responsible for the fact that the whole continent risks desertification.[15]

The pollution of surface water and the depletion of ground water by agriculture is situating the world on the threshold of a frightening water crisis.

> Seventy-three percent of the water used by humankind goes to agriculture.... Population growth and agricultural development have depleted and polluted the world's water supply, raising the risk of starvation, epidemic, even war. If today countries are poised to go to war over oil, the catalyst for future conflict will be water. In Mexico alone, some thirty million people, or forty percent of the population, do not have safe drinking water.[16]

Agriculture's contribution to the buildup of carbon monoxide, methane, carbon dioxide, and other gases in the earth's atmosphere threatens to disrupt the great rain-making system of our planet. Agriculture has led humanity into a blind alley, on whose walls are written inevitable episodes of famine and starvation.

FIGURE 39
*Young man making twine,
Anula group, Borroloola,
Northern Territory, 1901.
By simply feeding the plant
fiber between their hands
and thighs and rolling it,
the Aborigines produce a
braided twine of strength
and uniformity equal to
any woven on a loom.*

Already the world is consuming more food than it produces; only by drawing on international stockpiles of grain have poorer countries averted widespread starvation. But stocks are being depleted: from 1987 to 1989, global reserves of grain fell from a 101-day to a 54-day supply. If farmers in North America have favorable weather, stockpiles can be rebuilt, but more drought could put the global food supply in critical condition within a year or two.[17]

The prospect of mass food shortages holds an extra dimension of horror, given our long colonialist history and its frequent use of mass extermination. How can we be certain that this method will not be chosen again to "solve" socioeconomic problems, as it was in Nazi Germany and, earlier in the agricultural revolution, during the struggle to establish Christian orthodoxy and supremacy in Europe? Because the powerful Western industrial nations presently tuck their crimes of colonization neatly beneath self-righteous mottos of godliness, individual freedom, human rights, and democracy, we can be, in our hypocrisy, easily deceived. As the great Hindu poet Tagor warned, the West must recognize that "its civilization is built upon uncountable corpses."[18]

Traditionally, all members of Aboriginal society made their own simple wooden hunting instruments; with these they could feed themselves and, if necessary, maintain a completely independent existence. Aboriginal dedication to society and group is not, therefore, based on dependence and need, nor on the fears and ambitions that neediness engenders. Aboriginal individual economic autonomy is a life condition diametrically opposed to the vast network of international economic interdependency that entraps every member of modern civilization. Under the guise of free trade, economic interdependency has become the most recent source of warfare and cultural and environmental destruction.

To examine just one aspect of Aboriginal society, food procurement, in 100,000 to 150,000 years the Aborigines' impact on the fragile environment of Australia has been minimal. The country that colonialists confiscated from them was full of magnificent forests and rich with a variety of beautiful flora and fauna, extensive unpolluted waterways and rivers, and virgin, uneroded, salt-free, fertile soils. The land teemed with wildlife; the oceans were full of fish and seafood. Australia was a primeval garden where one could easily gather a nourishing and varied diet from nature. Hunting and gathering in Australia was never, as often depicted, a hand-to-mouth desperate survivalism. During the seasons of abundance, even in what would be considered the poorer environments of the western Australian deserts, food quests would occupy only an hour or two each day. Even during drought, a mere two or three hours of collecting by the women would provide a day's food for the entire clan. Their traditional way of life provided more time for the artistic and spiritual development of the entire society. Dance, ritual, music—in short, culture—was the primary activity.[19]

In our society, the average farmer or office worker has little time for these pursuits. The materialistic industrial societies are increasingly caught in a round-the-clock whirl in which people are trapped, day after day, in a breathless grind of facing deadlines, racing the clock between several jobs, and trying to raise children and rush through household chores at the same time. Agriculture and industrialism, in reality, have created a glut of material goods and a great poverty of time. Most people have a way of life devoid of everything except maintaining and servicing their material existence 12 to 14 hours every day.[20] In contrast, the Aborigines, who had no need for clothing, agriculture, or architecture, had at their disposal 12 to 14 hours a day for cultural pursuits, while their 2 to 3 hours of hunting and gathering provided a more balanced, varied, and nutritious diet than agricultural societies have ever achieved.[21] Aborigines achieved a higher way of life, both physically and spiritually, by maintaining their daily existence in conformity to the law of their Ancestors.

Many other aspects of tribal Aboriginal life challenge our prevailing concepts of the origins and meaning of civilization. For example, the

65

Aboriginal tribes, whose population is estimated to have been between 700,000 and 2 million at the time of European invasion,[22] inhabited every climatic region of this vast land: from the equatorial and tropical regions of the Northern Territory and northern Queensland to the cold climate of Tasmania, from the incredibly severe and difficult climates of the central and western deserts to the lush green abundance of the eastern seacoast. Tribal populations living under these diverse conditions for over 100,000 years maintained an extraordinarily consistent culture. Their chosen tools and forms of technology, their relationship to the environment in general, their world view, spiritual traditions, and mysterious initiations were in essence identical throughout this vast and varied continent. Along with agriculture, the colonialist drive is completely absent: there is no indication that the people from the severe desert regions ever tried to establish themselves on the abundant coastlines, nor did the northern tribes migrate to escape the incredible heat, nor the Tasmanians leave their much colder climate. Traditional Aboriginal culture in all the widely separated tribes was definitely shaped by precepts that were acknowledged as a universal revelation.[23]

FIGURE 40
The major known cultural areas of Aboriginal Australia.

Western historians and scholars have locked themselves into methods of thinking that are framed and limited by hidden value judgments. We adhere to the theory of evolution because our traditional thinking habits share the same structure as this theory. We believe that the gradual accumulation of data, experience, and analytical skills will eventually cause all our current problems and "unknowns" to fade away: weak or bad ideas will die off and good ideas will survive, in much the same fashion that natural selection works in nature. We believe that we learn lessons from history, and we believe that these lessons gradually modify our concepts until new value shifts emerge. We conceive of human development, and even the development of biological species, as "evolving" in the same way as do our ideas and knowledge structures. What we call Darwinian evolution, with its dependence on the idea of progressive sequences, is in reality a single, outmoded, linear, and analytical thinking method projected on the entirety of universal creation. We ignore the fact that behind our so-called objective history, progressive thought, righteous democratic values, and religious morality lurks a distortion that perpetrates suffering, genocide, and the wholesale destruction of life. The narrow interpretations of not just human origin but the origin and meaning of all creation has led present civilization into a sterile and possibly disastrous enclosure.[24]

> The West has grown positively sick of looking at itself, and it is trying to catch a glimpse of some vague "otherness," some potential alternative, some different reality previously hidden beyond the self-congratulatory mirrors of a stifled and windowless civilization.[25]

The traditional culture of the Aborigines is a rich storehouse of human and social forms and experience. It is of the utmost importance that in our vanity and ignorance we do not deprive ourselves of this legacy, which may contain the keys to survival during the perilous, war-torn darkness and pollution of the present era.

CHAPTER 5

REVELATION, PARADISE, AND FALL: THE MYTH OF THE GOLDEN AGE

If the fulfillment and delineation of the human person with a social, natural, and supernatural (self-transcendent) setting is a universally valid measure for the evaluation of culture, primitive societies are our primitive superiors.[1]

JARED DIAMOND

THE SOUTHERN CROSS

In the very beginning when Baiame, the sky king, walked the earth, out of the red ground of the ridges he made two men and a woman. When he saw that they were alive he showed them such plants as they should eat to keep life, then he went on his way.

For some time they lived on such plants as he had shown them; then came a drought, and plants grew scarce, and when one day a man killed a kangaroo rat he and the woman ate some of its flesh, but the other man would not eat though he was famished for food, and lay as one dead.

Again and again the woman told him it was good and pressed him to eat.

Annoyed, weak as he was, he rose and walked angrily away toward sunset, while the other two still ate hungrily.

When they had finished they looked for him, found he had gone some distance, and went after him. Over some sandhills, over the pebbly ridges they went, losing sight of him from time to time. When they reached the edge of the coolabah plain they saw their mate on the other side, by the river. They called to him to stop, but he heeded them not; on he went until he reached a huge yaraan, or white gum-tree, beneath which he fell to the ground. As he lay there dead they saw beside him a black figure with two huge fiery eyes. This figure raised him into the tree and dropped him into its hollow center.

While still speeding across the plain they heard such a terrific burst of thunder that they fell startled to the ground. When they raised themselves they gazed wonderingly toward the giant gum-tree. They saw it being lifted from the earth and passing through the air toward the southern sky. They could not see their lost mate, but fiery eyes gleamed from the tree. Suddenly, a raucous shrieking broke the stillness; they saw that it came from two yellow-crested white cockatoos flying after the vanishing tree—Mooyi, they called them.

On went the Spirit Tree, and after it flew the Mooyi, shrieking loudly to it to stop, so that they might reach their roosting place in it.

At last the tree planted itself near the Warrambool, or Milky Way, which leads to where the sky gods live. When it seemed quite still the tree gradually disappeared from their sight. They only saw four fiery eyes shine out. Two were the eyes of Yowi, the spirit of death. The other two were the eyes of the first man to die.

The Mooyi fly after the tree, trying always to reach their roost again.

When all nature realized that the passing of this man meant that death had come into the world, there was wailing everywhere. The swamp oak trees sighed incessantly, and the gum-trees shed tears of blood, which crystallized into red gum.

To this day to the tribes of that part, the Southern Cross is known as Yaraan-doo, the place of the white gum-tree. And the Pointers are called Mooyi, the white cockatoos.

So is the first coming of death remembered by the tribes, to whom the Southern Cross is a reminder.[2]

 SEED VANISHES and dies the moment it germinates, becoming externalized as a plant. At this moment, its power springs from latency to action as its physical presence disappears. The seed dies in order to physically manifest, whereas the plant manifests and then dies. If we can say that the death of the seed of archaic consciousness began with the introduction of agriculture, then it is important to discover how it has been retained in the collective consciousness of humanity and the earth. The "seed of the archaic" has been maintained, I believe, in the universal myth of the Golden Age.

The view that the universe is periodically created and destroyed and, like the earth's vegetation, dies only to renew itself, is an article of faith in Hinduism, Buddhism, Zoroastrianism, and Judaism, as well as in early Christianity and the religions of ancient Egypt and Greece. The world's cycle of birth and death and renewal occurs through a succession of four ages in which the initial age is the highest and most glorious, and the subsequent ages represent degeneration. One of the earliest texts to state this view is the Indian Atharva Veda, which bases its prophecy on revelations received 5,000 years ago.

The initial age is called the Golden Age. The Greek philosopher Hesiod wrote in the eighth century B.C.:

69

A golden race of mortal men was created at the beginning of time. The golden race lived like Gods, pain and suffering were unknown to them, death arrived like a self-induced dream, and the earth was fruitful without human toil. Food was plentiful, no wars or strife marred the happiness of human beings.[3]

Every continent and every known culture has a myth or story of the Golden Age. The allegories and metaphors of this myth all depict a time when humanity lived, naked and free, in a primeval world garden, created and given to them by a higher world of preformative ancestors. They all describe a time of purity and innocence when humanity lived in harmony with nature and the cosmos; when there was constant communication between humans, plants, animals, and all the creatures and forms of the earth, visible and invisible.[4] Everything was healthy and independent, and there was no need for tools, morals, compulsions, or fears. It was a time when worthy, capable initiates could achieve extraordinary, supernatural powers of mind and body.

The Europeans who discovered America believed that the paradise of human origins had been rediscovered. The discovery of Australia can be considered a return to an even more ancient paradisiac birthplace of humanity. It is interesting to compare an explorer's descriptions of the Indians of southern California with notations from Cook's journal on his first sightings of the Aborigines. Cook reported,

> They appear to be in reality far more happier than we Europeans; being wholy unacquainted not only with the superfluous but the necessary Conveniences so much sought after in Europe, they are happy in not knowing the use of them. They live in Tranquility which is not disturb'd by the inequality of Condition: the Earth and sea of their own accord furnishes them with all things necessary for life, they covet not Magnificent Houses, Household-stuff etc., they live in warm and fine Climate and enjoy a very wholesome Air, so that they have very little need of Clothing. . . . In short they seem'd to set no Value upon any thing we gave them. . . .[5]

Observations such as Cook's were discredited as preposterous by his biographers and often deleted from editions of his journals. His comments are almost identical to those of explorer Thomas Jefferies, who, on seeing Native Americans in California, perceived a similar vision of paradise.

> As they covet only the necessaries of life, with which nature has abundantly provided them, they scarce so much as think of its superfluities . . . the Indians are the happiest of all mortals . . .

they neither know, nor desire to know, those false enjoyments which we purchase with so much pains, and with the loss of that which is solid and real. And their most admirable quality is that truly philosophical way of thinking, which makes them contemn all the parades of wealth and magnificence.[6]

Based on these descriptions, we need not search for paradise in Elysian fields or nirvana; we need not construct extraterrestrial visitations, buried civilizations technologically superior to ours, lost continents, or space travel. To locate the Golden Age we need only understand the essential aspects of the old primary hunting and gathering way of life, of which there is no better example than the traditional Australian Aborigines.

The Golden Age always involves the idea of revelation at the beginning of time. Revelation can be defined as receiving inspiration or knowledge directly from a source that existed before this world. The belief in revelation presupposes that every form exists initially as an invisible potential within another. In contemporary physics, for example, revelation can be compared to the idea that tangible matter is a potential expression of energy; and energy itself is an expression of an even more subtle, more intangible order known as the field. Each, therefore, is an increasingly tangible actualization of its predecessor. The predecessor continues to exist to inform and vivify the new state. The same pattern can be seen in psychology: subtle insights contain potentials that become actualized as more comprehensible thoughts, and thoughts then become more structured and cohesive concepts that can then lead to material forms of expression. The patterns of manifestation of intellectual and material forms appear as a succession of metamorphoses, each a trope or symbol of its unseen predecessor.

In Aboriginal cosmology the universal manifesting field is consciousness, which simply externalizes or dreams the world of thoughts, forms, and matter. The Aborigines have built their initiatic culture entirely around this concept of revelation. Their language, way of life, and ceremonies keep them "tuned" to hear the stage that came before physical life. Maintaining this attunement allows the physical to resonate with the energy of its preceding state.

Most Golden Age myths depict a wondrous landscape or a life of magnificent power and pleasure that is lost or destroyed because of some disastrous change in human character. Cultures interpret this "fall" from the primal garden or paradise according to their particular needs. The Jewish philosopher Aristobolus was the first to define the fall in terms of sexuality—a theme picked up and carried to extremes by the early Christians. Esoteric Judaism and Christianity, like Buddhism, see the fall as mind that becomes attached to the appearance of the objective world.

71

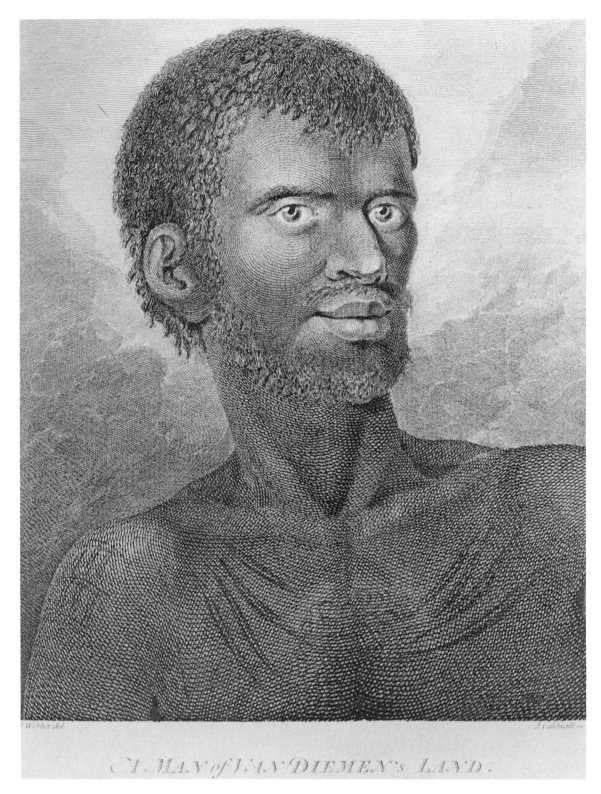

A MAN of VAN DIEMEN's LAND.

FIGURE 41
Engraving of a man of
VanDiemen's Land, present day
Tasmania.

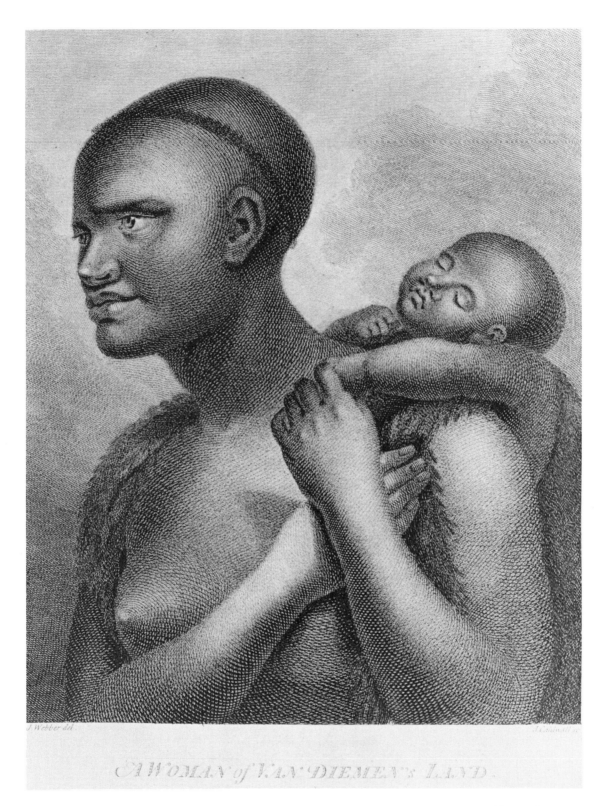

A WOMAN of VAN DIEMEN'S LAND.

FIGURE 42
Engraving of a woman and child of VanDiemen's Land, present day Tasmania.

For psychologist Carl Jung and mythic historian Joseph Campbell, the fall is human consciousness becoming caught in the ego. Egocentricity is a state of mind in which selfishness binds one to personal fears, desires, and will. Campbell claims that one overcomes the ego and captures the Golden Age by achieving an immaculate state of mind, free from desire, lust, and fear. In other words, paradise is equated with the peace and simplicity of a transcendental mind.[7] These three interpretations of paradise and the fall belong to the agricultural mentality.

For the Aborigines there is no fall; paradise *is* the earth in its pristine beauty. For them the earth remains the primordial garden, the all-nourishing mother who feeds all her creatures, grows them, and finally reabsorbs them. All that is earthly is a reflection or externalization of the events of the Dreamtime. There is no part of this existence that needs to be transcended, repressed, or gone beyond. Through ritual, the Aborigines express the entire Dreamtime Creation. There are many falls in the Dreamtime, the falls and vicissitudes of the Creative Ancestors, not of humans. The Dreamtime is reenacted in its entirety, with all the anger, rage, warfare, lust, greed, and control, in dance, ceremony, and ecstatic rites. Ritual creates a space in society for the full play of the Dreamtime: dark and light, cruel and beautiful, grandiose and impoverished. Developing these destructive and constructive potentials in ritual does not spill them out into the external world, to exhaust themselves and the earth in endless cycles of actualization. The constant use of ceremony and ritual in Aboriginal society accounts for the depth and intensity of the people's spirit and the simplicity and continuity of their material existence.

Ritual fuses in simultaneity the seed and the tree, the potential and the actual, the dreaming and the reality. In the Golden Age of the primal hunter-gatherer, revelation is a process of listening directly to the premanifest creation through the medium of the enduring beauty of a pristine earth. In the ages that follow, the people recall the metaphysical realm by invoking the essence of the Aboriginal, or Golden, Age.

The liturgies sung at dawn for thousands of years in the temples of Egypt recall the primeval beauty of the First Day, and were a constant reference to the Golden Age at the beginning of earthly creation. The first stage or beginning of every cycle was considered by the Egyptians to be the most sacred: the first hour of every day, the first day of the week, the first week of the month or new moon, the first month of the year. This initial moment was thought to be the most vigorous and most potent. The first day was symbolic of the capacity of the world, humanity, and the cosmos to perpetually renew itself.

The reverence and longing for the primal condition of earth and humanity, among other aspects of the mysterious Egyptian legacy, sug-

gest that Egyptian religion was a repository of much older hunting and gathering tribal and shamanistic cultures. The Egyptian religious practices, zoomorphic pantheon of gods, burial practices, concepts of death and rebirth, sorcery, magic, and medicine all have origins in the primal culture of the First Day.

In Hindu mythology the age that follows the Golden Age is called the Age of Treta; it is briefer than the Golden Age. In this age, integration and metamorphosis progress toward greater distinctness. Ritual becomes the intermediate between reality and the Dreaming, rather than a direct entering into the Dreaming. For this reason, the Treta Age is called the Age of Ritual. The Hindu third age is Dvapara, the Age of Doubt, in which separateness becomes so great that humanity loses confidence in its own spiritual relatedness to all things and resorts to agriculture as a means of providing for itself. It is an age of division, categories, and

FIGURE 43
Ceremony of Sacred Pole, Arunta Tribe, Central Australia. The pole symbolizes an invisible thread, which can be climbed to connect the initiate to the revelations of the Dreamtime epoch of creation.

REVELATION, PARADISE, AND FALL:
THE MYTH OF THE GOLDEN AGE

analytic judgment and reason, and it is accompanied by the beginning of material and emotional attachments (see Figure 54 on page 92).

The concluding age, the one we now live in, is the most degenerate, when separateness and division become open conflict. It is called the Kali Age; and in it, time itself becomes an incarnation of destruction. The Vishnu *Pranas*, a mythological text of the Hindus, described it this way:

> Kali brought sin into the world. In the Kali Age the proper order of human relations is reversed; social status depends upon the ownership of property; wealth has become the only source of virtue; passion and luxury are the sole bonds between spouses; falsity and lying are the conditions of success in life; sexuality is the sole source of human enjoyment; religion, a superficial and empty ritual, is confused with spirituality.[8]

Aboriginal cosmology, as well as these other similar traditions, is in direct conflict with the linear progression of Darwinian evolution. In each myth, wisdom and goodness stem from a single revelation in a Golden Age at the beginning of time. Prior to the seventeenth century, Western philosophy held the ideal of original primal knowledge, or *prisca sapientia*. This aspect of philosophy sparked the Renaissance in fifteenth-century Europe, when mysticism and ancient knowledge entered Europe, through Greece and the Middle East, and was translated by scholarly academies in Florence and Rome. The enlightenment that these texts brought fanned the flames of cultural rebirth in the minds of such men as Leonardo da Vinci. The Roman church persecuted and assassinated many of these scholars, cutting off this potential cultural transformation in its infancy. The European Renaissance can be seen as more of a stillbirth, or even an abortion, and the horrors of colonizing of the New World soon followed. Residues of this philosophy remained as matters for covert, exclusive intellectual study until the late seventeenth century. Sir Isaac Newton, one of the fathers of the modern scientific method, was caught between the ideal of the *prisca sapientia* and the rising tide of rationalism. He spent most of his elderly life gathering translations of ancient texts and scrutinizing them for hidden symbolism that might reveal some of this ancient knowledge.[9]

With the advent of the Industrial Revolution, the idea of pure and original revelatory knowledge was scorned as superstition by the promoters of industrial progress. Western philosophy then turned to a belief in the unquestioned supremacy of the present over the past, including the belief that knowledge will be continually revealed and increased in the future through the ongoing application of objective scientific methods. So thorough has the propaganda been that the ideal

FIGURE 44
Wandering Sadhus, traditional in India, resemble in many ways the appearance and comportment of the Aboriginal man.

of the *prisca sapientia* is completely forgotten. The doctrine of material progress, which is presently grinding us into exhaustion, can be seen as a reaction to an inner emptiness created by forgetting our exalted origins.

The naked, wandering Sadhus of Tantric India are another sect that expresses identification with the Golden Age. Their tradition results from looking back to prehistoric tribal shamanism. Tantric spirituality was practiced by these cults, who throughout Indian history rejected the confines and structures of villages and cities and, in remembrance of Aboriginal life, lived naked and free in the natural environment. Tantric yoga has elaborate disciplines for increasing the body's adaptability to the environment, giving the practitioner a degree of control over his or her body temperature, metabolism, and circulation as well as the ability to enter deep trance states. Such practices attempt to recapture the body/mind capacities of indigenous peoples. Twentieth-century India, in a sense, represents a particular spiritual tragedy. The knowledge and temperament of shamanistic vision is part of Tantric philosophy, but the human population has become swollen and the land nearly exhausted by the degenerating effects of millennia of agriculture.

Unlike Egyptian religion, Renaissance thought, or Tantric mysticism, the Aboriginal view does not go back to a Golden Age to evoke the First Day. The First Day is every day, and every aspect of daily life and ritual conforms to a Law that maintains humankind, all the creatures of nature, and the earth itself in its primal beauty and perfection—as it was on the first day.

THE RIDDLE OF THE TASMANIAN ABORIGINES

The Aborigines who inhabited Tasmania do not seem to fit the evolutionary theories applied to them. Although they were massacred by European settlers during the eighteenth and nineteenth centuries, evidence from eyewitness accounts, archaeological work, and geological cycles paints a picture of a people who adhered to and flourished under a way of life that closely followed the Dreamtime Law. Applying the Golden Age model of history and creation can explain this enigma.

Tasmania, an island a little smaller than Ireland, is separated from the southeast coast of mainland Australia by approximately 150 miles of turbulent ocean waters. Tasmania has a range of fauna and flora similar to that of mainland Australia as well as some species that are all its own.

Like the fauna and flora, the Tasmanian Aborigines were related in many ways to the Aborigines of mainland Australia but were in some

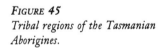
FIGURE 45
Tribal regions of the Tasmanian Aborigines.

77

FIGURE 46
Tasmanian Aboriginal camp, Maria Island. This group of Tasmanian Aborigines was sketched by the French naturalist F. Peron on an expedition in 1802. The French explorers showed great respect, both historical and scientific, for the Aboriginal culture, whereas the British saw the Aborigines as an obstacle to their exploitation and confiscation of the land and resources.

FIGURE 47 →
None of these tools found on mainland Australia were used by the Tasmanian Aborigines.

ways unique. The oldest skeletal remains discovered in mainland Australia are of the Tasmanian Aboriginal type, therefore, the cultural variations peculiar to the Tasmanians may also represent an older cultural form.

The Tasmanian Aborgines were unique in that no other known society had existed in isolation for so long a period. They were a small, lean, and muscular dark race with unusually heavy, curly hair and beards, which they loaded with grease and ochre, twisting the individual ringlets into tubular masses; these hung around the head like the strands of a mop, almost concealing the eyes. Unlike many of the mainland Aboriginal tribes, they were an uncircumcised race and practiced markedly different marital and burial traditions. They made a large number of hieroglyphic rock carvings, but the people were exterminated before the significance of any of these carvings could be transmitted.[10]

There were nine separate Tasmanian tribes, of approximately 500 to 700 people each. Although they had no fire-making tools, one tribal elder in each tribe carried a fire stick that was kept perpetually burning.[11] They did not mount any of their stone tools on handles and did not use boomerangs and spearthrowers, as did the mainland tribes. Sightings of the Tasmanian Aborigines were first reported in 1642, by the Dutch, and on six other occasions before the year 1802, when the British pastoralist invasion of Tasmania began.

In 1772, French explorers sighted some of the Tasmanian Aborigines, finding them an exceptionally peaceful, joyous, and open people. Accounts of them given to the French philosopher Jean-Jacques Rousseau contributed to his philosophy of the noble savage. Within decades, the noble savage became the ignoble savage, and the Aboriginal inhabitants of Tasmania were referred to as degenerate, bestial, and primitive.[12]

Systematic archaeological research into the Tasmanian Aborigines has been made particularly difficult by environmentally disruptive government policies. These policies have been responsible for hydroelectric dam projects that have flooded pristine mountain lakes and forests, along with important ancient Aboriginal sites. In spite of this, Tasmanian Aboriginal culture emerges as a distinct and interesting mystery not explainable through conventional theories. Questions still revolve around the following observations:

1. The Tasmanian Aborigines were found to have a much smaller assortment of tools than the mainland Aborigines. They did not use a boomerang, spearthrower, halved ax, fire-making implements, or bone tools for weaving.[13]

   Archaeological evidence has demonstrated that 4,000 years ago the material culture and customs of the Tasmanians changed dramatically. Although bone tools had developed among the Tasmanians, their use was dropped at about this time. Bone tools of the same variety were used on mainland Australia to make possum skins into cloaks for severe winter seasons. When Europeans first recorded Tasmanian culture, no Tasmanian Aborigine wore possum skins for warmth; they went naked except for small pieces of wallaby skin tied around their necks for decoration. Even though the climate was colder and wetter than in other parts of Australia, where skin clothing was occasionally or ritually worn, the Tasmanian Aborigines stopped using not only the bone tools for making clothing but also clothing itself.[14] The elimination of clothing is even more bewildering in light of the fact that no other known population survived in the same cold southerly latitudes (40 to 45 degrees) during the Ice Age.

2. There is also evidence from shell middens that up until 4,000 years ago the Tasmanian Aborigines ate scale fish. After that time,

An *OPOSSUM* of Van Diemen's Land.

FIGURE 48
Possum Dreaming. In Aboriginal belief, animals pass their quiet hours in viewing the dancing subtle energy fields that surround living creatures. The Aborigines developed their own human perception to be more like that of the animals: acutely aware of the physical reality, and also engrossed in the subtle energetic Dreaming.

this readily available food source was no longer part of their diet, and when European explorers offered it to them, they refused to eat it. Early settlers noted that Aboriginal women, who used sophisticated fishing methods, would ignore easy catches of scale fish and swim miles into the open ocean to gather abalone and other shellfish from rocky atolls.[15] It appears that the elimination of scale fish from their diet occurred uniformly among the nine widely dispersed Tasmanian Aboriginal tribes.

3. The Tasmanians' use of fire is especially puzzling. Although a tribal elder carried and maintained an ignited fire stick for each tribe, the evidence suggests that the Tasmanian Aborigines used fire only for ceremonies and for cooking meat. They seemed to have no capacity for making fire; if the tribal fire stick was ever extinguished, the only way they could regain the use of fire was to receive an ignited stick from another tribe. As a result, fire was a motivation for peace rather than war among tribes. None of the fire-making equipment discovered on mainland Australia has been

recovered from excavations of Tasmanian sites. On the small outer islands surrounding Tasmania, however, where the Aborigines went by boat for ritual purposes, there are stone hearths and evidence of fire making.[16] In spite of the colder climate, it seems that the Tasmanian Aborigines used fire-making technology not for practical and domestic application so much as for ritual and sacred purposes. At one time, they also employed fire in what archaeologists call "fire stick farming," which is the burning off of small areas of bush land to flush out small game and to encourage fresh plant growth, but this practice was also dropped.

The Tasmanians' minimal level of technology did not result in any deprivation or suffering. The first Europeans to see them reported that the Tasmanian Aborigines were a well-nourished, physically strong, radiant, and energetic people. They also spent more time in song, dance, and ceremony than did mainland Aboriginal tribes.[17]

4. Even more unusual were the Tasmanian Aborigines' racial characteristics—dark skin and thick, tightly curled hair—which seemed ill-suited to their cold climate. This is especially puzzling in light of the fact that tribes in the southern temperate regions of Australia tended to be lighter-skinned with less tightly curled hair than northern tribes.

Figure 49
Arabana man making fire by twirling the upright stick in a hole in the lower stick, near Peake Station, Northern Territory, 1901. Dried grass is positioned near the friction point and begins to smolder. This is but one of the many methods used by the Aborigines for producing fire.

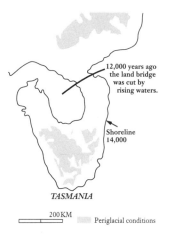

12,000 years ago the land bridge was cut by rising waters.

Shoreline 14,000

TASMANIA

200 KM — Periglacial conditions

FIGURE 50
Ice age in Tasmania showing the coastline at 14,000 B.C. and the drowning of the land bridge at about 12,000 B.C. (After Jones, 1977)

The accepted theory explaining the presence of an Aboriginal population on this remote island is that 15,000 to 18,000 years ago, during the last glacier maximum, there was a land connection between Tasmania and Australia. Over this land bridge the tribes of Aborigines are supposed to have migrated. When the Ice Age drew to a close in about 12,000 B.C., the land bridge was engulfed by rising seas. At this time, it is posited, 6,000 to 7,000 Aborigines were stranded in Tasmania. The gale-swept, stormy waters of the Bass Strait ensured that they had no contact with mainland Australia.

This theory exhibits a number of glaring flaws. The most important is the improbability of a population migrating toward the

FIGURE 51
Aborigines capture many tree-inhabiting species, such as possums, by climbing great heights, with extraordinary balance and agility, and venturing fearlessly to the end of a branch to pluck a sleeping possum from its perch.

pole during the Ice Age. Aboriginal culture, behavior, and world view has no tradition of migrating from one land area to another. No other explanation, besides this inherently contradictory one, has been devised to explain their existence in Tasmania. Recent evidence does suggest, however, that the Tasmanian Aborigines are the oldest of the three distinguishable types of Australian Aborigines. Evidence found in caves in the Tasmanian highlands moves the date of their occupancy from 20,000 back to 50,000 years ago, which further jeopardizes the Ice-Age immigration theory.[18]

5. Perhaps most perplexing is the Tasmanian Aborigines' consistent choice to expose themselves, naked, to a cold and inclement climate. From the Western perspective, no other aspect of the Aboriginal Law or discipline seems more of an aberration. Our fear of and retreat from cold has caused us to encase ourselves in layers of garments, architecture, and complex heating systems. The Europeans who first sighted the Aborigines remarked on the fact that the natives were uninterested in campfires, skin wraps, and small huts to protect them from the severe wind and rain of the frigid Tasmanian winters. The Aboriginal attitude toward clothing both fascinated and appalled the early European visitors. They repeatedly remarked on the fact that Aborigines of every age and both sexes never wore clothing of any kind at any time. Nudity as uncompromising as this was an affront to the repressions and inhibitions of the European colonists. Cook, in his first Tasmanian journals, concluded:

> They go quite naked both men and women, with out any manner of clothing whatever. Even the women do not so much as cover their privates.[19]

Explorer Banks was more philosophical in his comments.

> Of clothes they have not the least part but naked as ever our general father was before his fall, they seem no more conscious of their nakedness than if they had not been the children of parents who eat the fruit of the tree of knowledge.[20]

This unusual preference may be a key not only to the mystery of their origin and history but, as I will show in later chapters, to connecting them with the initiatic traditions of ancient cultures throughout the world.

The attitudes of the Tasmanian Aborigines toward cold reflected either a conscious discipline or an innate adaptation. The Tasmanian Aborigines' adaptation to cold may have been an instinctual residue

83

FIGURE 52

There have been six ice ages in the 120,000 years of the most recent glaciation cycle. During the last interglacial, prior to 120,000 years ago, the earth experienced a warm climate and consequently high sea levels. The sea stood five to eight meters higher than its present level. Until about 10,000 years ago the sea levels always remained lower than they are today. The two major lowerings (120 to 150 meters below present level) occurred in the last two major ice ages: 55,000 and 20,000 years ago. The cycle of the six ice ages is now reaching completion, and the sea level is returning to the height at which it stood 120,000 years ago. We are therefore approaching the end of a glaciation cycle.

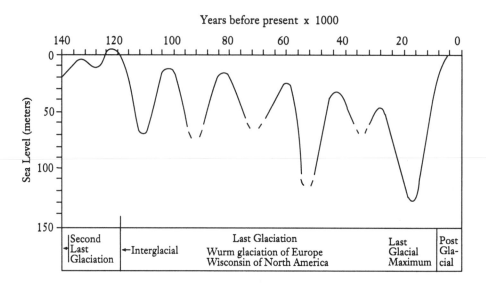

from their past history that allowed them to survive, as a seed survives the winter, the periodic occurrences of cold, isolation, and decline during the ice ages.

During the last three million years, which geologists have called an "ice epic," there have been six waves of glaciation, or ice ages, the last one reaching its maximum about 20,000 years ago.[21] Texts from prehistoric India, attributed to the indigenous Dravidians who inhabited the Indus Valley prior to the Aryan invasions of 3,000 B.C., speak of a similar cycle of destruction. They claim that humanity as we know it has appeared on earth, developing and attaining heights of artistic and scientific achievement, and being destroyed in widespread catastrophes, *six separate times*. These texts say that after the destruction of our present civilization humanity will go through seven more rises and falls before the earth extinguishes itself.[22] Biologists such as David Bellamy consider ice ages to be an important and positive punctuation in the cycles of the earth, cutting life back to its most essential forms and remineralizing and potentizing the earth's soil.

The Tasmanian Aborigines may represent the most remarkable survival achievement in the history of mankind. Even during the height of the Ice Age they did not desert the remote, windswept island, less than 1,000 kilometers from the great Antarctic ice sheet. They maintained a rich cultural tradition that included stone engravings, ritual cremations, songs, dances, and ceremonies while ice covered the mountains and valleys of their isolated island and huge icebergs floated past their coastline from the Antarctic.[23] Against the backdrop of what we would consider climatic duress, this culture left, on a long, ocean-exposed cliff face, the most impressive artistic site known from the prehistoric era. The designs and motifs are purely geometric and are deeply, almost sculpturally, engraved into the rock. This site is widely recognized as the oldest and most outstanding artistic achievement of any hunter-gatherer society.[24]

In rationalizing their exploitation of the Tasmanians, the invading European settlers labeled them a degenerate and pathetic race for whom extinction would be a blessing. During the first 70 years of European settlement, from 1802 on, a cruel and relentless genocide was enacted. Only shattered fragments of this primeval culture remain.

Applying the Golden Age image of history to the anomalies of the Tasmanians creates a new picture of human origins. Tasmania may actually be the land of origin to which the Aborigines remained spiritually and physically connected. The strong connection to the land is evident in all Aboriginal tribes, no matter what the environmental con-

FIGURE 53
The extensive cliffside Aboriginal petroglyphic carvings on the southwest coast of Tasmania constitute the oldest and largest prehistoric art site in the world.

ditions. The differences in characteristics between the Tasmanian Aborigines and those of the mainland suggest that they are an older, earlier people, perhaps as old as the speculated 400,000-year origin of *Homo sapiens* in Australia.

Calling the Tasmanian people "first" or "oldest" will bring cries of protest from academia, but, in the sense of creation through the Dreaming, *oldest* or *first* refers to the form that holds the most potential. As forms actualize or manifest variations and complexities, they move away from the original or older state. The Tasmanians maintained the simplest material existence of any people on earth. They are the oldest people of Australia, which is the oldest land. They preserve the Law in its greatest purity and simplicity, which places them as a symbol of the primordial archetype.

Using the Golden Age model instead of colonization as the means of explaining the spread of populations, migration can be associated with the idea of departure or exile from the sacred land of origins, based on deviations from the given "Law of the Land," or the universal plan of life. When we leave the Dreaming Law we also leave the Garden and enter into the cycles of time and becoming. This same theme is found in the mythologies of many people, including our own creation story of a garden of Eden in which the parents of humanity are exiled due to an infraction of a "given" law.

In summary, the less complicated tools of the Tasmanians may be a result not of their isolation but of their having returned to an older, more orthodox interpretation of the original Ancestral Law. The fact that the Tasmanian Aborigines had at one time eaten fish, used bone tools to make skin clothing, and used fire more extensively—all of which ceased 4,000 years before European settlement—may not mark a technological degeneracy, but rather a renaissance of the influence of the original law in their daily life and behavior.

Even among paleolithic societies, fire may have caused environmental problems. Much of the world's desertification may have been aggravated by the burning of great tracts of grasslands by prehistoric humans. The Tasmanians' self-imposed restriction on the use of fire may have been a decision of great foresight and environmental integration.

The rebirth of an older, higher philosophy or tradition is evident in many cultures, especially that of ancient Egypt. The cultural flowering that occurred in the eighteenth and nineteenth dynasties of Middle Kingdom Egypt was based upon a return to the artistic purity of expression of the first and third dynasties of the Old Kingdom. The Italian Renaissance may also be seen as a failed attempt to return to a previously enlightened age. The Aboriginal culture looked back directly to a metaphysical presence vibrating in the countryside, just as the Egyptian culture, in its pyramids, temples, and images, symbolically looked back to a past Golden Age.

To receive knowledge from the past—from the origin—and to be fertilized by it in such a way as to provoke a rebirth, requires a great depth of understanding and humility. I wonder how much further we must proceed with the calamity of our age in order to free ourselves from our self-destructive pride.

The world in Aboriginal cosmology was created perfect by the ancestral beings. Humanity's role was to keep the world in its original perfection by adhering to a revelatory Law. In following this primal knowledge humans will maintain, in society and in their physical bodies, the capacities to adapt to the changes in the earthly environment. The extreme simplicity of the Tasmanian Aborigines may reflect an older, more orthodox adherence to the ideal of the sacred value of the earth. Their uncompromising intensity in embodying the Dreamtime Law identifies them as the image of a seed for all human cultures.

CHAPTER 6

EARTH DYING, EARTH REBORN

The Morning Star is the son of the Sun Woman and the Moon is his wife. The children of the Morning Star and the Moon were the Ancestors of the Aborigines today.[1]

JENNIFER ISAACS

Once the earth was completely dark and silent; nothing moved on its barren surface. Inside a deep cave below the Nullabor Plain slept a beautiful woman, the Sun. The Great Father Spirit gently woke her and told her to emerge from her cave and stir the universe into life. The Sun Mother opened her eyes and darkness disappeared as her rays spread over the land; she took a breath and the atmosphere changed; the air gently vibrated as a small breeze blew.

The Sun Mother then went on a long journey; from north to south and from east to west she crossed the barren land. The earth held the seed potencies of all things, and wherever the Sun's gentle rays touched the earth, there grasses, shrubs, and trees grew until the land was covered in vegetation. In each of the deep caverns in the earth, the Sun found living creatures which, like herself, had been slumbering for untold ages. She stirred the insects into life in all their forms and told them to spread through the grasses and trees, then she woke the snakes, lizards, and other reptiles, and they slithered out of their deep hole. As the snakes moved through and along the earth they formed rivers and they themselves became creators, like the Sun. Behind the snakes mighty rivers flowed, teeming with all kinds of fish and water life. Then she called for the animals, the marsupials, and the many other creatures to awake and make their homes on the earth. The Sun Mother then told all the creatures that the days would from time to time change from wet to dry and from cold to hot, and so she made the seasons. One day while all the animals, insects, and other creatures were watching, the Sun traveled far in the sky to the west and, as the sky shone red, she sank from view and darkness spread across the land once more. The creatures were alarmed and huddled together in fear. Some time later, the sky began to glow on the horizon to the east and the Sun rose smiling into the sky again. The Sun Mother thus provided a period of rest for all her creatures by making this journey each day.

KARRAUR TRIBE

THE FILM *The Doors* (1991) opens with the nine- or ten-year-old Jim Morrison at the scene of a grim car accident, in which a large truck has collided into a pickup truck full of Native Americans returning to the reservation. The frightened boy peers out of the window of his family's car, his eyes locking onto the eyes of an elderly shaman who has been tossed onto the roadside and is dying. In the exchanged glance, the old tribal man's spirit passes through the boy's eyes and into his soul. Jim Morrison's life was, from that moment, possessed with a glimmer from the spirit of the eternal shaman. This spirit accompanied Jim on his meteoric rise to rock stardom. He used the shamanistic power of ritual to incite anarchy and to preside over the release of pent-up sexual energy. The rituals of ecstatic abandon associated with early 1960s rock music echoed the archaic voice calling many back to a living spirit that is inherent in the physical body and the earth. This message in sound began to vibrate in the unprepared consciousness of youth in America and throughout the world. Much of what was released in Jim Morrison's life and in the youth cult of the 1960s was unassimilable and had dire consequences for some of the lives it affected: the message of the archaic shattered the receptacle into which it was poured. Thirty years have passed since that tumultuous time, and the same seed in the depths of the unconscious and in the earth continues to press upward against the floor of our civilization. Our culture, the terminal phase of a long cycle, is inexorably drawn toward another beginning.

Indigenous means "born from" or "being an integral part of a place or region on earth." In our time the term *indigenous* has come to symbolize the rediscovery that our race is inseparable from earth and nature as a whole. In witnessing the dying of the natural world around us and in ourselves, we have at last been able to see that the earth is living. This is a significant stage in the revelation of the fundamental unity of life. In beginning to "re-language" and conceive anew the nature of the living earth, we may discover the passages of mind through which we reenter earth's dreaming.

EARTH'S BODY

In recent years the biological and earth sciences have developed a metaphor for the ancient concept of earth as a living organism, renaming our

planet and the biosphere *Gaia*, after the ancient Greek mother goddess. At last it is possible to speak "scientifically" of the earth as an organism that functions in ways similar to our own bodies. The Gaia concept brings our thinking close to an understanding of human origins that is compatible with that of the Aborigines.

For them, humans and the earth have physical and spiritual dimensions that are all symbolically reflected in one another. This relationship is like that of a pregnant woman to the child within her: the woman changes both physically and psychologically as the child develops, and the fetus derives all of its capacities to grow from the mother. As the earth's atmosphere and soil change in relation to the life on its surface, this life in turn reflects the changes that occur in its earthly milieu. An Aboriginal healer who had overcome a serious addiction to alcohol once underscored this relationship for me: "Of course the Aboriginal people are sick and drunk. We feel the earth as if we are within a mother. . . . When the earth is sick and polluted, human health is impossible. . . . To heal ourselves we must heal our planet and to heal the planet we must heal ourselves."[2]

If the earth is a living body, then its life (like all life) results from a concert of rhythmic activities. In all living creatures the music is the same; it is an echo of the voice of a wavelike movement that fills the universe. The vast, almost incomprehensible fields of force such as gravity move in this way, as do myriad rythmic patterns extending down to the infinitesimal pulsation of an atom. Vibrations of a higher frequency than light or of a lower frequency than the lowest audible sounds constitute the edges of other worlds of being.

Our hearts contract and swell as they suck in and pump out blood. Lungs breathe in and out, intestines open and squeeze. Sensations and thoughts are carried by tiny rapid pulsations that flee along nerve fibers. The brain is swept by endless waves of sleep, wakefulness, hunger, satiation. Wings flap up and down, arms swing left and right, back and forth; jaws open and crush down pitilessly; songs pour forth from the throat that, in hunger, swallows the death and sorrow of other creatures. The rhythms of copulation are everywhere, opening, closing, inflating, deflating, penetrating, withdrawing. These patterned vibrations permeate all of substance and life, providing the unifying resonance between people, nature, and the invisible worlds. An Aboriginal cave painting story also speaks of the harmonic integrating pulsation of life:

> Tree . . .
> he watching you.
> You look at tree,
> he listen to you.

He got no finger,
he can't speak.
But that leaf . . .
he pumping, growing,
growing in the night.
While you sleeping
you dream something.
Tree and grass same thing.
They grow with your body,
with your feeling.[3]

The cells of our bodies bear smaller versions of the universal cyclic activity. Cells form and disperse in rhythm, dividing into two and re-growing into a whole unit, only to divide again. Within the cell are molecules, atoms, and electrons, each in ceaseless motion, with each increasingly minute level of organization moving at faster frequencies. Our body vibrates not only to myriad cycles and rhythms within but also to the cycles of sun, earth, and planets. We are conditioned by the duration of day and night, the yearly solar cycle, the monthly lunation. Each heavenly body that affects earth and ourselves is itself sustained by larger rhythms.

If one cycle is selected from the grand continuum of pulsation, for example, the swing from night to day, it seems as if an "evolution" has occurred from darkness to light, as in the Old Testament. The single pulsation of a heart could be seen as an "evolution" from contraction to expansion, as some astrophysicists have postulated about our expanding universe. In the Ancestral Dreaming, each breath, each heartbeat of a living universe is part of an everlasting, perfectly integrated continuum. "Evolution" is a theory that arises from examining only a single fragment of that continuum. All forms of existence, be they individual or collective, are conditioned by a series of cycles contained within each other: to us an infinitesimal fraction of a second is an entire lifetime to an atomic particle, just as our lifetime is a split second in the life cycles of the earth, and the earth's life is a split second in the life of stars and galaxies.

The earth metabolizes, its charges and discharges parallel to the fluctuations of biological life and human culture. In Chapter 1, I mentioned the theory of the renowned French archaeologist Frobenius, who uncovered and reconstructed a very early phase in human culture before the recorded ages of stone and metal. The cultures he reconstructed had developed in the southern regions of the world and used a purely wood-based technology. Spreading and contracting in waves, these ancient people had profound, little-acknowledged influences on the cultures that left stone and metal tools behind them. The most outstanding example of these primal, wood-based cultures is that of the Australian Aborigines, who inhabit the southernmost continent. Among the Aborigines, the Tasmanians maintained the simplest, purest way of life and inhabited the southernmost portion of Australia. The pattern of spreading from south to north envisioned by Frobenius may have occurred in syncopation with the rhythmic expansion and contraction of ice masses. Glaciers spread from the poles in six periods of glaciation, each followed by interglacial periods in which life flourished. The 120,000 years of the Ice Epoch is concurrent with the approximate 120,000 years of Aboriginal culture in Australia. Both of these are in harmony with the 60,000 years of cultural oscillation that the ancient Dravidians called the Yugas, a period that extended from the Golden Age to the Age of Kali.

The cyclic patterns that govern our lives, the four seasons, and the inevitable cycle of life and death are but one substratum of universal cycles, which in larger waves delineate the cycles of civilizations as well as the larger natural cycles of expansion and contraction. Each level of cycle conditions the others.

The earth has two other prominent cycles with a south–north movement: continental drift and magnetism. The most profound is continental drift, in which the seven continents are tightly clustered in the southern hemisphere and slowly open upward and outward from the South Pole, spreading apart like the petals of a flower in bloom, then shrivel back to the south again. This movement happens on a 240-million-year cycle. The flow of land masses upward is a breathing out, the contraction southward an inhalation. Each phase of the earth's breath is a period of 120 million years. Continental drift itself may be a response tuning to

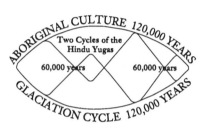

FIGURE 54
The traditional Hindu calendar and the glaciation cycles. The most recent ice age of 20,000 years ago coincides with the beginning of the Age of Doubt in Hindu cosmology, and the ice age of 55,000 years ago coincides with the beginning of the Golden Age. The retreat of the last ice age also coincides with the introduction of agriculture. In Hindu belief, the end of the six-fold glaciation cycle is concurrent with the end of the Kali Yuga and the beginning of a new age. The 120,000-year period of Aboriginal culture encloses two of the Hindu Yuga cycles and coincides precisely with the glaciation cycle. The two archetypal polarities, the "All-Mother" (Universal Feminine) and the "All-Father" (Universal Masculine) alternate their primary/secondary influence on humanity and nature, reflecting the earth's alternating magnetic polarity.

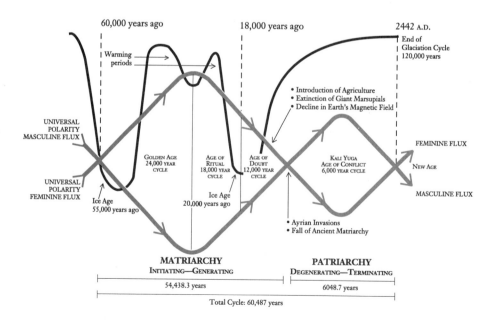

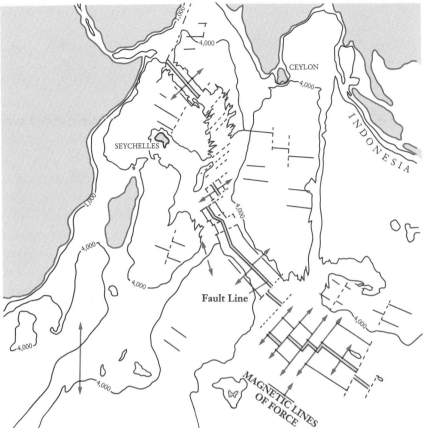

FIGURE 55
Magnetic lines of force lie perpendicularly to all the fault lines of the continental plates, forming a grid pattern over the face of the earth.

a cycle in which the solar system completes an orbit around the center of the galaxy, or Milky Way, every 280 million years.

Two hundred and forty million years ago there were seven great tectonic land masses packed close to the South Pole, forming a land mass called Pangaea. One hundred million years later, all of the continents had drifted north, some to the northeast, some to the northwest. Australia, however, maintains its connection and position close to the original geological formation, called Gondwanaland.[4]

The question remains whether the slow pulsations of continental drift are related to the other prominent cycle of the earth, the magnetism emitted from the earth's magnetic poles that alternates approximately every million years. The magnetic current circulating around the earth may be the dynamo that drives the constant rearrangement of the earth's crust. Recent developments in geology and marine geology are starting to suggest this. Magnetic lines of force lie perpendicular to all the fractures, rifts, and continental ridges on the ocean floor. These ridges, controlled by a magnetic grid pattern, allow for the expansion and contraction of the earth's mantle and the drift and dance of its continents and oceans.[5]

Beginning of age
of giant reptiles—
200 million B.C.

Mammals, birds
and flowers appear
—100 million B.C.

The planet as
she looks today.

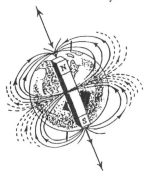

FIGURE 56
South–north continental drift
and the south–north flow of
magnetic energy. The continents
drift in a spreading south-to-
north pattern, as do the lines of
the earth's magnetic field.

Although there may be no definitive scientific answers to these questions, it is clear that the megaorganism of the earth experiences cyclic pulsations of varying rhythms and periods, all of which influence the climate and life of the entire planet.

THE MAGNETIC EARTH

The earth's magnetic field carries another important rhythm of the earth's life. It has long been accepted in Western scientific circles that the earth generates magnetic energy as if it were itself a gigantic magnet. More recently, space exploration research has revealed that the South Pole generates a positive magnetic energy and the North Pole receives energy through a negative magnetic field. The positive energies emitted from the South Pole spiral toward the North Pole; those traveling west move clockwise and those traveling east move counterclockwise. These paths cross and invert near the equator, to be absorbed into the negative North Pole.[6]

The magnetic field is stable for a period of approximately one million years. The stable phase is marked by mysterious punctuations, like those of an arrhythmic heartbeat, followed by a radical reversal of magnetic polarity. During a reversal, the North Pole, if it is presently negative, becomes positively charged, and the positive South Pole flips over to the opposite charge. Massive extinctions occur just after these field reversals. The magnetic extinction episodes wipe the slate clean, after which life can set off on a new pattern of development.[7] Fossil records of plants, fish, and mammals retrieved from ocean-bed drilling verify that the widespread appearance and disappearance of species correspond to these shifts in the earth's magnetic field. Dinosaurs were extinguished during one such magnetic collapse at the close of the Mesozoic Age 60 million years ago.

The last major shift of this kind occurred 700,000 years ago. Fossil records from excavations in the Antarctic have revealed a great dying off of organisms and microorganisms at that time. We are now approaching the end of a long period of magnetic stability, and there is evidence to indicate that we are in the initial stages of a reversal. According to Dr. Robert Becker, reversals that follow exceptionally long periods of stability eliminate all of the higher life forms, which had a long period of adaptation to the stable magnetic field.[8]

Dr. R. J. Uffen, a Canadian geophysicist, asserts that evolutionary surges occur at every polarity reversal of the earth's magnetic field. Evidence suggests that when the earth's magnetic field is at a heightened intensity, flora and fauna proliferate, as during the age of the great

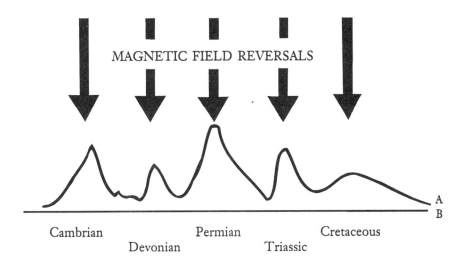

MAGNETIC FIELD REVERSALS

Cambrian　Devonian　Permian　Triassic　Cretaceous

A
B

FIGURE 57

Magnetic field reversals. The magnetic reversals are followed by a marked decline of plant and animal species. The rising peaks of the line (A) represent the numbers of new species, and the falling troughs represent the number of species that have become extinct. The geological time periods indicated along the horizontal scale (B) represent the end of each period. For example, the peak of the Cretaceous period marks the beginning of the decline of dinosaurs, and the end marks their extinction. The reversal at the end of the Permian period followed a long period of steady magnetic field in which no reversals occurred; the subsequent species die-out was exceptionally large. (Adapted from Sander)

mammals 80 million years ago. Other evidence shows that, as the earth's magnetism weakens through the ages, the remains of animals found in the earth's crust also grow smaller.[9] The earth's magnetism gradually declines in intensity as a period of stability comes to an end. Recent measurements of the average strength of the natural magnetic field show a gradual decline over the past several decades, which is consistent with archaeological evidence of an overall decline over the past 10,000 years or more.[10]

There is also evidence that geomagnetic polarity reversals could affect the amount and type of radiation that penetrates the earth's atmosphere, and that this radiation could cause massive mutations in the genetic material of every species of plant and animal on earth. This factor, if prove, could form the basis of an explanation for the disappearance of species. It is very unlikely, however, that severe mutation episodes are responsible for the appearance of entirely new species.[11]

These natural changes in magnetism and the side effects they have on the atmosphere take place gradually, over a long period of time. It is disturbing to consider, in comparison, the sudden changes industrial civilization has brought about in the last centuries: pollution and our global use of electromagnetic energy have affected both the atmosphere and the magnetic field.[12] It may be that industrial society is accidentally

MAGNETIC FIELD REVERSALS ON EARTH

⇢ Flow of Time ⇢

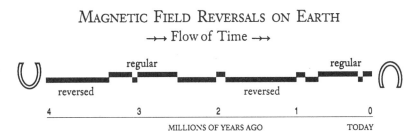

regular　　　　　　regular

reversed　　　　　reversed

4　　　3　　　2　　　1　　　0

MILLIONS OF YEARS AGO　　　TODAY

FIGURE 58

The Magnetic cycle. Each magnetic period lasts about 1 million years. Within this period there is a duration of magnetic stability, lasting about 500,000 to 750,000 years.

provoking a premature round of deep extinction, comparable to the way a damaged fetus brings on its own abortion. No one knows what the end result of our "civilized disruption" of Gaia's metabolism will be, but it is certain that we are radically affecting the two most prominent mechanisms—magnetism and atmosphere—that control her vast cycle of death and rebirth.

In light of this new model, we can conceive of a bridge of interaction between the magnetic life of the planet and biological and cultural developments of humanity.[13]

In summary, the flow of human civilization from the wood-based cultures of the south mirrors the south-to-north circulation of the continental masses. At one time over one-half of the earth's land masses were in the southern hemisphere, whereas now over three-fourths are in the northern hemisphere. The earth's magnetic lines of force flow in a similar pattern, from south to north, as do the continents. All of the cycles of the earth's body carry out its metabolism.

The Dreamtime myths mirror these interrelated patterns and cycles of earth and human nature. The myths begin with an interplay of great cosmic energies that move and shape the earth's crust (the cycle of drifting continents). The energies and cycles of earth then create, influence, and destroy all living species in rhythmic sequences (the magnetic cycles and the ice ages). These life cycles of the planet then have a profound and lasting influence on cultural patterns and the development of humanity.

The ancient Egyptians, who may have been a repository of early indigenous knowledge, refer to the sacredness of earth with a hieroglyph that reads *Ta Mari*. Literally translated, this means "the earth is the magnet of the sky," or "earth, the attractor of celestial energy." According to French Egyptologist R. A. Schwaller de Lubicz, the Egyptians possessed a knowledge of the great cycles that integrate human life and culture with those of the earth and with cosmic energies. De Lubicz translated a hieroglyphic passage that describes the symbolic nature and function of the four orientations north, south, east, and west.

> The Earth inspires [vibratory cosmic energy] through the North [Pole] and manifests through the South [Pole]. The South is the place of potentiality and the origins of manifestation. Through stages of actualization, the manifestation moves North as the movement from seed to fruit.[14]

The South Pole is a mass of earth surrounded by water, which is consistent with the Egyptian image of the south as the source of the

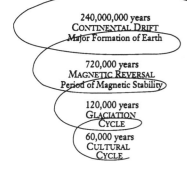

240,000,000 years
CONTINENTAL DRIFT
Major Formation of Earth

720,000 years
MAGNETIC REVERSAL
Period of Magnetic Stability

120,000 years
GLACIATION
CYCLE

60,000 years
CULTURAL
CYCLE

FIGURE 59
The harmonics of earth and human cycles. Within the grand cycle of geological formation or continental drift of 240 million years are the smaller cycles of magnetic stability (720,000 yr), the glaciation cycle (120,000 yr), and the human cultural cycle (60,000 yr).

manifest world. The North Pole is an empty, frozen ocean, consistent with the Egyptian image of the north as an energy receptacle.

José Arguelles, in his study of Mayan symbolism, reveals that the Mayans, like the Egyptians, based their entire cosmology on the four orientations north, south, east, and west, and that the south is the generative source in the cycle. "The South is the form which generates the seed."[15]

LIFE, MIND, AND MAGNETISM

The earth's magnetic field, like the fields associated with the human brain, is divided into two complementary hemispheres. The South Pole generates positive magnetic energy, which flows in a clockwise spiral over the southern hemisphere, while the North Pole absorbs negative energy, with magnetic lines that flow counterclockwise over the northern hemisphere. The geomagnetic equator of the planet, between the latitudes of El Salvador and Huancayo with lines converging on Peru, forms a neutral or zero-magnetic zone. We can assume that the inhabitants south of this equator are exposed to a prevailing positive-dominant polarity, and those in the northern hemisphere are exposed to a negative-dominant polarity.[16]

There is no doubt that celestial and earthly magnetism affects biological growth. This was first verified by the discovery of the relationship between the sunspot cycle and the fluctuation of growth rings in trees. It is known that the sun's magnetic field increases by 100 to 1,000 times during a sunspot flare-up. This disturbance in the sun's activity is transmitted through the earth's magnetosphere into the atmosphere, the biosphere, and then the solid earth, the lithosphere. Through this chain, the global, magnetic, and electric fields are altered. The same is also true of fluctuations that reach us from the moon and perhaps other planets.

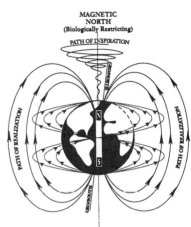

FIGURE 60
Earth's metabolism. The Egyptians considered the earth to draw in nourishing energy from the cosmos through the North Pole, digest that energy in its own interior, and re-emit energy from the South Pole for the manifestation first of land masses, then of the life of nature, and finally of human cultural development. The South Pole emits positive, life-supporting, magnetic energy, whereas the North Pole has an absorbing, life-diminishing field.

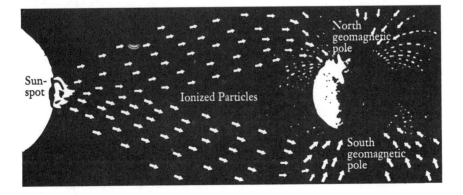

FIGURE 61
The earth receives solar radiation through its magnetic poles.

97

The growth of trees is accelerated during sunspot maxima; thus the eleven-year sunspot cycle is reflected in the increasing and decreasing width of the annual rings of trees. This effect is so reliable that archaeologists use it to date the establishment of ancient settlements.[17]

Although the earth's magnetic field is decidedly weaker than the magnets used in biological experiments, its effects are consistent. A large number of early clinical experiments have been performed in this field. In general, experiments indicate that animals and plants exposed to the positive energies of the magnetic South Pole show an increase in physical growth, an increase in the production of sugars and oils, a more rapid germination of seeds, greater metabolic warmth, an increased utilization of oxygen in animals and carbon dioxide in plants, and an increase in sexual strength, vigor, and fertility. In other words, South Pole energy proves to be stimulating in all aspects of physical life and growth, whereas animals and plants exposed to North Pole energy showed stunted growth patterns and weakened energy levels and biological functions. All conclusions point to the existence of two biological qualities of energy in magnetic polarization: the South Pole, or positive energy, which increases physical growth and development, and the North Pole, or negative energy, which arrests and inhibits life, growth, and development.

> In one experiment, fertilized eggs were exposed to a magnet for 10 hours and then placed in a hatcher. The hatcher had been fitted so that the South Pole magnet was in a corner opposite to the eggs. It was observed that the eggs, having been exposed to the magnet, hatched sooner than the 21-day norm. As soon as the chicks emerged, still wet, they proceeded immediately to the South Pole of the magnet in the opposite corner, where they cuddled up in front of the magnet as if sensing a kind of "motherly" strength.[18]

It is not simply a question of the South Pole positive being "good" and life-enhancing and the North Pole negative being "bad"; North Pole energy balances that of the South and provides the necessary control of growth. For example, infections or cancer exposed to South Pole energies have been proved to accelerate.[19]

Magnetic energies also seem to affect the psychological characteristics of animals.

> South Pole–exposed mice seem to bestow more care upon their offspring, both at birth and afterwards. They also exhibited cleaner living habits, suffered less labor pains and had an easier delivery of their offspring than did the North Pole mice.[20]

But again, it is a question of balance. Laboratory animals treated with South Pole energy exhibit superior physical condition and alertness up to a certain point in their growth. If this exposure is maintained for too long, however, they develop into voracious meat eaters and sometimes destroy themselves with overindulgence in sexual intercourse.[21]

The most intriguing generality drawn from early experiments that relate magnetism to the qualities of intelligence is that the North Pole energies stimulate the left hemisphere of the brain and the processes that underlie the reasoning analytical mind at the expense of biological and biochemical activity.

> We find that the North Pole [energy] (which is the negative energy), as to its effects on all biological systems, can and does possess the ability to pass through the head, the skull of man and animal, and act on the inner constraints of the brain. This acts to cause a stimulus to the left hemisphere of the brain, the reasoning mind itself. In our studies of this interaction we have discovered that when this form of energy passes unhindered into the innermost part of the brain it acts to arrest certain pressures on the brain by a reduction of inner and outer electromagnetic reactions to the brain. This relieves biological biochemical pressures as such from the thinking and reasoning mind. This then, as a result, has shown the ability of the man to think and reason more clearly and has aided in the learning capacity of the mind and the storing of that learning in the mechanical segments of the brain.[22]

According to this statement by Davis and Rawls, the North Pole negative magnetic field activity stimulates the left hemisphere of the brain. The left brain controls the type of functions that have dominated civilizations in the Northern hemisphere: an analytical and linear approach, sequential thought, abstract reasoning, and mechanical causation. This emphasis minimizes the organic, integrating, sensory intelligence of the right hemisphere of the brain. These qualities, which are stimulated by positive South Pole magnetic activity, are typical of early indigenous cultures such as that of the Australian Aborigines.

Although some details and terminology of these early investigations by Davis and Rawls have been altered somewhat by subsequent investigation, the flood of scientific research in recent years has more than justified the thrust of their pioneering work. To cite just a few examples from a rapidly growing body of research, directional experiments with 34,000 New England mud snails showed that they respond to both solar and lunar effects of the geomagnetic field. In 1975, it was found that bacteria have magnetic sensitivity and that each bacterium has a chain of tiny magnetic crystals within it. Living organisms respond more readily and

99

dramatically to weaker magnetic signals, such as those found in nature. Extensive tests carried out by physicist Zaboj Harvalik have demonstrated that human sensitivity to minute changes in magnetic fields can detect variations as weak as one hundred-thousandth of the geomagnetic field. Electromagnetic fields affect all kinds of processes within the human body. The pineal gland, for example, has been shown to vary its production of the hormones melatonin and serotonin when subjected to various orientations of magnetic fields no stronger than that of the earth (half a gauss). These hormones act on the nervous system in a variety of ways, including the control of all biocycles within the body. There is evidence that people under the influence of hypnosis or hallucinogenic drugs are highly sensitive to magnetic phenomena and sometimes actually perceive a static magnetic field as a flickering body of light.

Verifications of the influence of the earth's geomagnetic field in physical, psychological, and psychic aspects of our existence are becoming more common. The effect of electromagnetic and geomagnetic fields and currents on living things is one of the fastest growing fields in scientific research and constitutes one of the most innovative ways of thinking about self and earth. As Lyall Watson pointed out, "In 1960 there were just three papers on the subject in the scientific literature. By 1984, there were over 10,000. . . ."[23]

Drawing on the language of Aboriginal cosmology, this information might be summarized in this way: there is a flowing, interrelating energy realm, a dreaming world that surrounds living creatures and connects them to the magnetic emanations of the earth. The energy from the South Pole is the positive source, and it nourishes the earth-loving, earth-absorbed sense of reality. The North Pole is magnetically negative and draws the geomagnetism of the South Pole toward it, as well as pulling in magnetic influences from the heavens. The north awakens us, takes us from the living dreamflow of the earth to the fixed configurations of the conscious, analytical mind, and causes us to forget the Dreaming. Nonetheless, the balance of our thoughts, emotions, and bodies is influenced by subtle natural currents that connect us in various ways to Mother Earth.

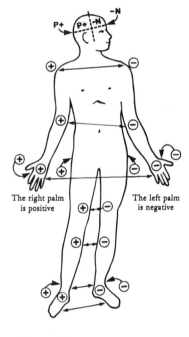

FIGURE 62
The human body is magnetically polarized, like the body of the earth; its polarization is bilateral, from left to right.

BLOOD AND IRON: THE DREAMING OF THE MAGNETIC COSMOS

The rhythmic cycles of growth for the earth and humans are driven by the pulsations of invisible fields of force, which Aboriginal tribal people call the ancestral beings or the Gods. These same invisible fields of force pervade our earthly environment, as well as the expanses of the universe. Contemporary astronomy now speaks of a universe pervaded by interstellar magnetic fields. These fields appear to be the most far-reaching media of communication, not only between stars, but also between galaxies.[24] At the same time that astronomy is becoming aware of the magnetic nature of the cosmos, modern physics has demonstrated that magnetic forces must exist in all substance. Matter, at its most fundamental level, is now considered to be a submicroscopic magnet.[25] More recently, biologists have become fascinated with the theory of self-organization in living systems and have found that magnetism is the most fundamental self-organizing property of life processes.[26]

Magnetism is an invisible web extending throughout the universe on every level, from atom to galaxy. Magnetic fields of influence integrate the universe, earth, and every living creature so that each communicates its rhythmic essence in resonance with all the others. Aborigines have always respected the force of magnetic energy, and they recognize the capacity·of blood and red ochre to increase their sensitivity to it.

An Aboriginal friend used this example to explain his people's concept of magnetism: "Psychic or spiritual fields are related to the material world in the same way that we conceive of a relationship of a magnetic field to its lodestone." He also said, "Living creatures are connected to the spirit or psychic fields through the blood flowing in their veins, while the earth's body is connected to these same fields, through its veins of magnetically sensitive minerals and crystals."[27] He told me an Aboriginal Dreamtime story that gives clues to the interrelationship of the earthly veins of magnetism and the veins of our bodies.

There was an ancestral dog, Mirindi, who lived at a time when the large reptiles ruled the earth. In the distant past, a huge lizard named Adno would climb every day to the mountain peaks and sing out, so that all could hear him, "Come out and fight, come out and fight. I dare anyone to challenge me." One day Mirindi grew angry with the lizard's tedious vanity and accepted his challenge. When Adno saw what a powerful and dangerous rival he had incited, he postponed the fight until after dark. Just before sunset, he wound a string of hair around the bone of his tail, so that his courage would not escape through his anus. He then called out to Mirindi, who leaped up from his sleep to receive the challenge. The dog tried to catch the lizard by the back of the neck and shake the life out of him, but the lizard ran underneath his jaw and bit the dog in the throat so that dark red blood spurted out. The blood falling from the ancestral sky formed deep red scars in the earth, which today are the deposits of red iron oxide with which the Aborigines paint their bodies.[28] Many Aboriginal tribes today refer to the red ochre they use to paint sacred totem designs as the "blood of the dog."

Earth Dying, Earth Reborn

The dog referred to in the myth is often thought to be the dingo, which appeared in Australia some 5,000 years ago. However, some of the stone cave galleries of western Australia, dating back 20,000 years, show paintings of a dog that appears to be the canine now known as the Tasmanian tiger.[29] This ancient Dreamtime story probably refers to this marsupial canine, a predecessor of the more recent placenta canines such as jackals, foxes, wolves, and dogs. The Tasmanian tiger was extinct on mainland Australia when the Europeans arrived and only existed in Tasmania, possibly its place of origin. The Tasmanian tiger was the most aggressive and predatory of the usually passive Australian marsupials. It was hunted into extinction by European ranchers in the early 1940s because of the toll it took on their sheep herds.[30] Almost cultlike attitudes survive today among Tasmanian farmers, who collect stories about sightings of the Tasmanian tiger.

FIGURE 63
The fabled Tasmanian tiger, the oldest known canine species and the predecessor of wolves and dogs.

The myth of Adno and Mirindi evokes an image of blood and death and associates blood with the earth's minerals. The Aboriginal name for red ochre is "clay mixed with blood," and blood and the mineral pigment red ochre are interchangeable in Aboriginal ritual. The Aborigines would pound and bake the red ochre, thereby chelating its iron compounds and making them highly sensitive to magnetic fields. Both red ochre and red blood contain ferrous oxide compounds, which cause cells and molecules to line up parallel to the lines of force of surrounding magnetic fields.[31]

In many Aboriginal rituals and ceremonies, red ochre is rubbed all over the naked bodies of the dancers. In secret, sacred male ceremonies, blood extracted from the veins of the participant's arms is exchanged and rubbed on their bodies. Red ochre is used in similar ways in less secret ceremonies.[32] Blood is also used to fasten the feathers of birds onto people's bodies. Bird feathers contain a protein that is highly magnetically sensitive.[33]

Blood used in this way is believed to establish a relationship between the dancer and the invisible energetic worlds. At sacred, initiatory male ceremonies, human blood is drunk in the belief that it contains a "seed" that emanates from the flow of blood of the Ancestors or Gods.[34]

The Aborigines, like all hunting and gathering people, are aware that magnetism is the basis of animal intelligence. To them, the blood of animals sympathetically vibrates with cosmic influences. Scientific research has verified this theory, noting that the blood's propensity for curdling and coagulating is directly related to energies received from the sun and the moon. Normally, the curdling index known as flocculation remains constant in men but in women varies with their menstrual or lunar cycle. In 1938, this index in both men and women suddenly began to rise. After years of research, the agent of this worldwide change was identified as the sun, for the peak of the sunspot cycle had begun in 1937. Changes in blood serum were noted as the sunspots crossed the center of the solar disk, a time when charged particles increased and were at the strongest point of their flow toward the earth. It was also discovered that blood-coagulating capacities decline during solar eclipses, when the moon stands between the earth and the sun, and that coagulation rates rise daily from sunrise on and drop at sunset. These changes are due to the fact that movements of the sun and moon are reflected in the earth's electromagnetic fields, which affect the blood's ability to coagulate.[35] For the Aborigines, this resonance between the circulation of the heavenly bodies, communicated by the earth's magnetism, and the inner circulation of man shows the sacred value of blood.

FIGURE 64
The iron molecule in red blood cells causes the cells to align along magnetic lines of force.

Animal blood is the basis for many Aboriginal food taboos. For example, among the Tasmanian Aborigines, the men ate only female animals and the women male animals, a taboo observed even in times of scarcity.[36] In most shamanistic traditions, the guides for psychic travel are animal intelligences evoked by the blood of a particular species.

In Plutarch's mystical writings, he refers to the "bone" or "core" of the gods as iron and lodestone. Symbolically, iron is the bone or mineral core of both blood and red ochre, and Plutarch associates this structure with the gods or heavenly beings.[37] Contemporary astronomer Fred Hoyle's observation of the formation of elements in the stars also shows that iron is the core of the celestial bodies.

Supernova explosions are believed to be triggered by the iron of the star's core collapsing and dispersing. Looked at symbolically, stars burst like germinating seeds, and the core iron, which completes the cycle of

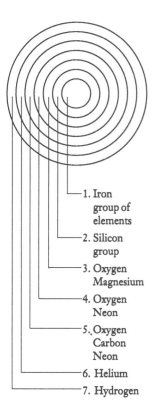

FIGURE 65
*Schematic drawing of the
seven zones of a star.*

1. Iron group of elements
2. Silicon group
3. Oxygen Magnesium
4. Oxygen Neon
5. Oxygen Carbon Neon
6. Helium
7. Hydrogen

FIGURE 66
*Manalagnenna. An initiated
man, one of the last surviving
Tasmanian tribal people.*

internal densification, converts back to helium, the original element that was formed in the heavens.[38] Iron completes the cycle of seven phases of densification, in a progression similar to the Dreamtime Creation, from invisible helium gases to the rigid fragility of dense, metallic substance.

The Tasmanian Aborigines applied red ochre mixed with the fat of wallabies and possums in wavy, energy-field patterns on their arms and torsos and through their matted, curly hair. They painted their bodies with the ochre on an everyday rather than a ritual basis, even though red ochre is in very limited supply in Tasmania. This fact suggests that they represented an older or at least a more orthodox form of Aboriginal spirituality.[39]

When European settlement blocked their access to natural sources of red ochre, the Tasmanian Aborigines were often seen desperately scraping rust from iron farm machinery or industrial equipment in order to make their body-paint preparations.[40] Native American lore suggests a possible explanation for this behavior. They believe that ochre, when rubbed on the body, allows the spiritual force trapped within us to flow outward, so they paint themselves for all journeys into other worlds as well as for tuning the body to the magnetic flows of the natural world in order to hunt. This is reminiscent of Carl Jung's insight that the sense of God or immortality is a spatial awareness of expanding and flowing into a frame larger than that of the body.[41]

The use of henna in ancient Egypt was based on similar beliefs. Although henna does not contain ferrous compounds, the red organic haemo pigment is believed to have properties similar to those of red ochre and blood. The use of henna as a cosmetic spread throughout the Middle East, North Africa, and India in later periods. Women used it on their fingertips to increase their sensitivity, particularly in selecting foods. It was also applied to the fingers of the dead to aid them in finding their way through the intermediate worlds. Henna was applied to the soles of women's feet and to men's beards to sensitize them to their mission and direction on earth. It was also believed to increase the magnetism of sexual attraction.[42]

Indigenous people believe that the blood of the gods, the subtle magnetic, celestial flow, circulates in the veins of the earth. This concept underlies the extensive occult science known as geomancy, the study of ley lines, for which John Michell is the most eloquent commentator.[43] A number of anthropologists and scientists have found that the Aborigines possess an acute sensitivity to magnetic and vital force flows emanating from the earth, which they refer to as songlines. Perhaps the oldest geomancy tradition, songlines are fundamental to Aboriginal initiatic knowledge and religion. Songlines are so named because they are maps written in songs, depicting mythic events at successive sites along a walking trail that winds through a region.[44] Each Aboriginal tribe inherited a network of songlines, and all travel in the lands of neighboring tribes was done along these lines. In previous epochs, according to John Michell, this appears to have been a sacred tradition throughout the world.[45]

Early anthropologists were amazed by Aborigines who had walked through immense desert expanses, unerringly finding their way to tiny water holes or distant mission settlements. One anthropologist has remarked that "no one has ever met a lost Aborigine." A friend visiting a tribal family in the Northern Territory was taken on a walk by one of the older men, along with two children five and six years of age. They walked for an entire day through uniform country of dense scrub and finally camped out near a sacred site. The two children had never made this journey before. Early on the day of their return the two children disappeared, and my friend became terribly concerned that they were lost. The older Aboriginal man tried to allay his fears by assuring him that there was no problem; they would find their way home. After returning to camp that night, my friend was about to report the missing children to the local police when they emerged from the bush into the firelight of the camp, joyous and unconcerned. Aborigines young and old seem to move through the countryside instinctively, in a manner comparable to what we now understand about bird and animal migration.

Biophysicists F. A. Brown and F. H. Barnwell have done extensive research on the biological effects of the earth's magnetic field, particularly as it relates to the sense of direction.

> There remains no reasonable doubt that living systems are extraordinarily sensitive to magnetic fields. By extremely simple experiments it is shown that highly diverse plants and animals may have their orientation modified by artificial fields of the order of strength of the geo-magnetic field. . . . The nature of the response properties suggest that the organism is normally integrated with its geo-magnetic environment to a striking degree.[46]

Sensitivity to geomagnetic currents is a function in animals that can be referred to as nothing less than an intelligence. Research on the amazing orientation capacities of homing pigeons revealed that these birds have a tiny crystal in their brain that is supersensitive to the earth's magnetic flow, which is received through feathers and nerves.

The extraordinary directional and navigational abilities of indigenous peoples echo the directional capacity that is universal among animals. The human sense of direction has weakened since the invention of the compass. The magnetic compass is an example of the externalization of

FIGURE 67
Henna was an important ingredient in the erotic traditions of ancient India.

1777

1842

1980

FIGURE 68
The changing pattern of the earth's magnetic field from 1777 to 1842 to 1980. The contour plots indicate the strength of the field at the boundary between the molten core and the mantle. The lines of force come out of the Southern hemisphere and flow back into the Northern hemisphere. The magnetic flux that flows into the core is represented by solid lines; the flux emerging out of the core is represented by broken lines. (From Bloxham and Gubbins, 1985)

the internal power of consciousness. This invention externalized energies and potentials that made possible what we view as historic events, such as the European colonialization of the world.

A simple scientific experiment has verified that a keen sense of direction is an innate capacity of human sensitivity to magnetism. The experiment involved dropping a busload of blindfolded people at scattered locations in the wilderness. Each blindfold contained a bar of metal that pressed against the back of the head; half of these bars were magnetized, the other half were not. The participants did not know whether they were carrying a magnet or not. All of the participants carrying the nonmagnetized bar were eventually able to orient themselves and find their way back, but none of those carrying the magnets were able to do so. The magnetic bar obviously interfered with a natural magnetic orientation within the human organism.[47]

The founder of the modern science of magnetism, William Gilbert, referred to the earth's magnetic field as its soul. Scientists consider the earth's magnetic field to be an energy emanating from the movements of the molten rock core of the earth's interior.[48] In Aboriginal terms, it is the force externalizing the inner dream of the earth. Magnetism is the voice of the earth's Dreaming; it controls the movement of continents, oceans, and plants and animals. It is a voice to which the Aborigines listen with great care—a voice to which our civilization has become completely deaf.

ECSTATIC RITUAL: A TUNING TO THE EARTH

The ability to sense magnetic fields is associated with psychic presentiments such as prophetic and intuitional messages and remote viewing, or clairvoyance at a distance.

> Some parapsychologists have found evidence relating spontaneous psi phenomena as well as dream telepathy to sunspot fluctuations, which affect the magnetic flux in the ionosphere. There is more psi during periods of relative quiet: the magnetic storms interfere with psychic resonant communication as they interfere with radio communication. This would be an example of negative resonance or dissonance between planetary and human vibratory patterns.[49]

In a far-reaching and detailed statistical study, the neuroscientist Michael Persinger has correlated the occurrence of various forms of

ESP—telepathy, clairvoyance, precognition, and apparition—with a worldwide index of geomagnetic activity. "Astounding correlations have been found between the faculties of telepathy and clairvoyance, particularly on days of quiet geomagnetic activity."[50]

The most remarkable evidence for the relationship between psychic phenomena and earthly magnetism is the fact that magnetic wave frequencies (known as the Schumann resonance) pulsating between the earth's surface and the ionosphere oscillate at 7.8 cycles per second. This is the lower end of the frequency range of the most common human brain wave, known as the alpha frequency. Alpha is associated with deep, intuitive, hypnogogic states of consciousness and meditation. More accurately, this means that in certain inner states our brain waves resonate with the rhythms of the earth; we are tuning into the vibration of the earth's voice.

The attention that the Australian Aborigines paid to the principle of vibration and earthly resonance can be seen in one of their most sacred initiatic rituals of creation. In several tribes of north Arnhem Land, this ceremony makes use of a ground painting in which the first Creative Ancestor is represented by a large circle of concentric red and white rings, like a standing wave field. The red rings are formed and hardened by earth mixed with blood that has been ritually extracted from the veins of initiated men. The white rings are also of blood and earth, but thousands of white bird feathers have been applied to their surface. From photographs of these rituals, there appear to be four wide inner circles and seven narrower outer circles (reminiscent of the modern cosmology of four universal fields and seven forms of energy). The circle is painted on the earth in a remote sacred place known only to initiated men, at the spot where the Ancestor is said to have emerged from the earth in the Dreamtime. The Aborigines described the event thus: "Though asleep, the ancestor was thinking. His desires flashed through his mind, causing animals to emerge from his navel and arm pits."[51]

The ceremony proceeds with three initiated men taking their place in the centre of a circle of young initiated men. The young men lie on the ground, pressing their ears and chests against the earth. The tribal elder in the center holds a large, heavy wooden pole that is also encircled from top to bottom with red and white colored rings. It has a crown of white feathers on top. The elder sits cross-legged with the pole in front of him; he raises and lowers it so that it pounds the earth. The pole is called *Numbakul*, which means the Eternal Naming. The alternating red and white colors of the pole, as well as the alternating, thumping sound, represent the principle of duality that manifests itself in all things, most transparently in the sexes.[52]

107

FIGURE 69
*Three North Aranda
tribesmen, ceremonially
attired, sit before a sacred
ground-painting representing
the Ilbalintja Soak, on the
Burt Plain, some 30 miles
northeast of Alice Springs.
This site is where the Great
Ancestor spirit energy first
emanated from the earth.*

The first line sung to the silent initiates is "May Numbakul reach to the stomach of the sky." This is sung as a mantra, alternating with "The earth is the stomach of the sky." As the sun sets the chanting stops. Assisted by the two men flanking him, the tribal shaman raises and lowers the pole, thumping the earth through the night. The silent group of young initiates lies utterly still and naked, absorbing and dissolving into the vibratory dream of the Creative Ancestors pulsating from the earth. As dawn approaches, the initiated men, seated quietly in the surrounding bush, begin to chant as if their songs arose from the heartlike beat of the pole thumping the earth.[53] The songs tell of the mysteries of the emergence of life and substance from the vibratory preformed realm of the Ancestors.

Aboriginal women have equally powerful ceremonies for entering mental states that are resonant with the earth's magnetic vibration, but anthropologists have not gained access to any of the traditional sacred secret rituals of Aboriginal women. In South India, however, naked village women take part in rituals in which they attain trancelike states while ecstatically moaning, wailing, and rolling incessantly on the earth through the night. These rites may be similar to those that Aboriginal women practiced for the purpose of entering the earth's magnetic field and drawing out its fructifying power.

To interpret these rituals, we can visualize the earth's magnetic field as it might be viewed from thousands of miles in outer space. This image allows us to contemplate the three primary and mystic relationships in Aboriginal cosmology: the relationships between space and consciousness, between rhythmic cycles and the patterns of life and mind, and between the body of the earth and the Dreaming of the Ancestors.

The earth rotates from day to night, just as the mind moves from the waking state to sleep and from conscious to unconscious. The earth's enveloping magnetic field is shaped by the force of the radiation emitted from the sun and other planets. These "solar winds," traveling at about one million miles per hour, sculpt the magnetic field into a tapering cavity called the magnetosphere. The magnetosphere is shaped like a serpent with its head on the daytime side, compressed into a flat oval 10 times larger than the earth's radius, and a tail, called the magnetotail, that sweeps behind to a distance of more than 1,000 earth radii. The compressed head of the serpent protects the planet from the fierce onslaught of solar and cosmic radiation, much as the skull protects the layers of brain within. The earth's own magnetic force at the North and

FIGURE 70
Earth and Mind. The earth's magnetic field is confined by solar wind into a comet-shaped cavity called the magnetosphere. As it moves through the cosmos, the earth processes energy through its magnetosphere. In much the same way, the conscious mind and the unconscious mind absorb and process information.

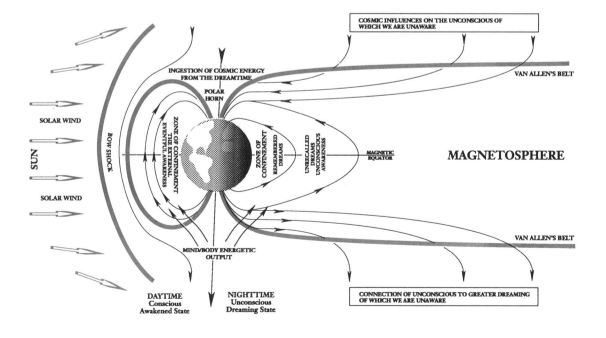

FIGURE 71
*Rock-shelter painting
associated with the clan hero,
the increase of natural species,
and "burial."*

South poles pulls the envelope of the magnetic sphere in toward the earth, forming the neck of its serpent body. The North Pole receives energy from the Van Allen belt, a ring of particles and cosmic radiation that have penetrated the weaker outer layers of the magnetosphere but are stopped and held by the denser inner layers. This belt of mixed cosmic and earthly radiation, like the skin of the serpent, is an active interface between this sinuous body and its celestial environment.[54]

On the daytime side (the conscious side of the mind), the energy drawn in by the North Pole from the cosmic environment recirculates through the earth's body and atmosphere, is interfused with the internally produced magnetic energy, and then circulates from the South Pole back to the North Pole. This digestion of celestial energy in the earth's field is reflected in the Aboriginal mantra, "the earth is the stomach of the sky." The tradition of Western astrology is based on the influences of the sun, moon, and planets on people; in the vision of indigenous people, we receive *all* celestial influences from the earth's emanations after they have been processed in her bowels.

The continuous loop within the head of the serpent suggests the activity of the conscious mind, which receives sensory input from the external environment, processes it within its internal awareness, and converts it into cognition and the active processes of conscious thought. On the nighttime side (the dreaming or unconscious mind), energy from the cosmos is also drawn in from the skin of the Van Allen belt. It flows into and activates the earth-generated field, then some energy flows back to remain within the cavity of the unconscious or magnetotail, some seeps back into the unbounded universe, and the rest is retained in the zone of confinement behind the shadowed or unconscious portions of mind.

The Aborigines possess a sacred science, one that seeks to fuse the energies of the earth and humanity to those of the cosmos. The medium of that fusion is magnetism in both its physical and more subtle levels of expression; its tools are blood and other sensitive magnetic conductors in the pigments of the blood of the earth, plants, and animals. This science of attunement opens their consciousness to enable them to communicate with the memory and mind of Earth. Their instincts, intuitions, and presentiments are based upon the ability to perceive and participate in the subtle energies and the subjective life of the entire natural world.

Figure 72
Shaman of the Aranda Tribe. It is believed his body is not like that of ordinary men but is filled with quartz crystals and endowed with incorruptible internal organs.

111

CHAPTER 7

IN THE WOMB OF
THE RAINBOW SERPENT

Long ago the old people used to tell the story of an orphan boy who was always crying and was eaten by the Rainbow Serpent. Once when he was walking around an old lady asked him, "Why are you crying?" The orphan said, "They refuse to give me any manburrangkali *lily roots.*" "Is that so?" replied the old lady.

Then that old lady went and got a different kind of lily root for him. The orphan was still lying down crying when she brought him back a bag full of yaldanj *lily roots.*

She placed the lily roots on the ground while she went and got some firewood. She returned and lit the fire and cooked them all. The old woman said, "Come and eat these yalkanj *lily roots.*" The orphan stood there and said, "I don't want those lily roots, I don't like them."

So he kept crying—he was walking around crying, so another man got up and went to get some bush honey. When he returned he showed the boy and said, "Come and eat some honey." The orphan stood there and said, "I don't want any honey, I don't like it." "Is that so?" said the man. "Okay, you just cry, and leave my honey alone."

So he just kept crying. Another lady then got up and said, "Let me go and get some long yams for him, otherwise he will always be crying." Then she went and got some long yams for him, filled her dilly bag, returned, put them on the ground, went for firewood, lit the fire, and roasted the yams. When they were cooked she said, "Come and eat some long yams." The orphan said, "I don't want those long yams." "Is that so?" said the old woman.

The people said to him, "Okay, you just cry, because you didn't want the long yams, the honey, the yaldanj *lily roots,* because you are always thinking of the taste of those sweet manburrangkali *lily roots,* because you have an insatiable desire."

Now there were lots of old people sitting there, and they said to him, "Why can't you stop crying? Will you always be crying then? Soon the

The Dalabon Aborigines hold that the Earth was originally an expanse of water, coloured as the rainbow, and that all life was held inside this female Rainbow Serpent.[1]

KENNETH MADDOCK

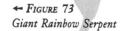

← FIGURE 73
Giant Rainbow Serpent

Rainbow Serpent will eat us." They told him this but he did not stop crying—he was always crying. He cried and cried.

Now there was a Rainbow Serpent at Miya, to the north. The Rainbow Serpent lifted up her head, looked around, listened very carefully, and heard him crying at Mayawunj in the south. That Rainbow Serpent said, "I will go south to that place and eat them."

Then the Rainbow Serpent started, she went underground and kept going, she was getting closer to them. When she came to them, she came out of the ground in the south, lifted her head and saw them. She said, "Ah, this is the place where that orphan is crying—this is where they are camping."

Then she appeared near them. The people had been looking to the north and had seen something like a fire or a light shining on them and they cried out in fear.

Then they told the men, "Quick, spear it! Do you want it to eat us?" They kept trying to spear it, but they always missed it, so they said, "That's it, bad luck. It's no good, the Rainbow Serpent will just have to eat us."

In fear they tried to run away. The Rainbow Serpent was watching them and hooked her tail around them all, the orphan with them. That Rainbow Serpent ate the orphan first, biting his head and swallowing it. Then she ate the others. This made the Rainbow Serpent from Miya full.

That is what happened at Mayawunj in the south—she went under the ground and was lying there with the people and the insatiable child within her belly sleeping in the south ready to reawaken.[2]

GUNWINGGU OENPELLI

I N THIS CHAPTER I apply the biomagnetic and geophysical concepts developed in Chapter 6 to an integrated vision of the historical development of humanity. Our collective and individual unfolding parallels the earth's, and these unfoldings are stimulated and guided by psychic-magnetic impulses associated with the magnetic life of our living planet. Let us imagine, in the context of scientific data combined with Aboriginal myths, how universal influences may have shaped the emergence of humankind and the species of plants and animals directly from their earthly habitation.

According to Aboriginal cosmology, the great Dreamtime Ancestors shaped the earth, its continents, mountains, oceans, and rivers, its lodestones and its veins of crystals, pigments, and metals. Their activities still

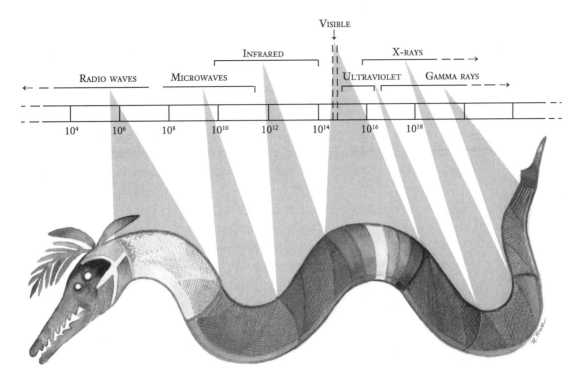

VISIBLE

INFRARED   X-RAYS

RADIO WAVES   MICROWAVES   ULTRAVIOLET   GAMMA RAYS

10^4 10^6 10^8 10^{10} 10^{12} 10^{14} 10^{16} 10^{18}

resonate in the shapes and energies that bathe the earth and all life processes. These energies are often referred to symbolically as the Rainbow Serpent, which, like electromagnetism and all energy fields, exists as a spectrum of various colors, frequencies, or powers.

The Rainbow Serpent is attracted to menstrual blood and will mingle with it to create life in the womb. The Rainbow Serpent is also attracted to rituals in which the tribal people are painted with red ochre. These rituals used the force of the serpent in their ceremonies to regenerate and increase the fertility of the dancers as well as the various plant and animal species. The Aboriginal myths of the Rainbow Serpent guide these rituals; the serpent is an energy figure symbolic of the sacred body of the earth and the preformative spiritual order of the universe. This image is the original appearance of creative energy in the Dreamtime.

The "serpent dreaming" myths are most prevalent in the sinuous river country of northern Australia, yet they are found in stories told throughout the entire continent. They are part of the oldest continuous documented religious theme in the world. The story-images are recorded in cave paintings going back more than 20,000 years. The serpent is always associated with vibration and flowing energy fields. In an ancient myth from Arnhem Land, the great ancestral Rainbow Serpent Ngaljod first created himself as the *ubar*, a long, hollow log. The *ubar* produces a hypnotic vibration and sound and is used as a musical gong in sacred ceremonies; it is considered an extremely sacred object. The hollow inside of the *ubar*, or Rainbow Serpent, is sometimes referred to

FIGURE 74
The Rainbow of Energy. The Rainbow Serpent is the first cosmological model for the spectral order of universal energy. The electromagnetic spectrum is a continuous range of radiation spreading from gamma rays to radio waves. Only a small portion of these energies is visible: the seven-color spectrum of natural daylight. All radiation has the same velocity and the same electromagnetic nature; the only differences between parts of the spectrum are frequency and wave length. The electromagnetic spectrum, like the Rainbow Serpent, is a profound metaphor for the unity that exists between the tangible and the invisible worlds.

115

as the uterus of the Great Mother, and the external form is referred to as the penis or the male form of the Rainbow Serpent. Sexual androgyny associated with the mythic Ancestor is often found in Aboriginal mythological thinking. For example, the sun, which is also related to the Rainbow Serpent, is considered feminine where it is a diffused, warming, nourishing agent of plant growth and life. This is especially true on the north coast of Australia, where the summer seasons bring heavy rains. In the severe desert regions, the sun is considered male since its overactive heat sucks up moisture and energy, burning and inhibiting life and growth.[3]

In one of the many creation myths of Egypt, the primal serpent Uraus also symbolizes duality, in part because many snake species have dual sex organs. The form of the Uraus was used in one of the initiatic crowns of the Pharoahs. The serpent's body, shaped into a crown of hammered gold, flows from the back of the head across the center of the skull, both dividing and uniting the two hemispheres of the brain. The serpent's face forms a third eye in the middle of the Pharoah's forehead. In the Old Testament, the serpent is associated with the duality of good and evil.

FIGURE 75
The Pharonic Serpent Crown. The embossed linen wrapped around the skull of the mummified Pharoah depicts the Serpent as the dualizing power, which both separates and cojoins the dual powers of consciousness in the right and left brain hemispheres. It may also symbolize the power of the union of the conscious with the unconscious.

Throughout the many serpent stories, either the earth and creation are pictured as being within the womb of the serpent, or the serpent is inside the earth. In one such myth, the Rainbow Serpent within the earth is the source and maker of new songs. Wawi, the serpent creature of the Darling River tribes, lives deep in the water holes and along the edges of the river bank. Like a wave field of energy, Wawi has the magical power to vary his size from very small to enormous. Only highly initiated men can visit this serpent monster. In order to do so, an Aboriginal man of high degree must paint his body all over with red ochre. He then fasts and begins a journey, following a rainbow into the wilderness for some days. When the clouds form a thundershower over the water hole at the end of the rainbow, the man of high degree knows he has found where Wawi lives. The man must dive into the water, where Wawi will appear to him and teach him a new song for ritual. The man must stay in these depths, repeating the song over and over until he has learned it. The song is a revelation of the mystery of life that he may bring back to his people. When the tribe sees him returning, painted red, they know he has been with Wawi.[4] The plunge into the deep unconscious is comparable to the metaphor used in many shamanistic cultures. The shaman enters the creative preformative realm and returns with revelations about the recurring seasons of new life, growth, and fertility. In other myths, all of creation plunges into unconsciousness or a cosmic sleep before beginning a new cycle.

Monsoon rains have high electromagnetic activity; the magnetic atmosphere undergoes radical changes before these storms. The atmospheric energies preceding the days of rain are believed to arouse not only the earth but also tribal peoples; this period is often celebrated with wild, ecstatic fertility rituals. In many parts of Australia, Aborigines continue to worship the great female serpent spirit today since she brings the wet season, with its teeming waters and abundance of wildlife, after a long dry spell.

The serpent rituals among the Aborigines are reminiscent of the ancient Egyptians' worship of the female goddess Hathor, associated with the rise of the life-giving waters of the Nile. In Egypt the rainbow was sacred to Hathor, who is also the nourishing principle of universal femininity. Hathor had a cow's body covered with vibratory waves similar to the Aboriginal designs painted on the body of the Rainbow Serpent. Like the Rainbow Serpent, Hathor also had a masculine component, which is symbolized by her piercing horns. It is said of Hathor "that everything that her heart conceived became at that very moment realized."[5] All her creations were completed in seven forms, like the seven colors of the rainbow.

> Seven propositions issued successively from her mouth and these seven propositions became seven divine beings, which fix the destiny of the world. . . . For all creation came into existence after she was born. It is she who touches the boundaries of the entire universe under her bodily aspect of surface liquid and under her real name of perpetual time.[6]

These descriptions of Hathor from an ancient Egyptian text could equally be the description of a rainbow. As the Aboriginal life-giving principle, the Serpent stands on her tail like a rainbow, revealing the celestial sources of her energy. The Aborigines describe her thus:

FIGURE 76
In ancient Egypt, Hathor the cow was a symbol of the nourishing life-creating energies, similar in mythic description to the Aboriginal image of the Rainbow Serpent.

117

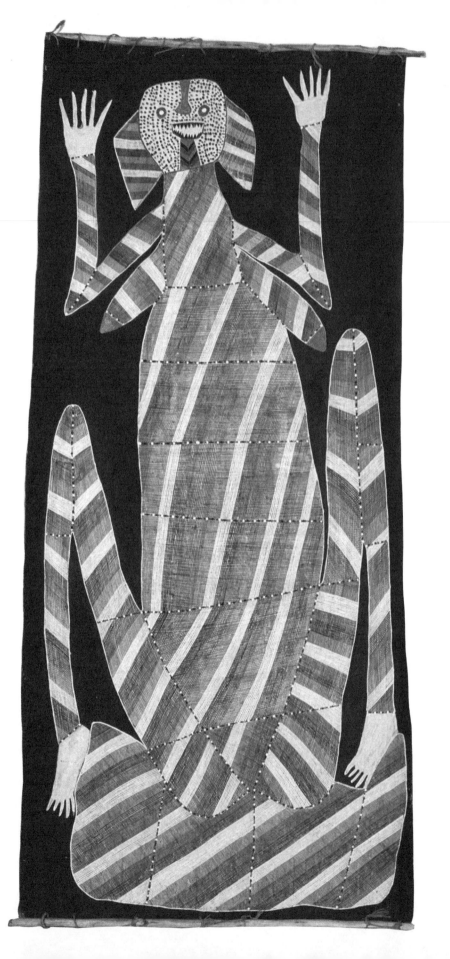

As the first Creator she taught the people the Laws and ceremonies, and failure to abide by these Laws will arouse her fury and desire for revenge. Many stories tell of her swallowing people who have not observed the taboos, or of causing natural disasters such as flash floods, earthquakes, torrential rains, or droughts.[7]

In both traditions the rainbow is a symbol that makes visible the hidden energies that stir earth and animals to fertility. These invisible forces control the patterns of weather and the cycles of animal and plant fertility; the Aborigines consider them the lawgivers of the earth, since they were deposited in the womb of life in the Dreamtime. The ancient Egyptian culture, which emerged within the cycle of agriculture, conceived of the body of the creative nourishing spirit as a domestic animal. The hunter-gatherer Australian Aborigines see the body of the nourishing spirit as a serpent energy that connects the earth with the celestial realms and is responsible for the increase and flourishing of wild animals and plants.

When the Rainbow Serpent is angered, impassioned, or sexually aroused she burrows into the earth, creating lines of magnetic energy and force that still flow today. In the Dreamtime she shaped the caves, valleys, and riverbeds. When the Rainbow Serpent touched the sites where the Ancestors had deposited their potencies, the forms and species of life arose. Over vast periods of time the Rainbow Serpent, like the earth's magnetic field, alternately extinguishes and re-creates life over the whole earth.

The myth of the Rainbow Serpent corresponds to the creation stories of the geophysicists: the last reversal of magnetic energy appears to have occurred 700,000 years ago, concurrently with a vast extinction or purification of life. This oscillation brought the spiraling, serpentine, positive magnetic field to the South Pole. Nourished by the life-enhancing South Pole magnetic energies, humanity may have emerged for the first time in this cycle in Australia, as mutation evidence indicates, some 400,000 years ago. The culture of the Australian Aborigines has remained intact in Australia throughout the duration of this cycle, as the generating seed.

THE SERPENT OF THE SOUTH: POTENTIZING, GIVING, MANIFESTING

The Kunwinjku people used the term rainbow *to refer to distinct Ancestral Beings. One of these, Yingarna, is described as the original creative being and is said to be androgynous. She is depicted as a large, dense, active field of energy. In some myths Yingarna's firstborn is said to be the Rainbow*

119

Serpent Ngalyod, whose long, flowing body is like an energy current and who is also androgynous. Yingarna holds Ngalyod within her stomach, along with all the other original ancestors of the Dreaming, just as Ngalyod holds within her stomach all of the creatures and things of this world.

The myth of Ngalyod often depicts her floating along river currents in a fish trap, creating and naming animals, plants, and sacred sites and giving land to people who emerge as she travels. (The fish trap can be imagined as the energy grid, the circulation of the earth's magnetic energy sets up in relation to the fault lines of the earth's mantle.) At the end of her journey, Ngalyod returns to her source and encircles Yingarna. The two are seen then as one rainbow. This concept is a powerful metaphor for the original dual creator and the regenerative powers of the rainbow.[8]

Let us symbolically apply some elements of the rainbow myth to the terminology of our creation story. Energies are received initially by the North Pole and mixed with the magnetism of the earth's interior. These energies are then regenerated by the South Pole, acting like a catalyst or invisible organizing principle in all processes of growth. As they pass over a particular region, these energies organize the earth's condition and the ambient energetic fields of a region into a milieu for the emergence of particular forms of life. This movement can be visualized as it is depicted in the myth of the great Rainbow Serpent: it flows from south to north along the lines of geomagnetic force, igniting the life potentials specific to a place that have been deposited there in an earlier metaphysical epoch. The original "seeds" of the Dreamtime may then attract the subsequent development of species toward qualities unique to that place.

The serpent is a dominant image in the Tantric or Kundalini yoga of south India. The subtle serpent energy is perceived as coiled at the base of the spine; it can be aroused so that it flows upward, opening up the powers latent in the various psychoneural centers of the body. The image of the Dreamtime Serpent coiling up from the South Pole and activating the latent creative powers of the earth reinforces the identity between the human body and the earth.

The Rainbow Serpent image may be used to explain some of the intriguing similarities that anthropologists have noted between a few indigenous tribes in India and the Tasmanian Aborigines. The two groups share linguistic, cultural, and physical characteristics. The Dravidian fishermen of the Madras coast use almost the same words for *I, thou, he, we,* and *you* as some Aboriginal tribes. Many other key words in the Dravidian dialects are identical to Tasmanian Aboriginal terms in both pronunciation and meaning. All of the Dravidian dialects are agglutinative, as are the Australian languages. Australian canoes are constructed identically to those of the coastal Dravidian tribes in India, and wild tribes in the Deccan region of India are the only culture known to use the boomerang outside of Australia (with the possible exception of ancient Egypt). The physical resemblance of the Dravidians to the Aborigines, particularly to the Tasmanians, indicates racial similarities as well.[9] Although this information was uncovered over 75 years ago, modern anthropologists tend to disregard it because it conflicts with currently prevailing theories.

What accounts for the presence of tribes of the same racial type as the Tasmanian Aborigines, with shared language and customs, in south India? Migration and colonialization are unacceptable explanations for the early expansion of human populations because these processes contradict the religious beliefs and demonstrated patterns of indigenous peoples. Another possibility, that the tribes moved with the Indian subcontinent as it broke free from Australia and came up to its present position in Asia, is also unsatisfactory.

Aboriginal cosmology, as well as the beliefs of other indigenous peoples, explains this question in a way that is worth considering. All tribal people throughout the world tell a similar story of human origins: human popu-

← *FIGURE 78*
Two examples of the ordinary boomerangs of the Aranda, Luritja, and Ilpirra groups of Central Australia. The specimen on the top is made by groups from Northern Australia. The boomerang is used to hit small game and birds in flight. In taking aim, the hunter calibrates the flight of the bird so that it meets in space with the curved trajectory of the boomerang.

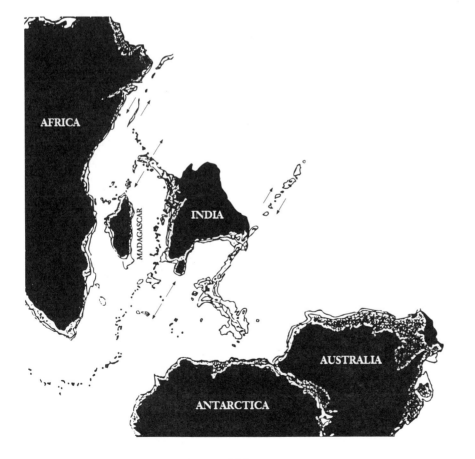

FIGURE 79
Land and culture. Seventy-five million years ago India was the last land mass to break away from Australia and from the ancient continent of the south, Gondwanaland (Australia and Antarctica joined together). The plate that carried India moved rapidly towards the northeast. Its impact with the land mass of Asia formed the Himalayas, thereby joining the two land masses but keeping India forever culturally separate from the development of the rest of Asia.

lations, as well as plant and animal species, arise directly from the alignments and energies generated by their particular locality. For the Aborigines, each tribe is an externalization of the vibratory essence deposited by the great Ancestors in the land from which it arose. Humans, animals, and plant life are the "dream" of the landscape where they originated. The quality and color of skin can adapt to a change in one's country or location, but essential vibratory affinities in blood and bone and language remain connected to the place where a person is born, grows, and develops.

> Each man he stay . . .
> stay on his own country.
> He can't move his country . . .
> so he stay there,
> stay with his language.
> Language is different . . .
> like skin.
> Skin can be different,
> but blood same.
> Blood and bone . . .
> all same.
> Man can't split himself.[10]
> BILL NEIDJIE, ABORIGINAL POET

Let us speculate further on why the village people of south India are so similar to the Tasmanian Aborigines. At the beginning of this magnetic cycle, the land of India was geographically close to Australia. It was the last land area to break away from Gondwanaland and, like a seed released from a flower, it drifted up and collided with continental Asia. During the Dreamtime, the prelife phase of creation, these two land areas shared many of the same energies. Therefore, the humans who arose from these lands also would have shared, in different proportions, many of the characteristics of blood and bone and consciousness of these once-close lands.

This brings us back to the tribal elder's statements earlier in the book concerning the origins and spread of humanity. I repeat his statement in full because each line may now be understood in the light of Aboriginal mythology:

> They say we have been here for 60,000 years, but it is much longer. We have been here since the time before time began. We have come directly out of the Dreamtime of the Creative Ancestors. We have lived and kept the earth as it was on the First Day. All other peoples of the world came from us. . . . People who farm the land or make buildings and keep animals—

these people do not belong to the spirit of this land and must go out from here because those things are against the Law of this land.

In Chapter 5 the terms "First Day" and "First People" were defined, not as chronological terms, but as references to a time and a people who reflect most clearly the metaphysical order that preceded the appearance of the phenomenal world. "The time before time began" refers to that timeless moment in which the Aborigines balanced their consciousness between the creative unconscious and the created world. The mysterious statement, "We have come directly out of the Dreaming," relates to an idea that science and religion have grappled with for centuries, the substantiation of invisible realms into matter.

Physicists David Ash and Peter Hewitt have approached this question in their recent book *Science of the Gods*, in which they speculate that energy frequencies faster than the speed of light comprise a world of super-energy and a super-physical reality. They claim that when these super-energies decelerate, substance and form materialize. They use a complex model based on this theory to explain the origins of the material world, as well as phenomena difficult to explain by mechanistic thinking, such as UFOs and the ability of psychics like the Indian guru Sai Baba to materialize objects out of "thin air."[11]

I believe the passage from the pure energetic continuum to a substantial world of atomic structure will never be understood by the conscious mind, no matter how avidly the priests of rational science search for explanatory mechanisms. The power to create substance and life out of pure energy belongs to the unconscious realms, to the Dreaming. The unconscious will always extend beyond the efforts of the conscious mind to unveil all its secrets. The unconscious levels of creation can be entered only through mystic doorways, through meditation or ecstatic dance, ritual, or dreaming. The conscious and the unconscious are the primal couple at the origin of creation; the entirety of creation comes into existence through the interaction of these two. If the conscious mind were to comprehend the unconscious completely, the two minds would be, in effect, identical. The primary twoness of consciousness would dissolve, taking with them all of creation.

The tribal elder's closing statement, "these people do not belong to the spirit of this land and must go out from here," may refer to the spiritual essence of people contained in a particular body of land since the beginning of time. This essence flowed away from the primal land of Australia with the continents that drifted north. In the Aboriginal myths, the metaphysical life-promoting rainbow energy, Yingarna, is at first a massive field (like the continental mass), which then differentiates

← *Figure 80*
The Aboriginal vision of humanity directly emerging from the energetic ambience of an earthly location.

into streams of essence. We can therefore replace the image of a physical exodus of human populations with this metaphysical theme and imagine, at the beginning of our present cycle of magnetic stability, the life-supporting magnetic energies flowing from the south, gradually bringing forth the physical manifestation of that preexisting essence. The golden peoples of the seed, the stable unchanging wood-based cultures, remained in place, just as the Australian continent remained close to its original southern position. The people of the plow and metal, of restlessness and strife (perhaps the insatiable child from the opening Dreamtime myth) emerged from the lands which, from their geological inception, contained the Dreaming of the north. As millennia rolled by and the earth's magnetic energy fields declined, the pristine harmony between earth and man degenerated. After the close of the Golden Age of our cycle, many possible movements and interactions between people can be imagined. For example, people may have migrated from south to north and then been influenced by the psychic and physical ambience of their new home. Their descendants may later have moved back from the north, invading southern regions, as with the prehistoric invasions of India by Aryans from the northern steppes of Persia and Iran.

Andrew Bard Schmookler, in his prize-winning study of power and civilization, *The Parable of the Tribes*, confronts the vexing question of the spread of human populations and relates it to why early humans left the earthly paradise of hunting and gathering to take up the toilsome practice of agriculture. He acknowledges—as few historians have—that the

FIGURE 81
The giant marsupials, spoken of in Aboriginal Dreamtime stories, became extinct 13,000 to 15,000 years ago. Before that time, the earth's stronger magnetic field supported larger forms of plants and animals and a more abundant variety of species.

step into agriculture was not an example of progress but rather an event forced on humanity by the combined effect of population growth and food shortages due to the earth's declining fertility.[12] Schmookler's conclusions remain reductionist, however, ignoring the most important lesson from the cosmology and histories of ancient indigenous people: for every physical explanation, there must be an associated metaphysical cause. Perhaps the metaphysical cause behind the adoption of agriculture is the life-promoting influence of the earth's magnetic field combined with the subtle psychic influence that the geomagnetic field exerts on human nature. In the Aboriginal vision, this magnetic field is the dreaming of a conscious, living planet. It is the earth itself, then, whose dreams materialize the cyclic rise and fall of nature and human civilization. *We are dreaming within a greater dream.*

Over 10,000 years ago, just prior to the fatal movement to agriculture in other parts of the world, fossil records show that the familiar Australian species of plants and animals—kangaroos, wombats, possums—all existed in a giant-sized form. These giant species suddenly became extinct. Scientists have evidence that at about the same period, the earth's magnetic field began to diminish. This agrees with archaeological evidence that plant and animal species flourish and grow larger when the earth's magnetic energy is stronger. The intangible cause of the worldwide decline in food sources approximately 10,000 to 15,000 years ago, which necessitated the development of agriculture, may indeed have been the diminishing force of the earth's magnetic field. Aboriginal legends refer to a time just prior to the disappearance of the large marsupials, when humans possessed greater psychic and visionary powers. The decline in the force of the earth's Dreaming may be a hidden cause for the gradual loss of meaning humanity experienced as its contact with the psychic power, emanating from within the world, declined.

SONGLINES AND THE BLOOD OF CULTURE

If early human populations did not spread and colonize, how did communication occur during the Golden Age, when people were spiritually grounded and inseparably merged with their earthly place? In any living organism, most formations are stationary. The trunk, branches, and leaves of a tree maintain a fixed position relative to their role in the growth and organization of the whole. A material such as sap or blood constantly circulates, carrying and exchanging energy and information. The sap or blood of human societies is culture.

The landscape of Aboriginal Australia mirrored a living organism.

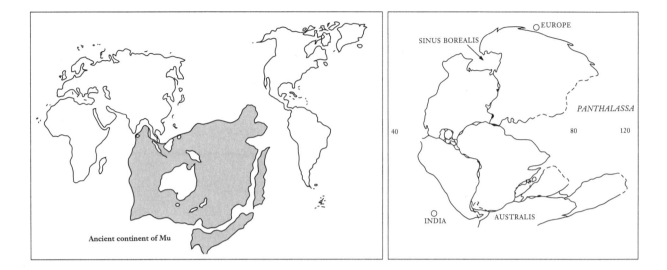

Ancient continent of Mu

SINUS BOREALIS   O EUROPE

PANTHALASSA

40   80   120

O INDIA   AUSTRALIS

FIGURE 82
The description of the ancient, mysterious continent to the south, named Mu, predates the scientific model of a continental mass called Pangaea, or Gondwanaland, yet is similar to it in many ways.

FIGURE 83
The universal land mass Pangaea may have looked like this 240 million years ago.

Each tribe was a stationary expression of the region of the earth from which it emerged; connecting these tribal regions throughout Australia was a circulation system called the songlines. Directed by a complex, unwritten calendar of ceremonies and rituals, tribal people would move along these songlines and interact with people of other regions. In earliest times, tribal movement was never an economic exchange of material goods. Only ritual paraphernalia, such as pigments, feathers, and carved sacred boards, were carried and offered as gifts.[13] Interactions were governed not by materialistic enterprise but by a quest for increased understanding of the mythic law of the land. At the time of the European invasions, Australia was a land with many separate and widely distributed tribes. Each regional tribe had its own linguistic, social, and ritual characteristics, but the entire continent shared a basic universal law and world view. This universal culture was like the blood that unites all the functions and parts of a living organism.

The magnetic songlines guided the physical, ceremonial journeys of the tribes. Initiated men and women learned to travel these subtle and invisible energy veins using their psychic or spirit body. Thus they were able to exchange songs, dances, and mythic visions of the ever-unfolding Dreamtime reality over great distances. Tribal elders claim that not only Australia but the entire earth, at one time, was linked through the songlines. People did not have to abandon their relationship with the beloved region that "grew" them to relate to the world as a whole. I believe that the similarities in the myths and cosmology of indigenous people from all over the world result from this type of worldwide spiritual communication.

In my life I have (unconsciously) followed songlines that carried me from south India, where I lived with Dravidian villagers for six years, to the homeland of the Tasmanian Aborigines. Perhaps the ancient invisible web of songlines still underlies the avenues of our search for understanding.

The origin of humanity in the south, as represented in the rainbow myths, is consonant with many other occult histories of the world, including the myth of the mysterious vanished continent of Mu. Colonel James Churchward was an unorthodox scholar who believed that the cultures of the ancient Egyptians, Chaldeans, Babylonians, Persians, Greeks, Hindus, and Chinese all derived from the culture of the lost world of Mu. Churchward and others describe Mu as having been a large continental island, roughly triangular in shape, with Australia at its center. The concept of Mu, the great motherland of the human race, appears in many legends and mythologies. The legend of Mu also parallels the Gondwanaland formation in the theory of continental drift.[14]

It is not my intention to use Aboriginal myths to support yet another unconventional theory of prehistory; rather, I wish to stimulate new thought about history in general. It is becoming evident that the present scientific concepts of history—prehistoric, historic, the Stone Age, the Bronze Age, the Iron Age—are inadequate, oversimplified classifications that contain many internal contradictions. The history of science and the history of occultism are equally replete with outrageous hypotheses. I believe that the inconsistencies in all these theories result from a failure to consider seriously the myths of the most ancient people in our contemplation of human origins. The Aboriginal myths provide us with a vastly expanded gathering of time: dreams and imagination are the faculty of the mind in which the unbounded configurations, the flowing patterns of time and space can be visualized. They may also guide us to increased understanding of the legends of many world cultures, including those of modern science.

THE SERPENT OF THE NORTH: ACTUALIZING, RECEIVING, INSPIRING

From the Van Allen belt the North Pole pulls some of the life-destroying radiation of the sun and cosmos directly into the earth and its atmosphere. The Inuits, among other indigenous people of the far north, are fearful of the aurora borealis (the northern lights), which are evidence of the polar inspiration of cosmic energy. The coexistence of this destructive radiation with benevolent solar and terrestrial energy consti-

IN THE WOMB OF THE
RAINBOW SERPENT

tutes the androgyny of the serpent. Together, these forces animate, nourish, and drive the seed through its cycle of flourishing and to its inevitable decline and death.

We can look at the biological and psychological effects of the earth's geomagnetic polarity metaphorically to understand the qualities that are peculiar to the developed societies of the northern hemisphere. Human societies living under the influence of the northern magnetic field exhibit a high level of development because of the increased effectiveness of the cerebral capacities. The technological and industrial superiority of the northern hemisphere has been accomplished through a diminution of the bodily functions (such as decreased sensitivity to sensory stimuli and lowered sexual appetite) and a proportional increase in the conscious activities of the mind and brain. Another way to image in a material sense the subtle flow from south to north (from potential to actualization) is to remember that much of the raw materials used to feed the industrial manufacturing of the north are drawn from the so-called Third World, the underdeveloped nations of the south.

Cold climates are associated with aggressiveness, progressive and dynamic change, and the use of metals, whereas tropical cultures are receptive, unchanging, earth-bound, and organic, like early wood-based cultures. The earliest examples of wood-based cultures are found in the cold southern climate of Tasmania, so these characteristics may be the effects of a force associated with the southern orientation rather than climate. This same division of characteristics was noted in laboratory animals who were exposed to South Pole magnetic energy. Therefore, we may imagine that magnetic influences on living organisms contribute to the formation of the underlying patterns in human cultural development.

Northern civilizations have moved, in stages, toward encasing themselves in glass and metal structures and rubber-soled footwear. Glass and rubber are dimagnetic (poor conductors of magnetism), and metal diffuses and disrupts human sensitivity to geomagnetic fields. It seems that as northern culture has developed, it has resisted the negative life factor associated with the geomagnetic north. Cultural development in the north has been marked by separation and isolation from the geomagnetic and atmospheric currents. Western civilization is now enveloped in artificially induced magnetic fields that disrupt the organic functions of the body and mute human sensitivity to the magnetic ambience of the natural world. In his recent book, *Cross Currents*, Robert Becker points to electromagnetic pollution as a cause of many diseases that befall modern people, including cancer, heart disease, arthritis, and schizophrenia. These problems will continue to worsen as humans bury themselves in an increasingly dense blanket of radiation from interna-

← FIGURE 84
Fire Dreaming.

129

tional telecommunication systems and the unending proliferation of electrical appliances, tools, and devices.[15]

"Green" architects are those who are aware of the danger of electromagnetic pollution in buildings and who recognize that architecture often separates and alienates people from their environment. These architects design houses that both reduce and insulate against electromagnetic fields while permitting greater communication between the inner environment of the structure and the outer world. This new type of architecture offers other benefits. Studies have revealed the enormous physiological changes that occur in going from indoors to outdoors, or vice versa: breathing and heartbeat change; digestion, perspiration, and excretory functions alter; hormonal activity associated with the light-sensitive pituitary and pineal glands are also affected.[16] Almost all the functions of the autonomic nervous system slow down when one is enclosed in a building or vehicle, because these functions are tuned to the subtle changes of natural light and geomagnetism.

The reduction in autonomic bodily responses encourages a shift away from sensory, intuitive awareness to an increased reliance on the cerebral, conscious, decision-making mechanisms of the central nervous system. Anthropologist and linguist Benjamin Whorf has noted that the Hopi Indians were well aware of the radical changes caused by moving from outdoors to indoors. The Hopi languages have the capacity to describe perceptual gradations in the intensity of experience. The English language has very few words (*very*, *slightly*, etc.) for indicating intensity; in contrast, the Hopis as well as the Australian Aborigines, have a number of suffixes that, when added to a verb, indicate a complex range of subtle gradation. The suffix denoting the most intense change in bodily reaction—for example, diving into icy water on a hot day—is also applied to the verb meaning to go out of a hut.[17] So-called developed cultures do not acknowledge such sensations or the psychological and physiological numbness that has resulted from our excessive use of architecture. To the degree that we insulate ourselves from the natural world and change our external environment, we change and isolate ourselves.

Movement north through time is characterized by clarity, separation, isolation, and a shift in focus toward the external material world. Following the decline of the great temple traditions of India and Egypt, the principle of separative vision was manifested in Greek rationalism. The Greek language adopted separative vision in its grammatical structure through the complete separation of subject and object. This linguistic form shaped the emergence of the civilizations of the Mediterranean, northern Europe, and the colonized New World.[18] The languages of these cultures presuppose an observer who is separated from the observed world; the noun, or subject, of every sentence is separated from the object by a verb, or action. The language we speak every day forces us to see ourselves as acting on a world that is other than and external to ourselves. Consequently, we cannot easily conceive of any other relationship between self and world. Concepts such as merging, multiple association, transparency of levels, or simultaneity of opposites are difficult to express with our language and are therefore difficult for us to experience.

THE FORGOTTEN CYCLE
OF THE POSITIVE NORTH

There are several possible mythic interpretations of magnetic influences and magnetic reversals. In the magnetic history of the earth, each approximate million-year period is marked by a positive South Pole domination, alternating with a similar period of positive North Pole domination. Perhaps in the previous cycle, between one and two million years ago, when the North Pole was emanating positive magnetic energy, a complete cycle of human development emerged and disappeared.

FIGURE 85
The ancient shamanistic people of the circumpolar North may hve resulted from a previous positive north magnetic cycle.

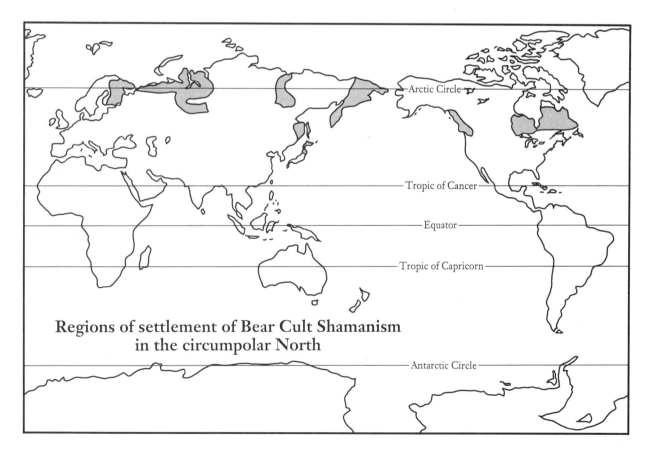

**Regions of settlement of Bear Cult Shamanism
in the circumpolar North**

Joseph Campbell has noted that shamanistic culture, similar in some aspects to Aboriginal culture, seems to have spread from the North Pole region; he calls these societies "circumpolar cults." The animals sacred to these cultures were the bear and the wolf. Such cultures include the Inuit of Alaska, the predecessors of the North American Indians, the early populations of Norway and Denmark, and others who settled across the Eurasian north, including the Caucasian indigenous populations of Japan and Siberia.[19]

The physical remains of these shamanistic cultures are less than a million years old, but some myths, such as those in ancient Indian texts known as the *Mahabharata*, speak of a cycle of human development prior to ours that originated in the north and spread southward across the continents. During this prior cycle, as in the present one, humans seem to have developed a sophisticated technology shortly before the cycle's demise. Some interpreters believe that the *Mahabharata*'s descriptions of gigantic chariots in the sky and iron thunderbolts are Vedic interpretations of reactors, rockets, and spaceships.[20]

Imaginative historians, such as Pauwels and Bergier, Zechania Sitchin, and Peter Kolosimo, speculate that an earlier cycle could have ended with devastating technological wars and human massacres. They also suggest that at the time of these catastrophes some populations escaped and migrated northward, where they reestablished the original homes of their ancestors, thus explaining the presence of an ancient circumpolar shamanism in the north. Kolosimo cites the Inuit folklore about certain ancient tribes "that were flown to the far north, at the beginning of time, on 'gigantic birds' made of metal."[21] Mysterious historical anomalies, such as the ancient Mayans or the tribes of Tierra del Fuego, might be explained as residual outgrowths of this far distant, earlier cycle.

Archaeologists today build their far-reaching historical theories on an excavated scrap of earthenware, the radiocarbon dating of a piece of bone, or even the analysis of a single fossil blood cell, but these scraps represent only a small fragment of what has been consumed through time in the loamy bosom of the earth. It is absurd to treat history, particularly prehistory, as an exact science. There is no direct access to the past; historical events are immaterial and are not subject to experimentation. All remains, records, and memories depend on subjective, interpretive, and linguistic mental processes founded on individual perceptions and shaped by limited or precommitted perspectives. Martin Bernal has stated the problem succinctly in his book, *Black Athena:*

> Twentieth-century prehistory has been bedeviled by a particular form of this search for proof, which I shall call "archaeological positivism." It is the fallacy that dealing with "objects" makes

one "objective"; the belief that interpretations of archaeological evidence are as solid as the archaeological finds themselves. This faith elevates hypotheses based on archaeology to a "scientific" status and demotes information about the past from other sources—legends, place names, religious cults, language and the distribution of linguistic and script dialects.[22]

The narrow foundation of the proof-based, inductive science of history leads to proliferation of competing renditions and theories. Academic contention does nothing to help us enter the spiritual vision and the multilayered symbolic language that are prerequisite to any knowledge of the Dreamtime. If, we respect the wonder of indigenous cultures and acknowledge their interpretation of existence as valid, however, then their myths and rituals fall open to reveal the web of interconnectedness beneath our segmented perception. These myths allow us to integrate, in a single perception, our spiritual, psychic, psychological, and physical perceptions of the world.

EARTH AND SERPENT REAWAKEN

The flowing patterns of geomagnetic energy are the psychic circulation systems of the earth's body. This invisible blood nourishes the cultural unfolding of the earth's unborn child, the human tribes, and is mirrored within her physical body by a multitude of branching veins of magnetically sensitive minerals and crystals. The human body is also enveloped in fields of subtle energy, which flow in resonance with its bodily blood. The harmony between the psychic and physical circulation of earth and man maintains a channel of communication, like an umbilical cord, through repeated cycles of death and rebirth. We observe this process as civilizations change and develop.

The gathering and hunting phase represents the fetus harmoniously secure within the womb of the earth. This phase is followed by the rapid trauma of labor and a continuing process of separation and externalization throughout life, represented by the development of agriculture and technology. The cycle culminates at death with a reabsorption or rebirth into the original whole. The same pattern is expressed in civilizations as an expansion into empire, decadence, and finally oblivion. These patterns repeat through vast cycles, each phase and transition written in the potential energy that earth and its people receive from preexistent cosmic and metaphysical forces.

Attempts to develop these types of integrated models are, for us, ideas in their infancy. I believe it is important that we attempt to translate metaphysical symbolic explanations for the life processes that are going on around us into contemporary language and thought. The overlapping webs of invisible lines of communication that exist among humanity, earth, and cosmos can return to our active consciousness only when we rediscover the myths, way of life, and language and thought patterns of society that will permit us to perceive the importance and meaning of the interconnectedness of all things. The Aboriginal culture is a reservoir for that which will help us regain the vision of the Dreamtime.

CHAPTER 8

SEED DREAMING

Present-day Western civilization and the traditional Aboriginal cultures are as Fruit to Seed. All life begins and ends with a Seed.

The Seed is the plan. Within lies the ancestral dreaming
of a species—a coded language guiding the unfolding of phases, the
emergence of characteristics.

The Seed is permeated with and surrounded by a field,
a preformative entelechy
drawing all growth toward a prescribed form and destiny.
Within the dreaming of the Seed pulses
the entire drama of genesis.
The Seed disembodies itself to objectify its internal forms
and forces. Germination is an explosion—
the unified body of the Seed
vanishes into the duality of root and stem.

The Root, a geotropic plunge
into the dark dream of the earth's night—
the power to transmute substance from the Unborn,
the kingdom of the mineral,
and bond it to the dance of the Living.

The Stem, Branches, and Leaves, a thirsty reaching—
absorbing the subtle breath and blood, life and light,
from the celestial realms, the Kingdom of the Ancestors
and of the Dead.

From the realms beyond, of the Unborn and the Dead,
the plant gathers its vital force.

Everyday, we observe a great mystery: everything that exists has a seed. Time is the duration between seed and fruit.

R. A. SCHWALLER
DE LUBICZ

FIGURE 86
The germinating seed.
Experimental demonstration of
the negative geotropism of the
stem and the positive
geotropism of the root.
Sprouting corn seedlings were
oriented in the manner shown
above. About 48 hours later
they had reached the condition
represented below.

The Flower, the sacred nexus of sexuality—here the two
oppositional yearnings for height and depth meet and merge.
In the fragile magnetism of the flower, the dream of union
is born in the image of a new seed.

The Flower—that which flows—
and flowing, the energies absorbed from earth and sky
pour forth like virgin blood in ritual deflowering.

The Flower soon dies, but the new seed within
has absorbed the knowledge and experience
of the past cycle and rests, dormant.

Dormancy—the death that is not death;
but the initiatory death. The sleeping seed is mummified,
sealed in its shell, its power of regeneration
a living immortality.

The Fruit emerges, first hard and bitter,
unaware it is impregnated with a new seed.

Mindless of the nourishing earth below, colored with
self-importance, the Fruit swells in the conviction
that it is the goal of the cycle.

Tenuously dangling in air,
its taste, texture, smell, color, and form
are the final externalization
of all the latent, innate powers of the Seed.

The Seed needs the fruit to complete and renew the cycle.
The Plant needs the fruit
as human life needs art and pleasure,
science and power,
opulence, refinement, and decadence.

The Fruit is the moment of individualization.
Alone,
it hangs between heaven and earth,
between detachment and indulgence,
achievement and debauchery,
self-actualization and self-destruction.

The Fruit sees from above the entire struggle of growth—
the limits of the branches' reach,
the trembling fragility of the proliferating leaves,
the withering of the flower of love.

The Fruit holds the perspective of joyous, amoral
ambivalence—
the end is certainly near
yet forever should be denied.

The Fruit's embodiment drains the entire plant of its life force
and triggers the decline and end of the cycle.

Its ultimate role is to carry the Seed safely to earth
and to manure the ground for the next germination.

Manuring has its dangers.
The Seed may be smothered in the lingering,
fermented decomposition of the Fruit.

Nothing regenerates from the Fruit itself but,
digested by the earth,
the Fruit is the womb of the new seed

N HIS BOOK *Black War: The Extermination of the Tasmanian Aborigines*, Clive Turnbull maintains that many of the British colonists who first stepped off the boats onto Tasmanian soil would today be classified as criminally psychotic. After centuries of colonial atrocities all over the New World, the cycle of seed to fruit reached its peak in the confrontation between these degenerate colonists and the Tasmanian Aborigines: by 1850, the extermination of this primeval people had swept from the earth the last rituals of human innocence.[1]

We are blinded by the delusions that rise from our hollow and rotting social order. It is vain pomposity to believe that humanity can advance while the earth and its native peoples, plants, and animals are enslaved, desecrated, and destroyed. The dream of human origins and destiny as an evolution from monkeys swinging in trees to men in space suits lumbering off to other planets is an adolescent dream of uninitiated men drunk on the power of the cerebral cortex. Unfortunately, the men who maintain this dream are the ones who hold economic, military, and political power today. Whether it be by sociopolitical revolution, economic disaster, or environmental catastrophes, the overturning of this power is the only hope for the earth. The change must occur while there is still time to nurture the seed and to prepare ourselves inwardly for the dream of regeneration.

It is important to recognize that the Aboriginal way of life retains the seed of human culture. It is of great importance to humanity to retain and protect this seed. The thwarted attempts by Aboriginal leaders and communities to obtain land rights over some of the uninhabited regions of Australia so that they can practice their traditional way of life is a significant issue for our entire civilization. Whether it is with us consciously or unconsciously, whether we proceed gradually or rapidly, the return of the seed—the reestablishment of our basic humanity, as well as the sacredness and beauty of nature—is the image of the future to which we should turn.

FIGURE 87
Nicholas Roerich, Human Forefathers, *1911. Nicholas Roerich's prodigious artistic output was inspired by a vision of archaic humanity. In this painting he depicts the close communication between shamans and animals in the Bear cults of the indigenous people in the circumpolar North.*

The closing of the fruit phase should leave behind an enhanced aesthetic insight and power. Perhaps artists see more clearly the true nature of the vast human transition that is upon us. The most eloquent exponent of the return to the Golden Age of indigenous tribal life is the Russian mystic, artist, and world visionary, Nicholas Roerich. Roerich saw "the Stone Age as the Golden Age of mankind when man and nature were in harmony and work and art were one. To him this was the essence of culture and the goal towards which mankind should strive."[2]

After the fruit decomposes and reveals the seed, a new cycle begins when the seed breaks its shell and the dormancy of imagination ends. For us, the shell is our fixed and sometimes unacknowledged assumptions and values. The shell has hardened from the influences we absorb consciously and unconsciously, from our language, our culture, and our personal needs and ambitions. These influences solidify and become our image of reality. To shed the shell, to view the world from a fresh perspective, we must risk turning upside down the most fundamental constructs of the past 10,000 years of civilization. To dream anew, we must see the shadows in all that we assume to be light. We must dare to see the degeneracy in what we have called progress. We must acknowledge the superficiality of our most precious treasures, the corruptibility of our ethics, the selfishness beneath our charity, the barbarism of our most exalted ambitions, the shoddiness of our values, and the disturbing vulgarity of what we call sacred.

We are conditioned and educated to believe that architecture, clothing, writing, and agriculture define civilization and culture; everything that preceded these developments were no more than primitive fumblings, until our forebears finally broke through the darkness and ignorance and then gradually evolved into our present "advanced" state. We must relinquish the model of linear progress from simple to complex, from primitive to advanced, from infantile to mature if we are to avoid the entrapments into which it is leading us.

Recognizing the Shadow

Are you willing to be sponged out,
erased, canceled, made nothing . . .
dipped in oblivion? If not, you will
never really change.[3]
D.H. Lawrence

Western psychology acknowledges that every characteristic of the human psyche contains a shadowed or dark side, in addition to a positive aspect. We can also look at human civilization this way. We have elevated agriculture to the status of greatest evolutionary leap of the human race, but the shadow of this step is becoming longer and more pronounced. The 10,000-year agricultural "experiment" has been carried out; its results include overpopulation, war, and the degradation of the planet. Our dream of the future must reach both before and beyond the shadows of this form.

Since the colonialist era, the image we have followed has been that of the rugged individual, the man on the land, the farmer pioneer, carving out his existence with his own hands while feeding a hungry, active, progressive world. Agricultural practices have bulldozed precious wilderness areas, industrialized the countryside, poisoned the soil and the air with toxic fertilizers and insecticides, wasted and polluted water, left huge stockpiles of food in some regions of the world while millions starve in others, and given us foods that—far from nourishing us—are implicated in the diseases that plague us. Agriculture today has the horrifying image of the burning of the Brazilian rain forests, the barren salt flats of Australia, and the wind-eroded plains of America and Africa.

Clothing has also attained an exalted position in our world view. We have invested it with our social status and our personal sense of style and beauty. Clothes define our sexuality, our vocation, and very often our identity. We have transferred our sense of modesty, purity, and dignity to the garments we put on our backs. The lack of it, in certain situations, can mark us as criminal or even insane. Sexual arousal has been programmed so that it depends on clothing or its removal. The shadow side of this civilized institution is that it has reduced our physical capacity to adapt and relate to our environment, it has added to the separation of mind and body, interfered with and repressed bodily functions and sexual vitality, and encouraged us to create a false sense of identity.

Architecture, the glorious accomplishment of human engineering, is in a sense the clothing of our social and domestic institutions. As clothing has, architecture has weakened our ability to adapt to nature and endangered our health and immune systems. It has given us a false sense of control over and possession of space. It is often an artificial show of power and wealth, isolating people in an encumbered life while encouraging acquisitiveness, selfishness, and a false sense of independence.

One of the hallmarks of civilization is the exploitation of minerals and the science of metallurgy. Gold, silver, steel, lead, uranium, silicon, and many other minerals have been mined, processed, and applied to an astonishing number of uses, from bombs to bridges to computer chips. With metallurgy we gained a technology whose potential for power, stability, and precision is matched by an equal potential for destruction. The contrasting attitudes of the modern mining industry and the Australian Aborigines highlight the differences between the two cultures. When extracting ochre from an exposed vein, traditional Aborigines walk to the site with heads bowed in silent respect. When returning with their ochre, they walk backward in their own footprints and cover their tracks so as to leave the site of this intimate contact with the earth undisturbed and sacred.[4]

The Aborigines consider the veins of ochre and iron to be the blood circulation system of the earth. In contrast, we are so alienated from the earth that we no longer understand our deep interdependency with it, although the connections exist in many unforeseen ways. Casualty statistics reveal exact parallels between the quantities of iron ore that are extracted from the earth and smelted into iron and steel and the flow of human blood in wartime.[5]

Minerals are turned into metals through the application of extreme heat and compression, a process that in every detail is a description of hell. This hell to which we subject the minerals of the earth inevitably turns back upon us as war. The metals industry, it seems, can only maintain growth and profitability during wartime and periods of armament buildup. The profitability of iron production declines even during peacetime economic booms. Automobiles, peacetime construction, and domestic appliances by themselves are not enough to sustain a healthy profit in the competitive world steel market. The barons of the iron and steel industries have understood this market reality since the end of World War I; for this reason, British and Australian iron producers ignored international agreements and covertly continued to provide Germany with steel in the period following World War I. Their compliance contributed significantly to the military strength of Nazi Germany.[6]

All the plants, animals, and natural substances that we have subjugated under the name of human civilization participate in our psychic and spiritual as well as physical makeup. What we do to the earth, we do to ourselves. Recent evidence indicates the bones of modern urban dwellers contain 40 to 100 times the amount of lead found in the mummified Pharoahs of Egypt.[7] The heavy metals floating through the bloodstream of those alive today are an underlying cause of many diseases, mental disorders, and criminal behavior.

The same process of fixation we have imposed on space and earthly substance is reflected in our mental processes by our predominant reliance on written language. Written language tends to dogmatize, reduce, and oversimplify our thinking processes while it inhibits our perception from flowing with the eternal ever-changing process of nature. Just as we alter and harden the minerals of the earth, we harden our thought processes in restrictive language forms and solidify our economic and industrial centers. We seem incapable of changing, in spite of the warnings of imminent disaster.

The magnitude of the transition confronting us requires a dream that releases us from these fixations and conventions—a dream that reaches to the seed essence that preceded all of civilization's accumulated growth, residue, encrustation, and dormancy.

CULTURE: THE SOURCE OF DIVISION AND CHANGE

In a biological sense, culture means a growth process occurring in a prepared nutritive medium. In terms of human development, the medium is the earth; human cultures originate from various places on earth because societies have related to and been nourished by those places in particular ways. Humankind has developed four fundamental ways of living on earth, which can be related to the four basic cultural types: hunting and gathering, herding livestock, village farming, and modern civilization, which combines the last two with extensive industry.[8] Culture can be defined as the relationship of a society to the primordial nature or law of the earth.

These cultural modes, I believe, are more important fundamental divisions of humanity than are the five distinguishable races. Race is based on relatively superficial variations of physical traits that are genetically inscribed and therefore cannot be affected by human interaction and communication. Culture, on the other hand, is an active, adaptable field of exchange that determines how people exist and function in the world. History provides many examples of populations of mixed races existing peacefully as long as the cultural mode was shared by mutual consent. When populations that follow different cultural modes are neighbors, however, they have different requirements from the land and a differing sense of environmental relatedness; they often clash. For example, agriculture and industry have been destructive to the land-tenuring needs of the hunter-gatherer; conflicts between pastoralists and farmers have occurred in many parts of the world. At present, industrial urbanization is encroaching on valuable and productive farm regions.

A recent television documentary dramatized the relative insignificance of racial differences beside cultural differences. The documentary tells the story of an urban black African who longed for the hunter-gatherer lifestyle and could not find it among his own people. After reading about the Inuit people of Greenland, he left his homeland and joined a family of Inuits, participating in their ancient way of life. Although he was black and nearly twice the size of the Inuits, he was accepted because of his dedication to their hunter-gatherer culture.[9]

Colonization and the wars associated with it are based on cultural rather than racial differences. Colonization comes about through the lack of respect for the indigenous culture, followed by its destruction and the imposition of another cultural mode. After the original culture has been obliterated, the colonizing culture attempts to destroy less tangible aspects of the indigenous culture, especially spiritual practices and language. Racial differences do not become an issue if the members of the subjugated race adhere to the imposed culture. However, racial and cultural issues can continue to be used as a source of division by the power-hungry who seek to maintain control while imposing their economic institutions. (The "divide and conquer" techniques of British colonialism are an example.)

The great influence that blacks have had on mainstream America, as well as their problems of assimilation, may be the result of cultural rather than racial differences. The power of African-American music, language, and values may stem from the culture's relatively recent connections with African indigenous, tribal culture. Public pressure since the 1960s civil rights movement has allowed some African Americans to assimilate the ambitions and goals of white middle-class industrial economy; with assimilation, racial conflicts diminish. When the economy falters or when African Americans are denied opportunities to assimilate into the dominant culture, the resulting problems are labeled racial, not cultural or economic. Native Americans, who suffer problems similar to those of African Americans, have never been allowed broad mainstream assimilation. Their recent increased efforts to protect their ancient cultural practices have been met with social, political, and legal conflict. Many Native Americans still remain on reservations and, like the Australian Aborigines, are among the "most regulated people on earth."[10]

If we are deluded—and many of us are—into thinking that what constitutes real differences among us are physical characteristics such as eye folds, broad noses, or freckly white skin, then we cease to desire to learn from the differences. Stressing racial differences tends to leave two options: the most common is suspicion or a separative reaction; the other is to virtuously ignore racial differences as if they didn't exist. But, if *cultural* rather than *racial* differences are recognized as the most important, then we have much to learn from our differences. By examining cultural differences we can exchange, modify, expand, even transform our horizons. We can evaluate the assumptions hidden within our mode of life by comparing them with those of another culture.

Western culture has made, through language, a provisional analysis of reality, without correctives, and holds resolutely to that analysis as final. The only correctives lie in all those other tongues (and cultures) which, by aeons of independent evolution, have arrived at different, but equally logical, provisional analyses.[11]

At least one of the races, the Capoids, who originated in northern Africa, is now extinct. The Australian Aborigines are considered close to extinction. The Caucasian, Negroid, and Mongoloid races have expanded their populations greatly.[12] The New World spread and advancement of these races, especially the Caucasians, was due not to racial advantages but to cultural differences. The outstanding advantage of the Spanish in colonizing South America, for example, was their utilization of domesticated horses and oxen, together with metal weapons and firearms. The domestication of animals, particularly as beasts of burden, was not practiced by the indigenous peoples of South America. The Incas' and Aztecs' culture and civilization was superior in many other ways, yet it could not survive the physical, material power the Europeans derived from their use of subjugated animals.

CULTURE AND THE CYCLE

The history of the world is written in cultural transformations that emerge as human society grows, just as a leaf emerges from a stem. Every successive form of culture releases some of the potency of the original seed. Each phase is not the linear predecessor of the next, but a distinct process within a continuous cycle. Each phase lives and grows simultaneously with the others until the fruit emerges, which marks the end of the cycle and a withdrawal of life processes.

The long epoch of the earth-mother civilizations, characterized by pottery and other forms of earthenware, may represent the rooting phase and process of the current cycle. The megalithic cultures, which built temples to the earth and erected massive stone obelisks that reflected the movement and patterns of the heavens, can be seen as the reaching upward of the trunk and branches. The inception of limited agriculture among a predominantly hunting and gathering people can be considered the leafing process. The cultivation of corn among the American Indians is an example of the release and manifestation of new potential in human society. But the innovation of agriculture also triggered distrust and war amongst tribes. The solidifying formation of the bud just prior to flowering may represent that moment in the cycle when agriculture and written language became the new standard of civilization.

The cultures of pre-Vedic India, the Sumerian fertile crescent, and Egypt all developed along rivers with flowerlike, spreading deltas, connecting them to the flowering of this cycle. In flowering plants, the formation of seeds takes place through an almost mystical interaction between the male stamen and the female ovules. The entire complex fertilization within the flower is guided by precise harmonic and geometric laws. It is little wonder that the "essence of the seed" was transmitted from the river cultures to those of the future in the form of music and mathematics.[13] The death of the flower may be associated with the invasions and rise to power of the Aryan conquerors from the north approximately 5,000 years ago.[14] When the flower dies the seed is occluded; what is generally called the historical period proceeds from this point with the formation, ripening, and decomposition of the fruit.

With European colonialization of the so-called New World, the fruit encountered but failed to recognize its own seed essence in the indigenous cultures. The conventional view of history has disguised the fact that the vital force of the seed is, and always will be, the source of empowerment for the fruit. The overturning of conventional history is revealing the astonishing gifts that the indigenous populations of North and South America contributed to the rise of European colonial empires. The foods that the Europeans adopted from the Indians altered the inadequate European diet, giving new vitality to a society that had been racked with famine, plague, and disease. Not long after the discovery of the New World, over half the foods eaten by Europeans had been "grafted from the indigenous Americans." In exchange for agricultural bounty that included potatoes, tomatoes, chocolate, sugar cane, peppers, corn, squash, and beans, the Europeans bequeathed to the Indian societies disease, alcohol, deception, dissolution, and genocide.[15]

European Australia, on the other hand, did not emerge as a creative leader in the modern world, in spite of its endowment with vast natural resources and other apparent advantages, such as the controlled population growth of a white, English-speaking society. One reason Australia lacked the dynamism required for leadership and modern development, I believe, is that settlers in Australia crushed and then completely ignored its indigenous heritage. They failed spiritually and materially to attain any of the innovations and originality that American society achieved from their greater interaction with Native American and black African tribal cultures.

Gold and silver blinded the Spanish to the extraordinary cultures of South America. They instead turned their attention to extracting the ores with the slave labor of the Incas and Aztecs. These minerals gave Europe the basis for a stable, standardized currency or, in other words,

FIGURE 88
Diagram of an ideal flower, shown in longitudinal section. The life cycle of a flowering plant occurs, like a musical octave, in eight distinct stages. As the spore (pollen grains) develops it is organized as a single cell with an internal division into three diminutive cells. This threefold division within a fundamental unity is a basic proposition of esoteric geometry and all esoteric spiritual traditions. In its subsequent divisions the spore passes through a series of three nuclear divisions, so that the mature female gametophyte contains a total of eight nuclei. One of these nuclei becomes the egg. Again, the flower is following the principles of numerology related to esoteric music, in which one eighth equals a musical tone. The remaining nuclei divide into musical ratios of two eighths, three eighths, and four eighths, each of these groups of nuclei performing specific functions in the fertilization process.

SEED DREAMING

the economic component necessary for expansion and trade. While the Spanish aristocracy indulged themselves into oblivion with the luxuries and refinements afforded by the mountains of precious metals stolen from the Americas, the more businesslike British throne established companies that amassed fortunes from slave trading and piracy. These companies became the prototype for international corporate organizations. Europe's addiction to cane sugar stimulated its production of sugar through large, disciplined, specialized groups of slaves; this provided the model for the factories of the Industrial Revolution.[16]

At the time of colonization, European medical science was floundering in maladapted and superstitious practices, which were all that remained of the ancient healing arts after they were destroyed by the fanatical "witch hunts." These remnants were informed and advanced by the healing traditions of the indigenous New World.

> The Indians provided quinine, the first effective treatment for malaria. They offered a sophisticated pharmacy that contributed much to modern medicine in the form of aspirin-related tree bark extracts, laxatives, painkillers, anti-bacterial medicines, petroleum jelly, and much, much, more.[17]

An even more important contribution may be the early colonial leaders' recognition of fundamental democratic principles in the caucuses, tribal gatherings, and organization of Native American society. Franklin, Jefferson, Washington, and other leaders built the American federal system on these principles. The ideal of the free and autonomous individual citizen, developed by romantic philosophers such as Rousseau, arose after Europeans made contact with the Indian nations and brought back eyewitness accounts of the independence and freedom of tribal people.[18] Recently, it has also been documented that the perfect, homogeneous socialist state that Marx and Engels envisioned was initially inspired by the genuinely egalitarian organization observed among hunter-gatherer tribes.[19]

By divorcing ourselves from the hyperbole and rhetoric of modern democracy, we can understand that the individual freedom we aspire to has thus far been realized only in hunting-gathering societies. Unless one has the knowledge and skills to obtain sustenance from the earth independently, it is absurd to build a psychology or a society on individual freedom. However much we pontificate on the importance of our individuality and personal freedom, our grip on such a reality is as flimsy as the plastic handles on our shopping bags. Agriculture and industry invite the human body and spirit into complete dependency on a system.

In Darkness the Dream
Discovers Its Source

The sages who set up societal forms in early Eastern and Middle Eastern agricultural civilizations conceived of society as an organism with interdependent functions. Each function, from digestion to respiration to circulation, was compared to the work of a particular caste. Castes, not individuals, were the fundamental unit of agricultural societies. The caste system in precolonial Europe had fallen into a state of hopeless corruption because of power struggles between the church and aristocracy. These conflicts were terminated by the revolution of the bourgeois (or mercantile caste) in France and America. The European statesmen of the New World attempted to embrace the ideal of the autonomous individual derived from the "noble savage." This cross-fertilized with their agricultural, caste-oriented society, creating one of the unacknowledged conceptual and structural flaws at the core of modern democracy.

Democracy, although derived from a Greek word, was never practiced in Greek society. The Greek caste system, like other caste societies, attempted to invest power in a spiritually or intellectually advanced elite that would guide the masses, much as the brain organizes and guides bodily functions. Democracy, in effect, is an inverted caste system that attempts to invest control and power in the masses. Democratic individual rights have now degenerated into a media-enhanced illusion disguising a world order dominated by a relentless commercial-industrial caste. The electronic media are so adept at deluding popular imagination that the flagrant hypocrisies of our system are swallowed by a gullible public. Some choice examples are George Bush's "kinder, gentler" America walking headlong into an economically motivated military conflict and Gorbachev sending Soviet troops to gun down innocent people in the Baltic States even as he accepted the Nobel Peace Prize. The destructive manipulation of people by media-perpetuated mass illusions shows that it is time to dream of a new image of human society and nature.

The Afro-Asiatic roots of classical Greek civilization are finally being revealed and accepted in academic circles. The germinal concepts underlying the expansion of northern European civilization derive not from white classical Greeks but from the tribes of old Egyptian, Indian, and Semitic cultures. The fundamentals of Western mathematics, philosophy, drama, poetry, and esoteric religion belong to the black and Semitic mystical traditions of Egypt and the East.[20]

The most original aesthetic development in European cultural history, abstract art, was the result of such artists as Picasso and other early Cubists looking at African tribal artifacts.[21] Later, abstract expressionists also derived their impetus and innovation from tribal images. The use of psychoactive drugs by romantic European poets such as Coleridge and Rimbaud opened the vision of the West to an inner world much as these substances are used in shamanistic rituals to induce trances. Remy de Gourmont, a French philosopher, made use of African kef and certain hallucinogens.[22] His profoundly introspective essays and novels were an early inspiration for Sigmund Freud, who also used drugs to open the doors of the unconscious, and gave birth to the most profound developments yet in Western psychology.

The shadows at the foundations of contemporary civilization are growing more obvious even as we rediscover the light we have received from our indigenous origins. The source of germinal principles and regeneration is the Eternal Seed. That seed, the genius of indigenous peoples of the world, was confiscated along with their land, and then distorted and exploited as the basis of the European New World. European historians have covered the tracks of this theft, blinding us with scientific racism in the guise of science and ethnocentric myths of white, Western superiority.

All of our technology is an externalization of powers innate in the human organism. Aerospace travel, computerization, electronic communication, the probing capacities of microscopes and x-rays, the remote viewing abilities of telescopes, and even nuclear fission are accomplishments that tribal shamans and mystics have experienced inwardly by cultivating the innate potentials of consciousness. The inner life knows none of the constrictions of time and space. The journey to other worlds and the adventure of exploring the universe beyond the earthly domain belongs to spiritual awakening, not technological development. The ancient myths assure us that when we reawaken in the reality of the Dreamtime, we will discover the expanse of cosmic time and space to be inwardly navigable and experiential.

The turn of the cycle back toward the seeding of our culture mirrors the return of that which has been repressed in our psyches. Carl Jung has said that aspects of human nature that are denied, repressed, banished, or discredited inevitably surface, initially in an unhealthy and destructive form.[23] Many of the modern world's symptoms of collapse, its degeneration, corruption, and addictions, can be attributed to the reemergence of the dark, long-repressed tribal aspects of human consciousness. The socially destructive use of drugs such as tobacco, alcohol, cocaine, hemp, and opium, which in tribal cultures often played a sacred initiatic role, show the dark side of our repressed tribal nature returning. The modern urban obsession with shopping is the dark return of the hunting and gathering spirit in which the corporate world replaces nature as the provider of all. The large numbers of homeless people living on the streets of modern cities are a shadowy remembrance of tribal bands. The final degeneration is seen in the numbers of dispossessed people sifting through the refuse baskets on city street corners.

Music with roots in tribal Africa has swept through Western society, effecting changes in sexual morality, body movement, and language, with sometimes liberating, sometimes destructive results. The healthy acceptance of nudity in domestic life and on public beaches, as well as its exploitation in pornography, can both be related to the early stirrings of the return of tribal attitudes.

Psychic channeling, witchcraft, paranormal experimentation, and many other popular occult phenomena can be seen as desperate gropings to restore the communication that tribal societies maintained between the psychic and physical realms. Even after three centuries of widespread rational education, people in every society of the world retain their interest in esoteric and occult phenomena. Many such involvements have been labeled with the "New Age" rubric. Statistics on the growth of interest in New Age phenomena serve as one indication of a return of consciousness to the psychic aspect of reality.

> Though it is hard to say exactly how many Americans believe in which parts of the New Age, the movement as a whole is growing steadily. Bantam Books says its New Age titles have increased tenfold in the past decade. The number of New Age bookstores has doubled in the past five years, to about 2,500. New Age radio is spreading.[24]

Related forms of some psychic or so-called New Age phenomena existed in the tribal mind as aspects of a spiritual science. Herbal medicine and alternative therapies, which reflect a return to tribal healing methods, are some of the forms already being positively assimilated in our society.

At this moment of crisis, the world's attention is turning toward the Antarctic, where an atmospheric hole is admitting life-destructive radiation. The incidence of skin cancer in Tasmania has increased 80 percent over the last four years, and the ozone depletion over the South Pole (where this cycle of human existence may have begun) threatens to destabilize global atmospheric conditions. High levels of ultraviolet radiation could destroy the ocean algaes and microorganisms that support the cycles of life. These factors indicate a cycle turning back upon itself to its origin.[25]

Concerned scientists, environmentalists, academics, and government agencies who are committed to "turning around" our social planning are often applying the same reductionist thought patterns that set civilization on its present course toward self-destruction. The return of the seed is not simply a matter of human choice, it is the inescapable law of cycles, and it cannot be dealt with by devising technological and economic solutions. Plans to reform our industrial economies into renewable-resource, ecologically sensitive societies are like confronting a hurricane with an umbrella. The issues extend far beyond economic and industrial modification.

James Lovelock, whose Gaia theory has been useful to environmentalists, retains the dangerous, one-eyed vision of a mind locked into an exclusively conscious, rational comprehension of the world. Some of

FIGURE 89
Waramanga man, Tennant Creek, Northern Territory, 1901.

Lovelock's other ideas, such as seeking our salvation through nuclear power and producing beeflike proteins from petrochemicals in huge vats, are narrow and dismal. Lovelock has proposed infecting the swollen herds of grazing cattle throughout the world with the degenerative disease myxomatosis. He claims that the death of the world's cattle populations would prevent them from further polluting the atmosphere with methane gases; where each one of them is buried, we can plant a tree, thus bringing down the quantity of excess carbon dioxide in the atmosphere.[26] This spiritless vision is typical of contemporary science and antithetical to the concept of a living earth. Humans have pitilessly exploited the endlessly nourishing propensity of cattle—as if the humiliation of herding, feedlots, abattoirs, and hamburgers were not enough, to propose infecting this species with a tormenting, degenerative disease is an appalling example of human perception blinded by the worship of the conscious mind. Lovelock may be planting trees, but he has lost the vision of the seed.

These first chapters have attempted to develop a parable, or a dreaming story, of the history of our origins. A dreaming story is not necessarily factual or moralistic; rather, it is designed to open thoughts beyond conventional horizons and make visible the patterns underlying the history of the cosmos, earth, and humankind.

In the rest of the book I will examine the mysteries, rituals, and symbolism of the Australian Aborigines, as well as the details of their traditional daily life. Everything in Aboriginal life—childrearing; food gathering, sharing, and cooking; marriage, infidelity, taboos, and the structure of family, clan, and tribe; burial practices; methods for dealing with crime—defines a world view utterly different from ours, yet urgently relevant to our need to transform the way we exist in the world. In this light, Aboriginal culture can be considered a guiding code, a seed, for the reemergence of our tribal soul and primal mind. The concept of the Aboriginal Dreamtime can release the shadows that constrain and disturb our inner vision. Once we confront and dispel these shadows, the fetters on our imagination will shatter and we can become children of the moment, free to dream the dreams of the next cycle in which humanity is reintegrated with the earth and the beauty and spirit of the natural world.

151

PART TWO

LIVING

THE

DREAMING

INTRODUCTION

LL FORMS OF LIFE spring from a tiny seed. The seed is the smallest of the many forms our bodies assume in the passage through life. For the Aborigines, the step from seed to birth and all of the phases leading to the end of life are viewed as a continuous expansion, a centrifugation in which the physical body, the mind, and the consciousness are continually opening and widening. Ideally, life is a process of dissolving the boundaries of comprehension, the self-centeredness of being, the isolation of embodiment, and the fears and neediness of separation.

The seed's separation and externalization into leaf and root parallels the division of mind and body, as well as the separation of the child from the womb of the mother. All of these parallels echo the archetypal movement on which all creation is founded, that is, the division of one into two. This profound separation at the beginning is healed through a life that reflects and maintains its congruity with the Dreaming. Birth is an initiation from the enclosed womb into growth and expansion within the formations of life. Death is the final expansion of living, a return to the unbounded existence from which we arose.

In Part II, the contours of this expansive vision of life are followed as the infant enters the world. A newborn Aborigine discovers a world in which his or her ego is allowed to establish itself, and all its needs, demands, lack of control, and excesses are tolerated. From this tiny beginning the new life is encouraged to expand in ever-widening spheres of existence: emotion, social awareness, sexuality, ritual, nature, and metaphysics. The goal of Aboriginal education is the extending, relating, and expanding of being, forming a kinship with the entire world, and maintaining that kinship through the ritual enforcement of the universal law of reciprocity.

Western education, in contrast, teaches increased definition, fixed identities, and categorization that limit and bind us to specialized vocations and professions. Our way of life increases separation and isolation through architectural confines and encumbering material acquisitions. Our capacity to expand and grow is limited by the built environment and the social institutions on which we all depend. Our involvement with the metaphysical and our need for abandonment and contact with otherworldly experience are put in boxes labeled art, superstition, religious faith, drug abuse, drunkenness, fantasy, or mental pathology. The reality of death is covered and denied, and its presence fictionalized. Death is considered antithetical to life rather than its inevitable conclusion. Let us look, as into a mirror, at the broad outlines of daily life for the Australian Aborigines as it has been lived for untold millennia. In that image, we may clarify the depths of our own alienation as well as the specter of rebirth.

CHAPTER 9

COMING INTO BEING

BIRTH AND THE SPIRIT
OF THE UNBORN

I N THE EARLY DAWN LIGHT that dusts the desert plain of spinifex grass with soft pink, two Aboriginal women, one very old yet strong and full-breasted, the other a young pregnant girl in the early stages of labor, leave their sleeping camp. They stop at a secluded place near a rock-hole water catchment. Luminous peach light swells along the edges of the night-somber red desert as the older woman digs a slight depression in the earth and makes a small fire of spinifex grass, adding some dried herb leaves from her string bag. She tells the girl to straddle the smoldering grass for a few minutes so that the aromatic smoke can engulf her naked body. Then, leading her to a nearby lone acacia tree, the older woman directs the girl to squat and begins to deeply massage her spine in a circular motion. The squatting girl presses her back firmly against the trunk of the tree to brace herself when she pushes, helping the baby in its descent from the womb. The tree imparts an energetic alignment to the mother's spine, a birth-giving empowerment from the earth. With strong weathered hands, the old woman scrapes out a hollowed depression in the ground between the girl's legs, an earthly receptacle to receive the newborn.

At the moment the child emerges, the grandmother has an important decision to make. If it appears to be premature, weak, or badly deformed, or even if the mother herself has been sick or weakened during the pregnancy, the old woman might decide to cover the child with sand and bury it in the exact place it was born. This child, though, emerges complete and squirming with life in the brilliant clarity of the desert dawn. Quickly the old woman bites the umbilical cord with her teeth; with one hand she lifts the newborn boy out of his earthen cradle, and with the other she buries the placenta in the depression. This spot is the place of the child's birth; it will shape his identity and his ritual obligations to the surrounding land for the rest of his life.

The old woman holds the child face down for a moment in the spinifex smoke. She rubs his body with ash and sand and cuts a piece of the umbilical cord with a stone tool, twisting it into a necklace that she places around the newborn's throat. This symbolizes a spiritual connection that will enable the child to learn the language of the sacred knowledge that reaches back, like a spiraling cord, to the great Ancestors and the beginning of time. Before she returns the child to the new mother, she walks out of sight and, holding the child close to her face, breathes into his nostrils his sacred totem names that establish the basis of his knowledge of, indebtedness to, and respect for the plants, the animals, and the earth. She then wraps the child in the bark of the paper bark tree and places him in a *parraja* (or *pitchi*), a curved wooden dish, next to his mother.[1]

The event of childbirth is essentially the same in most Australian tribes. The midwife's actions are both practical and symbolic. Smoking the baby with herbs and exposing it to ash have both hygienic value and significance for ritual purification.

Childbirth shares with the majority of Aboriginal ceremonies, called *corroborrees*, a physical and symbolic focus on fire. The flames symbolize the fleeting passage of life, but in traditional fire-making methods, smoke precedes the first spark and continues to rise until the last embers die out. Smoke is the symbol of spiritual existence that both precedes and follows life. Ashes are the symbol of that which remains of life after its departure to the realm of the dead. In their ceremonies Aborigines symbolically enact the fusion of life and death by covering their ecstatically inflamed bodies with the ashes of death while they dance in the smoke of the eternal spirit.

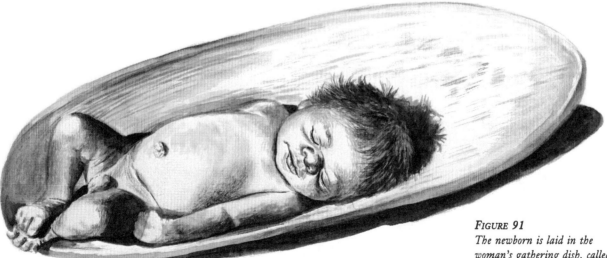

FIGURE 91
The newborn is laid in the woman's gathering dish, called a pitchi.

COMING INTO BEING

In some tribes midwives keep a fire burning day and night to warm the new mother. Babies are born with a pinkish skin tone; part of the rationale for smoking the newborn is to ensure that its fully darkened skin color develops. The Aborigines associate the pale skin of the newborn with the nonliving,[2] unborn, smokelike realm from which it and all of life have come; black skin is the color of earth and represents all that is alive and of the earth. The otherworldly paleness returns with death, in the color of bones, ash, or skin which turns ashen white when a body is cremated. Aborigines believe that black-skinned people have a whiteness of spirit inside them that sometimes breaks out as destructive, lightninglike emotion. White-skinned people, on the other hand, carry within them an earthiness that can suffocate or manifest as unmitigated materialism that becomes an inner darkness.

The symbolic inversion of white and black skin is similar to an ancient Taoist concept concerning the universal qualities of masculine and feminine. The archetypal female, like the black races, is passive, absorptive, receptive, and negative on the outside and light, fiery, emotive, creative, and positive within. The archetypal male is the reverse; like the white race, he is positive and externally active while being negative, passive, and potentially deathlike internally.

The association between white skin and beings from the realm of death was humorously revealed when an early missionary tried to discover the Aboriginal beliefs about the afterlife. He asked a tribal man, "Where do you go when you die?" The tribal man asked him, "Where have you come from?" Showing him a map, the missionary replied, "I have come from England." The tribal man shook his head and said, "Well, that must be where I go when I am dead."[3]

In many tribes, soon after the birth the midwife looks down at the healthy, perfectly formed baby and denounces it as bad, ugly, and useless. This is done to dissuade any malevolent spirit beings from taking an interest in the newborn. The mother and child generally remain in seclusion for a number of days; during this period the father and all other male relatives are strictly prohibited from approaching them. The father is responsible for gathering the mother's food, but his catch must be delivered to her by the midwife. This behavior reflects a fundamental Aboriginal respect for birth-giving as a power and capacity of women and as a distinctive charateristic of the Universal Feminine.

Like many tribal people, the Aborigines consider it very important that a child's first experience of life be an immersion in the warm, nourishing receptivity of feminine energy. For both males and females the path of life, like that of a plant, separates gradually from the enveloping Earth Mother in an arc that grows out and away from her at the same time that it is supported and nourished by her. The decline of life is a journey of return back to the embracing Mother.

Many food taboos apply to the period before and after childbirth. In some cases, the mother is not allowed to eat meat until the child's skin color darkens, or she may be forbidden to eat crabs while pregnant because the vibrational quality of the clawed creature might choke the fetus. Often the father observes a number of food taboos during the mother's pregnancy, from which he is released at the child's birth. The Aborigines believe that the father and mother are magically connected and that the father's austerities may determine the child's gender or help the woman have an easier birth.

Incidents have been recorded where the mother has returned to the camp and resumed her full activities within an hour after the birth, but in most cases she remains secluded in her birth camp for about a week.[4] When she returns to the camp she may remain with the midwife for a period before joining her husband. Except for his responsibilities for providing food, the new father continues to remain very much in the background.

The activities and behavior of each participant in the birth rite are directed by tribal law and have, with only slight variation, been rigorously observed for more than 100,000 years. These laws represent the responsibility of human society for attending to not only the physical demands of birth but also the psychological and psychic energies that are prevalent in every aspect of giving birth.

SPIRIT CHILD, SPERM CHILD

To the Aborigines, no occurrence is caused only by physical mechanisms, especially the events and processes associated with life. They tend to see all causation as a combination of physical and spiritual forces acting in harmony with energetic emanations of the earth. To the Aboriginal mind, the modern explanation of conception as the collision of a tiny sperm and egg is absurd. In their view, sperm may prepare the way for the entry of the child into the womb, but the spirit of the child appears in the father's dreams or inner awareness before conception. Determining the spirit origin of the child is more important than the biological mechanism, which, because of their deep involvement in the reproductive cycles of natural species, is self-evident.[5] Because of this "spirit child" concept, for years anthropologists wrongly believed that the Aborigines did not understand the function of the male sperm in pregnancy.

The spirit child often appears to a man while hunting, perhaps as a voice in the wind or water that calls to him as "father." It may come as a fleeting image as the man dives into the water to spear a fish or turtle. The spirit child may imbue a fish or other animal with its essence and allow itself to be caught so that the man will bring it to camp for his wife to eat. In most cases, the spirit child persistently asks the father to find or bring him to his mother. A similar pattern persists in the mental processes of our contemporary world, where it is usually characteristic of the male energy, from an archetypal point of view, to receive the initial, abstract, or intellectual concepts from unborn thoughts.

From knowledge imparted to him in initiation, an Aboriginal man recognizes at once when he has been contacted by an unborn spirit. When he has experienced this, after intercourse he may say to his wife, "I found a child yesterday, it's inside you now. I put it in just then."[6] It is the spirit child, not the sperm, that animates and directs the entire process of the "breaking of the egg" and the formation and unfolding of the fetus. When the spirit child enters a womb that has been prepared by the father through sexual intercourse, Aborigines say, "The spirit child has become a sperm child." (This Aboriginal view resembles the concept of morphogenetic fields in the new field biology.) Depending on the law of the tribe, a sperm child then enters a moiety, or subdivision of the tribe. In some tribes children enter the moiety of the father; in others, the mother's. This moiety describes a descent pattern that, through a parent, associates the child for life with totem Ancestors, animals, and plants.[7]

In other cases a spirit child is said to enter the world directly. The Aborigines believe that a woman may be spiritually fertilized by coming into contact with a power related to a specific place. A mother may attempt to attract a spirit child independently of the father by going to fertility caves where traditionally only women are allowed to go. Such caves in Uluru (Ayer's Rock) contain huge, phallus-shaped stones whose coarse surfaces have been rubbed smooth by women massaging every part of their body against them.[8] This practice is said to intensify their earthly magnetism and fertility. The women may then go and sit with their legs spread apart near water holes, rock formations, or clumps of trees where spirit children are often sighted in order to attract one into her womb. If a woman experiences pain or becomes sick and vomits after one of these outings, she immediately goes to her husband and divulges the exact place her illness began. The husband investigates the local myths to find out what Ancestral power visited and potentized that place during the Dreamtime. The potency of an ancestral being deposited at the spot where the mother experienced her symptoms is considered the conceiver of the child. Individuals whose mothers were fertilized by this

FIGURE 92
Ayers Rock, reportedly the world's largest monolith, is near the geographic center of Australia and is one of the most sacred earth temples of the Aborigines.

type of power establish an identity directly with that spirit power rather than adopting the animal totem of the father's or mother's clan. Spirit children thus form their identity affiliations differently than do sperm children.

Many people today feel that their biological parents are not the source and basis of their fundamental identity; their parents represent only an entrance point to life. These people often spend their lives seeking spiritual families or affiliations through which they may discover their capacities and inner identity. In this sense, the phenomenon of the spirit child is still an active part of human birth.

Animal powers, or the spirit associated with a species of animal, can also play a role in the conception of new life. For example:

> A man dreamed one night of the power of the essence of a species of yellow goannas, while hunting the next day he was invisibly assisted by this power and he captured a large yellow goanna. As he approached his camp his wife saw that he had someone with him, but the mysterious companion vanished before he arrived. The meat that the man brought back was really a gift from the spirit power of the animal and his wife was made ill

161

from eating it. The day after, the wife noticed the same mysterious stranger standing on a rock. He held a small bullroarer [whirling sound-making instrument] which he threw at her and she felt a small pain as it struck above her hip. The woman's husband together with his father-in-law deduced from these experiences that she was to conceive a yellow goanna child.[9]

Besides showing the importance of dreams, this incident illustrates an Aboriginal perceptual pattern and sense of reality. It demonstrates the integration of life processes with human consciousness and a spiritual alliance with earthly localities and plant and animal species.

Ancient Egyptian religion also believed in the spirit child and the conscious spirit entity who chooses the womb and the conditions in which to be born. In the tale of Satni, from the eighteenth dynasty of the Middle Kingdom, after a couple ate a certain plant in a place that was indicated to them in a dream, the woman conceived a child who was the reincarnation of a magician-sage.[10]

Aboriginal concepts of fertility are accompanied by social and psychological attitudes radically different from our own. Women consider their role in childbirth that of an agent, or temporary transit, for a being with its own spiritual preexistence. A woman knows that if a child is aborted or miscarried, the preexistent spirit will continue to exist and will find another opportunity to incarnate. The spiritual sense of conception reduces the personal attachment a woman has to the birthgiving function and to the role of motherhood. Although Aboriginal society collectively worships childbearing, women are not valued exclusively for that function; nor does childbearing play a big role in a woman's self-esteem.

Although it is the man's role to recognize and deliver the preexistent spirit from its unborn status to the womb, once the spirit is in the womb the woman decides whether or not the impregnation will proceed toward birth. Because of women's knowledge and unchallenged control over the physical process of conception and fertility, overpopulation never seems to have been a problem in Aboriginal society. They always maintained low, stable populations with densities proportional to their food-gathering capacities. Too many children or children born too close together would interfere with a woman's and her clan's capacity to follow the wandering life prescribed by the Dreaming.

Women take great care to space their pregnancies, nursing children for three to five years to inhibit conception. Aborigines believe, as did the ancient Egyptians, that the spirit does not fully conjoin with the fetus until it has reached a certain stage of development, usually 70 days after conception. During this period, older women carefully observe young wives to prevent unwanted births. Aboriginal women have a great store-house of methods for terminating pregnancy in its early stages, as well as a knowledge of herbs that act as contraceptives. The University of California is studying the contraceptive properties of *cynbidium madidium*, a plant known since ancient times by the Aborigines.[11]

Other explanations for the low, stable Aboriginal population are less credible. Starvation as a form of population control is very unlikely for three reasons: Aboriginal mobility allows for relocation to richer gathering regions, traditional diets contain many highly drought-resistant species, and tribal customs center on food sharing. Infanticide is not an important factor in preventing overpopulation. It is rarely practiced and only resorted to when absolutely necessary, as in the case of a birth handicap that would make strenuous tribal life an agony for the child. Given the enormous affection that Aborigines naturally have for children, the decision to smother the baby in sand has to be made by the midwife instantaneously, before the mother can see the child's face or hear its cries, because she would be so overwhelmed with compassion that she would prevent the deformed child's death.[12]

In light of Aboriginal childbearing and rearing practices, overpopulation is more likely to be a result of agriculture and the social and religious attitudes that arose with it. The Old Testament directed people to multiply and spread over the face of the earth. Human propagation became a means of conquering nature and acquiring land to establish secure, powerful agricultural settlements. Women became breeding tools for the expansion of a family-oriented patriarchal social order. This system took away from women their innate ability to monitor conception and childbirth and avoid the burdens of unnecessary birth.

Aboriginal men do not consider children a means of perpetuating their individual achievements. A child is not a personal possession of the parents, nor are the parents responsible for the child's character and fate. The child owes its birth to the entirety of nature and to the spiritual potential of the natural world. The child's family is its entire tribe, all of whom share a common parentage—the Ancestral Powers and Mother Earth.

Childbearing, therefore, is an incidental rather than a primary function of an Aboriginal woman. Her primary function is maintaining harmonious relationships between human and psychic energies within society, as well as the harmony of human society with the earth. Women are the hidden force behind the sacred attitudes that allow the earth to remain a generative field that nourishes and sustains life.

FIGURE 93
Aranda woman carrying child and digging stick while balancing a pitchi *on her head. Alice Springs, Central Australia, 1896. Child care does not interfere with a woman's hunting and gathering nor with her participation in ceremonies.*

Childhood—The Lust
for Embodiment

Without exception, the earliest Europeans to catch a glimpse of traditional Aboriginal camp life noted the boundless joy, exuberance, and independence of the children. No other people seem to be as lenient or indulgent toward children as the Australian Aborigines, and many anthropologists have declared it to be the most child-centered society they have ever observed. As soon as a newborn infant returns to the camp with its mother, he or she becomes the unchallenged center of attention. Older relatives and siblings as well as the parents continually shower the child with affection. From the beginning, a number of kin provide parental support. Although the child's actual parents have primary responsibility, the child's relationships spread throughout the entire clan or camp group. If the birth parents were to disappear, the child would experience no sharp loss.[13] Usually the child's name is given by the grandparents, who expend a great deal of time and energy caring for it. Children are never allowed to cry for any length of time; the parents and the entire clan see that their discomforts are quickly soothed or alleviated. Small children are breast-fed on demand, and they continue to suckle for three to five years. In spite of this, breastfeeding is not a burden on the mother, since a number of female relatives often participate in a multiple nursing arrangement. In a baby's early months, many women nurse and care for it. Older women, especially the grandmothers, often have older infants suck a clear fluid that women can produce even after menopause.[14]

Aboriginal women say that their generosity in giving nourishment to their infants was learned from the Wallaby Dreaming. At birth the newborn wallaby, like other marsupials, crawls into the mother's pouch and remains there for many months, suckling at will. In contrast, placental mammals must drop from the womb to the ground in a permanent and abrupt separation from the mother; often they must compete and struggle for the mother's nipple. A marsupial mother licks the in-pouch infant's "bottom" when it defecates, and drinks its urine, thus keeping the pouch clean and redigesting the nutrients. The animal's complete, undisdaining intimacy and the love of the mother for the newborn serve as a Dreamtime archetype for Aboriginal motherhood.

In spite of the flexible multiple parenting and nursing arrangements of the clan, the baby spends most of its time with its mother. When the child is very small it may lie in a curved wooden dish that the mother holds at her side or lays in the shade of some scrub while she carries out her hunting and gathering activities. Since children are involved in all

← *Figure 94*
Kangaroo. The gentle, in-pouch mothering of the kangaroo is a model for Aboriginal mothering practices, in which infants are allowed nearly constant contact with their mother's body.

Figure 95
Most Aboriginal children are able to happily feed themselves through hunting small lizards and animals and independent food-gathering by three to five years of age.

collective activities, the mother's social activities are in no way diminished by her child. During a *corroborree*, it is not uncommon to see a child perched on its mother's shoulders, its tiny fingers clutching her hair, sleeping comfortably as the mother dances. Children usually wean themselves with no deliberate strategy on the part of the mother. As soon as they can walk, children are allowed to run free and participate in all the food-gathering activities of their parents. The mothers give tiny Aboriginal children digging sticks, and they quickly learn to feed themselves on the spot from what they can collect. Their education begins with the mother pointing out edible plants, animals, and insects. At a very early age Aboriginal boys become adept at throwing sticks and stones and can capture small lizards, mice, and small birds. This propensity is encouraged in boys but not in girls. In other respects, in the early years male and female children are treated equally, with the exception that the mother may be even more lenient with a male child.

Aborigines openly and unaffectedly converse with everything in their surroundings—trees, tools, animals, rocks, and such—as if all things have an intelligence deserving of respect. Not only the mother-to-be but many members of the group may carry on a running conversation with the fetus as soon as it is established in the womb. The Aborigines believe that communication happens primarily on nonverbal levels, flowing as continually as life itself. The process of relatedness is not limited simply to linguistic exchange. A woman who served as nurse to the elderly Truganini (the last full-blooded Tasmanian Aboriginal woman, who died in 1897) relates that Truganini would carry on long, humorous, emotional exchanges with her oversized liver pill, trying to convince the pill to go down between her failed attempts to swallow it.[15]

From birth, nursing mothers talk to their infants about foods to be gathered and kin relationships with simplified versions of the words. They carefully tell a child what his or her relationship is to each of the people who come and go in their surroundings. The complex web of family relations that make up the kinship society allow the child to name its relationship to every person who enters its perception. There are no strangers, and the child has no sense of alienation from those around it. The kinship system encompasses not only the idea of family but also the idea of friendship. Everyone with whom one has even the slightest association is identified by a bond that is familial in quality. In Aboriginal encounters, anyone with whom a person is *not* connected through some widely extended kinship is considered "other" and is therefore avoided and treated with suspicion. There is no word for possession applied to a family relationship, such as "*my* uncle," "*my* husband," or "*my* grandmother." When referring to kin, Aborigines use an expression for which we have no counterpart; the literal translation, is "self/uncle," "me/

FIGURE 96
Waramanga child running with play spear, Tennant Creek, Northern Territory, 1901. Aboriginal children in their traditional setting are among the most joyous and spontaneous children that anthropologists have ever observed.

COMING INTO BEING

uncle," or "I/uncle."[16] The term implies that a kin relative is an integral part of one's own being.

Children learn to share the food they are given or that they have gathered themselves. Older relatives beg the children to share food with them or instruct them through games in the distribution regulations of their kin. For example, a male child may be told, "This is your sister and you call her so-and-so (kin designation). When you get older you must give her some of the meat you catch, and she will give you some of the vegetables she collects. And if her husband treats her badly you must take her part." The same child may be shown a female walking past and told, "She is one of your mothers-in-law, you mustn't look at her face to face. You must not speak to her. But later, when she is married, you will send her gifts of meat and if she makes a daughter she may give her to you as your wife."[17] Such casual instructions go on repeatedly, every day of a child's life, building up a sense of relatedness and of knowing one's place in the ever-widening world.

The kinship system is a network of relationships in which a number of people fill the same role. For example, besides the natural father, the brothers of the mother are considered father to the child. Before children can speak, they learn a sign language in which each relationship, be it sister, uncle, or brother-in-law, has its own hand gesture. Later in life, even across a crowd at a large gathering, an Aborigine can acknowledge a relationship to another person with a hand signal.[18] This complex network of relationships is the essential fabric of Aboriginal life; it replaces all sorts of social and legal institutions.

Aborigines view our mode of making friendships as part of an invisible kinship of which we are unaware. This web of relatedness, like their kinship system, is initiated at birth and is an inseparable aspect of the self. Because our social system has demolished the ancient kinship patterns and lines of ancestral relationship, we in the West must recognize our kin intuitively. However, genuine friends are, in effect, our kin. Aborigines believe that contact with those who are not kin is dangerous and can cause a loss of self.

A child grows not by learning or preparing for life but by actually participating in the life of the community. To the Aborigine, the social and natural environments were created together in the Dreamtime and are based on the same plan; children become familiar with the two together. Along with information about kin and the environment, grandparents tell children simplified versions of the myths associated with their part of the country. These stories often take the form of songs, dances, and sign language. The child's training is a preparation for the series of religious initiations to follow.

Aboriginal community is not based solely on psychological needs and material interdependencies; instead, a preexisting structure of relatedness supports, fulfills, and extends the sense of self. Aborigines do not need to develop self-definition and self-esteem from the community because those qualities are given as a birthright to each tribal member. They do not have to escape the conventions and demands of community to pursue inner development and spiritual growth, because their entire social system is structured to provide and support those features.

FREEDOM OF BODILY FUNCTIONS

A crucial step in socialization for children throughout the world is the process of learning to control excretory functions. In the traditional Aboriginal way of life, discipline is never used to accomplish this training. Older children contribute to the learning process by encouraging smaller children to defecate at a distance from camp. If encouragement fails, they might resort to lighthearted ridicule, but with great care not to offend the little one. In the next step, the child is encouraged to dig a small hole and cover the feces. Although Aborigines are extremely uninhibited about body functions, defecation is always carried out in strict privacy because feces can be used to great effect in sorcery. No restrictions apply to urination, however, and both children and adults urinate spontaneously in full view of others.[19] The psychological traumas resulting from rigidly enforced toilet training in Western society do not exist among the Aborigines; they still possess the ability to live openly with each other and with nature.

Aboriginal parents are for the most part extremely indulgent, going to great lengths to avoid denying their children anything they want. Adults endlessly pet and spoil children and tolerate a great deal of bad behavior, disobedience, and even abuse. Aboriginal parents have had to develop methods for releasing their frustration with disobedient children. For example, a mother may threaten her child with a thrashing "in spirit." This may mean simply taking a branch and hitting his footprints, or pointing out a tree to the child, giving the tree the child's name, and then releasing a great display of rage on the tree without ever touching the child.[20]

It is considered a great personal defeat for an adult to lose patience and slap a child. If punishment is definitely called for, as in the case of one child threatening injury to another, it can only be carried out by the natural mother or father. If someone else, even close kin, tries to reprimand a child, an intense clan dispute is bound to ensue.

In the West, the extensive damage wreaked by child abuse on the quality and direction of society is now being widely assessed. Recent psychoanalytic studies of Adolf Hitler and other mass murderers reveal close correlations between the violence they have perpetrated on society and what they suffered at the hands of their parents as children.

> A wealth of clinical evidence shows that the beatings and spankings administered in childhood have long-lasting harmful consequences, including suppressed anger, self-hatred, reoccurring depression, apathy, and stifling the compassion for oneself and others. The violence endemic in our society against children contributes to an adult's unquestioning obedience to authority and has been instrumental in the oppression of women.[21]

Aboriginal society can be a particularly rich guide for discovering nonviolent alternatives for parenting and discipline; their attitudes are based on a holistic metaphysical vision rather than psychological trends and shifting moralities.

Childhood emerges out of the depths of the spirit of the natural world and is inseparable from that world. Like the natural world, the child is to be adored, respected, and unfettered in every way. The child's growth is natural: it leaves the breast, regulates its body functions, and curbs its excessive demands as naturally as baby teeth fall out and are replaced by permanent ones.

Freeing the Emotions

Aboriginal children are allowed to vent all their emotions in every form, from wailing lament to colossal tantrums.

> Screaming and writhing on the ground, hurling whatever it can lay its hands on at the offending adult, the child, if able to talk, also lacerates the alleged oppressor with foul language drawn from a large supply of obscenities that children master very early in their speaking career. . . . It amuses other members of society, including the victims of these attacks, to hear tiny children who barely know which is what shouting epithets such as: you crooked penis, you stinking vagina, you hairy arsehole, and so on, ad nauseam. The usual reaction of adults to child temper tantrums is to cover their face and other vital parts as best they can while the assault continues and laughingly protest until the child gets what it wants or forgets and goes away.[22]

Aborigines allow the expression of unlimited egoism in early childhood. Unfettered, self-centered, even tyrannical behavior is considered appropriate for the infantile stage of life. To the Aborigines it is evident that babies are born with natural wilfullness and that they instinctively cry, scream, and otherwise focus their energy on having their needs met—usually by the mother's breast. As their mobility increases, children direct their activities solely on the basis of their own needs, desires, and ideas.[23] Aboriginal childhood education rests on the conclusion that the sense of individual motivation is the universal characteristic of infancy and early childhood and that what needs to be cultivated is a sense of relatedness. As the child matures, he or she is increasingly introduced to obligations to kin and society and, later, to the spiritual mysteries of the Dreaming. As a result of this natural progression, adult Aborigines are extremely mild-mannered, easygoing, and relaxed and have none of the armored defensiveness of the Western personality structure. Perhaps because of the freedom to release emotions given them as children, when the occasion arises adult Aborigines express their emotions with unrestrained intensity and then forget them. They do not harbor repressed feelings that can warp their relationships with their kin or with the metaphysical order.

In contrast, our modern societies have developed child-rearing practices and institutions that inhibit physical and emotional expression at the beginning of life and set the child on a course toward a disguised collective conformity. Western education and psychology perceive the development of the individual as a life-long process of incremental alienation and independence, first from family and cultural habituations, then from behavioral norms and social conventions, then from attachments due to unconscious complexes and projections.[24] Only an educated elite actually goes through the last stage of socialization and psychological education, but it remains a hidden agenda within the legally imposed public education of children. The dynamic of the American way of life depends on "abducting" children from their ethnic diversity in order to shape them into the image of contemporary Americans. Even today in many American public schools there are insidious slurs against the child who reveals an "ethnic" background by speaking two languages. Beneath the foundations of mass public education lies the image of the hero who breaks with old family values and succeeds as a modern American. This American ideal of the realized individual is inherited from the heroic myths of Greece and the Middle East. Ideally, this process culminates in the discovery of an internal selfhood in which free choice and autonomous action is the prize of life.

Thematically, Western education is the inverse of the Aboriginal method. While Aboriginal children are allowed complete expression of

171

their emotions and desires, they are gradually and subtly encouraged to move away from the bondage of self-centeredness toward an increasing sense of relatedness and a heightened sensitivity to collective and metaphysical realities. Throughout life, happiness is considered a process of enlarging identity through relatedness: to be is to relate.

In our society, the unbridled egocentricity that is repressed in childhood comes out in adult life in harmful ways—selfish concern for individual needs, materialistic aims, and appetites, often at the expense of others. Extremely infantile, egoistic characteristics prevail among those who achieve power, wealth, or fame in our society.

The child-rearing philosophy of the Australian Aborigines came face to face with its diametric opposite when Australia was brutally colonized by the nineteenth-century English working class. During the later Middle Ages, England had adopted patterns of cruelty, repression, and subjugation of children (consistent with the subjugation of plants, animals, and women that forms the basis of European civilization). Nurturing was replaced by establishing complete control and mastery over children. All forms of affection were prohibited. Children were forced to conceal their own bodies from themselves and others. Parents and institutions exercised control through the use of corporal punishment.

> The birch became the predominant penalty and children were commonly whipped in public until they bled. By the eighteenth century flogging occurred on a daily basis in England, where it was viewed as a way of teaching adolescents and children self-control.[25]

These inhumane practices have been handed down in our culture from generation to generation. Child abuse and severe methods of child discipline violate a child's innocence, vulnerability, and spontaneity and destroy the joy and freedom of the human spirit. The colonizing period that followed the Middle Ages in Britain and Europe decimated indigenous peoples who possessed these open, exuberant qualities—a process that characterizes the cruelty inherent in the Western family system. The institutionalized repression of children served as the prototype for civil justice based on a penal system. It has been possible to impose the dour prisonlike rigidities of the industrial system on humanity because abusive child discipline has obliterated the natural sense of freedom, sensuality, and spirited vitality from the imagination and replaced it with fear, guilt, self-denial, and self-hatred. The first immigrants to Australia were the products of the British penal system; the human instincts with which they might have appreciated or comprehended the beauty of the culture they saw were already beaten out of them.

The Freedom of
Childhood Sexuality

The competitive spirit and the attitudes and drives associated with it have no place in the life of tribal Aborigines. None of their games and activities involve competition. Children's games mostly involve imitating adult roles, especially marital relationships and sexuality. Games such as "husbands and wives," "making camp," or "secret meetings" allow children to live out and enjoy the actuality of their future instead of dreaming up ambitious fantasies about "another life."[26] When not running wild, shouting, and dancing, children play independently in loose clusters, where even the tiniest can be observed setting up little windbreaks, building mock campfires, pretending to cook, and often making rudimentary attempts at sexual intercourse. All games are structured around kinship relations, the names of which they have been learning since infancy. All children know who their potential husbands or wives or potential mothers-in-law or uncles are, and they address each other by these kinship names. Sometimes there are games of adultery in which a little boy runs off with the "wife" of another, dramatizing the typical illicit relationship referred to by the Aborigines as "elopement."[27] The erotic play amuses adults, but they also use it as an opportunity to instruct children about the correct sexual, marital, and extramarital patterns allowed within the kinship system.

The openness of the Aboriginal camp and lifestyle provides many opportunities for children to observe sexual acts among adults. Sexuality is considered a normal activity for all Aborigines; moral considerations only involve appropriate kin relationships. The sex act itself is never hidden from children (although adult couples tend to prefer privacy). Children sleep in the same camp as their parents, and sex is an open topic of conversation. An adult may playfully grab a child, calling him or her husband or wife, and pretend to make erotic movements and advances. As soon as infants are old enough to respond to the people who handle and talk to them, adults and older children may fondle and tickle their genitals, commenting on their size and shape and joking about sexual relationships.[28] This playful sexual openness between adults and children contrasts strongly to our society, which recently has begun to acknowledge that the denial and repression of childhood and adolescent sexuality causes sexual abuse of children. The only taboo about sex-related matters in some tribes is openly talking about semen or menstrual blood, which for the Aborigines are highly sacred.[29]

Very young boys soon muster the materials for making little toy shields, clubs, spears, and boomerangs. Girls do not play with dolls; they are not

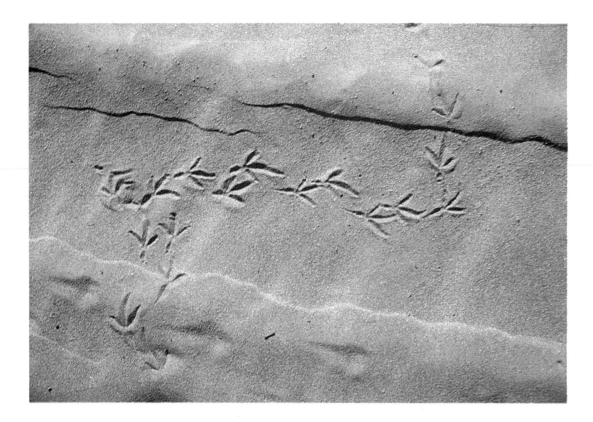

FIGURE 97
*The reading of tracks is an
important aspect of Aboriginal
education.*

raised to think of motherhood as their raison d'etre. Rather, girls spend time drawing lines in the sand and learning about the symbols that represent the hearth group and other spiritual images. They use these to spin yarns about family life, the exploits of people they observe in the camp, or stories modeled on those given to them by the elders.[30] These stories direct girls' attention toward human relationships, especially sexual relationships. Many adult women's rituals are love rituals, which also focus on influencing their personal relationships.

From a very early age, children learn to read footprints, and by the time they reach adolescence they can recognize the individual footprints of as many as 200 to 300 clan members. Tracking is one of the primary learning processes of Aboriginal people. Mind and perception are trained to observe every physical detail of an imprint. The Aborigines believe that, in addition to the physical appearance, a footprint has vibrations from which an attuned observer can gain extremely accurate information. In remote parts of Australia police still rely on Aboriginal trackers who, it is said, can tell from a tire track in the sand the time of day it was made, the type of vehicle, the speed, and the number of people in the car.[31]

In the Middle East, Bedouins with similar tracking abilities are employed by the Israeli army. This skill is handed down by the Bedouins over generations, and they claim it requires a special sense that cannot be taught without extensive initiation.[32] The symbolic importance of tracking lends support to the theory that the entire concept of writing and reading arose from the identification of human and animal tracks: "People initially contemplated the relationship of signs with earthly creatures and objects from observing the tracks in the earth left by animals, reptiles, birds, plants, and other natural substances."[33] Aborigines are masters at using and understanding symbols, but they did not develop a system of abstract symbols detached from a natural reality. They avoided the conceits, confusions, and delusions that the written word has introduced into human experience.

Aboriginal children take great delight in sleuthing the tracks of couples who are in the midst of a heated secret love affair. After tracking them down, the children spy on every intimate detail and later mime the events in front of the entire clan, to the utter embarrassment of the vicitimized Romeo and Juliet. Aboriginal couples prefer privacy for their sexual life, but it is a rare commodity unless they can convince children to sleep elsewhere. However, as children grow older the observation of sexual intercourse develops into their most absorbing pastime.[34]

FIGURE 98
Two Waramanga children, Tennant Creek, Northern Territory, 1901. The observation of adult sexuality becomes a major pastime of Aboriginal children as they approach adolescence.

The natural acceptance of sexuality in humans, from infancy to old age, has been amputated from our self-awareness by deep-rooted societal norms. The capacity to share the rhythms of pleasure openly and deeply, the ability to abandon self-consciousness in mindless ecstasy are to the Aborigines essential human behavior. In contrast, in our society children and adolescents are denied access to appropriate forms of sexuality and must seek it in fantasy or exploitative pornography. For us, public or family enjoyment of sexual activity is almost nonexistent, parents and adults hide their sexual enjoyment from the awareness and view of their children, the body is covered and all its functions—except eating—are carried out behind closed doors. The true pleasures of the body are often supplanted by titillation and commercial illusions.

In Western society, from childhood on we are trained to divert sexual energy into constant work and competition. Only in the arenas of sports, finance, and battle can heightened passions be publicly released under the contrived illusion of victory and defeat. Aboriginal tribal people do not derive enjoyment or excitement from competition—it is antithetical to their sense of kinship and reciprocity with all. For example, when indigenous New Guinean boys who were sent to mission schools were trained to play football, they adapted the game so that play would continue until each side had exactly the same score.[35] When Aboriginal boys were introduced to competitive football, the results were often bedlam and injury because, in their traditional society, aggression and confrontation were sanctioned only for the purpose of punishing those who transgressed Dreamtime Laws.

The uninhibited expression of bodily functions, emotions, and sexual imagination throughout childhood, in the presence of unremitting parental love and societal support, allows adult Aborigines a spiritual lust for life and the joy of fully inhabiting their physical bodies. The West's systematic repression of sexuality and emotions fills the personal subconscious layer of the mind with distorted, fantasized fears and desires. These subconscious attitudes solidify and remain with us throughout life, blocking capacity to live fully in our bodies and obstructing contact with the archetypal energies of deeper psychic levels.

FREEDOM TRANSFORMING

From about eight to twelve years of age, the wonderful freedom and openness of male-female relationships among children begin to shift. During prepuberty, the amount of time spent in erotic play begins to decline. Girls begin sleeping at the women's camp with their grandmothers or older female relatives, and the boys begin to separate themselves from the women's lives and activities. The boys are not yet old enough to join the men's camp, but by this age, they are already proficient in hunting small animals and lizards and often form their own camp group within the society, using their skills to obtain much of their own food. The male child begins his all-important separation from his biological mother as well as the maternal support of the entire society.

The differences between the activities of boys and girls become increasingly distinct as their proclivities develop. The boys' camp is allowed to keep the rewards of its hunting escapades strictly for the boys' consumption, but girls of the same age contribute the food they gather to the pool consumed by the entire clan. Such patterns encourage girls and women to be aware and responsible for the whole group; males are urged to develop more autonomy. In this way, Aboriginal society cultivates the equally necessary qualities of autonomous action and group interdependence. In times of emergency, danger, or rapidly changing environmental circumstances, a balance of both these motivations is necessary for survival.

The only absolute and consistent restriction placed on Aboriginal children is the prohibition against following adults when they depart to perform sacred initiatic rituals. Children are prevented from even going in the direction of sacred sites in the "men's country."[36] In the child's mind, this rule stands out against his or her otherwise idyllic freedom and magnifies the mystery and importance of spiritual activities, especially the men's. Throughout childhood, the shadow of the coming initiation develops the awareness that life is marked by an irreversible advance over a series of thresholds, a progress toward increasingly secret and sacred dimensions of life. Over these thresholds all must pass, and by them each person is irrevocably transformed.

CHAPTER 10

THE CYCLES OF INITIATION

RITES OF TRANSITION

ALL OF EXISTENCE passes through a succession of phases, each marked by a definite transition. Astronomers speak of the infancy, youth, maturity, and old age of stars and galaxies, acknowledging similarities with the stages of our own lives. For us, each life transition involves deep physical and psychological changes; the difference between one phase and another constitutes a new form or way of being. A former self dies and is replaced without disturbing the organic continuum of life. Cultures in which initiatic rituals are important view death as no different than other life transitions, except that in death continuity is maintained not by the ever-changing physical body but by the spirit.

Death is the greatest transition rite of all, and each life transition is a symbolic preenactment of death. The primary function of society as the repository of collective knowledge is to assist each member through these archetypal phases. Initiation expresses society's intent to make each phase change as distinct as that of a substance undergoing the change from solid to liquid, or from liquid to gas. In initiatic societies the name, appearance, social position, and level of responsibility of each person changes at each major juncture. For them, no surface quality should be carried from one stage of life to the next. In Aboriginal culture, the continuity that underlies these discontinuous phases of life is the Dreamtime; it provides enduring customs, kinship relationships, totemic ancestral identities, and a sacred topology, all of which have existed since the beginning.

Underlying the Aboriginal world view is the belief that people only reach fruition by accepting the risk and adventure of continual death and rebirth. In the Mardudjarra language, the novice *murdilya* (uncircumcised boy) is renamed *bugurdi* after being circumcised as part of his puberty initiation. The word *bugurdi* is formed from the combination of *bugu*, death, and *yudirini*, both being born and returning. The word *bugu* is

FIGURE 99
The three realms of Aboriginal cosmology and their relationship to the all-pervasive Dreaming.

applied to women during pregnancy, childbirth, and menstruation, indicating that women, by their very nature, continually participate in the initatic experience.

Masculine Energy and the Three Realms of the Dreaming

Male initiation, the "making of men," is a cultural imperative unquestioned in Aboriginal societies throughout Australia. Male initiation reflects their fundamental belief that all existence is divided into three distinct and equally real realms: the unborn, the living and dying, and the dead.

The realm of the unborn is a spirit world that existed prior to the appearance of forms and life. We are aware of the existence of the unborn within our own minds through a plentitude of thoughts, ideas, and desires that press against our consciousness but are never realized in the physical world. In a similar way, most plants and animals produce an abundance of seeds, only a few of which ever germinate. The unborn is a realm of potential energies that crowd along the boundary of life, pushing for entry.

The realm of the living and dying is the tangible world of nature. All living creatures embody the process of death: tissues, blood, and cells are constantly dying and being replaced. The outer skin of the body, our physical appearance in the world, is a layer of dead cells. The natural world is the child of an inseparable bond between living and dying.

The realm of the dead is the celestial abode to which the deceased travel after life. The identity of every living creature belongs to a place, a tribe, a species, a clan, or a family, yet each is also a unique entity in time and space. The Aborigines believe that the essence of each person calls together a particular combination of qualities and characteristics from these collective sources. Like a constellation of stars, these essential patterns originate in the realm of the dead. These coded forms organize specific expressions of life, and this essence of each distinct personality, at death, rejoins these eternal patterns as a star.

The dynamic of nature results from a blending of these three realms that is brought about by the mingling of male and female sources of energy. All three realms are present and active on earth. *To the degree that women, or the Universal Feminine, represent the power of life and giving birth, so too men and the Universal Masculine represent the power of death and the taking of life.* A necessary function of death is the hunting and killing of

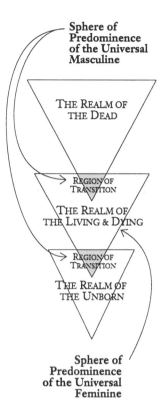

Sphere of Predominence of the Universal Masculine

THE REALM OF THE DEAD

REGION OF TRANSITION

THE REALM OF THE LIVING & DYING

REGION OF TRANSITION

THE REALM OF THE UNBORN

Sphere of Predominence of the Universal Feminine

Figure 100
The Cosmology of Sexual Energy. The qualities associated with the Universal Feminine are pre-eminent in the natural world of the Living and the Dying. The goal of the Universal Feminine is to bring forth the relentless yearning for life and to conserve, extend, and maintain life's growth and development. Male energy is affiliated with the forces of death and is directed toward the transitions that limit life's uncontrolled expansiveness. Male energy restricts, directs, and gives shape to life by controlling the ceremonies of transition from the unborn sources of life and the terminating transitions to the realm of the dead.

179

FIGURE 101
Demonstration by Aranda
man of spearthrowing, Alice
Springs, Central Australia,
1896. Sexual maturity for
Aboriginal men and women is
marked by strength, beauty,
and vibrancy.

animals. Death is inseparable from food—the life of every creature depends on the death of another. Without death to set limits, life would proliferate uncontrollably.

The connection between masculine energy and the "other worlds" of death and the unborn in Aboriginal society is shown by the dominant role men play in funeral and burial rites and their exclusive roles in the rites of increase. As discussed in Chapter 9, the spirit child generally appears to the father before it enters the maternal womb. Also, men of high degree are responsible for communication with the deceased and with the ancestral voices of the Dreamtime.

Among male ritual practices the rites of increase are extremely important. These are based on the belief that each plant and animal species has, in addition to its physical existence, a premanifest energy configuration known as "the spirit of the species." The sacred knowledge that men gain in their various initiations includes the place in their clan's territory where the spirit of a species (such as the kangaroo) originally manifests its physical form. Men also learn the vibrational rhythms and specific "seed sounds" that coagulate (increase) or disperse (decrease) the premanifesting energies of that species.

The belief that physical being emerges directly from an invisible vibration such as sound is related to what cognitive psychology calls synesthesia. In heightened states of consciousness a person can perceive the sound or name of something as a physical apparition; in other words, the sense mechanisms cross and people actually see a sound. Similarly, in Aboriginal cosmology, the earth's magnetism or Rainbow Serpent created the creatures of this world by pronouncing the name of the seed sound of that species at the place where the potency of that creature was deposited in the Dreamtime.

Aborigines maintain that the masculine role is *not* to act on the material world but to participate in the balance of natural creative forces on the metaphysical plane. To act on that which has entered the physical world is already too late; once spirit energy has materialized, a chain of reactions changes the entire pattern of nature. Ecological science shows the same thing from an inverse perspective: every time we change one thread in the fabric of nature, the whole cloth changes. The psychological practice of introspection acknowledges the same principle: controlling and directing one's thoughts is much more effective than dealing with them after they have been expressed.

Modern men are no longer initiated into knowledge that enables them to enter the deep states of consciousness, in which the premanifest world can be perceived and acted on. In its place, modern men attempt to dominate the physical world, constructing, regulating, analyzing, categorizing, mechanizing, and taking other desperate measures to control the natural world—the domain of the life-giving, life-nourishing Universal Feminine.

From the perspective of Aboriginal cosmology, overpopulation results from men's ignorance of their role in ritually maintaining the limits of the physical world as it balances between the terminating forces of death and the unlimited potential of unborn energies. Because of this failure, our existence is drowning in the reign of quantity—our world is plagued by massive overpopulation, on one hand, and mass extinctions through wars, disease, and famines on the other.

The cosmological importance of male initiation is the balancing and tempering of men's affinity for death with the life-sustaining qualities of the feminine and redirecting men toward the furtherance and fullness of life. "Everyone is born not only from woman but as a woman" may be considered a fundamental Aboriginal tenet of sexuality. An Aborigine once expressed it this way: "Women are born from nature, men are made by culture."[1] Earthly nature, or the physical phase of existence, is the domain of the birth-giving power of the Universal Feminine. Womanhood establishes itself readily in the natural flow and continuum of life. Men's otherworldliness, because it conflicts with life, must be dreamed into existence and carefully cultivated in the maternal ground.

The theme of male initiation is attracting some recognition in the context of the growing "men's movement." The poet Robert Bly, in his book *Iron John*, has brought the concept to a wide audience.[2] Bly con-

FIGURE 102
Woman with bowl. Food gathering and preparation by women provides a large portion of the clan's nourishment.

tends that the absence of the initiation of young men by older males in our society is central to the sexual and social problems of contemporary young men. He outlines eight stages of initiation that derive from the eight days in the mythic story of Iron John, a tale that has survived from pre-Christian northern Europe. Aboriginal initiation also consists of eight stages, and there are other symbolic and psychological similarities between the two traditions, as well as important differences.

Bly considers every child to have been wounded in some way or another—by stifling repression, denial, neglect, or lack of attention and affection.

> The young man investigates or experiences his wound—father wound, mother wound, or shaming wound—in the presence of this "wild man," this independent timeless, mythological initiatory being.... The ancient initiation practice gives a new wound or gives a calculated wound sufficiently pungent and vivid— though minor—so that the young man remembers his inner wounds. The initiation then tells the young man what to do with wounds, the new and the old.[3]

According to Bly, since the father figure in our society is imprisoned by his work in industry and commerce, his absence from the family causes his sons to be smothered in maternal energy, emotions, and outlook. Male initiation is the bringing of males from the world of the mother to the world of the father.

> "There is not enough father." The sentence implies that father is a substance like salt which in earlier times was occasionally in short supply or like ground water which in some areas now has simply disappeared.[4]

The problems Bly addresses are peculiar to the Western institution of the nuclear family as it evolved in agriculturally based society and solidified during the Industrial Revolution. As we have seen, in Aboriginal society childhood is not a wounding experience. Children are not beaten, neglected, or sexually repressed. Aboriginal children are open, active, and emotionally expressive—their world is filled with constant parental and group affection. In Aboriginal initiation, therefore, wounding goes far beyond personal psychological traumas.

Bly imagines that in traditional society young men had constant access to their fathers and that fathers and sons lived and worked together. This does not apply to traditional Aboriginal tribal life. The mature Aboriginal man is often away on long hunting expeditions or involved in elaborate, all-male spiritual ceremonies. On other occasions men will isolate them-

← *FIGURE 103*
One of the oldest Aranda men, 70 or 80 years old. He is oknirabata, a very wise old man, living in Central Australia. Older men in Aboriginal society perform the important role of introducing boys to a spiritual experience of the Dreamtime mysteries.

THE CYCLES OF INITIATION

selves from the clamor and vicissitudes of domestic camp life. It is not through familiarity but through otherworldliness that men convey the importance of spiritual life to preadolescent children. Introducing young men to their spiritual dimension is the primary role of the father. Although understanding male initiation in our own culture can be of great personal assistance, it may be more important in this time of crisis for us to discover the *universal* significance of these timeless rites of passage.

MALE INITIATIONS

The initiation process in Aboriginal society is much more elaborate for males than for females. The process of "making men," which begins with the circumcision initiation, absorbs a great deal of the attention and energy of the entire society. The stages of male initiation into adulthood extend over a period of several months and include a variety of activities that involve the efforts of many people and extensive planning and organization.[5]

The cycle begins as the older initiated men of the tribe keep a careful eye on the young boys' camp. Since no age records are kept, each boy is watched for the signs of sexual maturity, such as the growth of facial hair, pubic hair, or genitals. The boys feel scrutiny of the older men, and they both fear and long for their coming initiation. Somewhere between the ages of eleven and thirteen, a boy or group of boys may be considered "ripe." At this point the men seize them to begin the preliminaries for the circumcision initiations. If a boy is particularly headstrong or disrespectful of his elders, the older men may take him early to encourage him to grow up, or they may embarrass him by leaving him behind his peers as they proceed to manhood and he remains an uncircumcised boy. Deciding when to seize a boy finally lies with his mother or female relatives, although it is the men's duty. The women may choose to delay or hasten initiation if they feel it may benefit the child.[6]

Initiated men understand that life can be fully appreciated only when seen in relation to the other realms of existence, those of death and the unborn. Aboriginal male initiation imparts the knowledge of the transition from life to death. Dying is different from death itself. Aborigines hold that from the moment that life leaves the body, dying can take up to two or three years. In the circumcision initiation, boys are introduced to the methods of inducing trancelike states of consciousness, because trance ceremonies will play a primary role in their future as hunters and initiatic mystics. In the trance dances the hunter learns to identify with the fate of his prey. Wounding and the sacrifice of blood bring men in contact with the domain of death. Gradually, through ritual, men experience the entire passage from life to death. Higher stages of initiation enable men to die "while yet alive." In this way, men come to know how to assist themselves and others on the difficult spirit passage following death.

In Western society the willingness of young men to go off to war represents an innate need in the male psyche for initiation into a confrontation with death. The older men who maintain power in our patriarchal system exploit this fundamental male need to preserve their own political and material well-being.

In Aboriginal society, handing over the adolescent boy to the older men symbolizes the introduction of pain, death, and responsibility into the joyfully carefree and erotic woman-based security of childhood. The circumcision initiation confronts the boy with the two fundamental fears that inhibit his spring forward into manhood: the separation from the mother or the maternal ground, and the fear of death. These two fears are, in essence, one.

The effectiveness of initiation depends on the boy truly believing that he will, in the course of his initiation, encounter a Dreamtime power who will destroy him, and that after dying he will be restored to life. Each tribe has a myth that reveals the details of this process, which is enacted for the novice while he is in a hypnogogic state. According to the mythology of the Wiradthuri of southern New South Wales, boys who reach a certain age are handed over to Dhuramoolan, who is described as a direct relation of the All-Father. Dhuramoolan has a frightening voice, like that of distant thunder.

> Dhuramoolan pretended that he butchered the boys, burned them to ashes, moulded the ashes into a manly shape, and brought them back to life. . . . After every initiation some boys failed to return. Dhuramoolan's explanation was that they had fell ill and died, but the All-Father became suspicious and, by questioning the survivors, learned that he had been tricked. The missing boys had been eaten by Dhuramoolan. . . . The angry All-Father killed the deceiver and put his voice into the trees and into the sound emitted by swinging a bullroarer. The All-Father then told the leading men that from now on they would have to initiate the boys and use bullroarers to imitate Dhuramoolan. Women and children were to believe as before that the boys were destroyed and returned to life.[7]

To ensure that the young boys believe absolutely that they are to die to this world and be reborn in initiation, the entire clan enacts what anthropologists describe as a group theatrical deception. The boys' mothers and female relatives resist as the men abduct the boys for initiation. They cry pitifully, often gashing their scalps, and shout in desolation, "The Great Spirit will kill our sons!" while the boys are being carried away. The boys are threatened by the men that their life will be taken if they ever reveal to women or the uninitiated what transpires during initiation. The women, of course, have gone through these rituals year after year and are fully aware of every aspect, yet the men never break their vow of secrecy and actually proceed as if the women believe the boys are destroyed and then restored to life. In a circular deception, the women never admit to knowing anything but the mythic version of the initiation. The secrecy and exclusiveness of male religion depends on this conscious pretense and theatrical deception provided by the women.[8]

What we consider deception is not simply that in the Aboriginal mind. Their attitudes toward myth are in keeping with their doctrine of two kinds of existence: the existence of extraordinary powers and the ordinary existence of humans and other creatures. For the Aborigines the existence of a perceivable reality in no way excludes or eliminates the existence of the extraordinary reality of the powers. The physical enactment of initiation occurs simultaneously with a mythic form on the unseen level, just as the conscious and unconscious minds are always functioning concurrently. On an inner level the boys actually die to themselves and are reborn.

The ritual circumcision must precipitate deep changes on three levels of being: psychophysical, social awareness, and psychic or spiritual understanding. Although the ritual form varies in detail from tribe to tribe, most have seven or eight distinct segments or acts. The seven phases of ritual described here relate to the mythic Rainbow Serpent whose spectral body forms a bridge between earth and sky, between our perceptual world and the invisible realm of the Dreamtime Ancestors.

THE SEIZURE

Several boys are usually taken into the bush, where they are decorated from head to foot with blood from the cut veins of the older men. The blood-drenching of the novice symbolizes that he has begun his second emergence from the womb of life. The blood of initiated men takes on, in spirit, a life-giving power parallel to that of a woman's blood that accompanies a natural birth. Later, before any ritual scarring or wounding is inflicted on the young boys, the older men also sacrifice their blood to the process of the boys' transformation. An Aboriginal myth personifies this symbolic male birth-giving capacity as a serpent that swallows young boys and then regurgitates them as men. The birth canal of male procreative power is the mouth, which emits the spoken word, symbol of a spiritual birth through language and culture.

The initial abduction and blood-drenching is followed by several all-night sessions. The initiated men are covered in red ochre, blood, and feathers, and their painted faces are eerily lit by small fires. Their appearance is similar to that of Bly's mythic initiator, Iron John, who is colored with rust and covered with hair. The initiated are already "dead" to the world in which the novice has been living. Symbolically, the novice is being led by the "dead" through death; *it is only death that can bestow rebirth.*[9] *The threat and constant presence of death, which the living must endure, is compensated by a gift from death of a succession of new lives.*

Hour after hour, from early evening through to the next morning, the initial ceremonies are marked by slow, repetitious singing and dancing, accompanied by a droning, sonorous music. The novice is prevented from falling asleep but, kept on the verge of consciousness, he enters a hypnogogic state. During this time the older men repeatedly tell him, in chant and song, that he is now hearing the law, the truth, the reality of life, and that it is something powerful and dangerous and never to be revealed to the uninitiated. The boy is informed that the freedom of childhood is now to be left behind and that he is entering an initiation that will prepare him for a completely new world. To survive this transition, the novice must acquire a deep sense of passive acceptance. He must silently endure physical pain, making a strong commitment to obey his elders and forever guard the sacred laws of a world that has, until now, been invisible to him. Each tribe has a mythic story that reveals the details of its own initiatic process, which is related and dramatized while the novice is in the trancelike state. It can be the myth of

FIGURE 104
Arunta Tribesmen making up with feathers for a corroboree, Central Australia. The initiated men in ceremonial costume make a formidable image for the young novice to confront.

FIGURE 105
Group of Aranda men preparing for the welcoming dance, Alice Springs, Central Australia, 1901. Elaborate dance preparations also mark the beginning of the male initiation cycles.

Dhuramoolan, or other myths in which kangaroos or emus journey and have adventures with the Ancestors. In his state of heightened sensibilities, the boy receives these instructions and stories into his unconscious awareness at very deep levels. He is living the dream experience.

During the period of the seizure the boys fast and remain absolutely silent; they are referred to as the "ritually dead." When the seizure ends they are carried, like corpses, back to camp to the wailing women, who give them some nourishment. The women instruct them that now they must undertake a great journey, during which time they are not to feel homesick for their family. Symbolically, the boys must at this time leave behind all their emotional attachments. They are told they must go out into strange country and return with many unknown people so as to fulfill their ceremonial rebirth. The crying women very often hold their sons as if for the last time and gaze into their eyes, which are glazed and entranced. The boys' eyes reveal that they have left this world and been inducted into the mythic dimension of experience.

All the members of the traveling party that escort the boys don thick hair belts and paint themselves with red ochre, re-creating the traditional appearance of the mythic traveler. This aspect of male initiation unfolds in cultures all over the world; the wandering Aboriginal initiatic band has strong similarities to the wandering Shadus of India.

This trip, which in traditional culture could last for many weeks, has both a social and spiritual purpose. Distant groups that have not been seen in a long time are visited. Long-standing disputes are settled, information is exchanged, and gifts are made of message sticks, which are said to have a power compelling people to accept participation in the boys' initiation.

In each of the camps the boys encounter members of their extended family for the first time. The journey and acquaintance with the larger social network teaches the novices about hitherto unknown territory. Ceremonies are held and instruction is given throughout the weeks of the journey, so that the boys' inner knowledge expands concurrently with their experience of the countryside.

Joseph Campbell saw the journey into distant lands as a consistent component in heroic myths in many cultures around the world. Jungian psychologists interpret the mythic journey as symbolic of the inner growth from the ego to conscious selfhood. The myth of the hero's journey is among the oldest of humankind.

> In this myth the hero is the descendent of the sun god, that symbol of absolute authority upon which all life depends. The sun god continuously reasserts his absolute authority by the conquest of the forces of darkness that challenge his reign. . . . Arming himself in the name of the sun god, his shield a symbol of the sun, the son hero goes forth in the name of his father god to perform that essential patriarchal act which identifies him with the creator himself. . . . Against the hero stand arrayed the forces of darkness that in themselves can shed no light save as they receive it from the sun.[10]

This presentation of the myth obviously reflects the values and concerns of an agrarian culture. In it are conquest, possession, and exploitation of the earth in the name of the all-powerful, fecundating, solar Father-God. In the Aboriginal hunter-gatherer world the purpose of the mythic male journey is expansion of the seeker's inner world; it has to do with increased relatedness to clan, earth, and Ancestors. The journey increases the boy's knowledge of the inner structure of consciousness, respect for the psychic power within humanity, and human relatedness to the spiritual life of nature. In the Aboriginal male initiation the boy leaves his earthly mother and is introduced to the power of the Universal Feminine—the dark, invisible, unconscious forces. Conversely, in the Western interpretation of this myth, those powers are conquered, subjugated, and denied.

RETURN TO HOMELAND

As the group moves from camp to camp, relatives who will participate in the circumcision rite go with them, and the traveling red ochre group increases. The relative who has been selected to perform the operation of removing the youth's foreskin joins the group. This may be a maternal uncle or the husband of one of the boy's father's sisters. The selected relative will symbolically kill the boy and in compensation bestow on him one of his daughters for a future marriage.

In many tribes their destination is the site where the boy's father was born. Here the travelers are joined by the women and children of the boy's own camp, and the men prepare a large ceremonial ground for the circumcision. The sequence of the ritual is beginning to follow a pattern: the youth is introduced during the initial seizure to a trancelike state and the unknown regions of his mind; then, in the journey, he encounters the unknown regions of the countryside and the larger human society of which he is a part. After each of these stages, he is returned to the familiar world associated with women.

THE CIRCUMCISION

At the boy's camp, the ceremonial procedures are elaborate and complex. There is a meeting of many clans, whose members play a role in the ritual based on their degree and nature of kinship. Dancing and exchanging food and ceremonial gifts follow complex guidelines. Body painting and ritual dress are used in different ways for each day of the ceremony. The kinship system contains designations that divide the group into the active participants, who will seize and "kill" the boy, and the passive audience, known as the mourners. The ceremonial ground is set like a stage, with precise positions for fires, groups of people, sacred objects, and food, much like a medieval European village's passion play.

The young novice is led into the center of the ceremonial ground amid groups of grievously crying women, fiercely painted dancers, and blazing fires. At a moment of crescendo, a group of performing men rush toward the central fire and, bending over in front of it, form a human platform or table on which the boy is laid. The relative who is to perform the cutting leaps up and sits on the boy's chest, facing his penis and the conflagration. He pulls up the foreskin and twists it carefully, holding the head of the penis down beneath his thumb. The boy's grandfather gives him a boomerang to hold between his teeth to help him endure the pain. The operator cuts the foreskin with a sharp quartz tool, while the grandfather, circling the human altar, continually reassures the boy. This scene, performed for over 100,000 years in Australia, is probably the oldest altar-centered ritual celebration; it shares the theme of death and resurrection with the Christian Mass and other religious rituals.

The object of circumcision and the succession of male initiations that follow seems to be to test the degree to which boys have assimilated previous instruction in methods of suggestion and their ability to enter a self-induced trance, rising above the pain and fear of the ritual ordeal. The intention is that the novice, as much as possible, lies inert in a self-anesthetized state.[11] Aboriginal circumcision is, therefore, not a courageous demonstration of undergoing pain but rather of acquiring a psychic ability to rise above pain. This is only the first step in a long process in which some of the novices will, in advanced rituals, undergo an actual death, or near-death experience, yet remain alive.

The boy is then taken from the altar and kneels, silent and bleeding, in front of a fire where he is enveloped in smoke, just as he was immediately after his birth. The ceremonial ground rises to a frenzy of dancing, singing, and moaning, accompanied by the wild hum of bullroarers (wooden rods with lashes fastened to them that, when twirled, produce

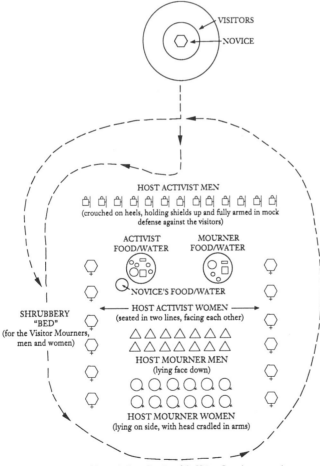

FIGURE 106
Schematic rendering of the positions of the participants on the circumcision ground at the moment the novice arrives. (After Tonkinson)

191

a low, humming sound). The novice's older brother tells him to open his mouth and swallow a good piece of kangaroo meat, warning him not to chew it. The foreskin is then sometimes dropped into the unsuspecting boy's mouth and swallowed. The grandfather tells the boy he has now devoured his own boyhood. Symbolically, the previous stage of life is not denied, surpassed, or destroyed, as it often is in our culture, but incorporated into his continuing growth. The grandfather tells him that his boyhood spirit, because it came before, is the father of his manhood. The foreskin of boyhood will impregnate him; grow inside him; make him strong, wise, and graceful; and give him the capacity to acquire skills. Aboriginal child-rearing practices ensure that the time of boyhood nurtures vital and fertilizing powers so that they may spiritually propagate the birth of manhood. By making childhood predominantly a wounding process, our society undermines the emergence of the mature male psyche. The body and blood of the Holy Eucharist, a literal symbol of rebirth through self-impregnation acquired by Christianity from the ancient Dionysian and Shivite shamanistic cults, may have originated in this aspect of Aboriginal circumcision.

The boy is then given two bullroarers. He has heard the hypnotic hum of this instrument throughout his childhood when the men would swing it during secret ceremonies outside of camp. He was always told that it was the voice of spirits. These bullroarers are presented to him as being his mother and his father. His grandfather instructs him that now, when he is in danger or needs food, he can no longer turn to his parents; instead he must communicate directly with the voices of the spirits. The role played by older men in Aboriginal circumcision rituals is not simply to break the boy's connection with the feminine world while introducing him to that of the male, but to introduce him to a new awareness of the spiritual dimension and an experience of expanded consciousness. Initiation is the beginning of a movement toward the Dreamtime and the extended encompassing states of reality that culminate for all in the realm of the dead.

In our society, children do not formally break with their parents, nor do they take part in symbolic experiences that can dissolve psychological and physical dependencies and replace them with spiritual knowledge. Our society is structured so that in times of hardship we have parental support to fall back on; our institution of inherited wealth also sustains parent-child interdependencies. By allowing parental authority and relationships to extend beyond the phase of childhood, we limit the expansive, explorative sensibilities that are necessary for an initiatic life— a life that embraces its opposite in both the physical and spiritual unfolding.

The Seclusion

After the cutting ceremony, the circumcised boys remain isolated in a camp together. As in a contemplative monastic order, they can communicate to each other only in sign language. During this period, as during the seizure, the boys are required to fast or partake of a very limited diet. The kin relations who played the killers in the initiatic drama make a symbolic peace with the mourners and bereaved relatives of the boys. Unlike the modern competitive rituals of sport and warfare, Aboriginal rituals always end by restoring a reciprocal balance between the interacting groups.

During numerous all-night dance ceremonies while the boys are in seclusion, the old men instruct the boys about the nature of the journey that people must make after death. Their stories center around the Dreamtime Ancestors who were transfigured into heavenly bodies such as stars, constellations, and dark holes. The myths that relate the stars to the realm of the dead usually include the southern constellations: the Southern Cross, the Pleiades, Canis Major and Minor, and the star Sirius. Tribal people continue to keep much of this type of information secret from probing anthropologists.

The Second Returning

When the boys' penises begin to heal, the camp of seclusion breaks up, and the novices return to the main campsite. Again, the boys are kept awake all night watching the dancing, which culminates in a wild crescendo in which the boys are raced from one small campfire to another. Their heads are held in smoke while the final purification chants are sung. A mock battle follows in which surrounding malevolent spirits are driven off by a shower of boomerangs thrown into the unknown darkness, just above the heads of the seated novices.

The initiated boys are finally returned to the women and children, to more lamenting and crying. At the conclusion of the ceremony, the mothers and female relatives appear tearful yet resigned as they confront their exhausted sons, still covered with the dried blood that symbolizes their rebirth. The boy sits before his mother, head bowed; he is alive, yet visibly altered. At this moment the mother accepts that her boy-child is dead and that their mother-son relationship has been transformed from one of love and intimacy to one of restraint and formal respect. The dead son has been replaced by a young man who, by virtue of having endured deep psychological and physical traumas, has achieved a new status in the world; he possesses new knowledge about the nature of the world and of life and death.

THE BETROTHAL

An important part of the initiation ritual is betrothal, a commitment to a marriage that will not take place for many years. It is the final stage of the male rite of passage. A little girl, often less than five years of age, the daughter of the man who performed the circumcision cutting or ritual murder, is carried by her older brother to the center of the ceremonial ground. The girl is placed next to her newly circumcised husband-to-be and a brief betrothal ceremony takes place. The boy holds his spearthrower across the little girl's chest or forehead and vows that throughout his life, he will hunt meat for her and both of her parents.[12] It may be 15 years or more before this marriage is actually consummated; in the intervening time, the boy will live in the unmarried men's camp and continue the initiatic process that, for some, leads to status as men of high degree.

ADVANCED INITIATIONS

The initiatic life is like a rainbow: each color or phase change releases a distinctly new quality from the continuum of being. Further initiations continue to break the bounds of fear and limitation, opening the door to the spiritual and metaphysical levels of existence.

SUBINCISION

An advanced initiation involving a genital operation called subincision is practiced by many but not all Aboriginal tribes and takes place several years after circumcision. It involves a much smaller ceremony that is also guided by myths concerning the kangaroo and emu, since both of these species have a distinct penile groove, similar to that of the subincised male. The operation entails splitting the ventral surface of the penis along most of its length, thereby exposing the urethra, which is then prevented from closing up when it heals. Its physiological side effects include splashier urination, like that of women, and reduced ejaculatory thrust of semen that may reduce but not prevent the capacity to father children.

The initial subincision provides an initiated man with a source of bloodletting for a number of rituals of increase throughout his life. In these rituals, men gather over the smoke of a fire and reopen the subincisions with a thorn, so that blood splatters on their thighs as they perform fertility dances.[13] Symbolically, the male genital blood parallels the life-giving power of female menstruation and elevates men to be, along with women, participants in the creative process of life. These

operations alter the penis so that its appearance and performance are more like those of the female genitals, thus raising the physical penis to a hermaphroditic phallic symbol. The more a man develops capacities to emulate symbolically the natural creative powers of the feminine through initiations, the higher his spiritual status. *Through initiation, the man balances his symbolic connection to death and life-taking with the image of one who gives birth to spiritual and metaphysical life.*

The subincision also contributes to a man's spiritual development in that the period of healing after each bloodletting ritual imposes on him intervals of celibacy similar to those a woman undergoes during her menstrual cycle, pregnancy, and the period after childbirth. Aboriginal spirituality, like all traditional cults that utilize erotic energy, recognizes that Eros is a force that comes and goes. The passage through many initiatic ordeals requires that the participant abstain from the erotic. When the period of initiation is over, the erotic returns with greater depth, and the initiate receives it with greater knowledge.

Some feminist writers, Barbara Walker for one, find the idea of men mimicking feminine birth powers worthy of scorn.[14] They may have some basis for their disapproval: in prehistoric Anatolia and the Middle East, after the advent of agriculture, male circumcision rituals degenerated to rather cruel and fanatical practices.

> The priests of Cybele, Aphrodite and other mother goddesses used to castrate themselves in imitation of Attis and Adonis. Their severed penises would be tossed into houses to bring fertility, or buried in a basket in the innermost and most sacred section of the temple after being painted and varnished.[15]

Castration (and in the Christian church, male celibacy) became synonymous with purity and control over one's physical nature among the Zealots and Gnostics; sublimated sexual energy was supposed to provide men with a spiritual power of creativity higher and more significant than women's natural power to give birth.

There seems to be a universal need in the male psyche to discover the creative processes that are appropriate for the aptitudes and temperament of the Universal Masculine. Without that discovery men tend to become drones, merchants, or warriors, blindly serving and protecting the life-increasing capacity of the Universal Feminine. Man has attempted to make the natural world (the domain of the feminine) his own kingdom, but the metaphysical purpose of male energy is far different. The health and success of a society depends on men discovering in the spirit realms of death and the unborn the true creative sources of the Universal Masculine.[16]

FIGURE 107

*Young Waramanga man
pulling out the facial hairs of
an elder, Tennant Creek,
Northern Territory, 1901.
Men learn in a trance-like
state to control their autonomic
response to pain. They are able
to have a kinsman pluck their
facial hair and forehead hair,
giving them a raised hairline,
without experiencing obvious
discomfort. This practice is
prevalent in the spring, as the
men wish to beautify
themselves for romantic
pursuits.*

For many contemporary men, artistic and intellectual creation fills this need by symbolically invoking processes of inspiration, conception, pregnancy, and giving birth. For example, architecture has been seen as the male attempt to re-create for himself a womb. Qualitative differences exist among the many expressions of the universal male drive to attain creative functions. In indigenous cultures, the male attempts to empathize with the procreative power of the feminine in order to emulate it spiritually and ritualistically. In Western society, men have tried to devalue and control feminine creative powers and to usurp them physically through religious and institutionalized authority, environmental manipulation, and technological and scientific methods such as test-tube conception and genetic engineering.

The Aborigines have a number of more advanced male initiations, such as the "sacred feast," which confers on a man the power to make symbols and sacred objects. Males also practice a number of minor initiations that vary from tribe to tribe, such as nose piercing, tooth evulsion, depilation (removal of body or facial hair, found mostly among noncircumised tribes), and cicatrization (scarring on various parts of the body, often referred to as sorrow marks). Besides their symbolic and psychological purpose, these practices provide males with the opportunity to exercise a hypnogogic trancelike state. As the psychic facility to induce a hypnogogic state matures, it promotes extraordinary physical control, particularly as it relates to the autonomic nervous system, and provides access to deep layers of the unconscious mind that are the doorway to death.

The Initiatic Wound

Initiatic wounding plays an important role in drawing, conducting, and constraining energies that originate beyond the field of perceivable nature. Many Aboriginal ceremonies involve ritual wounding, especially mourning ceremonies. Baldwin Spencer, the early Australian anthropologist, reported these observations of an Aboriginal burial in 1901:

> On the camping ground several men were lying *hors de combat* with gashed thighs. The wounds were bound to make sure they gaped widely. They had done their duty and henceforth, in token of this, would be marked with deep scars. On one of these men I counted no fewer than twenty-three that had been self-inflicted at different times.[17]

Many cultures refer to the wounding of men's thighs. Ritual wounding is not masochistic. The Aborigines and men of other cultures have been initiated into the process of hypnotically entering into the unconscious and autonomic levels of mind and body and deriving energy from them rather than just undergoing pain. The wild boar with his curved moon tusk wounded the heroes in Greek mythology, either in the thigh or genitals, just as the bull threatens to wound the thighs or genitals of the matador in the Spanish male initiatic ritual, the bullfight. Initiated men in prehistoric Canaanite culture were said to perform ritual dances while limping from their self-inflicted wounds.[18]

Figure 108
Waramanga man with gashed thigh the day after a man had died, Tennant Creek, Northern Territory, 1901. A keloid scar will result from the bound wound. The self-inflicted thigh wound is a means of embodying and releasing the psychological pain and suffering brought about by the loss of a loved one.

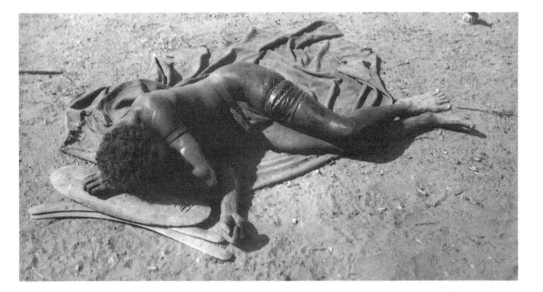

197

In Aboriginal ritual, self-wounding carries various symbolic meanings. Wounding at times of sorrow releases emotions from being trapped in the mind or body and places the pain of grieving on a physical level, from whence it can bleed into the earth and eventually heal. Wounding also allows spirit energy to enter the body and force out or replace withheld darkness. A man's bleeding thigh is like the blood of a woman's womb, both signifying the sacrifice required of life to create another life. The blood of women is thought to be the vehicle that carries the unborn spirit in its transit into this world; the blood of men accompanies and nourishes the spirits of the deceased on its journey to the next.

For the Aborigines, wounding and scarring of the body is considered beautifying because it displays the inner strength and courage of the person's spirit. Wounding is believed to strengthen that part of the body, giving increased depth and strength to the particular qualities associated with the wounded region or organ. Like the penis, a man must inflate himself to function creatively in the world. The inflationary nature of the male psyche is balanced by self-wounding, which deflates a man's concerns with the physical world so that he can return to his inner core. While recovering from their wounds, Aboriginal tribal men would have a period of isolation, silence, and inactivity during which they practiced symbolic methods of expression, such as bark painting. Modern males are unaware of the value of this rhythmic inflation (through increased power or productivity) and deflation brought about by initiatic self-wounding. As a result of constant self-inflation, modern man unconsciously brings on exhaustion, failure, and death.[19]

The male blood and body, as well as the unconscious levels of the masculine mind, conduct energy from other worlds. Men's development, and the disciplines they engage in, shape the metaphysical energy entering the world through them. In early history, not only mystics but kings, warriors, and merchants acknowledged that they were channels for metaphysical forces.

FIGURE 109 →
By learning to consciously rise above pain instead of physically absorbing and enduring it, the scarred Aboriginal warrior is a hero of the inner worlds.

Circa 1800 B.C., Hammurabi, the king renowned for this law code, ascended the throne in Babylon and began to extend its boundaries. According to his inscriptions the gods not only told him if and when to launch his military campaigns but were literally leading his armies:
"Through the power of the great gods
the king, beloved of the god Marduk,
reestablished the foundations of Sumer and Akkad.
Upon the command of Anu, and
with Enlil advancing in front of his army,
with the mighty powers which the great gods gave him,
he was no match for the army of Emutbal
and its king Rim-Sim. . . ."[20]

199

Megalomania and all forms of egotism delude men into thinking that the powers they express in the world belong to their individual physical and psychological natures. In 1990, Saddam Hussein resurrected the ancient idea of the ruler representing the power of Allah, but unfortunately his deceitful and clouded mind knew nothing of the initiatic disciplines that could make this possible. The ways a man utilizes his mind and body determine which metaphysical forces he disseminates through the world. The task of masculinity is more than mastering or releasing one's own innate nature; a man must mold himself into a balanced vessel and transmitter of metaphysical powers. Rationalism causes us to view this sort of concept as superstitious. But unless we have the means to understand metaphysical forces and can participate in regulating those forces, the Gods or the Ancestors will use the lives of humans as unconsciously as we use them. We need only look at the perilous condition of our world civilization to realize the dangers of permitting power to fall into the hands of uninitiated men.

WOMEN'S ROLE IN MALE INITIATIONS

The early European anthropologists who worked in Australia were all men and, especially the British, were educated in a male-dominated academic and scientific tradition. They tended to associate with and interview mostly Aboriginal men and painted a picture of Aboriginal society as being exceedingly male dominated. Recent work by a number of female anthropologists has begun to revise these misconceptions. They are discovering that Aboriginal women, besides having important initiation rites of their own, play a significant role in the male ceremonies.[21]

During the long period of the circumcision rites, women provide almost all of the food consumed by participants and visitors while men are busy with the complicated customs and ceremonial preparations. Although men apparently decide who will perform the cutting ritual, their decision follows the women's choice of a mother-in-law for the boy. Behind the facade of male bestowal customs, women actually maneuver the marital relationship based on their intuitions as to whether the couple would be happy together.

Without requiring the recognition ceremonially accorded to men, women understand the importance of their role. Anthropologist Diane Bell has reported that one evening, during the initial seizure of the boys, the mothers and female relatives reclaim the boy and for the entire night hold the boy in their arms, repeating over and over, "It is from a woman you are born, it is women who nourish you, and it is a woman whom you will marry."[22] These words embody the essence of the symbolism underlying the process of the making of men. Male initiation is primarily concerned with the relationship of men with the underlying ground of human existence, the eternal Universal Feminine. The boys are taken from women and returned to women. The severing of the umbilical cord, symbolized by circumcision, is immediately replaced with a phallic connection to a betrothed wife. Initiation requires that the attachment to the biological mother be severed, yet the sacred dance ground of initiated men is called the mother (*yagurdi*).[23] Male initiation is not a process of males becoming independent from or spiritually superior to women; rather, it means transcendence from physical dependency on women to a sacred responsibility toward the Universal Feminine, the earth.

Women in Aboriginal societies seem to have an unspoken understanding that in the natural order of things, the masculine psyche is secondary to, or removed from, the ground of organic creation. They accept that the fragile male ego requires constant external reinforcement, and they instigate and support male ceremonies that shape the male psyche so that it may function positively in nature and society. Women therefore condone, collaborate, and even dramatize the codes, prohibitions, and secrecy of male rites. Ronald M. Berndt (an Australian anthropologist who is respected by both academics and the Aboriginal people with whom he worked for more than forty years) relates a story that typifies these female attitudes. He was sitting around a campfire with a group of Aborigines, listening to a respected elderly man. The old man used a word with which Berndt was completely unfamiliar, and he asked an English-speaking Aboriginal woman what the word meant. The woman turned to him with a pious look and informed him that it was a word sacred to male language, which she was forbidden to even speak. The old man, overhearing the woman's response, nodded in proud approval. Several days later, Berndt accompanied a party of female gatherers. After narrowly missing catching a lizard, the same woman cut loose with a stream of profanity, every third word of which was the same sacred and forbidden word.[24]

Underneath their apparent submission to male pomp and ceremony, women maintain their balance of power *physically* by providing 80 percent of the food consumed by the tribe and *spiritually* through their own tradition of magic and sorcery, which men rarely dare to challenge. Although men apparently control most of the formal relationships in society, such as the bestowal of wives, women's informal control ensures that the entire society adheres to characteristics conducive to women's concerns for procreation, growth, and nourishment of life. The resulting characteristics of Aboriginal society—its stability, continuity, and interrelatedness—are in direct contrast to our modern male-dominated society, which is marked by violent upheaval, rapid change, progressivism, and discontinuity.

FEMALE INITIATIONS

THE TRICKSTER AND THE GIRL

Jalmarida and Baiangun were two sisters who lived at Dalingur by Arnhem Bay during the Dreaming era. One day they went out to collect cycad palm nuts, filling their dilly bags with the nuts. They dried them in the sun for two or three days, then pounded them, replaced them in the bags, and left them soaking in fresh water so they would be fit to eat. In the meantime, while they were waiting they went to Gudjindga and made camp there. Then they went down to a mangrove swamp to collect periwinkles from the mangrove roots.

Nearby there lived a man named Namaranganin. He saw the two sisters and followed them, watching them move across the swamp. Then he made the rain, to force them to turn back so he could catch one of them. Rain clouds gathered, lightning flashed, and the two sisters asked each other, "What has happened? Perhaps that man who followed us has made rain. What shall we do?" They decided to collect their periwinkles quickly to go back. Namaranganin, hiding behind a mangrove tree, kept watching them. The rain came down heavily and the thunder rumbled; they gathered up their belongings and ran toward the camp. Namaranganin thought, "Those two are coming now, I'll grab them and take them away." As they passed the tree he jumped out and tried to grasp them. The elder sister, Baiangun, escaped, but he managed to keep hold of Jalmarida, the younger. "This will be my wife, I'll take her away." He carried her off into the jungle. But Baiangun ran back to the main camp and told everyone, "Namaranganin has taken Jalmarida into the jungle . . . Namaranganin, the trickster, with his long penis!" All the men hurried off, following their tracks.

While this was happening Namaranganin, far in the jungle, had chosen a good place for a camp. "What are we going to do?" the girl asked. "We're going to make a big fire and a hut," he told her. He made a stringy bark house and built a fire inside, but Jalmarida would not talk to him. He kept trying, in one way and another, but still she refused to speak. At last he caused the fire to smoke, so that the hut was full of it. They lay down to sleep, but still Jalmarida was silent. The smoke continued to collect. During the night it became so dense that at last the girl awakened and asked, "Why does that fire make so much smoke, why doesn't it escape?" Namaranganin

replied, *"Yes, this is the reason, so that you will speak to me. I want to copulate now."* But Jalmarida answered, *"No, you can't do it, Dagurura is inside me, closing my vulva."* (Dagurura is a stone and a totemic emblem.) *Namaranganin got a stick, sharpened it, and wedged out the stone. As it emerged, a roaring sound came from the sacred Wonguri totemic water hole associated with it. Bursting out, the stone traveled to the water hole, entering it, while Namaranganin called sacred invocations relating to it. The Dagurura became a sacred emblem for the Wonguri people. The removal of the stone made it easy for human women to have intercourse.*

By now the other men who were tracking them had reached their jungle camp. They surrounded it with a ring of fires, preventing Namaranganin from escaping, then speared him and burnt him in a huge fire. But Jalmarida did not go home with them. She turned herself into a fly.[25]

All known indigenous cultures divide their cosmological realm into two—the primal couple—and the physical world into four—the primal

FIGURE 110
Aboriginal women, and the young girls to be initiated, decorate their bodies beautifully in preparation for the ceremonies.

203

FIGURE 111
*Through initiation, Aboriginal
girls attain the powers and
wisdom of the Universal
Feminine.*

elements. Parallel to the four archetypal masculine roles, hunter/ceremonial dancer and wanderer/mystic, in Aboriginal and other traditional societies the Universal Feminine manifests as the four archetypal roles, wife/mother and virgin/ritual prostitute. Each of these roles is maintained as a separate function in Aboriginal society and marked by a female initiation rite.

The female initiation rites are always related to biological changes such as menstruation, defloration, pregnancy, and childbirth.[26] Defloration parallels male circumcision as a rite of passage into adulthood and is also carried out through successive interconnected rites. It is preceded by several minor puberty rites celebrating the sprouting of breasts and other stages of physical development. Women mark these stages by gathering together and performing certain rituals and songs. In these ceremonies, the young girls are given their initial lessons in women's sorcery, known as "love magic." Girls do not undergo the long, formal instruction typical of male initiation, however, because they are by nature initiated into the mysteries of life.

The important defloration ceremony begins with the onset of the girl's first menstruation, during which she leaves the main camp and spends several days in a little secluded hut, some distance away, built by her mother or grandmother. The older women visit her, instructing her about sex and the way she should behave when she is married. During this time the girl observes certain food taboos. In many areas there is a prohibition against eating meat because it is believed that the animal species she ingests during her menstruation will suffer reduced procreation in the following season. This taboo holds for every menstrual cycle throughout her entire life.

The details of the initiation vary from area to area, but the general ritual is the same. At the end of her seclusion period the girl may be brought to a river, or billabong, for the second phase of initiation, ritual bathing or purification. In contrast to the seriousness that surrounds male initiation, the bathing is a joyful social gathering of female relatives who splash and dunk the girl in the water while the mother burns the seclusion hut. The girl is then decorated and painted before she returns to the main camp, where she is nominally given over to her husband and his kin in a small, unspectacular marriage ceremony. The time of consummation of the marriage remains a mystery to the young girl and may not happen immediately after the marriage ceremony. The parents and other relatives first spend some time sorting out the complex kinship arrangements every marriage brings.

There are variations on the defloration ritual, but like the male initiation, it generally follows a common theme. One day soon after the marriage ceremony the girl may go food collecting as usual with the older women. She is seized by a group of men, sometimes including her future husband and several others who are in the kin category of brother. During the seizure she addresses all these men as "husband," and they have intercourse with her, often gathering the semen and blood mixture and drinking it. In other cases, the fluid is retained as a powerful medicine. The defloration rite seems severe from a Western perspective; however, from early childhood Aboriginal girls look forward to this initiation, viewing sexuality as a joyous, integrated part of life. Therefore, most are eager to begin their sexual life. In these rituals men can release the archetypal "wild man" in a lustful, abandoned, fecundating ceremony. Before copulation begins, the vaginal orifice is sometimes penetrated by a sharp instrument, such as the rounded end of a boomerang. This is done in spite of the fact that it is often unnecessary to break the hymen, since the young girl's active physical life has commonly already dispensed with it.

The period of abduction and sexual ceremony with its associated ritual and dancing extends through the night to the following morning. After the abduction is over, the girl is decorated, using blood to attach white feathers to her body. Bands of charcoal may be painted on her body or she may be painted with yellow ochre, and is very often blindfolded. She then returns to the main camp and is presented to her husband; from this time their marriage can be consummated. The girl's new status is marked in several ways: she is given a new name, is treated as an equal by other mature women, and has greater freedom in camping arrangements and ceremonial performance.

Immediately after the defloration many tribes conduct a retaliation ceremony, which includes wild ritual dancing. At its conclusion, the abducted girl and her female relatives are permitted to take fighting poles and club any man in the tribe against whom they have developed a grudge during the previous year. There is no fear of reprisal for any of the beatings—sometimes serious—that the women hand out during this ceremony. This acts to ensure that the men are not abusive during the girl's defloration (unlikely, in any event, given their close kinship).

After the retaliation ceremony, the girl's body decoration is again changed; in some areas she is painted with red ochre, symbolizing that she is now empowered with the flow of menstrual blood. In some tribes, a crescent moon is painted in white clay below each of her breasts or on her stomach. This design symbolically regulates the menstrual flow, ensuring that it does not continue indefinitely and that it will reappear with each new moon. The girl is not allowed to wash or bathe until the red ochre paint wears off.

Menstrual blood is considered so powerful that women are forbidden to conceal that they are menstruating. They must observe certain rituals during menstruation, because the life-giving power of menstrual blood is matched by a lethal power that can be destructive to animal species and to young children of the tribe. The Aranda people of North Australia claim that the smell of menstrual blood attracts and excites the serpent, or fertilizing energy of the earth; the intensification of its presence surrounding the menstruating woman can disrupt tribal life. Menstrual blood is also highly revered and is the focal interest in much of Aboriginal religious life. Men do not react to menstruation with disgust or horror, nor are menstruating women labeled unclean, as they have been in the Judeo-Christian and Islamic traditions. During childbirth or menstruation, women are considered extremely sacred rather than ritually taboo.

Pregnancy and childbirth are considered other aspects of the complete cycle of female initiation and universal character. Each of these is held in equal importance and respect.

Life itself is the initiator for all women. With each child she bears and with each monthly menstruation, a woman accepts pain, depletion, and inner withdrawal. Her body and her state of mind undergo radical transformations and swings not only with the monthly cycle but also in the deep shifts in life roles. Women move from virginity to motherhood, and motherhood ends as abruptly as it began. The essence of initiatic death and rebirth are built into a woman's physiology. Her confrontations with pain, fear, and death are a necessary adjunct to her miraculous birth-giving role. The ritual cutting of the hymen, depicted in the myth at the head of this section, symbolizes the opening and outpouring of the universal gifts, those of pleasure, depth, nourishment, and life.

INITIATION AND SALVATION

Although female initiation is briefer and less elaborate than its male counterpart, it brings about equally important and irreversible physical, psychological, and psychic changes. The two rites are symmetric, however; for example, in some tribes the deflowering or hymen-cutting ritual is performed at exactly the same time as the male circumcision. In each case the novice becomes the center of a passionate ritual crisis that deeply affects not only the individual but many close relations. Family members from parents, grandparents, brothers, and sisters to more distant kin must undergo prohibitions and trials along with the novice. A relation may be obliged, by kin convention, to fast or abstain from certain foods or sexual activity for weeks or even months during the rites. Often mothers, sisters, or betrothed wives observe a vow of silence or scar their bodies in sympathy with the boy or girl being initiated. For each category of kin relation a special part of the body is allocated for scarring. For the rest of his or her lifetime, the kin whose initiation is represented on an individual's body by these scars can be contacted by touching that area and visualizing that person.[27] In this way, the shared initiatic ordeal remains a source of permanent psychic communication among kin. Initiation, therefore, awakens in each tribe member the assurance that all life transitions, including death, have complete empathetic support from the entire society. The fear of loneliness and sense of alienation of Western society would be inconceivable to the traditional Aborigine. No one is expected to endure the trials of life alone. The kinship system, as demonstrated in the initiatic process, is based on a deep, immediate sense of responsibility, not only for self and immediate family but for the entire society.

Psychologically, these adolescent rites serve to clear the unconscious mind of two universal sexual fears, rape and castration. Many of the primal interactions of the Dreamtime Ancestors involved rape and castration, and so they are embedded in the archetypal unconscious of each

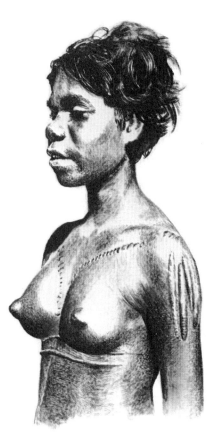

FIGURE 112
Body scarring emphasizes physical beauty as well as revealing a person's emotional depth and endurance.

207

human. Their ritual enactment reflects a basic tenet of Aboriginal psychology and cosmology: "All comes into existence through a passage from Dreamtime to the natural world." Subconscious primal events must be objectified in ritual so that life can fulfill its mythic amplitude and resonance. In contrast, in the subconscious of modern man the same dynamic interactions are left moldering to form self-involved complexes and projections, often triggering bestial crimes, perversions, or stifling life-destructive inhibitions. The purpose and meaning of initiation for individuals and society summed up in a statement that the apostle Thomas attributes to Christ:

> If you bring forth all that is within you, what is within you will save you. If you do not bring forth all that is within you, what is within you will destroy you.[28]

Western society brings forth or externalizes the world Dreaming in wilful, self-centered, environmentally destructive endeavors. The Aborigines externalize the original Dreaming through ritual enactment, marked by remembrance and respect.

Initiations draw together the physical and psychic realms in a reciprocal way. The ordeals and crises of initiation, such as body scarring, bring to a physical level the emotions of fear, sorrow, and loneliness that pervade our psyche during life's inevitable transitions and losses. Inversely, the physical body and its potent substances of blood and sperm are acknowledged for their spiritual and psychic power. Through initiation, as in life, the Aboriginal vision weaves together the psychic and physical realms into one body of life.

CHAPTER 11

ABORIGINAL SEXUALITY

URING THE EARLY TO MID-
1940s, the anthropologist Ronald Berndt recorded and studied the erotic
songs of tribes in northern Arnhem Land, who at that time were relatively untouched by the pernicious spread of Christian missions and
government assimilation programs. While Aboriginal sexual traditions
vary greatly from region to region, the Arnhem Land songs reveal certain underlying attitudes toward sexuality that are consistent throughout
Australia. By isolating three distinct types of song cycles, Berndt grouped
Aboriginal sexuality into three levels of experience: the social face of
love, the personal face of love, and the ritual face of love.[1] The social
face of love includes marriage, the activities that surround it, and rituals
of a lighter nature than the puberty rites. The personal face of love is
expressed through extramarital relationships that are conducted to fulfill
individual needs as opposed to those of the tribe as a whole. The ritual
face of love is the unleashing of wild, primal erotic forces of the Dreamtime
to establish a connection with the power of the ancestral beings and
nature.

Aborigines believe that the natural environment results from the sexual
potencies of metaphysical beings and that these potencies continue to
vivify the creatures and processes of nature. They also believe that the
quality, variety, and intensity of human eroticism can deeply affect the
surrounding life processes. The notion that the sexual energies of human beings and nature affect each other remains in our thinking today.
We acknowledge that moonlight, the thundering of waves on the shore,
the color and scent of certain flowers, or the shape and feel of stones
possess sexually stimulating qualities. The source of energy that triggers
sexual arousal varies from culture to culture. Because we are so accustomed to clothing, our sexual arousal is triggered by its removal. Since
Aborigines wear no clothing, they define the cause of sexual arousal
differently. For the Aborigines, subtle qualities of atmosphere and natu-

ral elements are considered the hidden hand of beings who triggered their sexual appetites. A gentle wind wafting through the pubic hair of a young girl is seen as a natural spirit force inducing the current of erotic energies to flow. The view that both humans and nature rely on metaphysical erotic sources persisted in all early societies before the crackdown on fertility rites by state religions, especially Christianity and Islam. In the dreadful course of events in Europe between the eleventh and sixteenth centuries, inquisitions and witch hunts destroyed the rites of exchanging sexual and erotic vitality between humans and nature. Both the emphasis and the restrictions Aborigines place on their sexuality are directed toward the reciprocal exchange between human sexuality and the erotic forces of nature.

The Social Face of Love

The selection of marriage partners reflects the complex system of kinship between clans. Each clan group is divided into two parts, called moieties. Some clans follow a line of marriage and descent through a matrilineal moiety, others through a patrilineal moiety.[2] This varies from tribe to tribe, according to the ancient law given by the Ancestors. In many areas throughout Australia, myths depict a very ancient period in which women controlled the social order and religious power; over millennia, men have confiscated this power from them in a variety of ways.[3] Matriarchal marriage and descent patterns are said to be left over from these ancient times.

All marriages are foreordained by the kinship system, and the observance of these conventions is of utmost importance to society. The kinship system provides a relationship category from which a marriage partner can be selected, the most frequent choice being what we might term a "cross-cousin." For example, in matrilineal clans the most common partner for a man is his mother's mother's brother's daughter's daughter, or, in our terms, the grand-daughter of the maternal granduncle (see Figure 114).[4]

The marriage possibilities at first seem extremely limited and "close blooded." The picture broadens, however, when we recall that a boy has not only a biological mother (blood mother) but several social or categorical mothers (all referred to as skin mothers). For example, in many tribes all of his mother's sisters are referred to as "mother"; besides these, his mother has skin sisters, thereby extending the number of individual girls who fit into the marriage category. To add to this complexity, a boy also refers to his betrothed wife's father's sister as a skin

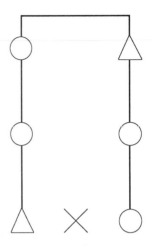

ARANDA RULE

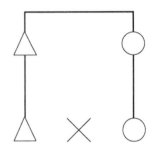

KARIERA RULE

Man △
Woman ○
Marriage ✕

FIGURE 114
The two most common marriage patterns in Aboriginal society. (After Maddock)

← *FIGURE 113*
Polychrome figures at Nourlangie Rock—an example of very ancient paintings from the Alligator Rivers Region of the Northern Territory. Many of the x-ray–image beings found in sacred caves are believed to have been completed in the Dreamtime by the Ancestors and then repainted by initiated men for thousands of years.

211

mother, which establishes another relationship pattern from which he can obtain future wives (Aborigines practice a form of polygamy).

In a patrilineal clan, the most common marriage partner is a boy's father's sister's daughter, again including all the skin and blood relationships. All clan groups throughout Australia are exogamic; that is, the partners must find a spouse outside the clan with whom they live, and the preferred choice is usually genealogically and geographically the most distant of all possible candidates.

Marriage occurs in two stages, betrothal and consummation. For boys the betrothal usually takes place as part of the circumcision ceremony, and many years of initiation intervene before the marriage is consummated. Aborigines prefer the betrothal of girls to happen at birth or in childhood; it should take place no later than during their puberty rites, after which the consummation of the marriage is almost immediate. Men and women are not recognized as adults by the rest of the community until they marry.[5]

Marriages are arranged by a formal bestowal, which is the prerogative of men. Women influence this process both covertly and through rituals called women's magic. The women's choice is very often based on the sexual attraction between the two young people, while the men tend to make marriage unions based on beneficial sharing arrangements or the extension of kinship alliances that might assist them during times of dispute. Loud intertribal and male-female arguments over these decisions can go on for weeks.[6]

The bestowal of women is also part of an intricate exchange system between men. This practice includes the transfer of goods and swapping of duties for ritual performances at their respective sacred sites. A man may bestow his daughter, his niece, in some cases his sister, and even his mother if his father has died. Men are constantly occupied with these

FIGURE 115

An example of the complex patterns of exchange made by older Aboriginal men in response to marriages or initiations. (After Maddock)

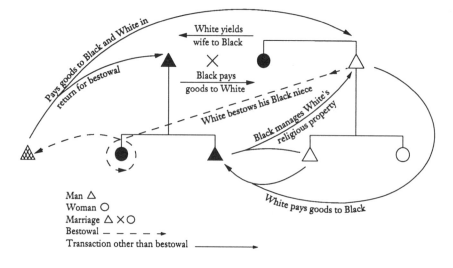

exchanges, and great care is taken that the deal is considered even between them.[7] The rights of exchange are based not on male ownership of women but on a mutual adherence to the original pattern of kinship law.

If reciprocity is not achieved, the harmony among clans can be upset; the ensuing disputes are often injurious to both parties. The bestowals are often conditional, over long periods of time, sometimes involving girls who are not yet born. For example, a man may say, "My daughter when she is born will be the mother-in-law to your son." Marriage bestowal agreements, though unwritten, are usually binding. At a later date, the agreement may be symbolically formalized. If a girl reaches adolescence and finds the arranged marriage unacceptable, she may make alliances with some sympathetic relatives or a brother, who agitates until new arrangements are made. This is unusual, though, because marriage holds many benefits for a woman without necessarily restricting romantic pursuits.[8]

Several small rituals or actions accompany the betrothal process. For example, mothers often set about making arrangements with potential mothers-in-law. In a woman's dance ceremony, the mother and the prospective mother-in-law confront each other and ceremonially settle a marriage partnership for their children by rubbing their breasts against each other.[9] Once this dance has taken place, the women begin putting pressure on the men to formally make the bestowal. A father may act out the relinquishing of his bond with his daughter to her future husband when the girl is secluded during her first menstruation. Outside her hut, the father waits for her to fall asleep. He attempts to creep up on her and plunge his spear into the earth between her outstretched legs. He then gives that spear to the man to whom he has given his daughter.[10] The father's spear penetrating the earth between the legs of his sleeping pubescent daughter is consistent with the Aboriginal belief in ritually externalizing all aspects of their subjective life, including the undesirable incestual attractions between fathers and daughters. In this way, the psychic atmosphere remains free of the complexes that are often associated with sexual repression.

The practice of male bestowal is repugnant to our present democratic and social ideals. In Aboriginal society, it is seen as a means of formally bestowing powers on men to compensate for their secondary role in the life-giving processes of nature. While they are secretly influencing bestowal procedures, Aboriginal women enjoy the fact that men bear the brunt of hostilities if the younger women are displeased with their arranged marriages.[11] A psychological benefit of bestowal is that it encourages men to consider women and their powers to give pleasure and nourishment and create life as the supreme gift of the great Ancestors. The Aboriginal marriage reflects the metaphysical sense of woman as the gift of life, to be bestowed and received, rather than a prize to be won or a possession to be acquired.

Psychologists have noted that universally, males tend to display a pattern of bestowal of women in one form or another. In our society, where formal bestowal is repressed, it emerges sublimally in the form of young men vicariously "bestowing" women by relating their sexual experiences with them, telling jokes based on heterosexual acts, or exchanging nude or pornographic photographs of women.[12] In contrast, the open exchange of women in Aboriginal society is accompanied by a strict code of male ethics: although they love to joke about sexuality, men never talk about intimate sexual experiences with wives or sweethearts. The bestowal of women in Aboriginal society supports a stable social order

FIGURE 116
The family unit maintains stability through the constant wandering of the hunting band and the many diverse kin and ceremonial relationships maintained in Aboriginal life.

based on nonpossessive attitudes. It also fulfills a more positive function than the repressive pornographic forms found in our society.

The Aboriginal marriage ceremony itself is extremely simple compared with the complex communal involvement in initiation and bestowal. One such ceremony was observed in the Aranda tribe of the Central Desert. Within a few weeks after her initiation, the girl quietly appeared before her husband. With no undue ceremony they sat in full view of other clan members going about their daily tasks. The man handed her a small cup-shaped piece of wood, part of the traditional fire-making equipment. He rapidly spun the other part of the implement, a small wooden rod, inside the cup, which she held close to some dried grass. The friction of the rod in the cup reached a temperature that ignited the grass. As the grass burst into flames, the couple looked into each other's eyes and the marriage was made.[13]

Older Husbands, Younger Wives—Older Wives, Younger Husbands

Marriage is decidedly different for women than it is for men. For all women in Aboriginal society, sexuality is their birthright. As soon as a young woman reaches puberty her marriage is consummated and she begins a full, active sex life, which often continues until death. All women are married right after the onset of puberty, and for the rest of their lives they will be part of a marital relationship. Women usually bear children very young, often avoiding pregnancy in later life. If a woman's husband dies, she is immediately bestowed to another man. Certain kinship laws require men to marry the widow of a specific relative. Sexual attraction between partners, which is highly valued by women, generally is more of an issue in these second marriages.

Women are generally considered—and consider themselves to be—sexually attractive even at very advanced ages. When this is not the case, older women have a repertoire of love-magic techniques for stirring up sexual interest. In many tribes, younger boys feel it is prestigious to have a sexual liaison with an older woman. It is considered undesirable, even dangerous, for a woman to be sexually frustrated or circumstantially cut off from sexual activity. As the Aborigines say, "It makes for bad magic."

Although Aboriginal women marry exceptionally young, Aboriginal men are prevented from marrying until they are quite a bit older, usually in their mid-twenties and sometimes as late as forty. This difference in marriageable age for men and women reflects the Aboriginal adage that women are shaped by nature, men by culture. Although women's innate understanding of life processes gives them the maturity to enter into marriage at a young age, men must be taught how their life force can be used to benefit the tribe and to connect the community to the realm of the Ancestors. Men must earn the right to marriage and sexuality through self-development and spiritual awareness. Therefore, women make bonded commitments only to initiated men. Men do not remain celibate during their long years of initiation, but marriage and any lasting sexual attachments are considered detrimental to their spiritual development. The long initiation of an Aboriginal man postpones the authority conferred on him by having earned the support, collaboration, and life companionship of a wife or wives. At the same time, the long delay intensifies his desire to marry.[14]

The pattern of delayed marriage for men and early marriage for women creates an excess of marriageable women for the older initiated men. This results in a pattern of male polygamy and serial monogamy for women. Older men generally have several wives, and women, who can have only one husband at a time, often move from one to another as their much older spouses pass away. Men are usually 20 or more years older than their wives. A man can take as many wives as he chooses, according to his skills and energy. There are early instances of Aboriginal men with 6, 12, and in one case 29 wives. For the man, each marriage entails increased ritual and kinship responsibilities and requires enormous fortitude, because a sexually dissatisfied wife may, if unable to find an extramarital liaison, generate unimaginable domestic disharmony. Many men choose to have only one wife, and these monogamous marriages often persist into the old age of both partners, with every appearance of devotion between them.

On the surface this marital pattern seems extremely male-dominant, but many anthropologists have found it to be a woman-centered social format. In many cases, the decision to invite a third person into a marriage is a mutual one. For example, a wife may encourage her husband to take a younger second wife to help with the food gathering, domestic chores, and child care. Polygamous relationships are usually harmonious; jealousy does not arise as long as the male is equitable in the sexual attention he gives his wives. This marital system allows young girls to enjoy the security and prestige of marriage to an older initiated man and close cooperative relationships with other women. Since older polygamous men seem to be less prone to jealousy, the girls are more free to have "sweetheart relationships." In addition, after childbirth many Aboriginal women prefer to wait from a few months to one or two years before resuming sexual activity. Polygamy gives them this opportunity without creating marital disharmony.

The Aboriginal marriage system, in general, allows for a great variety of sexual and relational possibilities. This flexibility takes into account social necessity as well as individual psychology. Young unmarried men experience the adventure of sexual liaisons, often with older married women. Older men have the rights and responsibilities of polygamous marital sex, and women have the opportunity to partake of both marital and extramarital relationships.[15]

The marital system enables the more energetic and aggressive "alpha" males to distinguish themselves by accumulating wives, but it obliges them to balance their excessive appetites with increased responsibility. It also allows another variation—as older husbands die and the women mature, the age pattern reverses and older widowed women are betrothed to younger males, who have just completed initiation and are ready for married life. The kinship system also requires a man to take as his wife the widow of his older brother, no matter how advanced her age. In comparison to modern open marriages and wife swapping, deceitfully carried out under the facade of an exclusively monogamous system, the Aboriginal system has obvious benefits.

Most Western objections to the Aboriginal marriage system center around the lack of individual choice in selecting marriage partners. Among the Aborigines, however, as in most traditional societies, marriage and

FIGURE 117
Aranda family with possessions in front of their bough shelter, Alice Springs, Central Australia, 1896. The man is smoothing a spear shaft and the woman is grinding seed. This is a typical family arrangement in which a man has a primary wife and one or more younger wives.

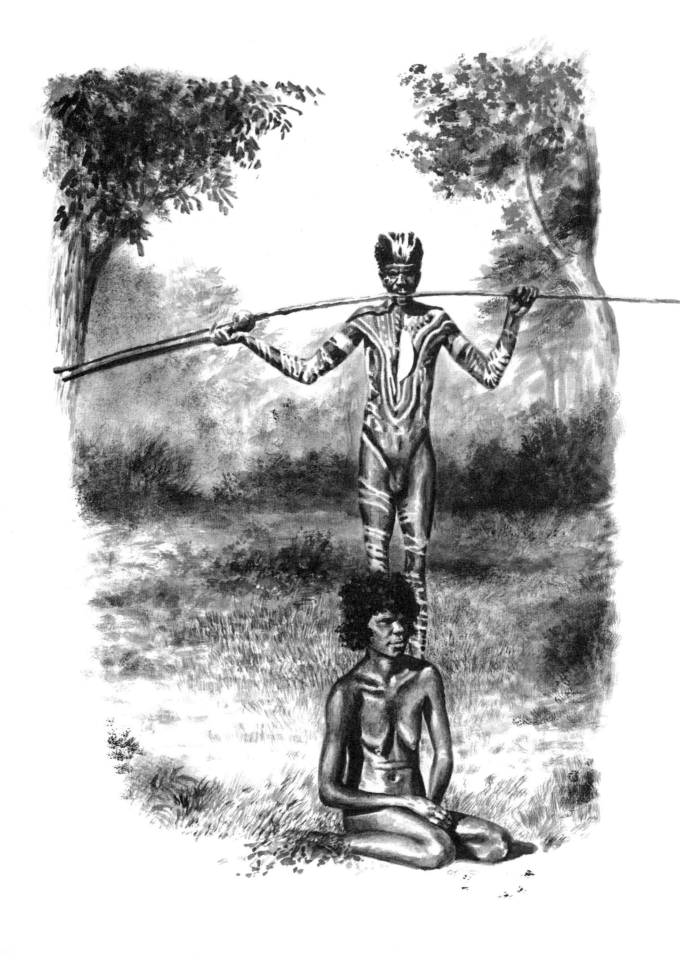

childbearing are not considered the domain of individual will or desire. The formation and arrangement of one's genetic material develop over untold generations and constitute the repository that one receives as a gift from ancestors both living and dead. For the Aborigines, their bloodlines spread backward through millennia, connecting them not only to a human ancestry but also to the totem lines of plants and animals and to the metaphysical Creative Beings. To them, their bloodlines must not become clouded but should echo clearly their full ancestral roots, since these embody an image of the order of the Universe. Any society that leaves the timeless connections of biological heredity to the instability of a marital system based on youthful sexual attraction is certain to invite its own destruction.

The major conflict in Aboriginal male-female relationships arises from the fact that people can only marry outside of their clan; one partner in a marriage must leave the clan and the locality to which he or she is spiritually connected by birth. By tradition, the woman always leaves to join the male's clan and locality. Her departure creates a great deal of heartbreak for her; these feelings are explored in this translation of an Aboriginal Dreamtime story of courtship.

> One man ran after one of the women and stood on her digging stick and gazed into her eyes and asked the young woman for food. The woman felt embarrassed because she had never been approached by a man like that before. He said to her, "Get up off the ground and don't be shy or frightened. From now on we shall dig together and we shall go everywhere together." He gently took the young girl by the arm and they continued together; as they travelled the woman left her country behind. She resisted and tried to return home. The man then beat the young girl's legs with a spear. As she lay naked, complaining of his cruelty, he began a ceremony to beautify himself so as to increase his appeal to her. He painted his body and scarred himself to produce sorrow marks which symbolised the depth of his experience and knowledge. He brought her an animal skin to warm her body and then sat with her. She tried to straighten herself but it still hurt too much. She looked back at her country but knew she must leave and go with her husband. The pain began to disappear.[16]

The girl's forced departure from her homeland can be compared to a boy's abduction and initiatic journey preceding his circumcision rites. The injury to the young woman's legs is an external manifestation of her being deprived of contact with her homeland. Her suffering is shared by her lover through his ritual self-scarring. Although the woman feels the pain of loss, she will gain the experience of living in another country. As

← FIGURE 118
Ceremonial capture of women. This Aboriginal ceremony, depicting the complete surrender or "initiatic death" that a woman undergoes when she leaves her girlhood to enter marriage, resonates with the Greek myth of feminine surrender, Eros and Psyche.

219

they continue together, she sees her husband's country like a mirage before her; her husband instructs her in the secrets and wonders of his land. Marriage pushes women to grow and encompass more knowledge by experiencing a variety of people and places; the accumulated wisdom of older women is highly respected.

The oppositional pull between land and marriage is a fundamental dynamic in male-female interaction. To counter his wife's longing for the land, a husband must continue to grow in knowledge and skill so that the attraction she feels for him flourishes. Most men do succeed in settling young wives in another country, but sometimes the husbands fail and are obliged to take up residence in the wife's country.

The pattern inherent in the Aboriginal marriage depicted in this Dreamtime story is similar to that described in the Greek myth of Psyche and Eros, in which Psyche represents the sacrificial characteristic of womanhood. Both myths acknowledge that the marriage arrangement is, for the woman, a totally different experience than it is for the man. Through marriage a man achieves heightened recognition and importance in society, as well as gaining a wife. For a woman, marriage represents a great loss which, mythically, is the archetypal death of a previous state of being.[17] The death of Psyche represents the loss of feminine independence and purity, which in the Aboriginal myth is symbolized by the loss of the homeland of her girlhood.

The relationship between land and sexuality is carried throughout the Aboriginal social order. Certain areas are designated male regions, where women are forbidden to go, and female country, where men are forbidden. There is a distinct separation of the sexes that is balanced by a complementary integration. The campsite of an Aboriginal band is divided into a women's camp and a men's camp, as well as a general camp in which husband and wife usually live together. During certain ritual occasions and certain phases in their lives, tribal law requires that they live in either the men's or the women's camp.[18] Association and relational living situations partake of a complex fluidity within the seemingly simple camp structure.

The tradition of Christian monogamy, now institutionalized as civil law in countries throughout the world, is shrouded in puritanical, almost fiendish attitudes. The early fathers of the Church, obsessed with celibacy as an ideal and with spiritual development divorced from acknowledgment of the flesh, saw women as the instrument of temptation for men and looked down on marriage as a lesser state. Exhorted to emulate Mary, the Virgin Mother, women were pushed into a passive role in religion and in marriage, which by the Middle Ages had developed into a socially accepted vehicle for the enslavement of women. Physical punishment of wives was publicly encouraged. The fifteenth-century Fra Cherubino of Rome wrote in his *Rules of Marriage*, "and if she doesn't work . . . take up a stick and beat her soundly, for it is better to punish the body and correct the soul than to damage the soul and spare the body. . . ."[19] This attitude became entrenched in European society. Through the nineteenth century, British law decreed that acts of assault, illegal if committed against a stranger, were acceptable in the eyes of the law when committed by a husband against his wife. Over the centuries, married women were considered the property of their husbands, little different than livestock. Through the middle of the twentieth century, American law upheld the legality of wife beating: "The legal system cannot invade the sanctity of the home in order to stop husbandly violence."[20] Even now the law may refuse to recognize a woman's right to protection in her own home.

Our society is still attempting to redress the inherent imbalances and distortions in the Western monogamous marital system. Feminists and other advocates for women's rights are bringing about change, but progress is slow. For many women and men, modern marriage remains a frustrating and unsatisfactory social institution, marred by high divorce rates, bitter child custody battles, infidelity, domestic violence, child abuse, and high rates of impotency and sexual dysfunction—to say nothing of boredom, isolation, and social sterility. Certainly some of the basic concepts underlying Aboriginal marriage, which was able to combine social stability with wide individual flexibility, are worthy of examination as models for transforming our structuring of male-female relationships.

The Personal Face of Love

Extramarital and premarital sexuality are an integral part of the marriage system. The kinship system designates relationship categories that are favored for romantic or "sweetheart" relationships. Most frequently, a man pursues romance with the daughters of those classified as (skin) sisters. The kinship system clearly disqualifies other relationships as incestuous, particularly between a man and his mother-in-law. Although they are accepted and even encouraged, extramarital relations must be carried out in great secrecy—no easy task in the close-knit fabric of Aboriginal society. The requirement of strict secrecy supports apparent marital stability while intensifying the sense of adventure associated with romantic liaisons. It also forces lovers to exercise their extrasensory abilities in communicating with one another. Dreaming of illicit pleasure intensifies the power of psychic projections; romance thus serves as

221

an excellent training ground for developing psychic and extrasensory skills.

The mind invariably projects the content of repressed complexes in the unconscious onto the external world. Making the projecting process conscious, and directing, focusing, and strengthening the associated energies, can affect the natural course of events. The highly charged fantasies that lovers exchange together with the risks they take in contacting each other produce an atmospheric energy that the Aborigines refer to as "love magic."

The institution of male polygamy sets the stage for romantic adventure. An older initiated man with many wives may sleep with his wives in a spiral around him. If one of his young wives is caught up in a passing affair, she may vie for a sleeping position away from her husband so that she can slip off more easily to meet her lover. Camp gossip usually

centers around sweetheart affairs, and they are often the cause of shouting matches and name calling.[21]

Illicit affairs are also an inspiration for Aboriginal songs, many of which emphasize erotic play and are designed to stimulate erotic behavior. Other songs tell of men and women giving secret signals to their desired partners through a magical power called *Djarada*. In one song, a man prepares a bunch of feathers (which are magnetically sensitive) from the throat of an emu. The man throws the feathers on a fire and sings over them as they smolder. The force of the *Djarada* singing wafts the smell of the singed feathers toward the man's sweetheart, and the force magically enters her vagina and tickles her. Aroused, she immediately goes out into the bush and joins him, and they play together. The psychic projection described by the song is similar to the physical property known as sympathetic vibration: when struck, a string tuned to

FIGURE 119
Sexuality finds expression in a variety of groups and circumstances, both in a ritual context and in personal life. Gusty, raunchy, vivacious spirits of nature, known as the Mimi Spirits, taught sexuality to the Aborigines in all its diverse forms.

223

middle C in one piano causes the middle C string on another piano, perhaps in another room, to begin to vibrate. The singer imagines his lover's vagina in such a way that the vibration of his fantasy physically affects the woman's sensations. The smoke of the burned feathers serves as the vehicle that transports this psychic projection. Another song presents a different form of *Djarada* love magic, or the projecting of a psychic energy:

> A man leaves the camp in search of the place where the girl he desires has defecated. Finding it, he sings a *Djarada* song while putting a stick into the middle of it and moving it up and down to signify coition. Then he partially defaces her footmarks, rubbing out the imprint of toe and sole and leaving only the heel. Facing in the direction opposite the way her original tracks were leading, he superimposes his own footprint, leaving her heel so that it appears to be joined to his front foot. Later, when the *Djarada* power has had time to work, the girl sees the singer, and makes a sign that she will meet him in the seclusion of the nearby bushes.[22]

Contemporary researchers are developing a theoretical basis for understanding how the processes of mind and matter interact and reestablishing that bodily products such as blood, hair, and feces retain the vibrational essence of the person or organism that produced them. Such diverse fields as quantum physics, biophysics, parapsychology, hypnotherapy, and medicine provide a conceptual ground for reevaluating the mind-body relationship (see Figure 179 on page 347). In recent decades a number of alternative health therapies, such as radionics, homeopathy, acupuncture, and polarity, have been renamed "energy medicine"; clinical research in these fields often verifies the direct effect of psychic energy on the physical.[23]

Ideally, romantic liaisons in Aboriginal society are short-lived and do not interfere with marriage, although occasionally they can. In some cases the couple may attempt to elope, which can entail great risks, such as punishment from angry relatives or malevolent sorcery directed at the couple by her husband or his kin. Some elopements do succeed, usually after much turmoil and controversy. The abandoned husband may eventually relinquish his wife if he is compensated in some way by the other man and his family. The elopement is gradually recognized as a marriage after the necessary adjustments are made to the kinship system. If the eloping partners have an unacceptable kin relationship, they risk severe physical punishment, even death.

Divorce is rare, but when called for, it is accomplished in a simple ceremony. For example, if a woman is terribly unhappy in her bestowed marriage or if the husband is excessively cruel to her, her family may intervene. Her elder brother presents the husband with a small braided strand of her hair and requests the release of his sister. If the husband cuts the strand of hair the divorce is effective, but if he keeps the strand intact, more deliberations and gifts may be required to dissolve the marriage.

Occasionally, betrothed couples who are impatient for the male's initiatic commitments to be completed engage in premarital sexual affairs. These affairs are accepted as long as the man fulfills his commitment of providing the girl and her family with food.[24] The practice of a young man contributing to the nourishment of his wife from her very early childhood is referred to as "growing a wife." This custom underscores the fact that the parental relationship is not primary. The sexual and marital bond, maintained from early life, carries rights and responsibilities and a sustained life-long involvement.

From all that has been observed of early Aboriginal life, extramarital relationships seem to have added a special dimension of excitement and pleasure, provided scope for individual choice and attraction, and given opportunities to exercise the telepathic aspects of love magic and psychic projection.

The Ritual Face
of Love

The basis of ritual eroticism in Aboriginal culture is the union of the human life force with the vital energy that permeates all of nature. The

FIGURE 120
Spirit women running. From a bark painting in Arnhem Land, Northern Territory. This image captures the spirit of the lusty, free, joyful sexuality of Aboriginal women.

225

forms of the natural world—trees, soil, rocks, clouds, and rain—are for the Aborigines interrelated with the forms and processes of human bodies and minds through actual exchanges of energy.

Erotic love poems describing the monsoon-related fertility rituals in Arnhem Land weave together the human psyche with the psychic content of the living universe. These poems depict a succession of ceremonial rites that culminate in ritual copulation among the palm trees. The duration between seasonal rains, so important for these tribes, is measured by the passage of menstrual cycles. Ritual intercourse is performed with young girls who menstruate during the monsoon—preferably virgins whose first menstruation coincides with the life-giving rains—to capture and reinforce the rains' power.

The monsoon ritual begins just as the clouds accumulate, before the monsoon. To the Aborigines the smell of the flowing blood and sperm enhances the power of the feminine clouds to attract the phallic, fecundating, lightning snake, provoking the life-giving outpouring of the monsoonal rain. The association of smell with the spiritual world is basic also to the mystery traditions of India and Egypt. The nose has direct neural connections with the powerful pituitary and pineal glands. Like animals, which have extraordinary olfactory sensitivity, our unconscious reactions to odors determine many of our actions and decisions.

Fertility rituals require a relaxing of the collective consciousness so that people may experience the vital identity between natural processes and those of the human body. These rituals are therefore preceded by collective rituals, such as the fire ceremony, which incite individual and tribal consciousness to expand beyond the boundaries of the perceivable world. These ceremonies continued for many days, bursting the conventions and patterns dominating ordinary life. The ceremony culminates around huge poles wrapped with combustible palms, which are ignited so that a scorching shower of sparks falls over the dancers as they move to and fro in wild abandon.

During these ceremonies, the strictly observed customs and taboos of everyday life are overturned. In one ritual of the fire ceremony, a man might break the strict avoidance pattern with his mother-in-law by copulating publicly with her, even though he is normally forbidden to speak to her or even look in her direction. In other ecstatic rituals men imitate copulation with each other in dance, and women, using a digging stick or fighting club as a phallus, mimic copulation or sodomy with the men. The group obtains release from the strictures of ordinary social behavior by turning the everyday world upside down and allowing the human psyche to merge with the inner world of nature. In this frenzied transition from the world of human society to the metaphysical, people become attuned with the world of the uninhibited Dreamtime Creators.[25]

FIGURE 121 →
Fire Ceremony, Central Australia. In Aboriginal ceremonies of ecstatic abandonment, the restrictions of the social order are temporarily ignored.

226

Although the Aborigines traditionally reject any form of utilitarian or domestic architecture, the tribes in Arnhem Land build huts raised on poles for ritual sexual practices: the poles represent the phallus, and the leafy interior of the hut is the womb. This same tradition is also found among the ancient Shivites of India and in ancient Egypt, where the phallus of Osiris functioned as the pillar of the temple. Aboriginal ritual huts are considered the oldest form of the entire tradition of temple building.[26]

A condensed version of an Aboriginal erotic song cycle, which describes the ritual evocation of the monsoonal rains, is reproduced here. It describes how the dance and ritual copulation begins within the huts and concludes in an ecstatic frenzy on the earth, among the cabbage palms.

Within those huts, at the wide expanse of water
They are always there, at the billabong edged with bamboo
Making them as they sit on the floor at the open doorways
They are always there at the wide expanse of water, at the place
 of Standing Clouds, the place of the Sea Eagle,
The place of Coloured Reflections, where the western clouds
 arise, towards Milingimbi.

"I am making my sea-eagle nest float in the rising waters of the
 billabong.
I am making it, and later the lightning will play on its roof and
 on me inside,
For its tongue flickers along the horizon, and thunder rolls along
 the bottom of the clouds,
I am preparing for you, clouds massing along the horizon: using
 my posts, my forked sticks and my rails.

They dance invoking the rising western clouds
They dance, calling the invocations
We saw their chests heave, as they called the invocations
Branches tossed aside and flung back.
The voice of the wind calls the open water,
Rain streams down their chests, and the wind flings it away:
Cold west wind, flinging away the branches.
It is our wind that we feel, the cold west wind!
Retracting our penises and calling the names of the country.

Hear the sound of their buttocks, the men moving their penises
For these beautiful girls, of the western tribes
And the penis becomes erect, as their buttocks move
They are always there at the place of Standing Clouds, of the
 rising western clouds,
Pushed on to their backs, lying down among the cabbage palm
 foliage.

Semen flowing from them into the young girls
For they are always there, moving their buttocks.
They are always there, at the wide expanse of water
Ejaculating, among the cabbage palm foliage.

Blood is running down from the men's penises,
Blood running down from the young girls, like blood from a
    speared kangaroo
Running down among the cabbage palm foliage
Blood that is sacred, running down from the young girl's uterus:
Flowing like water, from the young girls of the western tribes.

Thunder rolls along the bottom of the clouds, at the expanse of
    water
Thunder shaking the clouds, and the Lightning Snake flashing
    through them
Large Snake, at the billabong edged with bamboo—its belly, its
    skin and its back!
Thunder and lightning over the camps, at the wide expanse of
    water
The tongues of the Lightning Snake flicker and twist, one to the
    other
They flash among the foliage of the cabbage palms
Lightning flashes through the clouds, with the flickering tongues
    of the Snake.
It is always there, at the wide expanse of the water, at the place
    of the Sacred Tree.

Water flows from among the cabbage palm foliage,
Rain water flowing, foaming and white
Flowing down from the roots of the cabbage palms
Sacred water, foaming, spreading across the billabong.
Rain water flowing down, banking up with foam,
Sound of running water among the cabbage palms.[27]

Aboriginal ritual sexuality, whose dynamism is so boundless that it
excites and vitalizes all of nature, is based on a love for the earth and
earthly life. It is not a love instigated by exploitative desire, conserva-
tionist zeal, or environmental piety. It is a love for the earth that expands
from sexual passion, which is generated through man's lust for woman,
the living presence and symbolic image of the earth. Likewise, woman's
lust for man is generated through her yearning to be connected with the
archetypal Dreamtime, or the metaphysical.

Ritual sexuality is used not only to generate interchange and harmony
between humans and nature but also to show reciprocity and peace
among diverse tribes. An example of this type of ritual is what anthropologists call "wife lending." Men are often separated from their wives
or out of contact with women for long periods because of the travel

demanded by hunting and the religious duty of maintaining many distant sacred sites. When a hunting band encounters the campsite of another tribe, the ritual practice of wife lending is utilized to promote goodwill and a sense of generosity between the two groups. This ritual minimizes the possibility that a band of hunters may raid and pillage a settled campsite. Out of respect, the wandering band approaches and waits at a distance from the campsite so they can be clearly seen. The unmarried hunters and men who have been separated from their wives for a particularly long time lie down on their backs on the earth. At sunset, or just before nightfall, the husbands of the host tribe send out some of their wives, who approach the prostrate visitors and lie on top of them, staring into their eyes.[28] Aboriginal women have no opportunity to decline ritual copulation, which, aside from the practical aspect of forestalling raids, contains a sacred obligation, meaning, and purpose.

A similar image is found in Hindu mythology in the description of the copulation of the primal male and female archetypes. Paraviti, the eternal feminine, sits astride the male principle Shiva and relentlessly stares into his eyes during the copulation that generates the Universe. The woman, positioned on top of the visiting male hunter, captivates his upward gaze with the peace, pleasure, and harmony of the world reflected in her glistening, surrendering eyes.

The role of ritual prostitute is recognized and respected equally with the other spiritual and physical manifestations of the Universal Feminine, virgin, mother, and wife. In Aboriginal culture, as in others, the woman who serves as ritual prostitute reenacts the archetypal union of the male and female principles; she engages in copulation not for personal fulfillment but to allow the Universal Feminine to flow through her to the man and to all of creation.

Aboriginal men are intensely possessive and protective of their wives, but the ancestral law obliges them to condone rituals that allow women to enter into the anonymous, open, unencumbered sexuality of the ritual prostitute. As in the bestowal of women for marriage, men have the formal prerogative of lending their wives as a gesture of tribal harmony. In return, women can express the full spectrum of female eroticism on these infrequent occasions of anonymous sexuality. The roles of wife and mother do not permanently restrict a woman's expression of the archetypal roles of ritual virgin (as in the monsoon ceremonies) or the ritual prostitute (as in the lending or fire ceremony).

The effectiveness of the Aboriginal marital, extramarital, and ritual sexuality speaks for itself. Among early-contact tribes there was very little evidence of wife-beating, very few illicit marriages, and no evidence of prostitution for pay, female sterility, or homosexuality. Female homosexuality did not exist, although women typically spent much time together while the males were away hunting and performing rituals. Although women were habitually very intimate and sensual with each other, with a lot of touching and sitting in groups close together, there were no indications of sexual or erotic overtones. There are incidents of ritual male homosexuality among the early-contact tribes, but no authenticated cases of sodomy in everyday life. Masturbation among young boys was treated lightly, usually with a warning from the older men that it would "weaken" them.[29]

Only a few examples of the rich variety of sexual expression in Aboriginal society are discussed here. Nevertheless, they suffice to show that the rituals, customs, and institutions of Aboriginal sexuality, which the people say were given to them at the beginning of time, allow men and women to fulfill subtle, profound psychological needs and maintain fluid yet stable community bonds. Above all, Aboriginal sexuality powerfully involves the individual in the spiritual dimension of themselves and nature.

CHAPTER 12

DREAMTIME AND THE SENSE OF BEING

BORIGINAL INITIATIONS foster an encompassing sense of unity with the metaphysical world. In contrast, our sense of being has grown to be inseparable from, and limited by, our individuality. Our development focuses on personal memories, feelings, and preferences, and our progress is increasingly governed by personal goals and ambitions. We often present ourselves to others in terms of our distinct office, rank, or function within various groups and institutions which are considered of secondary importance. When personal interests are transcended in favor of the group, it is still the individual who is rewarded. Likewise, in deviations from the collective norm, it is the individual who is punished. The individual is the basis for social justice and morality—the entire structure of democracy is (ideally) organized around the protection, betterment, needs, and pursuits of the individual. The concept of the free individual is similar to that of a modern economic system. Both place high value upon autonomous, self-determined motivation, and action, and the right to expand and better one's own interests. A living cell with these characteristics would be diagnosed as cancerous.

The seed of the social sense of individuality was sown in mythic structures such as that of the conquering hero. It found fertile ground in the values and orientations of two major world religions, Buddhism and Christianity. Over time, these religions came to promote individuality by concentrating on personal salvation and enlightenment.

THE ORIGINS OF INDIVIDUALITY

A society's adverse impact on the environment is directly related to the extent to which it encourages the modern Western image of the individual. Exaggerated individualism is inseparably linked to the excessive patterns of materialistic consumption and waste. For example, although the population of America represents approximately 5 percent of the world population, the United States consumes 25 to 30 percent of the world's raw materials. The average white Australian's lifestyle has 60 times the environmental impact of a Third World villager; 17 million Australians have the same impact on the environment as one billion Third World villagers.[1] The idea of an ecological revolution is implausible unless attitudes change toward individuality and the separative ego in Western psychology. Since no other culture has had such a gentle effect on the natural environment as that of the Aborigines, an understanding of their lifestyle and self-awareness can make a vital contribution to our environmental thinking.

Individual is derived from the Latin root *individuus*, meaning divided into parts or fragments, and related to the Latin root *invidia*, meaning to envy or, more precisely, "to look wantonly upon that which is outside one."[2] Where did the worship of individuality begin? Many believe it began with the Industrial Revolution and competition for personal wealth and achievement.

Ancient Hindu texts point much farther back into history, claiming that the teachings of Buddhism set the groundwork for an exaggerated value of individuality.[3] A significant influence on Buddha himself was a teacher of Jainism (an ancient North Indian millenialist religion) named Mahavira (540–468 B.C.). He impressed the young Gautama with the idea that each person possesses a material, individual soul (*jiva*). Every act committed by an individual is believed to produce a karmic coloring of the soul—light colors for virtuous deeds, medium tones for minor offenses, and dark shades for major transgressions. At death the soul's coloration determines whether the person will be reborn as a higher human or even a god or as animals, plants, or the prisoners of hell (these would be the dark-colored souls).[4] The idea that through this personalized soul and its karma the individual extends beyond death into other lifetimes decisively promoted the power and value of individuality. It is now widely accepted that Jain teachers also influenced the early Gnostic Christians, in whose ideas individual karma and the darkening of the soul became mixed with the Judaic idea of sin. In 325 A.D., the Council of Nicea rejected the idea of reincarnation and the transmigration of souls, a tenet of some Christian sects, and replaced it with the idea of a permanent heaven or hell for the individual soul.

Both Buddhism and Christianity discouraged individual metaphysical speculation or any personal involvement with the intermediate spirit realm associated with nature and the earth. Christianity pared back the spiritual content of the universe to the relationship of the individual with a single, transcendental God and his semihuman son, whose teachings

were transmitted solely through an ordained priest of the centralized Church. The institutional forms of Buddhism and Christianity, as well as Islam, have had esoteric mystic sects which avoided the emphasis on individual purity and self-mastery. These include Tibetan tantricism, medieval alchemy, and Sufi dervishes. All of these have maintained some essential elements of ecstatic rites.

The main thrust of Buddhism, however, is on the individual's acquiring the capacity to deny and escape from the transitory, desire-driven world of the physical body through meditation. Buddhist meditation and Christian prayer place the individual at the center of spiritual life. Although the ego is considered the source of evil and suffering, it is nonetheless the center of attention. The monastic and cloistering processes are designed to eliminate worldly contact with society and sensual contact with the external environment and to turn the attention to the individual's inner thoughts and mental activities. Mastery of these activities of mind and perception is considered essential to achieving the ultimate state through meditation. The result of monasticism is that the human world is left to its own illusions and impurities, while the individual seeker establishes an isolated contact with the absolute. The "infolding" process of prayer and meditation is in stark contrast to Aboriginal spirituality which, through ever-deepening perception, opens outward to empathize and identify with every aspect of a living, active world.

Despite the differences between Buddhism and Christianity, many of their side effects are identical. They both abandoned the search for an understanding of life, nature, and the cosmos, at least for the majority of their followers, and forbade rituals in which people could experience a connection with the spirit energy of the dead and the unborn and the forces of nature and the netherworld. Both religions profess contempt for natural, earth-centered, ecstatic rituals and exaggerate the importance of individual morality by emphasizing personal sin and personal salvation. Alan Watts reflected on the implications of these religious beliefs which evolved into modern individualism: "Our skin-encapsulated egos are a most lonely and isolated center of being. It gives rise to alienation, fear, and the need to either dominate or be led."[5]

In both Buddhism and Christianity, the focus of adoration was the individual teacher as much as, or more than, the wisdom of religious doctrines. This furthered the importance of the exemplary ego and self-development as a fundamental religious goal. The ego on a collective level becomes the separate nation-state. In the Christian and Buddhist worlds alike, political entities emerged and assumed God-given rights to extend their separate material powers, just as a monk is free to expand his individual spiritual power. Empire-building and colonialism express the collective expansion of autonomous individual growth. The glorification of the independent rights of nations and individual egos has provided a context for continual war and conflict in Europe and Asia, where these religious philosophies prevail. In contrast, the Aboriginal world view is founded on a sense of self and society that offers a completely different basis for the relationship between humanity and the metaphysical.

SELF AND EARTH—*NGURRA*

Paradoxically, in the Western world people derive their individuality from combinations of collective identities: sex, race, social class, vocation, nationality, or religion. In contrast, the Aboriginal sense of personal identity is derived from only one context, the idea of *place*.[6] In the Pintupi language a place or country is designated *ngurra*. It may seem contradictory that a sense of place is so important for people who move so regularly and rarely camp in the same place twice. The confusion increases when one considers the vast, empty, only moderately contoured continent of Australia. To the casual observer, no other culture seems as impartial to place and location as the Aborigines. A wandering hunting band may at any time of day and for no apparent reason cut a few branches of scrub for a windbreak, shape an indentation in the earth for a fire, and in a matter of minutes create a camp in otherwise wild, unmarked country. Conveniences like a shade tree, a river bank, or a circle of stones rarely seem to influence the selection. The prominent criterion is never to camp in the same place twice and never to camp where another group has done so recently. The Aborigines feel that the earth's energies become fatigued when it supports domestic processes for too long.

The Aborigines make almost no distinction between wilderness and space appropriated for domestic functions. When they set up a domestic place, the Aborigines express the same freedom that typifies their effortless walking stride: while traveling through enormous, sometimes treacherous, expanses, they convey the familiarity and centeredness of being "at home." Yet *ngurra*, the sense of place, is a word of great importance that contains both physical and metaphysical connotations. Unraveling these apparent contradictions reveals a distinct dimension of the Aboriginal world view and sense of identity.

The entire earthly environment is *ngurra*, or "country," "camp," or "place." Places are formed only through the activities of powerful mythic beings. The Ancestors made land formations by making camp and carrying out other activities of daily living. The Aborigines' daily activity of making camp reenacts the same process by which the landscape was formed in the Dreamtime. They believe that in the act of making camp, they again cause the place and surrounding country to come into being.[7]

Thus *ngurra* describes both the physical *place* where they return to share food, dance, and sleep and the metaphysical *act* of "dreaming" the country into existence. The mythic formative events of that place are sung and danced at night by the campfire. Stories about the acts that resulted in the formation of the hills, rocks, water holes, and local animal species are reborn in the swaying, earth-stomping movements of the hunter-gatherers. To the Aborigines, place is inseparable from the original activities that gave it form. Reliving those activities in performance makes *place* inseparable from *meaning*. All experience of place and country is culturalized. Relating to space in this way enables people to establish a home or camp almost anywhere they may be with no sense of dislocation.[8] The question of identity, of *who* I am, is resolved in the Aboriginal consciousness by knowing the full implications of *where* I am.

In demarcating a certain place, the Dreamtime Ancestors deposited a particular potency that stimulates the campers' memory of Dreamtime events to guide their rituals. The Dreamtime stories are the only form of information the Aborigine must commit to memory. All moral codes, spiritual beliefs, and societal obligations are embedded in the Dreamtime stories. The landscape is thus the externalization of cultural memory as well as the memory of tribal and mythic forebears.

The songlines comprise chapters of a Dreamtime "book" of songs, dances, and stories. Each story tells about the formation of a place, and each place tells a story through its topography and subtle energy. This nexus of land and Dreamtime culture is a memory that humanity shares with the earth. With the earth as memory, Aboriginal consciousness is free to focus solely on the power of immediate perception.

Place is also the Aborigines' criterion for judging trust and honesty. They might say, "One's words and thoughts must stand in the same 'place' as one's body; otherwise, the mind is crooked and truth destroyed."[9] A Pittitinjarra man described to an anthropologist what went on in his mind as he gave instructions on the location of a hidden water hole: "My thought travels there and sees things as it goes and comes right back, but spirit and mind stays here with this body . . . they never leave this place." In contrast, Western consciousness is trained to coexist with a mind split off from the body, oblivious to place, and engrossed in concerns, fears, fantasies, generalities, and other abstracted mental activities.

As the Aborigines pass through successive initiations, they receive ever-increasing knowledge of the origin, meaning, and potency of places in their surroundings. As they travel and expand their cultural knowledge, memory and the spatial world expand together as an extension of self. An Aboriginal friend told me that in one of his most profound initiations, in a state of deep trance, a tribal elder transmitted to him the experience of his body extending into space so that it encompassed the entirety of his tribal land. The songlines that criss-cross the landscape flowed as his own veins and arteries, the swamplands were his glands, the grass his hair. During the trance, the elder painted his body with the symbols and locations of the water holes, the sacred sites, the centers of animal increase, and all the distinct features of the Dreamtime landscape. This experience, he assured me, was not symbolism but part of a deep sense of identity.[10] Internalized mythic knowledge and its topographical image, painted on their bodies in initiations, are the only graphic maps of their countryside the Aborigines possess.

Before white settlement the continent of Australia was organized into at least 200 different tribal lands, but they had not the slightest external boundary demarcations. Big Bill Neidjie, a Kakadu Aborigine, expressed this sense of country:

> I feel it with my body, with my blood. Feeling all these trees, all this country . . . when the wind blows you can feel it. Same for country . . . you feel it. You can look, but feeling . . . that put you out there in open space.[11]

Each Aborigine knows his country as he knows himself, through his own body and the internalized images of his dreaming places—these *are* his identity. There is no Aboriginal story that does not make reference to places, and land formations are never discussed without reference to their mythological stories.

Due to the mystical interrelationship of these two most profound realms of existence—the physical body and the extended body of the surrounding environment—the notion of possessing country or of land as a separate object has no place in Aboriginal consciousness. There are no words denoting possession in Aboriginal languages. A male Aborigine may speak of "holding" his country, referring to obligations he has inherited for maintaining certain sites, but he never speaks of ownership. Like the human body, the country is considered nonsegmentable. There are distinguishable features such as thigh, abdomen, and chest, but they form integral parts of a continuous living being. An old Aborigine said of the ever-present barbed wire fences in rural Australia, "White man's fences strangle the music of the countryside, just as clothes strangle the music of the body."[12]

The present ecological effort to reestablish a bond between human societies and the natural environment seems superficial compared to the Aborigines' deep identification with nature. For over 100,000 years, this deep connection has prevented Aboriginal culture from exploiting the earth's environment; we must seek to understand this level of identification in transforming our relationship with the earth. Bioregionalism,

237

the practice of relying on resources from one's own region rather than world resources regardless of relative need, is a philosophy that aims at developing people's respect for the particular place where they live. If our irresponsible exploitation of the earth is replaced with a social order in which people again derive their sustenance directly from their surrounding environment, human societies can transcend the obsessive concerns with the individual and again learn to treasure the earth.

SELF IN MOVEMENT

The Aboriginal notion of space and identity is interwoven in a way utterly strange to the Western mentality, as is their concept of movement in relation to space and time. The Dreamtime stories contain, in

addition to moral, spiritual, and psychic understanding, all kinds of practical information. A story may direct a hunting band to places where the lilies bloom, where turtle eggs hatch, or where wild yams ripen. The clan follows the stories from place to place without a calendar. They may visit a site, make camp, perform rituals, and hunt and gather the yield of a particular region, much as we move through a yearly calendar of work punctuated by holidays involving ritual celebration and seasonal foods. The outstanding difference is that the Aborigines move through space, and we move through time. Aboriginal stories, be they about life or the Dreamtime, focus on place descriptions and spatial directions rather than time designations such as *when*, *before*, or *after*. For example, in the course of a journey of a few miles along an approximate 180-degree arc the names of 38 separate spatial directions are marked as sites in a ritual walk at the base of Uluru (Ayer's Rock) in central Australia.[13]

FIGURE 122
Tjitjingalla ceremony, performed by the Aranda on the four evenings of April 27–30, 1901, Alice Springs, Central Australia. The dancers' bodies and faces were decorated with ochre and plant down. Leafy twigs were tied around their ankles. The head-dresses were made of sticks, covered with human hair string and topped with emu feathers.

The Aborigine's deep affinity for the primacy of spatial experience was reiterated thousands of years ago in the Rig Vedas of ancient India.

> Space is greater than fire, for in space are both sun and moon, in it are lightning, stars, and fire. The power of Space; one calls, one hears, one answers; in Space man rejoices and does not rejoice. Man is born in Space, man is born for Space. Achieves Space kingdom, worlds rich in light, unconfined, for striding out bodily and as far as Space reaching, so far will it be granted to him to walk at will.[14]

Aboriginal and western thought share an interdependency of time and space, but our deep yearning and spiritual search for the elusive "present moment" and "eternal life" seems of no consequence to the Aborigine. For the Aborigines, the present moment and eternity have been physicalized as place. One is alive in the moment by being utterly grounded and centered in space.

Life depends on the earth's yield of water and food—this has never changed. The food of the hunter-gatherer is often eaten in the exact place where it is gathered or caught. Not a generalized idea of earth but the combined energies surrounding a particular place have produced the nourishment that sustains life. The hunter regards the energies of a particular place as the highest of gods. Seen from this perspective, agriculture has robbed us of a living, immediate spiritual contact with the earth. As we pick our food from store shelf or garden, our minds project forward so that the food is consumed in time, not in place. None of our attitudes toward nature—not our passionate possession of real estate, not the poetic inspiration that some derive from nature and wilderness, not the growing concern of many for our threatened environment—can replace the depth of spirituality that results from the immediate transferral of a spirit potency from earthly place to physical body. This is what the Aborigines call *ngurra*.

The Aborigines divide existence into three realms: the unborn, the living, and the dead. The realm of the living distinguishes itself through the primacy of meaningful forms in space. In contrast, the realm of the dead exists in the sky, where relationships are primarily temporal. Westerners also have a temporal concept of the sky in that we measure astronomical space in units of light years. The Aborigines believe that the mental, conceptual energy that dominates white civilization circulates like the disembodied dead, through time, rather than space—otherwise how could we tolerate the ugly, polluted state of our spatial milieu? An Aboriginal friend got this point across to me while we were walking down a corridor in a particularly grim Australian government building—one that reeked of bureaucratic sterility. As we entered an office my friend said, "Think for a moment, what are you opening?" "A door," I said, and he chuckled. Then he said, "What's in your hand?" "Just this bunch of papers," I said. "No," he said, "those things are trees. Trees that lived and grew, each with its own particular place on earth. Now they are flat; they have no space and no life. You took the trees away from the place on earth where they lived, but in return the trees have locked you up in little compartments of time, where you sit and tremble with fear for survival and mistake that trembling for the pulse of life itself. White man's system will be enclosed in the realm of the dead as long as you do not feel the difference between a door, which means survival, and a tree, which means life."[15]

Aerospace technology, international travel, industrialization, worldwide electronic communication, and mass media have flattened the contours of cultural expression so that each place is becoming more like every other place in the world. The value of a place is measured by how long it takes to get there. Time is the dynamic that drives all of modern life as space becomes increasingly dead, fixed in architectural structures, quantified and imprisoned in the brittle boundaries of ownership.

For the Aborigines, time is absorbed in the cycles of birth, growth, decline, and renewal of the living creatures that inhabit a particular place. The eternal aspect of time, the Dreaming, is also absorbed in the actuality of space and is identified with the untouched enduring formations of earth.

For Western man, the destruction of wilderness and the extension of fixed or structured space is the foundation of our time-measured civilization and personal identity. Both wilderness and the unconscious threaten the bases of our sense of self and our culture. For the Aborigines, the loss of wilderness is not only the loss of identity, but also the loss of contact with the eternal truth and meaning of existence. Spirituality depends on intensity of life in the land, and when it declines so too does the spiritual potential and depth of humanity. The Aborigines move across an almost imperceptible boundary between campsite and wilderness in the same way that they move between the conscious and the unconscious—between the physical world and the eternal Dreaming. They accomplish these transits with the ease and joy of a walk in a wild country seething with life and meaning, or a dance in shadowed firelight vivified with mythology.

241

CHAPTER 13

THE ABORIGINAL KINSHIP SYSTEM

THE COMPLEXITY of the Aboriginal kinship system emphasizes how the individual is integrated into his or her surroundings, social as well as natural. The network of kin relations provides all Aborigines with support and responsibilities, much as their relationship with the earth does. In our system, individual awareness is distinct from collective involvements, sometimes even in conflict with them. In the Aboriginal world view the individual and the collective are the contracted and expanded form of one continuous being.

KINSHIP AND SOCIAL ORDER

Claude Levi-Strauss once remarked that mathematically representing the structure of an Aboriginal kinship system would demand the most complex nonlinear formulas and equations—and even they might not suffice![1] Much has been written describing the intricate overlapping patterns, networks, and transformations that weave together Aboriginal society from generation to generation.[2] Only a very simplified, structural explanation is within the scope of this book.

The intricacy of the Aboriginal kinship system contradicts the idea that the Aboriginal mentality is free of abstract categories. Anthropologists and mathematicians describe kinship in terms of categories, but for the Aborigines kinship is not an abstraction. From their earliest memories, they experience kinship through close intimate relationships with living people. The kinship system in most regions is an elaborate pattern of interlocking categories based on nearly 20 different relationship terms: mother, father, elder sister, elder brother, younger sister, grandmother, and so on. The major difference between Aboriginal kinship and the European family system is that each Aboriginal kin term includes not only blood relatives but categorical or "skin" relations. For example, a man recognizes as his father not only his biological father but also his father's brothers, while he refers to his father's sisters as aunt. A child also recognizes his mother's sisters as mother, while he refers to his mother's brothers as uncle. Classifying more people in each category without reducing the number of categories expands family genealogies so that almost every associate in daily life is a kin relation. The average European-style family forms a family group of 30 to 50 people, including distant cousins; the Aboriginal kinship system generates groups of 300 to 500.[3]

The Aborigines believe that their kinship categories were established in the Dreamtime. As a young person grows and comes in contact with more distant tribes, he is constantly filling in these categories with an ever-extending family. Every kin relationship carries specific obligations, rights, and respect that were also predetermined in the Dreamtime. Some of these responsibilities can be economic (providing food), ritual (performing rites at a relative's father's burial site), or educational (a grandmother instructing a child about sexuality or menstruation). Other responsibilities are purely social, such as the obligations to attend a relative during illness or to participate in initiation ceremonies. Another class of kinship relationships have a purely spiritual nature and involve such duties as passing on a sacred language or signs to a younger group member as he or she reaches a certain stage of initiation. Just as every member of Aboriginal society is given self-sufficiency in gathering food as a cultural birthright, so too are all social and relational requirements given at birth through the kinship system. The personal, intimate interaction outlined by the kinship system is set in larger group structure called the tribe or language group. Within the tribe is the smaller ceremonial group known as the clan, and within that, a smaller hunting or camping group called a band.

The predetermination of life relationships found in the kinship system can be seen as a symbolic reflection of organization in the natural world. All living substance is made up of four simple elements, hydrogen, carbon, nitrogen, and oxygen, that combine according to predetermined laws of chemistry. Plants grow and express a great diversity of forms, patterns, and substances because the chemical interactions of photosynthesis provide a uniform, stable foundation. Natural processes in general achieve their freedom and diversity because they are based on predetermined laws at the more fundamental levels of organization. In a similar way, Aboriginal individual freedom is based on a set of socially predetermined laws that they believe were laid down at the same time as the laws of nature. Culture and nature mirror each other, as they have from the first day of creation: "The kinship classifications made by Aborigines appear rather to manifest a passion for order that has driven them to try to apply to the whole world a single system."[4]

KINSHIP AND EMOTION

While working with the Pintupi people of the Western Desert, anthropologist Fred Myers discovered that human emotions serve as an invisible organizing energy beneath the intricate structure of the Aboriginal kinship system. Emotions are cultivated in a way that upholds both the spiritual and daily order of the society.

As a principle of collective organization, emotions play a large role in the Aboriginal kinship system. Each of the approximately 20 kin categories falls into one of five types of behavioral patterns, ranging from complete avoidance (mother-in-law/son-in-law) to complete informality, or the so-called joking pattern. The latter is usually shared by grandparents and grandchildren or by a man and his maternal uncle or his nephew (the son of one of his sisters). For a woman the joking pattern applies to a paternal aunt or a niece. Informal or joking behavior includes dirty jokes, gossip, sarcastic snipes (especially aimed at one's avoidance relations—the original mother-in-law jokes), complaining, self-pity, jostling, giggling, and all sorts of letting-our-hair-down nonsense. The sharing of this level of communication establishes an intimate, unpretentious bond across several generations, exposing the younger generation to mature, light-hearted insights into the reality of human behavior. The relationship between son-in-law and mother-in-law typifies the classification of complete avoidance. Members of this relationship category can never converse, be in each other's presence, or look in each other's direction, even at a great distance.[5]

Between the behavioral polarities of complete avoidance and joking are three graduated categories: restraint, moderation, and lack of restraint. The restraint mode includes, for a male, his biological mother, who moves from a pattern of complete informality to restraint immediately after the boy's initiation. Restraint is also practiced between males and any female kin relation who is an eligible marriage partner prior to marriage, and between males and their skin fathers (the biological father's brothers), who are eligible to perform the cutting in their circumcision rites. Following initiation and marriage, both of these relationships change to a lack of restraint pattern. Generally, deep enduring relationships develop between a man and his wives, and between him and his uncles or skin fathers.[6] Throughout life, the relationship between elder brothers and their sisters and elder sisters and their brothers fall into the highly restrained pattern.

Strict social regulations are a means of limiting incestuous relationships. The kinship system works to eliminate unhealthy attachments to family ties (brothers to sisters, parents to children) at the same time that it permits continuing interaction of family members into adulthood, as part of clans and hunting groups.[7] The kinship patterns reflect a keen awareness of the psychological problems associated with incestuous attractions: not only the physical expression of incest but its psychological forms can disturb the sexual energies on which both biological and spiritual creation depend.

KIN BEHAVIORAL PATTERNS (MALE EGO)

Avoidance	Restraint	Moderation	Lack of Restraint	Joking
Wife's Mother, "Wife's Mother"				
	Elder Brother			
	Elder Sister			
	"Female Cousin"			
	Daughter, "Daughter"			
	Mother, "Mother"			
	Father's Sister, "Father's Sister"			
	Wife's Brother			
	←— Father, "Father" —————→			
	←— Son, Sister's Son —————→			
		"Elder Brother"		
		"Younger Brother," "Younger Sister"		
		"Elder Sister"		
		Mother's Brother, Wife's Father		
		"Sister's Daughter," "Son's Wife"		
		Mother's Brother's Son, "Mother's Brother's Son"		
		Father's Sister's Son, "Father's Sister's Son"		
		Unrelated Female		
		←—— "Wife's Brother" ————→		
			Wife, "Wife"	
	←—————— "Sister's Son" —————————→			
	←—————— "Mother's Brother" —————————→			
			Father's Father, "Father's Father";	
			Son's Son, "Son's Son"; etc.	
			"Mother's Mother";	
			Daughter's Daughter,	
			"Daughter's Daughter"; etc.	
				Unrelated Male
				Male Cousin

FIGURE 123

The five major kin behavior modes and the distribution of the kinship categories. Arrows indicate the approximate range of behavioral variations occurring within these categories. Note that some of the patterns of behavior change as a result of the initiation and marriage of an individual. The names in quotation marks, such as "Wife's Mother," signify the classificatory kin, whereas those without (Wife's Mother) signify the blood relationship. Many of these relationship patterns apply equally to women. For example, all the heterosexual relationships are mutually transposable, such as brothers with sisters. Relationships such as Wife's Brother, in the case of a female, becomes Husband's Brother; also, for the female, the Mother's Brother would be parallel to the Father's Sister, Sister's Daughter would become Brother's Son, and so on. There are, of course, many variations depending on tribes. For example, with the Tiwi people the brother-sister relationship is one of avoidance, rather than moderation as shown in the figure. (After Tonkinson)

Aboriginal socialization and regulation of human emotions has even more profound implications. The kinship system designates a relative to whom one can turn to share emotion. If one is grieving or suffering a severe embarrassment, there is always a relative one can rely on to share dramatically in the expression and release of that emotion. Emotions are not treated as subjective and individual, as they are in Western society. Emotions are not personal or private but universal, common to all cultures and times, and perhaps the most enduring and immediate shared form of communication. The Aborigines view emotions as embedded in a dramatic social process. The sense of being trapped alone with our subjective feelings is a result of Western society's focus on individuality, and it contributes to our sense of alienation from others. We conceive of emotion as an aspect of our internal life to conceal or to use as an agent of personal expression. In contrast, for Aborigines sharing emotion is an empathetic relational activity by which one enters into an identity with others and with society as a whole.

Emotional energy and its dramatization is the basis for childhood education in Aboriginal society. What might be called the "emotional nakedness" of the Aborigines promotes psychic identity with the entire society rather than fortifying a subjective sense of individuality.

Aborigines believe in a complete concordance of the physical and psychic worlds. In the physical universe the nuclear expansive or explosive forces balance the isolating constriction of gravity. Emotions act in the psychic universe much as nuclear forces do in the physical: they expand, radiate, promote interaction. By exaggerating and strengthening the presence of emotions in social life, tribal people maintain active relationships with as many as 500 or more people. They radiate emotional energy beyond human relationship into communication with plants, animals, and the earth itself.

COMPASSION—THE EMOTIONAL GROUND OF BEING

The first emotion the Aborigines cultivate is compassion. For them, the feeling of compassion extends beyond a moral sense; it is the summation of their sympathetic and empathetic sensitivity to the surrounding world. Sympathy is feeling accord with the emotions of another, whereas empathy is the power to project one's being into the emotional state of another or to allow another state to enter and be felt. Compassion is sympathy or empathy accompanied by a desire to help alleviate the plight of another. From compassion flows a group of emotions called public or social emotions. The public emotions are divided into two modes. The first comprises sorrow, grief, and nostalgia, which are limited by the emotion of revenge; the second consists of modesty and respect, which are contained and enforced by ridicule and the sense of embarrassment.[8]

The teaching of compassion begins from the first moment an infant grabs some food or object and brings it to its mouth. The mother or any other relative, usually female, repeatedly uses these moments to plead with the child to share what it has with her. Of course, the mother never takes away what the child possesses or denies it anything it desires, but she finds many opportunities to pretend to be in great need of the infant's generosity.[9] Reinforcing this constant dramatization by the mother is an open society in which people actively share everything with each other. Whenever a weak, ill, or harmless person or creature passes the child's path, the mother fusses over it and showers it with attention, even if it is a scraggly lizard: "Poor thing," the mother declares with great, heartfelt emotion.[10] Food is never denied to anyone or any creature that is hungry. The child experiences a world in which compassion and pity are dramatically directed toward the temporarily less fortunate. The constant maternal dramatization of compassion in the early years orients a child's emotions toward empathy, support, warmth, and generosity.

It is not important that these dramatizations be "sincere." For Aboriginal sensibilities, emotional energy pervades a world that is saturated with the emotive energy of the Dreamtime Ancestors. Projecting emotions, even through pretense, evokes a flow of energy that catches "the heart" of both the viewer and the actor and creates an intensity and harmony required for that moment to live. Any adult who does not show emotional empathy with the surrounding world is thought to "be like a rock" and is considered to be "not quite human."[11]

An incident that demonstrates the Aboriginal sense of compassion occurred during Australia's bicentennial celebration. The Australian government had the bad taste to commemorate the landing of Captain Cook in 1788 rather than the ratification of the national constitution, which occurred in 1901. Cook's landing was, of course, not the birth of a nation but rather the beginning of the genocide of the Aboriginal people, and Aboriginal leaders protested the selection. The Australian government sponsored an elaborate charade in which a fleet of ships identical to those sailed by Captain Cook left London in time to arrive on Australia's shores on the 200th anniversary of Cook's landing. The Aboriginal community organized a day of mourning, attended by Aborigines from all over Australia, to protest this vulgar display of support for colonialism. An Aboriginal friend of mine who was attempting to elicit Aboriginal community support against this celebration stood with a group of elders on the headlands overlooking Botany Bay, where one of the fleet would pass to reenact the initial "discovery of Australia."

My friend said half-jokingly to the old Aboriginal men, "You have boys in your community who are great swimmers. They should sneak out there and attach some explosives to the side of the ship and blow a hole in it."

One old Aboriginal man shook his head in response, "No, we can't do that, 'cause then we would have to swim out there and save all those white gubbas from drowning."

My friend sighed, "Those are the very attitudes that allowed the whites to rape and destroy our people, our land, and our culture. And those are the attitudes we have to lose."

The old man smiled and said, "But if I lost those feelings I wouldn't be Aboriginal."[12]

I shudder to think how this compassionate, humane, and dignified culture was ripped apart by the blind greed and punishing desperation of a colonialist convict mentality, and how the ancient, open spiritual freedom of the Australian continent was converted into a penal colony.

MODESTY, RESPECT, AND EMBARRASSMENT

FIGURE 124
The Aboriginal personal ritual for expelling anger reflects the mythic figure of the dark and destructive feminine power, known in India as Kali, who released her rage in a similar way.

In the Pintupi language, the cultivation of a shared identity is called *walytja*. Its purpose is to extend to the entire world the child's concern and involvement with its kin. The child's elders discourage the expression of any emotion that detracts from the sense of the world as an extension of the self, such as greed, jealousy, selfishness, and envy. The means of preventing the display of these emotions is community singing and dancing. Whenever negative emotions begin to discolor the collective atmosphere, ceremonies are immediately called for. Song and dance function as important regulators of social harmony. Everyone is encouraged to set aside private pleasures and hostilities for a time of community singing and dancing known as a *corroborree*.[13]

Socially negative emotions themselves are not repressed, but their public display is discouraged. Antisocial emotions such as anger can be expressed either privately with the appropriate kin or in solitary rituals. An anthropologist described an Aboriginal woman who became obsessed with anger and jealousy. She went off by herself, tied her ankle to the base of a tree with a cord, and went into a howling, flailing fury for days. She flung her own feces, drank her own urine, and pounded the earth until the emotion was expelled.[14]

Aborigines present to their society only "public" emotions; the public display of "private" emotions such as animosity, ambition, or egotism is considered vulgar and unrefined. Everyone has full and clearly defined emotional roles to play that are determined by the kinship system. Anyone who fails to carry out his or her role in the drama of emotions destroys the theater of daily social life. If egotistic concerns distract someone from the emotional relationships that people must provide for one another, that person is treated like an actor who has forgotten the lines. The negligent performer is then severely embarrassed and ashamed.

Social situations that normally accentuate ego-centered roles are handled with great care to avoid the embarrassment associated with publicly revealing private feelings. For example, no Aborigine would ever carve a sacred object or even complete a body painting alone without requesting the participation of another tribal member, to avoid the appearance of personally identifying with the work of art. If a situation arises in which one person must address a group, the person does so only after many self-effacing apologies. People who make too much of themselves or take themselves too seriously incur a great deal of ridicule. Such attitudes prevent the development of any political hierarchy based on individual power or authority. Even the most respected tribal elders speak with authority or take an official stance only by making constant references to Dreamtime stories and the ancient laws they imply. If occasions arise that oblige elders to address a group, they often sit facing the other way or looking down at the ground, giving repeated assurances that "they are only telling a story." Ideally, growth and maturity mark a decline in egocentric behavior and the exposure of "private" feelings.[15]

SORROW, GRIEF, AND REVENGE

Sorrow and grief are also highly dramatized in Aboriginal society. Both men and women wail and lament long after the death of a relative. The tearful demonstrations continue until, as the Aborigines say, "they become empty of grief." Grieving is sometimes accompanied with ritual wounding. Bloodletting, like emotion, is an outpouring of spirit into a larger reality. In the dramatization of sorrow, both spirit and blood escape the body in acknowledgment of the suffering and death that universally befall humankind.

The feeling of sorrow expands from the individual and society to include a relationship to the land. When someone dies, the places of conception, birth, initiation, marriage, and death of the person receive as much respect and attention as the deceased relative. In this way, grieving moves beyond the individual's death and becomes more a catalyst for remembering places and the events and myths associated with those places. The rule in Aboriginal society is to avoid, for a long time, the place where a kin died, until the memory has faded in intensity. Approaching the death site of a recently deceased relative would imply

FIGURE 125
Bound-twine figures,
djondjon, *traditionally placed in a camp deserted after death, both from Western Arnhem Land. Usually, one is placed near a dead person's hut in such a way that the short arm points to where the corpse was placed on a platform, while the long arm indicates the direction taken by the people who have left the camp.*

FIGURE 126
Waramanga man releasing woman from a ban of silence following a death, Tennant Creek, Northern Territory, 1901. After a long period of mourning, when the wife is assured that the spirit of her deceased husband has sufficiently faded from the earth's atmosphere, a kinsman of her husband will offer the heel of his hand for her to bite. At that moment she is released from her vows.

disrespect. Aborigines would say, "I cannot go there or I will become too sorry." During their absence from these sites, the Aborigines dramatically express nostalgia for the features of that countryside.[16] Often, the demonstrations of grief are not spontaneous or authentic, yet they express a continuing relationship that the living have to the dead.

Widowed women also express sorrow publicly by maintaining vows of silence, even after remarriage, for months and sometimes years after the death of a husband. Baldwin Spencer reported a great number of women in each tribe who were observing these vows and busily communicating in sign language.[17] In Indian yoga, vows of silence are believed to instigate rapid inner changes; this aspect of silence would benefit Aboriginal women, who must completely restructure their lives when they move from one marriage to another.

Displays of sorrow are performed not only to express personal loss but to forge an identity with all others who have experienced the same grief. The rule of sorrow and compassion does not apply when a serious crime has been committed against the transcendental values passed on by the Dreaming. Sorrow is then suspended, and avenging or killing the person responsible for the infraction becomes a duty and an honor. Those who violate the Dreamtime Law, say the Aborigines, will be "killed without sorrow."[18]

The Aboriginal attitudes toward emotion create a social and moral basis for society in stark contrast to our own. The differences between the two can perhaps best be summarized by comparing human society to changing views of the human organism. Western societal structure is comparable to the traditional biological concept of the body: it is organized around the brain and central nervous system, and the brain is considered a hierarchal, centralized control system. All the neural and chemical messages either originate or are processed in the brain center and then disseminated to control and maintain the rest of the organism. This concept of the body developed in the late nineteenth and early twentieth centuries, along with centralized systems of power, both socialist and capitalist.

More recently the body has been seen as a self-organizing, self-maintaining integrated whole. New emphasis is placed on the interconnectedness of parts and the self-sustaining, autonomous capacities of each cell and tissue and their symbiotic relationship to each other. Each cell expresses an intelligence that indicates an internal sense of its own identity and meaning within the symphonic play of the whole. This image of an organism is much closer to the order of Aboriginal society.

In Aboriginal tribes, the source of organization is deep within the emotional center of each individual, which the Aborigines locate in the solar plexus. This internalized source of emotive power is directed and modified by the sensitivity to, and knowledge of, one's social and natural surroundings. The organ of this sensitivity, the Aborigines believe, is the ear. Hearing or listening to—not thinking about—the external world is considered the major activity of intelligence and understanding. The verb *hear* is the same as the verb *understand;* in Pintupi language it is *kulininpa.*[19]

The sole authority outside innate feelings and perceptions is the transcendental law of the Dreaming. Arbitrary, external, institutionalized authority, fabricated by men to control other men, has no legitimacy in the Aboriginal world view. The motivational drives and emotive force of individuals do not stem from an aggressive, self-contained, egoistic self; they are internal energies that are immediately objectified and projected outside the self in a play of relatedness with other members of the society. Aboriginal identity is a product of an expanding field of deeply empathetic relationship with the entirety of the living world and the timeless beings who created it.

KINSHIP AND RECIPROCITY

Beyond the kinship conventions, no other law enforcement is required in Aboriginal society. There are no chiefs, kings, or headmen. Tribal elders receive great respect, but they do not have an authoritarian or judicial role. All disputes are resolved by kinship structures of reciprocity. Kinship is a more pervasive and powerful force in Aboriginal Australia than anywhere else in the world.[20] The kinship system of sharing and reciprocal exchange supplants the activity we call trade, replacing it with a complex system of gift-giving dictated by the kin relationships. Gift-giving can include a mixture of bestowal of sexual favors, religious or initiatic services, or meat and vegetables given in exchange for alliances in disputes. All exchange of services and goods can take place in one transaction.

All adults have ongoing commitments to one another. Every service accepted must be repaid, every gift must be compensated in kind. Aborigines can often be seen with hands extended, one palm facing up, the other facing down, moving them up and down in a balancing motion. This signals a sense of balance, or evenness, in an exchange, and on this simple gesture hangs the entire communal life.

An anthropologist once presented an Aboriginal tribal man with a row of nine evenly spaced matches. He removed one from each side and asked the Aborigine to comment on the difference. His response was that there was no difference. The maneuver of removing one from each side was repeated twice, and on each occasion he claimed there was no difference in the configuration. The nine matches were then put back in place and the anthropologist removed one from the right-hand side, at which the tribal man exclaimed, "Everything is different, the balance is gone."[21]

The significance of exchange to Aborigines lies far less in the value of things exchanged than in fulfilling the act of reciprocity itself. These attitudes cannot contrast more with the obsession with quantity afflicting our society. Aboriginal values go beyond holding the quality of things in higher esteem than their quantity; they value the quality of the *interaction* of people involved in exchange.

Everything in Aboriginal society works against the accumulation of personal possessions. Since they live naked and are continually journeying, it is desirable to keep only a few useful tools. In the lifestyle of the Aborigines it is not only desirable but necessary for people to own only what they can carry. The combination of their mobility and their psychology of reciprocity produces unacquisitive, unpossessive, and uncompetitive personalities. Status relates directly to the capacity to take part in reciprocal exchanges. Initiation and other social institutions, such as marriage, allow men greater initiative in making exchanges. The religious life of men, more than women, is devoted to ritual exchange. One group of men may give another carved sacred boards or a dance or ritual song. These may be reciprocated by gifts of spears and boomerangs.[22] The importance of these acts is the renewal of the invisible lines of communication and relationship between groups of men. The invisible reality is of primary importance to the Aboriginal imagination.

Aboriginal society acknowledges that differences and opposing perspectives are fundamental to life. Conflict caused by differences is minimized by the spiritual evocation and tangible demonstration of the principle of reciprocity. All of life is a matter of giving and receiving. Each breath, each morsel of food, each joy and achievement results in a depletion of some other being. The fullness of each gain must be acknowledged and returned in kind. The act of giving and receiving is emphasized ritually, for the harmony of the world depends on it.

Modern society does not use ritualized reciprocity to overcome differences. Instead, we clothe our identity in large group affiliations—race, religion, nation—that we believe have the same goals and acquisitive needs and drives as we do. Within these more powerful group identities, we expand our control and protect our self-interest. Western modes of exchange are geared toward achieving increased advantage over others, both collectively and individually. Clearly this approach has not eliminated differences, only expanded and deepened them, and the conflicts that result grow more and more devastating. The Aboriginal model of ritualized reciprocity as a means of sustaining differences while evoking a sense of unity holds rich potential for elaboration within any future social order.

CONFLICT AND KINSHIP

Violence within the context of the kinship system has an accepted place in Aboriginal life. If exchanges are not reciprocated, quarrels, sorcery, and even killings can occur. Broken commitments are treated very seriously, because if they are allowed to accumulate they threaten the very fabric of the kinship system. Boys are not permitted to fight until they are initiated and married.[23] Fighting and self-defense, like the right to be sexually active, are ideally withheld and conferred only through initiation. For an initiated man, fighting becomes a part of his duties, offered as a service to those for whom he bears responsibility.

INDIVIDUAL DISPUTES

One interesting method of settling private disputes is the "dark argument" procedure observed among the Mardudjara tribes of the Great Central Desert. At night, when the members of the band separate into their campfire groups, the participants in a dispute shout and air their grievances, often standing at a considerable distance from each other. Under the secure cover of darkness each participant shouts, screams, and wails his or her complaints. In the dark, their outpouring of emotion is unrestrained, and the chance that weapons will be thrown is virtually nil. These verbal shouting matches can go on for hours, but generally the participants tire and go to sleep before dawn; most often, by the next day the incident is forgotten.[24]

Sometimes individual disputes stir interfamily or interband conflicts. Quick-tempered outbursts can flare up and lead to blows. Women are often the first to dive into the fray to quell the situation by hanging on to the necks of the men. An enraged man may find himself dragging around three or four screaming, moaning women who want to prevent him from resorting to weapons. He soon forgets his adversary in trying to free himself of the women.[25] The image of aggressive, individualized male power—characterized by the Kung-Fu artist, the all-powerful chief, or the warrior king—cannot be realized in the context of the Aboriginal kinship system, in which the entire community moves against this type of behavior.

On the other hand, men rarely interfere in fights between women, perhaps because women are forbidden, by kin law, to touch any lethal weapons such as the spear or boomerang. Women can arm themselves only with light clubs, but this does not prevent their fights from having great violence and intensity. Without directly intervening, men may gather around the combatants and attempt, through more subtle means, to indirectly diffuse the ferocity of the battle. Far fewer conventions apply to female conflicts, perhaps because Aboriginal women show a remarkable capacity to drop the dispute once the air has been cleared, whereas men seem to carry on vendettas for a long time. Women have been seen relaxed and chatting amiably together, bloodstained from wounds they inflicted on each other that same day.[26]

If grievances and quarrels are such that verbal procedures are not successful, then men can resolve them only through a reciprocal squaring of accounts. For example, if one man spears another, the offender should offer his thigh to be speared by the classificatory brother of the dead or injured man. If the offender for some reason fails in his obligation to be ritually speared, the kinship system then permits a younger brother of the offender to settle the account by offering his own thigh to be speared.[27] This gesture brings an end to the trouble, preventing a revenge attack against the community. The boys' initiatic ritual wounding trains them to expand their threshold of pain and acquire a capacity that can serve as a peacemaking ritual gesture. Aborigines believe that males have as much excess blood in their system as women, who lose it during menstruation. They also believe that the substances produced by an organism that are unnecessary to sustain its own life (excess blood, sperm, and perspiration) are gifts from the ancestral beings and can be sacrificed in rituals to establish a reciprocity between humans and these higher forces. Crossing the pain barrier through ritual scarring leads to practical health advantages in acquiring such skills as self-surgery. An initiated person can remove from his or her own body thorns, spearheads, animal quills, or stingers. The practical aspects are secondary to the main purpose of these initiatic practices, which is to allow one's being to flow out beyond its normal boundaries and to increase one's exchange with both the physical and psychic realms.

DISPUTES AMONG TRIBES

Hunting and gathering necessitates fragmentation into small, somewhat isolated hunting bands who are closely attached to certain localities. It is natural that caution and suspicion sometimes develop among Aboriginal groups that have been isolated. Differences between people are exaggerated by distance and language variations and, combined with habitual isolation, they create the tendency to be distrustful of strangers.[28] When breaches of behavior occur, it is commonplace for a group to scapegoat an outside group, usually one with whom there has been prior conflict. In cases of illness and death there is always a suspicion of sorcery by another group or band. Other offenses that can cause serious quarrels include a member of one group or band eloping with a wife from another band, the theft of a sacred object, the failure to reciprocate adequately in some intergroup exchange, or unjustified revenge or ambush.

The acts of clan revenge are called "feather-foot attacks," and they occur when a group of Aborigines believe that an unforgivable infraction of kinship law has occurred and must be severely punished. The group does not rely on gods, karma, an afterlife, or universal justice to intervene; they take the responsibility for maintaining the Dreamtime Law into their own hands. When the offender's guilt is unquestionable, revenge is relentless. The group who carries out the revenge is chosen according to its kinship relation to the victim. Each member of the group forms brooms out of bird feathers, wrapping them around each ankle so that as they walk, the feathers will erase their footprints. The presence of feather-foot marks in a region signals that an execution is underway. When the fugitive sees such tracks, he knows from tradition that his demise is inevitable. Under these conditions people often die of fright or self-suggestion arising from their own guilt.

FIGURE 127
Aborigines design and craft their implements with meticulous care for detail. Each embellishment has Dreamtime symbolic significance. The renderings, while always adhering to tradition, have definite individual qualities.

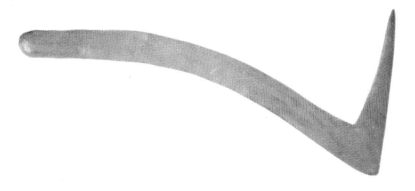

255

FIGURE 128
The Makartta, or feather-foot party, is a band of men whose obligation is to revenge a crime and establish law and order.

FIGURE 129 →
Short decorated stone axe, Milingimbi tribe, 1967, Arnhem Land, Northern Territory. Long-flaked quartzite axe or pick, Warramunga Tribe, circa 1910, Central Australia. These exemplify the beautiful craftsmanship of Aboriginal weapons.

To begin with, the members of the feather foot party *Miringnu* perform magical rites such as going through the enactment of spearing, often drawing an image of their victim on the ground, or moulding clay and giving it the name of the victim. They use a bone from the dead man they plan to avenge to tell them which direction they should take, then set off in snake-like formation to the victim's camp, surrounding it in a traditionally prescribed way before killing him with spears or boomerang.[29]

When the clan of the offender accepts the offender's guilt, it often turns him over to the executioners, thus preventing revenge against the entire group. The aim of all violent punishment in Aboriginal society is for the enemy to suffer the same injury that he or she has inflicted.[30] Most of the crimes that are considered serious are connected with sexual liaisons or spiritual responsibilities; because they directly threaten the kinship-based social order, they are dealt with severely. Crimes that involve property, ownership, or theft of material goods are rarely committed.

As in individual conflicts, reciprocity is the means of evaluating disputes between groups or tribes. Group disputes in particular are not easy to resolve in the stateless society of the Aborigines. There is no chief, no judiciary, no formal institutions, and no judgments that are binding on all parties. For resolving conflicts among clans, the typical method is an open forum. Men and women of the disputing groups assemble in a large circle and openly air their grievances. They are required to present their account to the entire assembly. If no reciprocal compensation is agreed upon, they disband and await a second or even third meeting. This process generally diffuses the tension.

Dialogue between conflicting parties and the statement of grievances stresses an excessive use of kinship names, thereby emphasizing the interpersonal or interfamily connections. The offender addresses his accusers as "uncle" or "brother" or by a totem animal that he shares with them. This contrasts with Western legal systems, which disguise all parties with abstract titles—defendant, witness, state. Aboriginal linguistic strategies usually achieve peaceful settlements because they enable the contenders to acknowledge their relatedness to each other.

For offenses that seem particularly explosive, other measures are used. Sometimes a band may punish the offending member of their group in full view of the offended party. If the offender is a man, his own group may force him to stand in front of the wronged group unarmed except for his shield. He is showered with spears and boomerangs until the offended group is satisfied. If he is particularly agile and is able to fend off the shower of missiles, which many Aboriginal men can do successfully, the offended group closes in on him and wounds him with clubs and jabbing sticks. If at this stage the punishment becomes too harsh, the home group comes to the aid of their guilty member. When the two groups actually begin trading missiles as well as verbal insults, women from both groups intervene and defuse the situation.[31]

The Dreamtime Law states that men may never engage in disputes when they are in men's country or at sacred sites. Men can only enter into conflict and violence in the mitigating presence of women. Women's intervention usually restores calm.[32] Men in our society, however, are encouraged to group together in conventionally all-male arenas—war, competitive sports, and business deals. The possible positive benefits from male-dominated conflicts in modern society are diminished by the unalleviated contentiousness that dominates them. Violent punishment is also forbidden at all sacred sites and requires the presence of women, by whom it is often modified. In some cases, intergroup rifts fail to be

settled by any of the methods described, and the most powerful source of resolution must be employed. This method shifts the sphere of exchange from the physical to the spiritual level and is carried out by men at a sacred site, where physical punishment is prohibited. It is the purest symbolization of the ideal of reciprocity. Robert Tonkinson witnessed this ritual while living among the Mardudjara people:

> Many boomerangs had been thrown and several men on both sides were badly cut, as were several women who had intervened. When calm returned a meeting of all the men decided to settle the dispute for good by means of cutting and exchanging sacred boards by men from the two groups. The following morning men of the two groups went out together and spent two days cutting and shaping two huge wooden boards from a river gum tree, each board measured 20 feet long and 18 inches wide. Once properly shaped and smoothed, they were ceremonially exchanged. Then each group set to work carving intricate patterns on the board given to them by the other group. This task alone took teams of men several weeks to complete. They worked in separate locations but remained within the sacred territory. Once both sides had completed this mammoth task, they reassembled for a common feast. Each group ate seed cakes and meat provided by the other group and they drank coagulated blood that had been extracted from the arms of members of the opposing group which they ingested by kneeling and drinking from small depressions in the ground. Having eaten the food and drunk the blood provided by their adversaries, they re-exchanged the two carved boards and this gesture puts a mark of finality on the conflict. Any attempt to revive this conflict is henceforth unthinkable, because the Dreamtime Beings, who devised this method of settling their disputes, never again fought each other.[33]

The behavior implicit in this ritual exchange of ceremonial boards typifies the values expressed in what are considered the highest ethical teachings, those of Buddhism and Hinduism. The Aborigines shift the arena of confrontation to a higher metaphysical level and replace conflict with cooperation. The same procedure can be found in the Buddhist text the *Dhammapada*, considered one of the most advanced of ethical teachings. What the *Dhammapada* views as the flaws of nature—hatred, jealousy, and anger—can never be appeased if the judgment takes place at the same level as the conflict: "For in truth in this world anger is not appeased by anger, injury is not appeased by injury, hatred is not appeased by hatred. Anger, injury, and hatred are appeased by love alone."[34] The Western prison system ignores this ideal and in so doing inversely verifies it—the modern penal system has proven to be a breeding ground for more crime.

FIGURE 130
Shields from Western Australia. The tribal shield is a symbolic implement: it is used not for warfare but for the ritual settlement of disputes.

The Aboriginal approach differs from the Buddhist in allowing enactment of the physical and psychological levels of conflict before moving to the metaphysical and spiritual. Buddhist monasticism propounds the development of rigorous internalized controls, which keep these emotions from ever arising in the physical world. Newer schools of Western psychology provide techniques for the acting out, or venting, of repressed conflict and aggressiveness, more effectively alleviating these states for many people than the arduous Eastern monastic methods of meditation and self-mastery.

A famous episode in the Hindu text, the *Bhagavad Gita*, closely parallels the Mardudjara rite reported by Tonkinson: Arjuna, the warrior, climbs onto his chariot and enters a great battlefield. A dialogue between Arjuna and the mysterious driver of his horses moves the question of conflict and aggression in human affairs through three stages of examination.

In the first stage, crime, destructiveness, exploitation, and deceit in human affairs must be punished and balanced by human action and not be left to the intervention of the gods, some eternal retribution in hell, or a metaphysical balancing of karma through reincarnation. On this point both the Hindu and the Aboriginal views are the same. Arjuna enters the battle with the idea of righting a wrong and upholding honor— "a tooth for a tooth," "an eye for an eye." This level of ethical awareness is expressed in the Aboriginal rite that permits the wronged to retaliate against the wrongdoer.

As the battle progresses, Arjuna is overwhelmed by the violence and suffering of the conflict, and his mysterious driver leads him through discussion to the second phase of ethical judgment. Arjuna experiences the unity of substance between the victors and the victims, the wronged and the wrongdoers. He weeps, saying, "These are my brothers, they are of the same flesh and blood as I." This phase, which might be called the awareness of unity, has its Aboriginal counterpart in the constant references to kinship in settling a dispute and, later, in the exchange and drinking of blood by adversaries.

At the third stage Arjuna decides to quit the battle, but his driver leads him to see that the structural and metaphysical principles out of which the creation of the world originated require oppositional factors: action/reaction, right/wrong, dark/light, tension/release. Creativity and growth require the manifestation of destruction and decline. The driver of the chariot then reveals himself to be Krishna, the god of creation and love, and he implores Arjuna to see that this earthly conflict is only a reflection of the universal law of creation. He insists that Arjuna discover the higher universal truth underlying the event and begs him to continue in battle. In fighting on, Arjuna represents the mature human conscious-

ness that integrates the physical and the metaphysical, the particular and the universal meaning of existence.[35]

This stage of awareness is represented in the Aboriginal rite by the reciprocal exchange of sacred boards. It acknowledges that the great Creative Ancestors, in addition to the forces of love and creativity, required the devices of war, conflict, and dissonance to maintain balance and harmony in the world. What we observe in Aboriginal society is an embodied ethical order that integrates what our civilization considers the highest type of theoretical ethical discourse.

Another solemn rite used by the Mardudjara men to prevent or atone for conflict is called *barlgalu*, the penis-holding rite. This ceremony may take place in the camp area only if women and children lie down on the ground and cover their faces, since they are not allowed to witness it. It is based on the painful male initiatic practice of subincision, which bonds men to a shared level of spiritual understanding.

> In this simple rite one group's members sit with their heads bowed while the men of the other group walk among them and grasp the hand of one of the seated men, pressing their penis into the palm so that the urethral incision can be felt.[36]

The giving and accepting in this conciliatory gesture signifies a bond of trust and shared sacrifice between the groups; it almost always ensures peace and a lasting settlement. The Aborigines believe that obedience to Dreamtime Laws about dispute and reciprocity guarantees continuing fertility, stability, and security of the entire society.

Aboriginal customs are aimed at preventing the expansion of conflict beyond direct reciprocation. In our culture we have enlarged the sphere of conflict to abstract entities such as nations and states. One way out of the escalating scale of human conflict would be to engage ourselves in the world in such a way that we understand that any unreciprocated gain, injury, or acquisition contributes to the disruption and imbalance of all of life and nature. The entirety of our universe incarnates in each one of us. In the physical world, as in the metaphysical, the ritual gesture of giving and receiving has a cosmic significance far surpassing any legal or moral connotations.

CHAPTER 14

DREAM, EARTH, AND IDENTITY

Once upon a time the whole country was flat. There were no hills at all. There was a buck kangaroo called Urdlu and a buck euro called Mandya who both lived in the plains called Puthadamathanha. These two used to travel around together in the same country. One of their favorite foods was the wild pear root. In fact, it was they who gave it its name ngarndi wari.

Urdlu the kangaroo and Mandya the euro dug for tucker (food) in separate holes. Urdlu found a lot of tucker, but Mandya found only a little. Urdlu, however, wouldn't tell Mandya where his hole was. Poor Mandya was getting thinner and thinner and Urdlu was getting fatter and fatter. In the end Mandya came to Urdlu and said: "Give me some of your mai" (mai is tucker). Urdlu said to Mandya: "There's some mai in that bag there. You can take that." As he ate it, Mandya said, "This is really good tucker! Where did you get it?" Urdlu said with a wave of his arm, "Oh, I found it over there."

FIGURE 131
Kolobarra, the kangaroo spirit, in an x-ray painting by Ngulayngulay Murimuru, a leading Oenpelli bark painter, in the Collectors Gallery exhibition. The paintings of the Aborigines reveal not only their vision of normally invisible energy patterns but also their capacity to look through the surfaces of creatures to their inner workings.

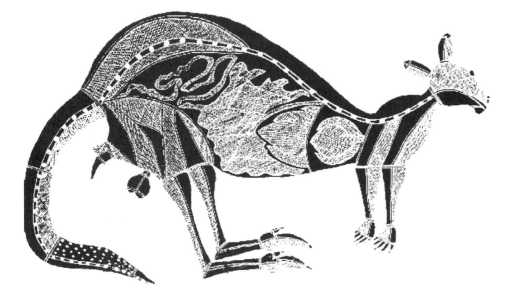

FIGURE 132
The sharp division between the plains and the mountains is vividly described as resulting from the activities of great Dreamtime ancestral animals.

The pair of them went to sleep. In the morning Urdlu got up and went to look for water. While he went around looking here and there for water to drink, Mandya got up and went to find the hole where Urdlu got his tucker. He picked up Urdlu's tracks and followed them. He went along steadily down the track made by the kangaroo until he came to his hole. He dug out a big heap of tucker from it. He was so pleased he stayed there digging and eating without even looking up.

Urdlu came back from having a drink. "Now where on earth has the old fellow got to? I know, he's gone to my hole!" He took off after Mandya. He tracked him. His fresh tracks were there, all the way down to the hole. He could see where Mandya had dug up the dirt as he went along. He sure had dug up the dirt! When Urdlu arrived at the hole Mandya was so busy digging he didn't even see Urdlu coming. Mandya was digging like mad. Urdlu called out, "Why did you come to my hole?" Mandya said he was starving and Urdlu was mean not to tell him where there was tucker. He just went on eating. Now this made Urdlu really angry, so the pair of them were soon having a big fight all over tucker. Mandya pulled at Urdlu's arms. He stretched his arms, he stretched his fingers, he stretched his legs.

They got very long. Then Urdlu pressed Mandya's fingers and his legs; he pressed his back, his chest; he thrashed him. Then they separated.

The wounded Mandya went off to Vadaardlanha to camp. While he was lying there trying to go to sleep, his hip started to hurt. In fact, he had a sore. He reached down and took out a little stone from the sore. He blew on it and in a flash hills came up from the plain. Indeed, several ranges of hills came up. The more Mandya blew, the more hills kept coming up.

Meanwhile Urdlu headed down towards Varaarta (Baratta). He moved that big flat (plain) along as he went. He was lying out there on the flat when he looked back and saw the hills coming down the plain. He said, "Hey! What's the old fellow up to? Over that way there's a big range of hills coming up! If he keeps that up I won't have anywhere to live!" So, with a big sweep of his tail Urdlu pushed the ranges back to where they are now. You can see where this happened, up there north of Vardna-wartathinha. That big flat never gets any grass on it. It's called Urdlurunha-vitana (kangaroo's flat).

Urdlu then made Munda (Lake Frome) so that he would have a permanent supply of water, but Mandya was jealous about this and put salt in it. Right to the present day kangaroos cannot drink from this lake because of the salt.

Mandya was up there in the hills behind Vadaardlanha. From there he looked back and said, "Look at the way the old fellow moved that big plain along!" And as Mandya looked back he turned into a spirit. He is called Thudupinha, and you can see him sitting up there today. Below him the ground is red where his wounds bled after his big fight with Urdlu. This place is called Mandya Arti (which means Mandya's blood).[1]

T HE DREAMTIME STORIES are always related to enduring features of the living landscape. This Dreamtime creation story tells how the rocky Flinders Range in southern Australia was formed and then pulled away from the adjacent plains by the magnificent sweep of a kangaroo's tail. It explains how Lake Frome (called Munda by the Aborigines), an important lake in the region, came into being as a salt lake and where the pointed hills surrounding it came from. The story also tells us something of the diet of two similar macropod marsupials, the large red kangaroo of the plains and the smaller mountain-dwelling euro, or wallaroo. It explains how they came to look so different and why their habitat is so distinct.

This story reiterates the central Aboriginal ethic concerning food sharing, introduces a favorite Aboriginal food—the root of a wild pear—and emphasizes the all-important skill of tracking.[2] On the surface Aboriginal Dreamtime stories may appear simplistic, but to someone who speaks the language and knows the culture they are rich in implication, hidden symbolism, and assumed knowledge. They trigger vast storehouses of cultural and natural information.

THE ONTOLOGY OF THE DREAMTIME

The Dreamtime is difficult for Western minds to comprehend. Looking at the etymology of three words from the Pintupi tribes of the western Australian desert can help to open up this highly sophisticated ontology and provide a key to their world view.

In Pintupi the word for Dreamtime or Dreaming, *tjukurrtjana*, can be translated as the absolute ground of being or the fundamental universal continuum from which all differentiation arises.[3] Through the stories handed down by untold generations, Aborigines are constantly made aware of the continuum underlying the Dreaming and the forms and events of the perceivable world.

Quantum physics and modern psychology both recognize the concept of a metaphysical continuum beneath the tangible. The quantum continuum is a universal field that underscores all other levels of energy and matter. All particles and rhythmic processes of energy arise from this field continuum. The fields themselves are a mystery, but their existence is apparent from their undeniable effects, such as those of the gravitational and magnetic fields. Beyond these effects and the fact that fields always emanate from, or are associated with, a form (a planet, magnet, galaxy, universal curvature, brain, or body), we know nothing about them. Fields are an invisible state or active condition of pure space. Like the unconscious mind, they are an unmanifested realm, known to conscious perception only by their effects. Carl Jung maintained that underneath all activities of mind is an endless flow of consciousness of which we are unconscious; like the Australian Aborigines, he compared it to the state of dreaming.[4]

The fact that the Aborigines use the term Dreaming to denote the fundamental basis of their cosmology is in itself significant. To the Aborigines the most profound or ultimate level of being is not the heaven of Christianity, or the mathematically perfect laws of the mechanists. It is not the ideal realm of the classic philosophers, the galaxies of outer space of the materialists, the divine beatitude of Hinduism, or the nir-

vana of the transcendental nihilist. It is a natural dimension of our normal sleeping state. To designate the ultimate trancendent state the Dreaming signifies to the Aborigines that this "other world" is an intimate indispensable aspect of the tangible world, just as sleep and dreams are to the waking state.

THE DREAMING AND THE TANGIBLE, NOTHING MORE

In direct semantic opposition to the Dreamtime, or *tjukurrtjana*, is the Pintupi word *yuti*, which means the actual, perceivable, phenomenal world. The *yuti* comes into being as soon as the creative phase of the Dreamtime concludes. *Tjukurrtjana* and *yuti* constitute two distinctly different, yet equally real, levels of existence. The *yuti* includes events that have been witnessed or are, in principle, witnessable. Only phenomena that have been experienced through one or more of the five physical senses are *yuti*. The word *yuti* is used to emphasize the experiential relationship to the environment. If a tribal man were searching for his spear, his wife might direct him to it with the phrase, "There it is over there *yuti* (visible)." By leaping from behind a bush into sight, a hidden kangaroo, *ringu*, becomes *yuti ringu*. An event or entity perceived in a dream or vision may also be considered *yuti* if the dreamer can convince someone else that he actually witnessed it while dreaming or in a trance.[5]

The perceivable world, *yuti*, is conceptually synonymous with truth and reality, *mularrpa*. The entire universe and all of Aboriginal experience is divided by this polarity—*yuti/mularrpa*, the perceivable truth and *tjukurrtjana*, the Dreamtime.[6] The two modes of thought are of equal weight yet mutually exclusive, so that if a hunter returns to camp and joins a group in the middle of a conversation, he immediately asks whether they are talking *yuti/mularrpa* or *tjukarrtjana*.

This polarity is not static. People, laws, customs, and animals are said to have originated in the Dreamtime, along with the creative titans and gigantic beings. The phrase used by the Pintupi tribe, "from the Dreaming *tjukarrtjana* all this becomes real (*mularrpa*)" acknowledges that creation is considered a movement from an original subjective phase to an objective world. Aboriginal culture and conceptualization situate themselves in an ever-moving passage between two planes of being. Unlike many of today's world religions, which reject the physical world and sensual experience in favor of transcendental or ideal states, Aboriginal spirituality considers the sensual experience of the physical world the only means to realize the truth, beauty, and reality of the metaphysical creative powers.

In contrast to our way of thinking, there is no category or word in Aboriginal languages for an intermediate position between the super-reality of the archetypal Dreamtime epoch and the actual physical world. There is no word or concept for fiction, fantasy, or personal imagination—something that does not occur or is not perceived is a lie, pure and simple.[7] Any story that does not directly refer to tangible perceptions or to the original Dreamtime stories is considered deceitful or just plain silly.

A story that illustrates this point is told by an early-contact Catholic missionary. The priest had decided that in one grand gesture he would change the "uncivilized, primitive" behavior of the Aborigines who had been forced to live on his mission. One day he took a group to a nearby stream, where he commenced to baptize them, telling them that the splash of water would remove the invisible stain of sin that was upon them, and from that point on, they would be and act like completely different "civilized people." The following Friday he observed one of the baptized Aborigines enjoying a meal of kangaroo steak from an animal he had just captured. The priest said to him, "You know that since you have become a Christian it is wrong to eat meat on Friday." The man smiled and said, "This is not meat, it is fish." The priest was angry and told him he was compounding the sin by lying about it. The Aborigine looked at him very sternly and replied, "Last week you sprinkled water on me and told me I had changed into a completely different person, so I did the same thing with this kangaroo. Sprinkled water on it and changed it into fish." He then laughed as if he had pleased the missionary by going along with his joke.[8] The Aborigine did not dismiss this magic out of hand, but the baptismal splash did not produce any change he could see, nor was this so-called transformation recorded in his Dreamtime stories or in the topology of his country.

The stark division in the Aboriginal mind between the Dreamtime and the perceivable world, with no intervening concepts between them, has been interpreted by psychologists and anthropologists as representing a deficiency or poverty in Aboriginal thought. Psychologist Ronald Rose, who did extensive testing on tribal Aborigines in the late 1950s to measure ESP and intelligence levels, concluded, "The outstanding difference in Aboriginal thought is that it completely lacks the faculty to generalize and to think inductively."[9]

Aboriginal languages reflect the cultural emphasis on experiential awareness, or *yuti*. For example, Aboriginal dialects have hundreds of names for each particular type of tree, and they have names for many individual trees. In the case of fish and animals, there are sometimes separate names for the same fish or animal at different stages of its breeding cycle. The vocabularies of Aboriginal dialects are so enormous that it has been virtually impossible for Western minds to master any of their languages. Linguistic studies prove that the richer a language is in names, the more it disposes the mind to observe and record ever finer distinctions.[10] In spite of this linguistic power to distinguish each aspect and each individual plant, tree, or animal, Aboriginal languages have no words for abstract, generalized categories such as tree, plant, or animal.

The ability to generalize (from which, at its highest level, we derive our physical and natural laws) is the most prized faculty of our so-called advanced mental development. Mathematics has been exalted as a scientific language because it provides the mind with its most powerful tool for generalization.[11] As an inductive thought process, generality creates nonexistent classes, categories, or linkages based on observed similarities between separate, particular things. For example, because a number of trees have bark and leaves of a similar shape and color, they all belong in the eucalyptus category. A generality is not applicable to any specific perceivable case, though. Categories of phylum, species, and family are useful guides for naming. However, every animal and plant, even those of the same species, responds to its external environment and its own inner nature in subtly different ways. It is by means of these minute variations that plants and animals tell us about themselves and the intimate invisible connections they have to a particular place. Unlike the abstract nomenclature that refers to little other than an imposed system, this knowledge is essential to a living experience of nature. As Bertrand Russell dryly and succinctly stated, "The class of elephants is not an elephant."[12]

A recent scientific experiment has emphasized the problems inherent in generalization. The National Research Council of Canada attempted to measure the gravity-induced acceleration of a falling body. It spent years building a shielded laboratory to eliminate all extraneous factors. All electric and magnetic forces were eliminated, and precise temperature controls were installed to avoid any expansion or contraction. Millions of dollars were spent to eliminate any vibration, friction, or oscillation and to create ideal insulated and replicable conditions for measuring the acceleration of a falling metal bar. In spite of all this effort, each and every experiment produced slightly different results. Even the averages of one series of measurements were different from the averages of a second series. "Even in doing something as straightforward as [measuring] the fall of a metal bar, nature conspires to introduce fluctuations into each individual event. . . . The laws of nature work exactly only in the imagined laboratories of the physicists' minds."[13]

The propensity to approach the diversity of the natural world with a categorical eye has the effect of lumping together all our different perceptions, thereby obscuring the nature of reality. In a sense, generalization is related to the activity of mind called fantasy. Fantasy is the faculty that forms representations of things not actually perceivable. In their elaborate form, fantasies tend to distort, exaggerate, or embellish reality, whereas generalities are the contracted or reductive form of fantasy. This dichotomy is often referred to as art versus science, belief versus factuality. We don't happily acknowledge generalization—this lofty product of empirical observation and rational induction—as fantasy, but to the Aboriginal mind it is just that: neither *yuti* nor *tjukurrtjana*. Consider that *generality* and *general*, the hierarchal military title, share the same word root; indeed, generality places the mind in a position of power above and in control of the multitude of perceived particulars. Scientific thought has in effect replaced the realm of the archetype (to the Aborigines, the Creative Ancestors) with the mental faculty of standing above the phenomenal world and reducing it to comprehensible regularities. In the words of physicist Eugene Wigner, "Physics doesn't describe nature, physics describes regularities among events and *only* regularities among events."[14]

The intellectual and linguistic practice of reducing and generalizing characteristic of Western thought actually reinforces a physiological filtering mechanism in the lower brain stem, called the reticular formation. This part of the brain cuts down and selects the images and impressions that reach the brain from the great flood of information that comes in through our senses.[15] Neurobiologists now believe that our generalizing, reductive patterns of thought may be overactivating this physiological system. Because our mode of thinking limits the forms we perceive through generalization, we are less able to perceive direct reality and less open to new experiences. There is a great deal of evidence supporting the theory that thought patterns act formatively on the brain or, in other words, that the act of thinking changes the thinker. In contrast to the conventional belief that the brain creates thoughts, it seems that thoughts affect the patterns of neural circuitry in the brain.

That the brain is structurally and functionally changed by the thought processes and other mental activities flowing through it has yet to be incorporated into our sociological and psychological theories and—more important—into our educational methods. Once language patterns and brain activities are established through regular practice, the metabolic pathways and the neural networks are altered and subsequently shape our view of reality. World view, language, and thought patterns then act to reinforce one another. Everyone that speaks the same language or uses the same thought processes is therefore disposed to see the world in a particular way.[16] Generalizing and categorizing are cerebral activities that stimulate a brain activity that reduces perceptual richness and intensity.

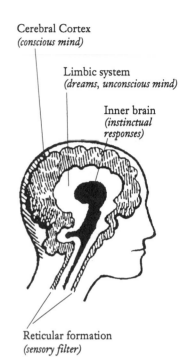

Cerebral Cortex
(*conscious mind*)

Limbic system
(*dreams, unconscious mind*)

Inner brain
(*instinctual responses*)

Reticular formation
(*sensory filter*)

FIGURE 134
The reticular formation acts as a filtering mechanism for the flood of sensory impressions before they reach the brain.

269

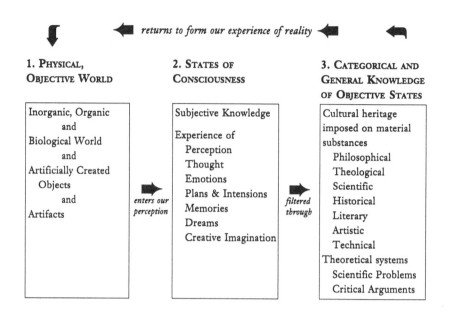

FIGURE 135
This model, after Carl Popper, shows the interraction of our perception of (1) the physical world with (2) the subjective states of consciousness and with (3) the linguisitic and cultural categories of our objectifying mentality. In effect, we project these categories back upon the physical world, thereby changing and reducing our perception of reality.

returns to form our experience of reality

1. PHYSICAL, OBJECTIVE WORLD

Inorganic, Organic
and
Biological World
and
Artificially Created
Objects
and
Artifacts

enters our perception

2. STATES OF CONSCIOUSNESS

Subjective Knowledge

Experience of
Perception
Thought
Emotions
Plans & Intensions
Memories
Dreams
Creative Imagination

filtered through

3. CATEGORICAL AND GENERAL KNOWLEDGE OF OBJECTIVE STATES

Cultural heritage
imposed on material
substances
Philosophical
Theological
Scientific
Historical
Literary
Artistic
Technical
Theoretical systems
Scientific Problems
Critical Arguments

Modern Western society increasingly filters its selection and interpretation of the world environment. Any world view that disconfirms our consensually conceptualized screen is considered ignorant, superstitious, or crazy.[17] We assume erroneously, in our generalities and belief systems, that the answer to a problem in one situation or one culture can be applied to all.

By rigorously connecting language and thought to careful perception of the natural world, the ancient Aborigines escaped the rigidification of the brain that results from contrived conceptual activity. As the Aboriginal mind matures it is initiatically introduced to revealed knowledge in stages; this knowledge symbolically depicts the activity of the invisible realm. With each initiation comes a new vocabulary or language that enables them to comprehend these mysteries. These timeless, revelatory languages are always connected to the tangibility of the earth's topography; in this way, the physical world retains its hidden psychic content and the psychic world is verified in the physical symbols of nature.

Figure 136 explains the inclusiveness of Aboriginal modes of perception, which, in contrast to the linear flow (Figure 135) of the Western perceptual process, are integrated into a cycle. The power and presence of the *tjukurrtjana* (the Dreaming) is always revealed in relationship to the *yuti* (the perceivable). Earth is like a two-sided mirror: internally, in its subtle energy and symbolic structure, it absorbs and reflects the metaphysical drama of creation. This reflection, through the earth's external forms, echoes in human consciousness, which sees itself and discovers its own meaning, along with the source and meaning of nature. The earth's topography is a magic mirror through which humanity,

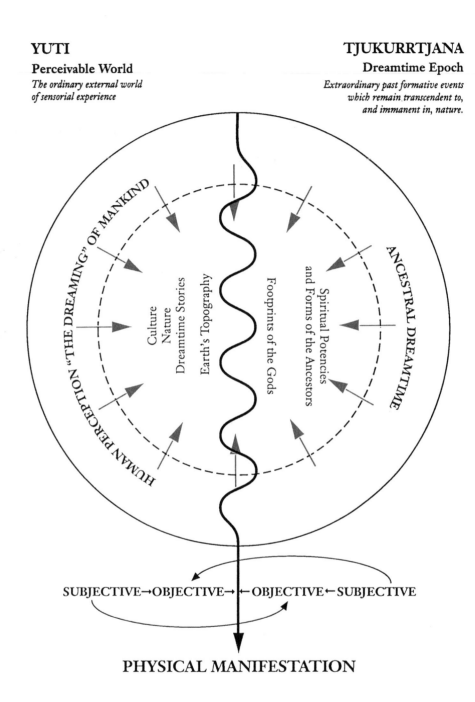

YUTI

Perceivable World

The ordinary external world of sensorial experience

TJUKURRTJANA

Dreamtime Epoch

Extraordinary past formative events which remain transcendent to, and immanent in, nature.

HUMAN PERCEPTION "THE DREAMING" OF MANKIND

ANCESTRAL DREAMTIME

Culture
Nature
Dreamtime Stories
Earth's Topography

Footprints of the Gods

Spiritual Potencies
and Forms of the Ancestors

SUBJECTIVE→OBJECTIVE→ ←OBJECTIVE←SUBJECTIVE

PHYSICAL MANIFESTATION

FIGURE 136

Although the Dreamtime epoch concluded in the past, its vibratory residue continues to power ongoing creation. The outer ring of the right-hand side of the circle represents the creation epoch or Dreamtime. The inward-pointing arrows, from this region, represent the residual potencies of the Ancestors, which have been deposited in the earthly environment. The irregular center line represents the forms and topography of the countryside. The Dreamtime stories and rituals associated with and emanating from the landscape and the creatures of nature enter and fill the Aboriginal perception of reality. These perceptions are returned (arrows from the left) through language, law, behavior, and social instruction that reflect the essence of the Dreaming.

nature, and the Creative Beings all reflect each other in a circle of reciprocity.

In Western thought, generalities are used to make sense of the world around us, but they impose an order on reality rather than connecting us to the world's living presence and the metaphysical dimension from which it arose. This leads to stereotyping; making assumptions; heartless, often totalitarian government; and political standardization of human

271

society. The scientific mind seeks to find truth through what is considered objectivity, by measuring certain phenomena in the physical world. By using mathematical formulas to develop and bolster generalizations, science gives our society limited and temporary technological power over substance and natural processes. But even modern numeric and geometric formulations contain inherent reflections of the metaphysical, archetypal realms and creative principles. A common example is the relationship Einstein discovered between energy, mass, and the speed of light. Unfortunately, the power of mathematics has been diverted away from the metaphysical to the physical and mechanistic and from an expansive, integrating view of reality to a narrow one.

Although the confusion between generalities and archetypes goes unaddressed in mathematics and physics, the work of Carl Jung has successfully elevated generality to the more richly metaphorical concept of archetypes. Archetypes have lent a universal dimension to the way we understand psychological and subjective processes and enhanced our fictional creations. Unlike the Aborigines, for whom the Dreamtime Ancestors are very real, most psychologists believe Jungian archetypes have no independent existence but are merely projections of the personal or collective unconscious.

The concept of projection in modern psychology is an inversion of Dreamtime cosmology, in which the Creative Ancestors "projected" their dream into the actual forms of the physical world. Projection can be described metaphorically by comparing mental activity to that of a film projector: all the activities, desires, and innate structure of the unconscious mind are like the film rolling inside the projector. The contents of the unconscious are projected onto the world as the images on film are projected onto a big screen, and they appear to the conscious mind as external reality.

Human qualities that are too nasty to acknowledge within ourselves tend to be projected on, and attributed to, others. For example, a teacher who perceives a good-natured, energetic classroom as hostile and aggressive may be projecting his or her own fears and insecurities or an unacknowledged hostility toward children onto the class.[18] Many people who engage in peace marches or demonstrations against war are probably projecting their own hidden, denied aggressive tendencies or anger onto society. Problems caused by this type of projection are not simply psychological but cosmological. We are ignorant of the role of the unconscious, or the Dreaming, in the creation of external reality.

All aspects of human nature that are repressed, denied, or unfulfilled, whether through education, society, or interpersonal relationships, develop into "complexes" in the unconscious and tend to be projected onto our experience of the external world. One of the most common is the hero complex. Seeing oneself as heroic is often a part of adolescent development: the need for recognition, attention, or acceptance is crucial during the awkward, bewildering, sexually complicated transition from child to adult. In Aboriginal society, puberty initiation rites place each young person at center stage in tribal life while he or she undergoes a heroic journey and struggle of initiation, emerging from it courageous and victorious. Western society accepts only a relatively select group of young athletic or academic achievers as "heroes."

Exalting "heroism" while denying it to most of the population promotes the development of a hero complex that is projected in various ways on the external world. Modern entertainment exploits the repressed hero complexes of adolescents by fueling their imagination with pop stars, film celebrities, and other commercially exaggerated figures. Adolescent girls who, in our society, have less opportunity than boys to excel and achieve heroically, project their needs and resources onto a succession of admired males or fantastic fictional heroes. Often it is only later in life, perhaps due to a disillusionment that serves as an awakening, that women surrender these exaggerated external projections and discover the need to begin their own heroic journey.[19] The projection syndrome abounds in the psychological makeup of Western society because of its inherent repression and denial. Indeed, just as our technological developments externalize the inner powers of consciousness, the enormous popularity of films, television, and other projected images may itself be an externalization of the projection process endemic to Western psychology. Mothering complexes, savior complexes, control complexes, inferiority complexes, and sexual complexes—all of these have gained such a grip on our psychological outlook that, in a sense, we are possessed by complexes as one might be possessed by spirits.

These are negative aspects of unconscious projection; the positive aspect acknowledged by Jungian psychologists is that projection allows otherwise unconscious dimensions of our being to enter our conscious awareness. In addition to repressed complexes, we also harbor in our unconscious universal psychic forces, qualities, and emotions that are hidden from normal consciousness. In Jungian psychology, projection is not something we do but something that happens to us; as we divulge our personal complexes these universal forces can pour forth projections and manifest their qualities in our lives and the lives of others. Because these energies become ensnared in our personal complexes in the unconscious, we conceive of them as originating within us. In contrast, Aboriginal society provides an open avenue for expressing these archetypal forces in the physical world through endless rituals and ceremonies. The Aborigines recognize these energies as having an extraordinary independent existence originating with, and projected by, the Dreamtime

Ancestors. Dream, ritual, and trance are the modes by which the deepest unconscious forces are expressed as an active, accepted, constant part of Aboriginal reality.

MIND AND LANDSCAPE

When Westerners generalize about the physical environment, we categorize it with terms defining country, state, or regions. Aborigines do not apply such abstract terms to their environment but refer only to specific land formations. When Aborigines have to describe an area or give directions, they use a language strategy indicative of their world view. For example, if one tribal man is directing another to a place where a type of quartz crystal can be found, he begins by naming one near-by land feature to establish the locality, such as a prominent mound or significant tree.[20] He may then sing a line of a Dreamtime song that tells of a great Ancestor whose exploits occurred around or through the quartz-covered area. The sites he names in the fragment of song coincide with the extent of the stone deposit. While he is singing, he carefully observes how much the listener seems to be understanding. Mixing together oblique physical and metaphysical references to define a spatial area is consistent with the Aborigines' sense of reality.[21] This type of direction intensifies the relation between the land and mythic creation and allows the speaker to act on clues to the listener's cultural or initiatic level and his familiarity with the countryside in question. Aborigines relish oblique references because they encourage individual expression that adds to the possibilities for humor and cleverness in conversation. There are innumerable engaging ways to convey a single piece of information: the line of a song might well be replaced with a fragment of a dance or a tale of a fire or a death that occurred years ago in that vicinity.

Generalities, categories, and regional terms are ways of expressing abstract or imaginary boundary definitions. This form of artificial segmentation of either mental or physical space is antithetical to Aboriginal patterns of thinking. They do not create names or empower boundary descriptions that do not occur in nature. In contrast, we live in a mental world shadowed by fantastic boundary creatures such as nations, religions, social classes, and political parties. These function as binding configurations in which humans confine and limit themselves and, at worst, destroy one another.

The difference between our sense of boundary conditions and the Aborigines' is rooted in our differing attitudes toward a metaphysical reality and, ultimately, toward death. Our drive to impose generalities, categories, and fantastic projections on the world around us expresses the need to withdraw from the intensity of the actual moment and to define the living uniqueness of nature with fictitious constructs or the familiar categories of our language and science. We have closed ourselves off from the multilayered, spiritual dimensions of existence. Death is the point at which we must confront the metaphysical, the Dreaming. We are frightened by death because it represents layers of being we distrust and repress. Traditional Aborigines, because of their grounding in nature and their uninterrupted contact with the eternal Dreamtime, do not share this fear with their white conquerors. The Aborigines have the courage to live within the realm of "the swift-perishing, never-to-be-repeated moment."[22] No intervening agency, such as restrictive perception or architectural armor, stands between Aborigines and the naked intensity of physical reality. They confront the wilderness and wonder of creation through the unfiltered perception of the Dreamtime Creators.

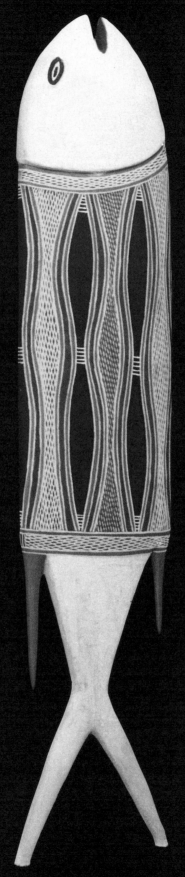

Sacred Kingfish Totem

PART THREE

TOTEMISM

AND

ANIMISM

CHAPTER 15

TOTEM AND SOCIETY

GOOLA-WILLEEL, THE TOPKNOT PIGEON

Young Goola-willeel used to go out hunting every day. His mother and sisters always expected that he would bring home kangaroo and emu for them. But each day he came home without any meat at all. They asked him what he did in the bush as he evidently did not hunt. He said that he did hunt.

"Then why," said they, "do you bring us nothing home?"

"I cannot catch and kill what I follow," he said. "You hear me cry out when I find kangaroo or emu: is it not so?"

"Yes; each day we hear you call when you find something, and each day we get ready the fire, expecting you to bring home what you have killed, but you bring nothing."

"Tomorrow," he said, "you shall not be disappointed. I shall bring you a kangaroo."

Every day instead of hunting, Goola-willeel had been gathering wattle gum, and with this he had been making a kangaroo—a perfect model of one, tail, ears, and all complete. So the next day he came towards the camp carrying this kangaroo made of gum. Seeing him coming, and also seeing that he was carrying the promised kangaroo, his mother and sisters said, "Ah, Goola-willeel spoke truly. He has kept his word and now brings us a kangaroo. Pile up the fire. Tonight we shall eat meat."

About a hundred yards away from the camp Goola-willeel put down his model, and came on without it. His mother called out, "Where is the kangaroo you brought home?"

"Oh, over there." And he pointed towards where he had left it.

The sisters ran to get it, but came back saying, "Where is it? We cannot see it."

"Over there," he said, pointing again.

"But this is only a great figure of gum."

"Well, did I say it was anything else? Did I not say it was gum?"

"No, you did not. You said it was a kangaroo."

"And so it is a kangaroo. A beautiful kangaroo that I made all by myself." And he smiled quite proudly to think what a fine kangaroo he had made.

But his mother and sisters did not smile. They seized him and gave him a good beating for deceiving them. They told him he should never go out alone again, for he only played instead of hunting, though he knew they starved for meat. They would always in future go with him.

And so forever the Goola-willeels, the topknot pigeons, went in flocks, never more singly, in search of food.[1]

BEHOLDING—NOT POSSESSING

 RELIGION MEANS RE-LINKING. The totemism that is central to Aboriginal religion describes the linking of humanity, nature, and the gods. The natural world is guided by the same principles and patterns that guide the formation of human culture and society. Aboriginal social order, ritual, and myth are inspired by and celebrate the bonds of mutual life-giving between nature, humankind, and the Ancestral Dreamtime powers. Nature gives life to humanity, and through culture humanity gives meaning to nature—together, they give body to the invisible life of their Dreamtime Creators. This entire reciprocal process is totemism. Totemism can be seen as animating lines of identification flowing from the origin through all things, forming an invisible web on which the species and societies of the earth grow, nourish, and reflect each other.

Totemic identification forms the basis of the three major social groupings: the tribes, the clans, and the bands. The larger social group is a tribe with between 500 and 1,000 members who share a common language; it can extend over several regions and land areas. A tribe maintains consistent customs, laws, and rites that distinguish it from nearby groups. Tribes are not easily defined, however, since there is much crossing over and interchange between groups. *An Aboriginal tribe is not an isolated group that owns and defends a specific territory and lives largely within set boundaries conserving resources for its own use.* People move frequently between tribes, which are linked by marriage, ceremonial interactions, and the sharing of resources. This lack of clear boundaries has troubled anthropologists. Many believe that Aboriginal tribes are better identified as linguistic units since they distinguish neighboring groups from their own through subtle differences between dialects, not through distinct territorial boundaries. For example, the lands of three tribes in the Western Desert have a common border. Each of these tribeal languages attaches a prefix before the word *tjara*, and this prefix designates what we would call a tribe. Literally, *tjara* means "having" or "holding" an area of land, and the prefixes designate three distinct dialects. The prefix *pitja* means "coming"; thus the tribal name of the Pitjantjatjara people means "coming to hold the land." Many words in the Pitjantjatjara dialect have the same prefix. The prefix of their eastern neighbors, the Yankuntjatjara, means "going" or "releasing." The Ngaatjatjara in the west use *ngaatja*, which means "remaining with" or "this."[2] These three groups are named as if each group were a different verb in a single phrase describing the relationship of humanity to earth.

Tribes are divided into a number of smaller groups called clans, usually numbering several hundred people. Each clan is associated with a particular animal species and manages an area of land that serves as a sanctuary for the spirit of that particular species. Each clan has an obligation to preserve the stories of its totemic species and ensure the performance of ceremonies related to them. One clan is considered to be descended from the kangaroo-man Ancestor of the Dreaming, and members of this clan have a special relationship to the kangaroo and the land, stories, and ceremonies of the kangaroo Dreaming sites. Other clans have similar relationships to the emu, the native fig, and the wild yam.[3] The spirit of the species is believed to flow from the spirit world into the physical world at a particular site within the sanctuary. The stories contain the secret songs and vibrational rhythms, words, and dances that stimulate the fertility of that species when performed at the sacred site. This spirit of the species actually *possesses* the region, not the clan that represents it. If the possum population is low in places hundreds of miles from the region of the ringtail possum, emissaries from distant tribes travel along the paths of the songlines carrying sacred boards to the elders of the clan of the ringtail possum. They ask the elders to perform more increase ceremonies at the site believed to be the spiritual generator of the ringtail possum species.

According to Aboriginal legends, all animal life in Australia has remained marsupial through the intention and influence of tribal elders who practiced the sacred rites of increase of the marsupial spirit since the Dreaming. Unlike the aggressive predatorial placenta mammals that emerged in other parts of the world, marsupials are peaceful, nocturnal creatures, which do not prey on humans or any other species. Because of these nonpredatory marsupial characteristics the night in Australia is safe and open, and much of Aboriginal cultural life takes place by the light of stars and the moon. The darkness of night holds some dangers, but they are spiritual, not physical. During the early contact period the

FIGURE 138
Bark painting from Oenpelli in Arnhem Land: two kangaroos facing and touching hands. The Australian Aborigines believe that through ceremonial intervention they maintain the spirit of the land within the qualities and characteristics of the gently nocturnal marsupials.

Aborigines would be found sleeping from dawn until noon after having danced all night. This behavior drew antagonism from the early colonists, who were already conditioned as drones of the industrial revolution.[4]

In many religious rituals, a man identifies himself by painting clan designs on his body and performing dances associated with his animal spirit power and the lands which his clan forages. Place is symbolically integrated into his dance; even though he may be far away from his own tribal land, the dance allows him to achieve an inner state that transports him to the place of his species power. The Aboriginal consciousness rises

FIGURE 139
Historical ceremony, Kangaroo
totem, Musgrave Rangers,
Northwestern Australia. Each
region contains a site from
which the spirit of an animal
species arose. These sites are
the location of male increase
ceremonies.

above the sense of separation through the symbolic resonance between the dancer and the place of his animal power.

The next social division is the band, a smaller group of people who camp, forage, and range together. Since people must marry outside their clans, very often husbands and wives live in bands composed of members of different clans. A band may hunt or forage over several clan estates by asking permission from the clan elders who are responsible for that estate. The clan's relationship to an area of land is predominantly religious and spiritual, but a band relates to an area mostly through the gathering of food and other necessities.[5] The Aborigines express their relationship to clan country by saying, "My country is the place where I can cut a spear or make a spearthrower without asking anyone."[6] In our terminology, a clan could be said to manage a land area, while a band utilizes a land area. The overlapping functions of band and clan are characterized by numerous reciprocal procedures of interchange, sharing, and formalities of respect that minimize any disputes. The reciprocal relationship between the two complementary group identities of band and clan keep any fixed singular relationship from developing between groups of individuals or between a group and its environment.

In addition to totemic identifications based on groups' relationships to land regions and animal powers, tribes are also divided into moieties, which provide each person with a second animal identity. Moieties are derived not from land but from parental descent. In some tribes, called patrimoiety tribes, children enter the moiety of their father; in matrimoiety tribes they enter the moiety of their mother. Moiety membership is fixed and remains so for life. The totemic animals and plants that are used for moieties always belong to contrasting classes, such as white cockatoos and black cockatoos. In all rituals, people sit in circles according to their moiety of origin; the black cockatoo moiety always faces the white cockatoo moiety. Since people marry outside their moiety, this affiliation cuts across marital bonds.

In many tribes, the physical environment is also divided into these oppositional classes. For example, the Aboriginal tribe in Arnhem Land is divided into two moieties. One moiety is the *dhuwa*, meaning "spearthrower" (a carved shell-like wooden tool that guides the thrust of the spear); the other moiety is the *yrritja*, the spear itself. Some areas of tribal land are *dhuwa* and others are *yrritja*. Whales and sharks are *dhuwa* and sea gulls and barramundi are *yrritja*. These allocations play an important role in ceremonial taboos and exchanges.

The land and animal associations established through moiety identification incur differing sets of rites and responsibilities than those associated with clan identification. Thus each individual's identity is built on symbolic multiple connections to the environment. *No one owns or possesses anything of earth or its living creatures, and Aboriginal languages have no words or concepts for ownership.* The Aborigines conceive of their relationship to the earth as "beholding" their country: they observe a network of mutual rites and obligations from which each person derives acknowledgment, self-esteem, and identity. Early anthropologists Spencer and Gilling described the practice of beholding in this way:

> Clans or moieties are bound together by a rule of reciprocity. Among the Kaitish and the Unmatjera, northern neighbours of Aranda, anyone who gathers wild seeds in the territory of a totemic group named after these seeds must ask the headman's permission before eating them. It is the duty of each totemic group to provide the other groups with the plant or animal for whose "production" it is specially responsible. Thus a man of the Emu clan out hunting on his own may not touch an emu. But, if, on the other hand, he is in company he is permitted and even

FIGURE 140
Spearthrowers, Western Australia. The spearthrower is an aesthetically graceful, highly utilitarian implement. The hook end of the spearthrower is placed in a notch at the back end of a spear, giving the hunter extra leverage in hurling.

283

supposed to kill it and offer it to hunters of other clans. Conversely, when he is alone a man of the Water clan may drink if he is thirsty but when he is with others he must receive the water from a member of the other moiety, preferably from a brother-in-law.[7]

Other totems further expand and enrich a person's identity and interrelatedness to the world. Some tribes have sex totems, which identify an emblematic bird or animal for each sex. Conception totems relate each person to the mythology of site where his or her mother first realized she was pregnant. Birth totems do the same with one's place of birth.[8] Each person's sense of individuality is based on many interrelations, which results in far-reaching yet well-defined human associations.

Personal names derive from a physical part or characteristic of the clan's totem animal. A member of the possum Dreaming clan may have a name such as possum's tail or possum's tooth or possum's climb or walk. Each part and characteristic of every animal has a separate term. Each of the many totemic groups to which a person belongs contributes a different name to the person. The function of the anatomical part in the body helps define the group function of the person who acquires the name of that part. Thus the multiple associations are united in the idea that every individual is part of an embodied whole.[9]

The totemic social system, like a living organism, is made up of overlapping, interdependent relationships and functions: the parts of a society exist in relationship to each other and to the whole. All divisions, all identities have permeable boundaries. Like natural systems, Aboriginal individuals and groups do not exist defensively within exclusive bounded regions such as egos and nations. There are no fixed impermeable positions, either in the sense of self or in society. The rules of totemic relationships have been handed down from the Dreamtime as unchanging metaphysical laws, forming an invisible structure infused with the diverse animating spirit of all the species of nature.

CHAPTER 16

TOTEM AND IMAGE

LIKE SEXUALITY, Aboriginal art takes three forms: personal art, social art, and sacred or ritual art. Underlying this threefold expression is the primordial couple, or sexual polarity. All graphic elements have gender; for example, the circle is feminine and the straight line is masculine. The twofold, gender-based division extends to the various methods of execution as well as the allocation of some methods and images to the visible world and others to the world of the Dreaming.

Image and Intimacy

Personal art is predominantly, but not exclusively, made by women, and its designs center on camp (*nuggara*) and all the activities associated with camp. Their symbols and images are overtly sexual, telling stories of love, lovemaking, the fertility of favored gathering sites, the women themselves, and their daughters. Women usually draw these intimate images in sand while telling stories from their own lives or from their dreams.[1] Shared with the immediate members of the women's community, this activity is the enjoyable focal point of the campmaking tasks. The association between camp and storytelling follows the precedent of the Dreamtime, since the great Ancestors also camped and told stories and, in so doing, brought the world into existence.

The symbols used for women's storytelling developed into the images prevalent in today's Aboriginal "dot" paintings. These symbols are always associated with a narrative, so, although they must refer to an actual physical thing, they must be simple enough to be drawn and erased quickly in time with the flow of the story. In our culture, films are comparable to the Aboriginal art of drawing images and telling stories in the sand. Just as the sequential nature of film causes one image to be

FIGURE 141
Dot painting of witchetty grub and other Aboriginal food sources. A women's painting of the radiating trails leading from campsites to the gathering sites of favorite foods, whose fertility is symbolized by concentric energy circles.

replaced by another, films affect the popular imagination briefly and then fade.

Over the years, a few sand signs have taken on universal significance in Aboriginal art. For example, a "U" design represents a person involved in an action, and the tools next to the "U" (a spear, digging stick, or fish trap) designate the action. Many symbols drawn with a story are created on the spot, to fit a particular story and a particular audience. The storyteller fabricates and defines her symbols as she communicates them, which makes all symbols highly contextual.[2] Such immediacy encourages the listener not to memorize but to visualize anew with each story a connection between a symbol and its object or action.

One consistent aspect of this otherwise mutable symbolic process is that most objects, people, and landscapes are drawn as if seen from above. This aerial perspective connects the storytelling to dreams or other altered states in which consciousness is projected out of the body.

Men apply the personal mode of art in a more specialized way. A man is given a number of personal stories by older kin that he can use to attract women. These love stories usually tell, in intimate detail, the romantic exploits of a great Dreamtime Ancestor.[3] The symbols associated with these love stories are generally clever, humorous, or erotic, and the innuendos sexually arousing. The stories become part of a man's charisma, and women may be drawn to him through curiosity about his reputedly great stories.

IMAGE AND SOCIETY

Social symbolism appears in both women's and men's ceremonies as body painting. Body painting raises the personal presentation of imagemaking to a communal level. It is a sensuous, tactile form of social interchange in which stories are shared as the body is painted; the combination of touch and hearing increases the empathetic power and intensity of this form of communication.[4] In women's ceremonies, the body carries the story into dance and actually releases the emotional content surrounding the adventures of love and the tragedies of loss.

No form of Aboriginal visual art is meant to stand alone, whether it be a sand image, a body painting, a sacred board or stone, an earth sculpture, a painted tree trunk or wooden sculpture, a painting on rock or bark, or any other traditional art form. Visual arts have a language that is always associated with, or parallel to, other languages: myths, stories, dance, song, or ritual. In the Aboriginal view, the meaning of a symbol is inscribed in one's awareness only when it is absorbed through languages that affect both mind and body.

The Aboriginal way of interweaving a multitude of languages is clearly reflected in earth sculpture, a social art made by men. A group of men

FIGURE 142
Ceremonial earth sculptures represent topographies created by the Dreamtime Ancestors. They may extend for acres in order to complete a mythic cycle.

287

shape the land into a relief map. The myth being depicted determines the size of this earth sculpture. Some earth sculptures, especially those created for initiation rites and some funerary ceremonies, recreate an entire myth cycle and can extend over several acres. While the men work on the design together, they sing the related chants and perform the dances associated with the forms they are building. The songs and dances explain the many levels of meaning in the simple linear and circular design elements. No social or ceremonial art is ever preserved as an *objet d'art*. The actual work of art is destroyed after it has supported a ceremony involving many different levels of being.[5]

Aboriginal art uses a palette of four colors ground from red, black, yellow, and white earth pigments. There is no name or concept for blue or blue-green in the Aboriginal vocabulary. All the colors of natural

FIGURE 143
Body painting is the most fundamental expression of social art.

daylight are tinged with blue from the refraction of light as it travels through the atmosphere; hence, the blue of the sky, the blue of the ocean, and the blue-greens of the plant kingdom are all considered an infusion from the Dreaming, which permeates all things. Earth colors are associated with the tangible world—the *yuti*—whereas blue and green reflect flowing, mutable sky and water and the changing cycles of leafing and flowering plants. This division marks the transition from the invisible ultraviolet to the tangible infrared of the rainbow, in other words, the transition between the Dreaming and the physical world.

Other forms of social art are the large carved boards that men exchange during the settling of disputes and the paraphernalia men fabricate from sticks, hair, and feathers for kinship exchange and healing. There are also message sticks—carved branches that are carried great distances to announce ceremonial events between distant clans. As with ceremonies, some art—the sacred boards, carved stones (*churingas*), and bark paintings—is classified as sacred and has practical, social, and ceremonial functions. Other types of art are classified as secret sacred and are shrouded in mysteries that are withheld from all but the initiated.

Transformation and the Sacred Image

Several characteristics mark a work of art as sacred. Sacred art always implies transformation: the transformation of pure energy into form, the transformation of ancestral powers into animals, animals into humans, and humans, through ritual costume and body painting, into the ancestral beings and their animal powers. The cultural heroes or great Ancestors, through their acts of miraculous transformation, created the species, varieties, and order of the world. Transformation in sacred art recalls the potency of the Dreamtime. Aboriginal sacred art designates transformation in a number of ways; for example, a kangaroo in a painting may wear a hairbelt or other item of apparel strictly associated with humans.[6] Such attributes indicate consciousness transformed into a spirit of another species. In Egypt these transformations were represented in exactly the same manner: the gods were pictured as humans with animal heads or animals with human attributes or accessories. The Aborigines depict another level of transformation by painting cross-hatched patterns inside or surrounding the bodies of animals and humans. These represent the subtle energy fields that underlie, surround, and interconnect all things in creation.

Transformation or metamorphosis is the basis of the entire sacred symbolism. A circle, for example, may represent many things: a circular

FIGURE 144
The didjereedoo is the world's
oldest musical instrument. In
addition to ceremonial use, it is
employed primarily as a method
of studying nature. The player
deeply empathizes with the
sounds of nature and reproduces
these through this flute.

path, a water hole, a fruit, a fire, a yam, or a tree base. The circle relates not only to a physical object but, through that object, to the metaphysical creative power of the earth: to a water hole as well as the specific regions of the earth from which the spirits of various species emerge; to a woman's breast as well as to the rain that falls from the heavens in response to the earth's hunger. In other words, the circle ultimately represents the source of all life and nourishment.

Underneath the soil surface of a locality where wild yams grow profusely, the Aborigines visualize concentric rings of energy that account for the productivity of that piece of land. These invisible geometric configurations are referred to as *guruwari* and are often drawn in the earth during the most secret sacred ceremonies.[7] The concentric rings are raised and stabilized by mixing the earth with human blood. Alternate rings are decorated with bird down. The Ancestors created and deposited many such energy configurations that account for the fertility of the earth, and this energy drives the continuous transformations that we experience as life. By grace of this power, the food we eat is transformed into our own flesh, the sunlight is transformed into trees, plants, food, and flowers. In a sacred vision, all of life is a symbol in a state of transformation; each moment is transforming itself into the next.

The motivation for schematizing and symbolizing in Aboriginal art is not abstraction as we know it. Each form is simplified only to the degree that its interrelationship with other forms and other worlds becomes evident. The Aborigines perceive all of existence in congruent layers from metaphysical to physical dimensions. Totemic art depicts this layered structure of the world, with each layer being a different manifestation of a metaphysical seed power. Western science sees the totemic world in a materialistic way in which all levels and complexities of life descend from a single original DNA code. Western art comes closest to the totemic essence of symbolism in abstract expressionism, where the detail and definition of images are removed, allowing simplified images to form associations within the viewer's consciousness. Abstraction arose in the West as a reaction against the literal use of image and detail that developed after the Renaissance. Although abstract expressionism had a profound effect on Western aesthetics and thought, the main tendency of Western signs and symbols is toward singular, unambiguous, unchanging connotations. For the Aborigines, the opposite is the case. The only accurate symbol is ambiguous because, like all of life, it conjoins many meanings and many levels at once.

As with imagemaking, Aboriginal music also unites consciousness with the invisible laws and energy patterns of nature. Aboriginal art is perhaps most accurately described as a method for gaining knowledge of nature and its invisible Dreaming. An example is the playing of the didjereedoo, a long wooden flute, perhaps the oldest musical instrument on earth. Traditionally, an Aborigine would go into nature and listen intensely to animal sounds, not just voices but also the flapping of wings or the thump of feet on the ground. The Aborigine would also listen to the sounds of wind, thunder, trees creaking, and water running. The essences of all these sounds were played with as much accuracy as possible within the droning sound of the didjereedoo. For the Aborigine, the observation of nature immediately requires a state of empathy, which leads to an imitative expression. Dance follows the same process: each movement of an animal is acutely observed and re-created so that the steps of the dance represent the dancer's knowledge of and identity with the natural world.

IMAGE AND INTEGRATION

The ambiguity and the transformative properties of both life and symbol are fundamental to the Aboriginal sense of reality. In sacred art, the Dreamtime Ancestors actually live within the transformative images. The image is the vehicle, indeed the body and presence, of the fertilizing power of the Ancestors on earth. The positive ambiguity of the image allows it to capture the spirit of invisible transformative powers. Sacred images exercise that power by inciting transformations in the thought and awareness of viewers. The fish trap, in Aboriginal art, symbolizes the capacity of an image to trap the transformative spirit; that is why the Rainbow Serpent energy is often represented within a fish trap.[8] Ancient

FIGURE 145 (BELOW) & 146 (NEXT PAGE) Bark painting of a grouper fish and a shark. The fish trap in Aboriginal thought and the bird net in Egyptian symbolism symbolize the capacity of consciousness to capture the fleeting, mutable ideas and meanings associated with the creatures and activities of the natural world.

Egyptians used a net for capturing birds in the same way: the subtle, the volatile, the ever-moving is captured or contained in a symbol.

The Aboriginal use of symbols can be applied to the unresolved questions about the relationship of an object to its image that persist in contemporary thought. A classic example is the image used to describe the nature of light. The "fish trap" for describing light is sometimes a particle—an infinitesimally small packet of light (photon)—and sometimes a wave or wave field. For a while, historically, the particle was a dynamic model that spawned advances in the understanding of matter as well as progress in both applied and theoretical physics. Nearly a century ago, this image began to be replaced with the wave theory of light, which has generated more technological progress as well as a more unified theory of energy and matter. One image of light is not true and the other false; each explains some aspect of light. One possible explanation of this ambiguity is that one image or symbol is effective in one phase of individual or collective development, and another image of the same phenomenon is more potent at a different stage. It is assumed that light contains a spectrum of qualities, some of which correspond to the *particle* image, while others correspond to that of the *wave*. The image itself may actually complete the externalization of a particular quality that is innate in the force field of light. Therefore, by consciously changing their view of reality, people are actually contributing to changing the actual parameters of the world.

To state the issue another way, the consensual validation of an image in the collective mind produces an energy that activates particular qualities from the multitude latent in the natural forces. In *Beyond Supernature*, Lyall Watson developed historical evidence to support this idea, using the example of the history of tuberculosis. From 10,000 years ago until the end of the nineteenth century, this disease was responsible for dev-

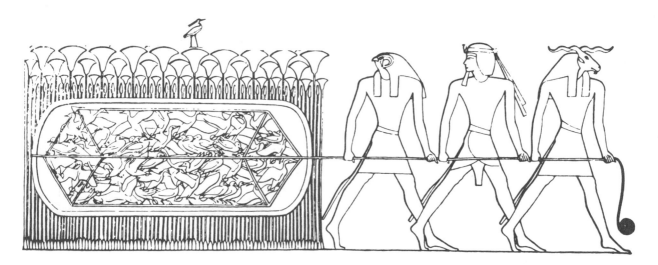

astating epidemics throughout the world. The image that most people had of its cause was a mysterious, amorphous, sickly ether or atmosphere that swept through cities and countrysides. In 1882, Dr. Robert Koch triumphantly announced that he had discovered that the cause of tuberculosis was not an invincible, invisible agent but a tiny bacteria, so weak that exposure to sunlight could destroy it. That very year, before any medical action was taken, the death rate fell to one-third its previous level.[9] Did the change in paradigm change the way people were affected by the disease, or did it actually change the powers of the organism itself? Indeed, can the two things be separated? Perhaps the phenomenon and its representation draw energy from the same channels of influence.

After a century of success in treating fatal diseases through a biochemical approach, a century which saw such deadly diseases as cholera, pneumonia, and bubonic plague rendered curable by antibiotics, we have come to attribute the cause of all sorts of diseases to bacteria—and now to viruses as well.[10] In so doing, we may have empowered the image of disease causality to the extent that viruses are practically omnipotent. Consequently, new uncontrollable epidemics stand at our threshold. As the microbial theory of disease reaches its zenith, recognition is growing that disturbances in mental and emotional energy may be a more fundamental level of disease causation. The bioelectric bases of living organisms is being explored in this context, and the cause of disease is beginning to be related to electrical or radiation disturbances.[11] The pendulum seems to be swinging from the particle paradigm (bacteria and viruses) to the field paradigm (wave) of causation.

IMAGE AND RENEWAL

For more than 100,000 years, the Australian Aborigines would periodically repaint the cave-wall images of their Ancestors, who were considered the active agents behind the forces of nature. This was done in the belief that renewing the image strengthened the force that the image represented. The ancient Egyptians also defaced or reestablished images and hieroglyphs on their temple walls, believing that this increased or restrained the activity of those forces in the physical world.

The integration of psychic, imagistic, and physical forces that is just emerging in our scientific world view agrees with the Aboriginal world view. The Aborigines see psychic energies as causatively involved in every natural process and event from sunlight, wind, and rain to human fertility. Sacred art and ritual play an important role in the congruence of a multilayered universe and the cycles of harmonic transformations from the Dreaming to the physical world.

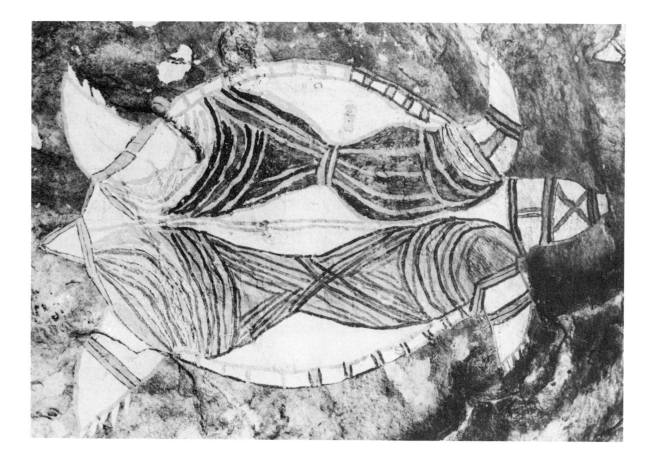

FIGURE 147
An Australian Aboriginal rock painting. In the ancient turtle totem of Aboriginal Australia, the dome-like curved shell symbolizes the sky in its relation to the square flat underside, which is symbolic of the earth.

The living world does not reduce to images or language. The actions and reactions of life occur in an immeasurable variety of intertwined relationships. The perceivable world (*yuti*) can only be spoken of in fleeting images drawn in sand. Its truths can only be transmitted through the laughter and imagination of a woman telling a story to a child. It is the flowing unformed world whose inner energy existed before symbols, before the "naming." The ancestral powers through Dreamtime events, created separate, definite things by naming them; therefore, the symbols and language of sacred art can touch the otherworldly ancestral powers. The Ancestors' consciousness was so wide, powerful, and concentrated that it could swallow great multitudes of the incomprehensible plentitude of the experiential world, devouring them into a single word, image, or species. Symbolizing or naming retains the connection to death and devouring that it has had since the Dreaming. The experience dies to itself as soon as it becomes word or image. The naming mummifies the experience, converting the mushrooming confluence of the actual into a reflection suspended in the veiled mirror of language. Reality and meaning escape the entombment of experience—they fly through the grid trap of sign and symbol. Their fearful desertion permits the inner

← *FIGURE 148*
Aboriginal rock images have been painted and repainted for at least 40,000 years.

FIGURE 149
The basic graphic elements of the phosphenes are comparable with those found in early Tasmanian petroglyphs.

vision to catch only a glimpse of them fleeing. The death of experience in words can be like any other death—an initiation. Words and symbols, if understood as death and initiation, allow experience to be reborn in human consciousness as fresh awareness in each generation.

Before European contact, all sacred art in Aboriginal culture, except for some cave drawings, was purely geometric. The figures of crocodiles and emu birds and kangaroos were added only after European contact because, as the Aborigines say, "The Europeans have no power to visualize." In the subtle variations of cross-hatched energy fields, the Aborigines read knowledge of animals, maps, clan affiliations, and entire mythic stories.

Tasmanian Aboriginal glyphs exemplify this Aboriginal geometry. They bear a striking resemblance to a set of designs called phosphenes that have emerged from research in cognitive psychology. *Phosphene* comes from the Greek word for "light shows," and they are produced by excitation of the retina. Everyone who has received a severe knock on the head has seen flashes of light that seem to originate within the head. Such light patterns can also be seen when falling asleep or meditating with eyes closed. Airplane pilots report seeing similar apparitions when

FIGURE 150

A bark painting from Yirrkala, Arnhem Land, in Australia's Northern Territory, illustrating the track of the mythical goanna, Tjundu. *It is painted in red and yellow ochre, white clay, and ground charcoal. The meandering line represents the mark of the goanna's tail, and the herringbone pattern, the sand that runs down the slope as he walks along the crest of a drifting sandhill. The earth's pigments—red, yellow, black, and white—make up the limited palette of traditional Aboriginal art. The traditional artists painted the complex linear grid patterns with brushes made of six strands of human hair twisted together.*

flying across expanses of empty sky. Astronauts have reported viewing phosphenes so tangibly in outer space that they were first believed to be caused by heavy light particles. Phosphenes appear when the opened eyes have had nothing to see for an extended period of time. Delirium tremens, fasting, high fever, hyperventilation, migraine headaches, and simple eye pressure can produce variations on the basic set of fifteen patterns.

Clinical tests indicate that children between two and four years of age see phosphenes in such a way that they seem as real as the external world. Given a crayon at this early age, children are apt to draw patterns that have a distinct phosphene character. Evidence suggests that animals are frequently absorbed in this form of visualization.[12]

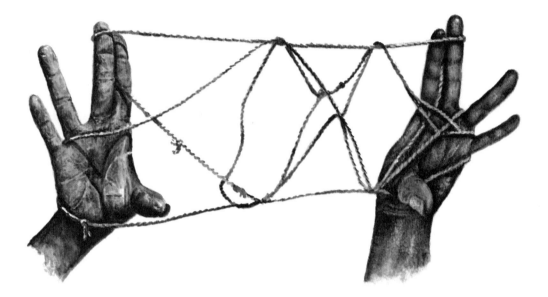

Cat's cradle, a game in which a looped string stretched between the fingers of both hands is manipulated into a succession of patterns, is played throughout the world. It has long been known that this game originated in Egypt, but it has recently been discovered among tribal people as widely dispersed as the Pygmies of the Belgian Congo, Native Americans, and the Australian Aborigines. These peoples have played this game as far back into their history as they can remember. In Aboriginal culture, the string is made from braided strands of human hair, and each successive design instigates the memory of a cosmological myth. The storytellers stare at the various patterns and relate the mythic drama associated with each design. The designs produced resemble phosphenes.

Hallucinogenic drugs induce states in which phosphene viewing is particularly vivid. Henry Munn, who lived with the Mezatec Indians of New Mexico, reported that the shamans always begin their hallucino-

FIGURE 151
The making of string figures is an old art form that flourishes among Aboriginal people, especially in northeastern Arnhem Land. These geometric patterns stimulate the remembrance of complex mythic stories and events.

genic healing rituals in a completely dark enclosure, in which similar patterns to the phosphenes begin with intense vividness. For the shaman, they announce the beginning of a transcendental experience. The shaman speaks in the darkness, describing to those present the meanings that spring from the hallucinations. The shaman's words arise directly from the vision without any intervening thought process.

> Gradually colours begin to well up behind closed eyes. Consciousness becomes consciousness of irradiation and effulgences, of a flux of light patterns forming and unforming, of electrical currents beaming forth from within the brain. At this initial moment of reawakenment, experiencing the dawn of light in the midst of the night, the shaman evokes the illumination of the constellations at the genesis of the world.[13]

Munn claims that the essence of the shamanistic tradition lies in language, the making of the word. His essay supports the idea that shamanism is the origin of all philosophical traditions that adhere to the precept, "In the beginning was the word." Munn describes a shamanistic ritual in which the shaman receives inner images and instantaneously emits the word for them. For the listeners, also in a hypnogogic trance, these words ignite lines of relationships between things that otherwise appear separate and unrelated. The healing power of the shaman is directly related to the ability of his visionary words, which draw together that which has been pulled asunder. The highest level of shamanic healing, according to Munn, lies in the capacity to provoke new understanding of both self and the world.

The mytho-poetic descriptions of inner patterns danced and sung by entranced Mezatec shamans are also the source of cosmological images that correspond to the elemental or natural world. Munn reports that the shaman's expanding, subjective state spreads through his vision, so that his interior contains all that is outside.

From a scientific point of view, what are these inner light shows? Phosphenes are believed to originate primarily in the retinal-optical track and the brain. Scientists think they are images reflecting neural firing patterns in the visual pathways, which makes them very important cognitive images. After nearly a century of research into human perception, neurophysicists agree that these spatial, temporal, neuroelectrical light patterns are the only input that ever reaches or stimulates the brain. The consciousness of the human species converts these geometric neural patterns into the images of an experiential world. This process is similar to the way Aborigines read into their pure geometric images stories of places, people, events, and things. We are able to perceive the world because the spatial-temporal patterns of our neural activity resonate with the spatial-temporal patterns underpinning the external environment.

This kind of imagemaking provides another way to think about the Dreamtime creation. The Creative Ancestors made the world in a similar way, forming and shaping the creation from the symmetries and geometries of a preexisting energy continuum. The Aborigines maintain within their bodily existence the universal geometry of creation, activating it through sacred images and rhythmic movement. In contrast, the extraordinary capacities of Western civilization to geometrize space, time, and energy can be seen as the projecting or externalizing of the innate, ancestral order of the mind of nature.

CHAPTER 17

HUNTER-GATHERERS AND TOTEMISM

CHICKEN HAWK SUCCEEDS IN STEALING FIRE

Little Chicken Hawk (Djungarabaja), Big Hawk (Bugaidjma), and Dog (Mojin) were camping together on a high hill at Dilg in Madngala and Maranunggu country. Dog went out and collected sour yams and sweet yams. Returning, he said, "Brother, break a special stick for making fire. We'll twirl it to make fire to cook this food." Dog twirled it but broke it, tried another and broke it. He couldn't get it right. "Better I should go out and get a live fire stick so we can have a good fire."

He went off to a camp and hid behind a pandanus tree. A lot of women

had been out collecting yams and bush foods, and now they came back to the camp with them. They made a fire, preparing an oven and arranging the stones for baking. When the wood had burnt down they brushed aside the burnt-out pieces, leaving the glowing coals. Dog jumped forward to take a fire stick; but the women saw him and chased him away, saying, "There's no fire for you." He returned home and told the others, "It's no good, I'm too big, they all saw me." "Try again," they demanded. He went back to the women's camp and hid behind the pandanus again. As before, the women returned from food collecting and began to make an oven. Dog tried again to get fire, but again they drove him away. He returned to the others. "No, I'm too big. They always see me." Dog's hands were sore from twirling the fire sticks, so he said, "You go, Djungarabaja!"

So Little Chicken Hawk went to the women's camp and hid behind the pandanus. The women returned from the bush, as before, and began to prepare an oven. But this time they looked around for Dog, and, knowing that he lived with Big Hawk Bugaidjma, they looked for him, too. The presence of Djungarabaja escaped them; he was small. Satisfied, they continued with their oven making; they scraped out the wood and placed the large glowing logs to one side. As soon as they did this Djungarabaja swooped down and took up a piece of glowing wood, crying out, "Diid . . . Diid!" The women rushed forward, but he flew off with it. As he went he dropped some charcoal, broken by his beak as he held the fire stick; today there are charcoal

FIGURE 152 & 153
Demonstration by Aranda man of spearthrowing. Alice Springs, Central Australia, 1896.

patches stretching from Birangma toward Djungarabaja Hill (almost parallel to the Dilg Hills).

Back in camp he found that Dog, impatient at waiting, had eaten his yams uncooked. "Ah!" Djungarabaja scolded, "you have eaten them raw, and here I've brought fire!" That is why the dog doesn't talk, as chicken hawks do, and eats his food raw: he could not wait. But those three still remain at that place, dreaming; at Djungarabaja, named after Little Chicken Hawk.[1]

KINSHIP WITH THE SPIRIT OF NATURE

FOR THE ABORIGINES, eating is a sacred act; it represents humanity's deepest communication and kinship with the life-giving forces of the earth. Like all acts of communication, it is based on the Dreamtime Law of reciprocity. Hunting and gathering are considered the basis of developing the physical and spiritual potential of human nature. The great hunt is the means by which the spiritual powers of the earth and sky educate humanity. Animals and plants nourish the body, and the process of hunting, foraging, and preparing imparts dexterity, physical skills, and intellectual and spiritual knowledge.

Aborigines' tools are few and simple: for hunting, men take a few spears, a spearthrower, and sometimes a boomerang; for gathering, women use only a simple sharpened digging stick and a curved wooden bowl. To ensure an adequate, balanced diet, all Aborigines have to develop extraordinary alertness, perception, and physical dexterity. The animals they hunt, especially wallabies, kangaroos, and possums, are extremely agile and fast. Except in some of the fertile coastal regions, edible plant varieties are unrecognizable except to a trained eye; many varieties contain poisons or tannins and therefore require careful handling and extraction. Besides being able to handle their simple tools skillfully, the Aborigines must have an encyclopedic knowledge of plants and animals and a keen sense of the elements, such as wind conditions and seasonal patterns.[2]

Knowledge of the plant and animal world is obtained by two methods: long, careful observation and deep, empathic states of ceremonially induced trance. The most powerful hunters are also spectacular dancers and singers who can imitate the movements and sounds of animals and birds. Aborigines spend long hours watching and listening to animals. By imitation, they imprint these animal characteristics in their own neuromuscular systems during days and nights of ceremonial ritual and dance.

One such animal dance ceremony was observed and photographed by Gillen and Spencer. More than 30 naked men gathered in a large circle. One by one, each man performed the dance of the animal to be hunted while the others sang and slapped their buttocks to create a percussive beat for the dancer. The slapping sound was so loud that it could be heard for miles across the surrounding desert. The dance continued for hours, with each man dancing frenetically until he dropped from exhaustion. The eyes of the onlookers soon became glazed with entrancement; their penises were erect in a state of ecstatic arousal. Finally, after the last man had performed the animal dance and collapsed in exhaustion, the entire group leaped on him, emitting a loud abandoned cry. The next day the hunt began.[3]

The animal sounds and movements, learned through dance and song, are employed as lures and decoys during the hunt. The intelligence and sensibilities of the animal become alive within the consciousness of the hunter and his kin. *In this way, the quarry first becomes part of the hunter in spirit before becoming part of him in flesh.* The spirit life of the animal species is thereby extended in exchange for its physical death. The Aborigines believe that if this reciprocity is not fulfilled, nourishment may have destructive effects.

During the rise and spread of agriculture, people lost the knowledge of the spiritual reciprocity between hunter and hunted, eater and eaten. Postagrarian religions transformed the understanding of the balance

FIGURE 154
Bush Tucker. A handful of honey ants, a sweet delicacy prized by the Aborigines.

FIGURE 155
The ecstatic dance in which hunters enter into the spirit nature of their prey. In a hunting and gathering society the individual is materially independent, yet crosses the boundary into the spiritual dimension through the collective body of his clan or tribe. In contrast, the individual in our agricultural society is materially dependent upon the collective, and isolated or independent during spiritual experiences. These two cultures are materially and spiritually the inverse of one another.

between the nourishing and destructive qualities of foods into rigid restrictions. The ancient Indian Vedas declared, "Hunger is death and Lord and Master of this world. The eater, while eating, is being eaten."[4] It became widely accepted in later forms of Hinduism and Buddhism that the negative impact of plant food was much less than that of animal food, which generated an association between vegetarianism and spirituality. For the Aborigines, who maintain spiritual communication in their food-procuring ritual, such restrictions are meaningless. They partake of foods from every realm of nature: mammals, birds, reptiles, insects, land and water roots, tree and grass seeds, vegetables, fruits, fungi, algae, and eggs.

Hunting and gathering demand both exceptionally keen powers of observation and a subconscious mind highly developed through ritual trance, dance, and song. This state of awareness is recognized in most spiritual traditions as knowledge by identity.

The European settlers were amazed not only by Aboriginal perception, knowledge, and physical prowess but also by their ability to identify with and enter into their environment. There are accounts of Tasmanian Aborigines who, when fleeing from white settlers, assumed a crouched posture that made them indistinguishable from the trunk of a tree, extending one arm so that it looked like a branch. A person standing a short distance away could not distinguish the body from a tree stump. British sealers forced Tasmanian women, under threat of torture, to catch and kill seals for their skins. The native women would swim to rocks where a group of seals were resting, climb up on the rocks, and make sounds and movements that perfectly mimicked those of the seals. Their ability to enter into the essence of the species was so great that the seals mistook the women for other seals and were easily clubbed to death.[5]

This form of intelligence emulates the consciousness of the Dreamtime, in which each state or process interfused with another. The flow between states of consciousness is described in the final chapter of the Egyptian *Book of the Dead*. In this passage an initiate, after passing through a ritual death, completely masters the ability to externalize his consciousness in an identity with the beings of the gods (who are animals). In Chapter 42 of the *Book of the Dead*, the deceased says,

> My eyes are the eyes of Hathor [the cow]
> My lips are the lips of Anpu [the snake]
> My belly and back are the belly and back of Sekhet [the lioness]
> My phallus is the phallus of Osiris [cyclic time]
> My hips and legs are the hips and legs of Nut [the cosmic ocean][6]

Knowledge by identity—the absorption into the forms and consciousness of the surrounding world—is the meaning of the Sanskrit word for enlightenment, *prajnana*. This capacity or state of awareness became the goal of many Eastern meditation traditions. Its unacknowledged sources were the methods the hunter-gatherers used in their ritual preparation for the hunt.

The fundamental imbalance between our civilization and the natural environment can be traced to our total reliance on the objectifying, analytical mind, along with a lack of integration of this conscious mind with unconsciousness. We learn to establish our assessment of the ex-

FIGURE 156
Hunting the fleet-footed marsupials with only simple wooden implements requires great physical dexterity and mental concentration and perception.

305

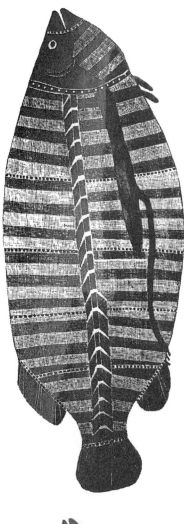

ternal world solely through the conscious mind, thereby isolating the object from the subjective. The Native American philosopher Jamake Highwater remarks that this permanent alienation is built into our language structure. In phrases such as "That is bread," subject and object are simultaneously linked together and held apart in a fixed state of separate being by the word *is*. Highwater states that in Native American languages the same experience would be expressed as, "In my perception for the moment, bread." This phrase acknowledges that bread has been earth, water, and sunlight, that it has lived as plant, grain, and flour. Bread is bread only in relationship to the beholder, who, in the devouring, realizes an identification in both body and spirit.[7]

Any creature that does not sleep dies. That is to say, nature and reality require a communion of conscious and unconscious, waking and dreaming, visible and invisible. In dreams the objective world becomes invisible and the subjective world visible. This universal oscillation *is* the existence of consciousness. The grammatical structure of Indo-European languages is based exclusively on the separation of the perceiver from the surrounding world. Therefore, our entire experience of space/time relationships is governed by our conscious mind. This represents a distortion of the nature of reality, a fundamental imbalance in our culture.

As they grow older, Aborigines learn more sophisticated approaches to hunting and gathering through initiations, to add to the physical abilities they develop during youth. Mature Aborigines are given initiatic knowledge of certain poisonous herbs that can be mixed into streams or water holes, stunning the fish in the water or the mammals who drank from it and facilitating their capture. Another cunning method is mimicking the calls and sounds of the animals to lure them within range.[8]

Older or more initiatically advanced Aborigines employ fishing methods that are grounded in spiritual awareness. They know that the sounds of clapping music sticks near the water will draw fish. These tapered sticks are tuned by varying their thickness and density to make sounds that attract a particular species of fish. In some cases, the proportions and shape of the tapered music sticks are similar to those of the species of fish they are meant to attract. Aborigines also communicate with dolphins, known to help them capture whatever species of fish they desire on a particular day. They scoop water into their hands and clap them together rhythmically, sending a signal to nearby dolphins, which drive a school of fish toward the Aborigines' waiting nets.[9] Another method used by older initiates, or men of high degree, is the capacity to catch the gaze of an animal and temporarily hypnotize it, preventing it from fleeing. The progression in hunting methods, from acute physical skills to an increased reliance on acquired knowledge culminating in psychic methods of capturing prey, vividly shows how the Aborigines spiritualize their relationship with nature.

Animals and plants are considered the embodiment of the world-creating forces, the Dreamtime Ancestors. Their physical presence on earth represents the spiritual presence of the gods. In their superior capacities of smell, sight, and hearing, animals take in and use a much greater amount of sensory information than humans do. In terms of perceptual intelligence, animals are more highly developed, godlike beings. The present alarming rate of species extinction is viewed by the Aborigines, indeed by all indigenous people, not simply as a diminishment of "useful genetic pools" but as a withdrawal of spiritual force from the earth and from humanity.

A profound delusion underlying modern scientific philosophy can be traced at least in part to the sixteenth-century logician René Descartes, who claimed that animals were no more than blind brutes or instinctive machines.[10] In the name of such reasoning, we have justified the exploitation of the animal life around us. Some scientific research is now undoing the great error of applying mechanistic models to animal life. Clinical evidence related to rapid eye movement shows that animals, birds, and reptiles dream vivid dreams, just as we do. Animals communicate, prepare remedies from natural substances to cure their own diseases,[11] act morally and altruistically toward their kin,[12] and think, reason, plan, and solve problems.[13] We have no justification for holding up our particular forms of intelligence and communication as superior to theirs.

Scientists have not yet been able to locate the source of our own intelligence. The brain receives only mechanical and electrical nerve impulses; nothing goes on in our supposed organ of intelligence except on/off neural signals. There are no sounds, no images, no thoughts, tastes, or concepts. The brain receives no sense qualities of external objects in a physical or chemical way.[14] We have no idea where the seat of the sensory perception of a spatial temporal world can be. Judging by the material evidence, there are no emotions within us, no imagination, no memory, only complex electrical and nerve patterns.[15]

Scientists are finally realizing that our powers of intellect, like those of animals, cannot entirely be explained by the functions of the physical body but may be influenced by superphysical or metaphysical phenomena. Contemporary biologists postulate the existence of morphic fields, which are similar to the Aboriginal preexistent spirit force associated with each species. The anatomy of the eye is very similar throughout the animal kingdom, yet the spirit of each species utilizes this structure to view the world in its own unique way. The logical conclusion is that the world exists only in the perception and intelligence of the multiplicity

HUNTER-GATHERERS
AND TOTEMISM

307

of creatures who observe it. There is no standard progression in species: each creature perceives a facet of the world and all together they cause the fullness of the world to come into existence. The wonders of the world are not reducible to human intelligence. For the Aborigines, the joy of life is to enter into the spiritual intelligence of all species and to share in life's diversity through the unique intelligence of each of its creatures.

FIGURE 158
Women's gathering is a graceful, joyous activity, in which they obtain food from land and water plants.

MEN AND WOMEN IN THE QUEST FOR FOOD

The natural male-female complementarity forms the basic unit of Aboriginal society. The male physical aptitudes and temperament equip him for the demands of hunting larger game. The female capacity to visualize and integrate complex patterns of plant growth aid in the discovery of plants, seeds, and small reptiles and mammals. Although men spend long hours hunting, their return is relatively small compared with women's. Women's gathering normally produces between 80 and 90 percent of the Aboriginal diet, which is 70 to 80 percent vegetarian. As with giving birth, the woman's role in providing nourishment is primary, the man's secondary. The male-centered bias of our culture has ignored this fact—indigenous people ought to be thought of as gatherer-hunters.[16] Anthropologist Catherine Berndt has recorded Aboriginal women explicitly declaring their pride in their role and identity: "We carry digging sticks, not spears. We are women, not men!"[17] This simple statement embodies an important principle overlooked by much of modern feminism; women have innate powers far greater than any they could derive by emulating men.

Men and women as a group decide the clan's food-gathering strategy for the day, depending on weather conditions, locality, and the direction of their wanderings. While the men's hunt and its associated rites are cloaked in seriousness, the gathering parties of women and children set off in a relaxed, jovial atmosphere. Gathering never entails any pressure or sense of urgency; it is not, unlike agricultural harvesting, considered a battle against time or the elements. Even during severe dry seasons the food quest is not disproportionately time-consuming, rarely requiring more than three or four hours. Foraging is always interspersed with leisure—sleeping, playing with small children, and idle chatting. Ritual dance and song occurs not only in groups at prescribed times but spontaneously by individuals in the midst of harvesting. Women feed themselves and their children as they go along, later sharing and distributing or exchanging their harvest with other members of the clan.[18]

The spontaneous informality of women's foraging is in direct contrast to the male hunter's role. The moment a man kills a kangaroo, a complex formal system of distribution goes into effect. Male polygamy entails multiple in-law relationships over long distances in all directions. Each of these kin ties involves food-sharing obligations. After the kill, the

FIGURE 159
Every detail of the procedure of hunting, including the lifting, carrying, cooking, and dividing of the prey, was outlined in the Dreamtime stories.

hunter sits unobtrusively to one side as each of his kin relatives steps forward to claim one of the fixed number of pieces into which the kangaroo has been butchered. The Dreamtime stories describe a specific cut of meat for each of the kin categories. The hunter himself eats last, if at all, usually claiming only the entrails. Paradoxically, the prime cut goes to his mother-in-law, with whom he shares a strict avoidance relationship and of whom he only speaks in the most insulting terms.

This hunter receives his prescribed share of meat when his kin makes a catch. Formal sharing is a compulsory activity for Aboriginal men, even when not necessitated by circumstance. This convention demonstrates that food sharing has nothing to do with sentiment or preference; it is a way of reaffirming the all-important web of reciprocity on which the life of this society depends.[19]

All of these gathering and hunting regulations are detailed in various Dreamtime stories and reflect societal attitudes about the universal, contrasting characteristics of men and women. The pattern of reciprocity holds in every aspect of Aboriginal hunting practices. For example, each animal species is believed to arise from a particular place, where Aboriginal men go to perform increase rites that appeal to the spirit of the species. It is forbidden to kill an animal in the region surrounding the site that is sacred to it. Aboriginal women reciprocate in what appears to be a more practical way: when digging up the desert roots they call yams, they always leave an end portion in the ground, which they say impregnates the earth to give birth to more.[20]

The spiritual dimension is also respected in cooking and food preparation. Ideally, an animal is cooked and eaten as close as possible to the place where it was killed; all things, including food, are more sacred by virtue of being in place. When a speared kangaroo or other large animal is roasted whole on an open fire, it is first exposed to roaring flames for 10 minutes, during which time the spirit of the animal escapes to the metaphysical abode of its species. After the initial roasting the bloated carcass of the animal is removed from the fire, its fur scraped off, and its intestines removed with a sharp stone. It is then returned to a bed of hot coals and cooked on each side for 20 minutes. The warm, partly cooked blood is thought to have magic properties; the men drink it in a post-hunt ritual and rub it on their spears for continued accuracy.[21] Cold-blooded reptiles, on the other hand, are always cooked until they are black and crisp. Other cooking methods, such as baking in ashes, steaming in ground ovens, or boiling in seawater and tortoise shells, all have ritual and Dreamtime connotations. Aborigines usually gather to eat only one main meal a day in late afternoon; during the day everyone snacks while they hunt and gather.

The greatest impact of the Aborigines on the environment is their practice of burning off small patches of country. This promotes the propagation of a variety of food plants, since the seeds of many edible plant species only germinate as a result of fire. The Aborigines relate this burning practice to initiation, calling it a "death" that incites new life. Fires serve the additional purpose of flushing out game so that it can be hunted more easily. The men chase the kangaroos, and the women the smaller marsupials. These methods, called "fire stick farming" by anthropologists, are highly controlled and are implemented only by men who have the responsibility for totemic rites in that particular region.[22] The Aborigines learned fire stick farming from the myth of the Great Ancestor chicken hawk, who used fire to catch marsupial rats and mice. An early anthropologist claims to have seen a chicken hawk swoop down and pick up an ignited branch from a fire Aborigines had set. From aloft the hawk dropped the smoldering ember into some grass, igniting its own fire to assist it in capturing prey.[23] This is an exceptional example of reciprocity between the mythic Ancestors, humans, and animals, and of the fusion of the physical and metaphysical dimensions of the hunt.

EARTH, SPIRIT, AND NOURISHMENT

An Aboriginal tribal woman stood watching a missionary as he anxiously tended a garden of wilted, insect-ridden plants. Shaking her head in dismay, she remarked to anthropologist Ronald Berndt, "You people go to all that trouble and worry, working and planting seeds, but we don't have to do that. All these things are there for us. . . . The ancestral beings left our food for us. In the end you depend on the sun and rain just the same as we do. But the difference is we just have to go and collect the food when it is ripe. We don't have to make all this other trouble."[24]

Whether desert or seacoast or tropical forest, the Aborigines treat the earth as if it were a paradisiac garden. They trust completely in their ability to meet all their physical needs through their relationship with the spiritual dimension of the natural world. Aborigines understand the potential of food cultivation: on occasion they remove seeds from a wild fruit tree growing near a sacred site and plant them close to one of their camps. However, this is done not with the intention of one day harvesting fruit but rather of bringing some of the spiritual energy from the sacred land closer to home.[25] Without question, gathering and hunting is for the Aborigines a metaphysical truth, a conscious choice, and a preferred way of life.

With the adoption of agriculture, populations became increasingly geographically fixed, their survival dependent on regional fertility and

FIGURE 160
Woman with U-shaped bowl. The gathering and wandering life of the Aborigines develops the physicality of women with strength and beauty.

311

weather patterns. The earth was seen as something to be cleared, exploited, and managed at will. As the source of rain and weather, the sky became the orientation of all prayer, rituals, and quests. Calling to the sky for salvation persists today in the form of space programs and fantasies of interplanetary colonization.

The physical immobility of agricultural settlement had far-reaching intellectual and metaphysical ramifications. The weather gods of the sky together with the yearning for a static cosmic order that would behave in a regular, predictable manner dominated religious imagination. These characteristics of the agricultural mind-set remain as the basis of mechanistic science and religious thought today. Anything that affected the growth of crops positively was considered good, and anything that had a detrimental effect, creating famine and starvation, became an absolute evil. Agriculture first encouraged and then required a structured moral polarity to replace the deep empathic participation of the hunter-gatherers as the foundation of religious sensibility. Written language developed along with agriculture and can be considered its counterpart in the realm of communication. Rather than being a milestone of progress, written language and agriculture marked the beginning of a cycle of decline—a sclerosis of mind, body, and spirit.

Are there other dreams to replace the nightmare of agro-industrial civilization? Revisionist ideas are becoming more potent now that our present system is collapsing. All creation begins with a dreaming phase: The romantic, back-to-nature, "whole-earth" movement of the 1960s is being transformed in the crucible of the 1990s' ecological crisis into farther-reaching plans for an environmentally sustainable future. Bioregionalism, biodiversity, and bioremediation are attempting to redirect our course toward an integration with the source of our life, the earth. On a grass-roots level, some people are developing seed stores of wild edible plants for reintroduction into an uncultivated environment. Others are attempting to reintroduce wild birds and animal species into their previous habitats. Cities and countries are finally beginning to reconsider their approach to energy consumption and waste. It is unlikely that the return to greater balance will be so direct that we avoid a passage through massive collapse. The force of imagination behind these social and individual gestures is more important than the external act—it is planting the seed of a new creation.

CHAPTER 18

TOTEM AND MIND

The Frog Heralds

When Baiame ceased to live on this earth and went back the way he had come from Bullima, up the roundabout ladder of stone steps, to the summit of Oobi Oobi, the Sacred Mountain, only wirinuns, or clever men, were allowed to address him, and then only through his messenger, Walla-guroon-bu-an.

For Baiame was now fixed to the crystal rock on which he sat in Bullima, as was also Birra-nulu, his wife. The tops of their bodies were as they had been on earth, but the lower parts were merged into the cyrstal rock.

Walla-guroon-bu-an and Kunnan-beili alone were allowed to approach them and pass on their commands to others.

Birra-nulu, the first wife, was the flood-maker. When the creeks were drying up and the wirinuns wanted a flood to come, these men would climb up to the top of Oobi Oobi and await in one of the stone circles the coming of Walla-guroon-bu-an. Hearing what they wanted, he would go and tell Baiame.

Baiame would tell Birra-nulu, who, if she were willing to give her aid, would send Kunnan-beili to the wirinuns, bidding her say to them, "Hurry to tell the Bun-yun Bun-yun tribe to be ready. The ball of blood will be sent rolling soon."

Hearing this, the wirinuns would go swiftly back down the mountain and across the woggi, or plains, below, until they reached the Bun-yun Bun-yun, or frogs, a powerful tribe with arms strong for throwing and voices unwearying.

This tribe would station themselves, at the bidding of the wirinuns, along the banks on each side of the dry river, from its source downward for some distance. They made big fires, and put in these huge stones to heat. When these stones were heated the Bun-yun Bun-yun placed some before each man, laying them on bark. Then they stood expectant, waiting for the

blood ball to reach them. As soon as they saw this blood-red ball of fabulous size roll into the entrance to the river, every man stooped, seized a hot stone and, crying aloud, threw it with all his force against the rolling ball. In such numbers and with such force did they throw these stones that they smashed the ball. Out rushed a stream of blood flowing swiftly down the bed of the river. Louder and louder rose the cries of the Bun-yun Bun-yun, who carried stones with them, following the stream as it rushed past. They ran with leaps and bounds along the banks, throwing in stones and crying aloud without ceasing. Gradually the stream of blood, purified by the hot stones, changed into flood water, of which the cries of the Bun-yun Bun-yun warned the tribes so that they might move their camps on to the high ground before the water reached them.

While the flood water was running, the Bun-yun Bun-yun never ceased crying aloud. Even to this day, as a flood is coming, are their voices heard, and hearing them the Daens or blackfellows say, "The Bun-yun Bun-yun are crying out. Flood water must be coming." Then, "The Bun-yun Bun-yun are crying out. Flood water is here."

And if the flood water comes down red and thick with mud, the Daens say that the Bun-yun Bun-yun or flood-frogs must have let it pass them without purifying it.[1]

FROM FIXATION TO
THE UNBOUNDED

LAUDE LEVI-STRAUSS'S ground-breaking work, *The Savage Mind*, argued that the academic, "mainstream" definition of totemism is based on false ethnocentric assumptions. Prior to the appearance of his work in 1962, totemism had been conventionally viewed as a confused attempt by primitive, prerational, preliterate people to establish some sort of systematic thinking. In forming his views, Levi-Strauss considered all of the anthropological research on totemism among diverse indigenous populations, especially Native Americans and Australian Aborigines. He proposed a new view of totemism as a rich, multilevel system of logic that is in no sense inferior to our own, only very different.[2] The major features he identified are listed here.

1. *Aboriginal totemic logic or thought process is based predominantly on perception of the natural world rather than on concepts or language.* Examination of indigenous peoples all over the world has revealed their extraordinary and inexhaustible knowledge of plant and animal characteristics, habits, and behavior. They also dis-

play a phenomenal ability to recognize and name any plant or animal from a slight fragment of leaf, fur, track, dropping, piece of egg shell, or sliver of wood. Their passionate attention to the living environment results in a dense, rich vocabulary, with distinct terms for every variety as well as for every anatomical part of each variety.[3] Some indigenous languages have 40 or 50 terms signifying particular shapes of leaves. Also common are a vast number of terms for describing gradations, such as specific names for the position of the sun at each hour of the day.

The incentive for this attunement to nature can be attributed to the gathering and hunting mode of life. Being alive, to the Aborigines, means daily wandering, searching, and exploring of the surrounding world. As they walk through the countryside, Aborigines repeatedly stop and taste the fruit of an unfamiliar plant, smell its leaves, and, without destroying the plant, dig out and examine roots, break and examine a stem, and taste and smell the sap, often rubbing it on their bodies. They intensely observe any bird, animal, or insect in their vicinity. This sensory exploration is carried out almost automatically; discourse while walking often involves sharing information about plants, and their food, medicinal, or ritual value.

Linguistic categories and logic build on this rich storehouse of perceptual knowledge. All perceptions are organized around place, not around abstract categories of genre, species, or variety. The taxonomy of animals and plants is built into the prefix of the name of every plant or animal food. For example, Aborigines on Cape York Peninsula use the prefix *nai* to designate all flesh food and *min* for all vegetable food. Similarly, the prefix *yuk* is used for all woody trees, *koi* for string or fiber plants, and *wakk* for grasses. The most important classification of any plant or animal is its association with the place where it is usually found. These classifications are also built into the word, sometimes as a suffix signifying dune country, beaches, or brackish water.

Living as a hunter-gatherer is an experience saturated with many details, each of the utmost significance. Theoretical organization of that experience into static generalities and abstract categories has no relevance to this life and would only interfere with the constant attention to the properties of a living world that is necessary for survival.

2. *Categories derive not from a singular characteristic but from a multitude of characteristics.* We classify cabbage and broccoli as a family of plants called crucifers, based on their characteristic crosslike branching pattern. This family of plants is isolated from another

group of plants, onion and garlic, whose classification as liliaceae is also based on their growth patterns. Cabbage and onions could be linked by their smell or by the fact that they both contain high quantities of sulphur. In addition to classifying a plant in terms of its shape, Aboriginal logic would classify the same plant according to its smell or color, its size or habit of growth, or its growing season. An onion could equally fall into the same classification as a piece of quartz because of its translucent white color, as a stone because of its smooth round shape, or as an artichoke because of its successive layers. A black and yellow wasp could fall into the same category as a snake with the same colors or markings. Things are not locked into isolated categories by singular qualities or definitions. "Classifications" are fluid, and everything shares a multiplicity of relationships with everything else in the world through an expansive, poetic field of analogy.

3. *Aboriginal logic is synchronic rather than diachronic.* In every known system of thought, all perception, and therefore all means of classifying, proceeds from basic contrasting pairs. The initial contrast is *self* versus *other*. All of experience reflects this primary opposition as diametric opposites, such as dark and light. Much of Western and Eastern thought is based on fixed dialectic oppositions such as the biblical good and evil and the Eastern concept of yin and yang. As we have noted, the moiety division of Aboriginal tribes also reflect this divison (black cockatoo and white cockatoo). But the dialectic logic of most indigenous peoples has been perceived as inconsistent. For example, in some Aboriginal tribes the white cockatoo moiety opposes a moiety representing a mountain cave, and the black cockatoo in other tribes opposes a particular kind of tuber or yam. At first ethnologists considered these irregularities to be examples of primitive muddleheadedness. The same apparent illogic has been found in the moiety divisions of African tribes and Native Americans. Closer examination has shown that these classifications do make sense, and that the anthropologists lacked the rich knowledge of plants and animals that is second nature to tribal people. For example, the Aborigines knew, as their observers did not, that white cockatoos are the opposite of mountain caves because black cockatoos always build their nests where caves are available; that black cockatoos oppose yams because these plants have a white and yellow flower, similar in color to a white cockatoo, which opens at the same early morning hour that the white cockatoos sing. In addition, caves and tubers are related because they are both embedded in the earth. This

type of logic, which is based on several relational principles operating simultaneously, is called *synchronic* logic; it flows from a greater knowledge of the natural world than the simplistic, singular, oppositional relationships of *diachronic* logic.

Our procedure of forming fixed diachronic oppositions based on singular or limited sets of qualities gives rise to a false theory of hierarchy often supporting the self-glorified ladder mentality of the West. Once we establish a diachronic opposition, such as *simple* and *complex*, we invariably interject a sequential movement or evolution from one to another. For example, die-hard Darwinists proclaim that evolution is a "fact" based on such evidence as comparing human anatomy (*complex*) to that of a frog (*simple*). There are indeed remarkable similarities, since both humans and frogs have the same muscles and bones and almost identically functioning digestive tracts. But are we obliged to assume that the more complex form logically evolved from the simple? Evolutionists have forgotten that there are nonsequential ways of creating a relationship based on observed similarities.

Throughout history, healers have prepared remedies from the parts or secretions of toads or frogs, particularly for treating conditions of the colon and intestines. Interestingly, many of the more than 2,500 varieties of toads have an intestinal tract twice as long as any other amphibian of comparable size. Inspired by the striking similarities between human and toad intestinal functions, as well as the known medicinal effects of toad preparations on the human intestines, the renowned physician, acupuncturist, and homeopath Felix Mann engaged in a synchronic thought process as valuable as the diachronic evolution from simple to complex. Mann noted that often patients with colon disorders or intestinal problems grow to look like toads, with voluminous bellies, lethargic habits, short necks, and bumpy skin eruptions. Intestinal disorders in humans often manifest in a physical form that suggests that everything is being concentrated or trapped in the belly. Frogs and toads themselves have a shape that accentuates the intestines—a voluminous belly, no neck, strong legs that can effectively and quickly move their disproportionately large abdominal cavity.[4]

In mythic or totemic thought, the toad is an externalization of the archetypal universal function of digestion, carried on equally in the convoluted organ of the intestines as in the convoluted hemispheres of the brain. It is as if the colonic forces of a universal being in the totemic kingdom are embodied most extremely in the toad.

If I might be allowed to exaggerate a little, I would say that a toad is nothing but a human colon; those forces which in the human are concentrated in the colon are in the animal kingdom concentrated in the toad. It might be said that from the point of view of living forces the whole toad has become a colon; the animal is bubbling over with colonic forces so that the whole of it has become transformed into a large intestine.[5]

Mann also describes the human types that reflect the totemic forces symbolized by the toad.

He was born to look like a toad. When he is healthy and full of life he looks like a toad; his wisdom comes from the depths of his belly. . . . [however, when he is deficient in toad force] he has lost this force that springs out from the depths of his belly. His colon and the rest of his body, which are normally permeated with this force, are now dead and are either hypoactive or function in an autonomous manner without being permeated by the function of other parts of the body. This type looks like a dead toad, like an ashen colon, which has already burnt the fire of its life.[6]

If we allow ourselves to see beyond the singular sterility of sequential thought patterns, there are a multitude of ways to connect the similarities and differences that abound in the natural world. The toad totem carries amazing qualities of existence. The toad has a set of tubercles on the backs of its hind legs that form a highly efficient digging tool. With these a toad can dig down from 2 to 10 feet to create a minimally ventilated habitat in which it can hibernate, surviving drought, cold, and other severe conditions. When the toad does emerge from this hibernation, or initiatic death, it can survive the most adverse climatic conditions known. Toads have night vision that allows them to see in virtual darkness. They can breathe through the entire surface of their skin and can reprocess and reabsorb their own urine, allowing them to go for long periods without intake of water.[7]

All of these characteristics make the toad an ideal candidate for space travel, far superior to the human astronauts with their lack of physical adaptability, their dependency on machines and medicines, and their comparatively high intake of food, air, and water. In fact, the space program had to devise mechanical methods to imitate the totemic toad capacity to reabsorb urine so that the astronauts' urine could be purified and reused for drinking water during space expeditions. Toads are synchronically linked to space travel in the sense that many shamanistic cultures use chemicals excreted by toads for hallucinogenic journeys. Other toad excretions may instantaneously cause death—our final departure into space. Since the evolutionists and mechanists can devise no long-

FIGURE 161
The extraordinary physical attributes of the common toad elevate them to be a prime candidate for leading evolution into interplanetary development.

term future for humanity other than migration to another planet, perhaps it is time to revise the ladder of evolution. Rather than continue to defend the singular elevation of human cerebral intelligence (which is already responsible for the desecration of this planet), we might admit that toads are much better equipped to lead the thrust into future interplanetary evolution.

4. *Aboriginal totemism allows for a shift of experiential levels within a classification system.* Totemism is a logical system in which animals perform the function of defining similarities and relationships among all the varieties of experience in our perceptual world. The Aborigines envision the parts of a single animal as different levels of experience. In a wedge-tailed eagle, for example, the flesh, blood, and organs denote kin relationships in the physical world. The distinctive behavioral characteristics of the eagle are used to describe human psychological characteristics or are imitated in order to empathize with the animal, and its beak, feathers, and claws—the more permanent parts of the bird's body—represent spiritual or metaphysical connections. Thus, within one framework, analogies can be drawn between physical, psychological, and spiritual levels of experience. If a tribal person wears the feathers of a wedge-tailed eagle, it usually signifies that his relationship to the bird is spiritual and so he cannot eat its flesh. A tribal doctor may carry with him the claw of an eagle, which has

FIGURE 162
Ceremony of the Eagle-Hawk totem. Almost all of the Aboriginal dance movements are based on observation and imitation of animal movements and behavior.

FIGURE 163
An Oruncha ceremony. In this secret sacred dance the initiated men are performing as wizard beasts. Their horn-like headress represents the lethal pointing sticks of shamanistic sorcery. This dance has been related by Joseph Campbell to similar imagery found in the Stone Age cave paintings at Lascaux. In both cases the wizard-beast played the mythic role of the shaman's trance-vehicle for entrance into the dangerous regions of unconscious experience.

First arrangement

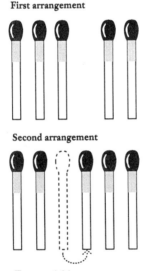

Second arrangement

FIGURE 164
The Aboriginal in viewing the second arrangement remembers to include the previous and reports: "There are two sets of three things, two sets of two things, and one three-making thing."

psychic healing powers in that it can uplift energies; a hunter may prepare himself psychologically for hunting by performing an eagle dance.

The multiple levels of recognition that make up Aboriginal perception were revealed accidentally during a series of logic and intelligence tests an anthropologist performed in the early 1950s. He was attempting to discover whether Aborigines were capable of consistently visualizing and identifying the abstract concept of groups. He placed five matches on a table. The first three matches were vertically aligned and evenly spaced. The remaining two matches were placed in the same orderly arrangement as the first three but separated from them by a significant gap.

According to abstract Western logic—reading from left to right, naturally—this arrangement represents a group of three and a group of two. The anthropologist asked a tribal Aborigine what he could say about this arrangement. The Aborigine responded, "In this place there are three matches and over here there are two matches." This answer was encouraging to the anthropologist, despite the fact that the Aboriginal subject failed to describe these things as purely abstract, quantitative groups.

Next he moved one match from the group of three, placed it in the group of two, and again asked the Aborigine what he saw in this arrangement. A response consistent with Western logic would be, "Now there is a group of two and then a group of three." The Aborigine's response was, "I see two groups of three matches and two groups of two matches, and one 'three-making' match."[8]

In his second response, the Aborigine soared far beyond our narrow fragmented mode of perception. We are conditioned to see fixed and isolated quantitative aggregates that exist as if distinct from any previous condition, as well as from any ongoing transformative process. We fail to see qualitative process-related differences, such as the one "three-making match" being different from those that are stationary. Our logical habits cause us to fall into a static, uniform, quantitative interpretation. In contrast, the Aborigine perceives the matches as inseparable from the transformative process performed by the anthropologist. His vision not only retains what is in front of him but integrates it with an invisible a priori state. The Aboriginal view integrates past and present, qualities and quantities, objects and process, visible and invisible, sequential and simultaneous.

We who are dominated by a monolithic, scientific world view based on one-dimensional or severely limited patterns of logical relationship might open up our thought processes by even a cursory exposure to those of the Aborigines.

5. *The qualities by which things are categorized are never separated from living totality.* For the Aborigines, every quality that exists on a physical level relates to a quality manifested on psychic or metaphysical levels. For example, physical qualities such as weight, translucence, warmth, and wetness also reflect emotional, psychological, or spiritual conditions. Every objective quality or state has a subjective component, since the visible world is everywhere fused with the Dreaming. This premise underlies all mystical traditions. The eleventh-century Sufi mystic, Al-Ghazzali, said, "The visible world was made to correspond to the world invisible, and there is nothing in this world but is a symbol for something in the other world."[9] Basic to all mystical traditions is the classifying of objects or qualities in contrasting pairs and then unfolding parallel lines of contrasting pairs based on sympathetic correspondences of basic qualities.

A diagram basic to all mystical traditions is two interlocking quadrants. The four corners of one quadrant display the fundamental qualities in oppositional pairs: dry opposed to moist, warm opposed to cold. Surprisingly, the German anthropologist C. G. von Brandenstein established that this principle is also the basis of totemism

FEMALE	MALE
Yin	Yang
Earth	Sky
Water	Fire
Body	Mind
Mother	Father
Substance	Form

FIGURE 165
The initial creative powers, the All-Mother and the All-Father, leave the imprint of their universal polarity resonating in all things throughout the world. The horizontal relationship between pairs is contrasting, and the vertical relationship in two parallel lines is a succession of correspondences.

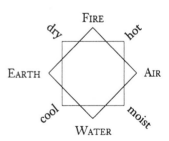

FIGURE 166
The four primary elements and the four archetypal qualities are the basis for the "science of correspondences," which is the foundation of knowledge in many esoteric traditions throughout the world.

TOTEM AND MIND

among Australian Aborigines.[10] The Aborigines have expressed the same polarity of four basic qualities, dry opposing moist and warm opposing cool, in which the dry corresponds to active male and moist to passive female. The Aborigines base a whole thought pattern on the symbols of a warm-blooded kangaroo couple, made up of one active male and one passive female, and a cold-blooded goanna couple, one active male and one passive female. They represent the four qualities as four animals with distinctive characteristics: the active male desert kangaroo, *Karimarra*, "sharp maker" or penetrator of the passive female hill kangaroo, *Paltjarri*, who is pliable and mild, and the active male desert goanna, *Pannaga*, tense, vicious, and poisonous, married to the passive, lazy female wetlands goanna, *Purungu*, who is massive, inert, formless.

ANIMAL SPECIES	ABORIGINAL NAME	QUALITY
Active male desert kangaroo	*Karimarra*	warm/dry
Passive female hill kangaroo	*Paltjarri*	warm/moist
Active, vicious male goanna	*Pannaga*	cold/dry
Passive, lazy female goanna	*Purunga*	cold/moist

Figure 167 compares the Aboriginal system to Western mystical systems and the basic system of the yin/yang categories of Chinese philosophy. In each of the four quadrants, the Aborigines place the beings, things, and phenomena that share the two basic qualities of that quadrant. The upper elements are the "heavenly" warm bloods, the lower elements the "earthly" cold bloods.[11]

QUADRANT 1: Dry/Hot	QUADRANT 2: Hot/Moist	QUADRANT 3: Dry/Cool	QUADRANT 4: Cold/Moist
Choleric: hot, light, thin-blooded, rash, overbearing, brutal	Melancholy: warm, heavy, thick-blooded, gentle, quiet, pliable, yielding, childlike	Sanguine: cool, light, thin-blooded, active, fast, sinewy, stretched, slender, tough, muscular, dry, hard, cold, sober, calculating	Phlegmatic: cool, heavy, thick-blooded, lazy, massive, plump, fat, glandular, doughy
Sharp, hot, bitter, dangerous	Calm, clear, sweet, mild, deep, palatable	Dry, hard, stony, metallic, cold, sour	Watery, soft, slimy, spongy, salty
Sun, fire, heat	Moon, fresh water, gentle breezes, cirrus clouds	Moon (occasionally), cold	Sweat, dew, seawater, and many plants.

The complexity and sophistication of Aboriginal classification methods went unrecognized for so long because *Aborigines do not separate qualities from the physical or living entities that express, embody, or carry those qualities.* Their thought patterns are consistent with the reality of the physical world in which there is no quality that is not generated by a substance or thing. We obscure this reality in our thinking processes because we routinely refer to a quality such as warmth as if it had no connection to a substance or entity. Our language allows us to move from the concept of a warm body to the disassociated quality of warmth. Splitting qualifying terms such as adjectives from nouns reflects the fragmentation of our experiential world. It allows us to forget that the warmth of our homes is not an abstract quality but is generated by the burning of a substance whose exhaust pollutes the atmosphere. It also allows us to forget that trees that are logged and chipped and cattle that are slaughtered for hamburger are not raw materials but are inseparable from qualities no different from those we attribute to our minds and bodies and consciousness.

Our language has induced in us the belief that qualities are separable from their physical expression in a living world. This is the "magic" underlying photographic and cinematic images. We receive from these images impressions of qualities disassociated from the living subject. Photographed glamor, sex appeal, horror, and injustice are qualities that impress our consciousness with a singularly simplistic perspective, letting us form partial fantasies based on detached qualities. These partial realities are easily manipulated by others for commercial and political gain.

The hypocrisies of Western religious beliefs also follow from the splitting off of spiritual or ethical qualities from the people and societies that profess those beliefs. For example, is it not a fallacy to believe that the ethical qualities basic to Christianity—purity, poverty, charity, humility, devotion, submission to God—exist apart from the materialistic and capitalistic institutions, societies, and individuals who proclaim themselves Christian? Is it not equally fallacious to suggest that the peace, justice, and harmony of Islamic doctrine can stand aloof from the constant war, torture, and inhumanity of the Middle East? Monetary currency is perhaps the best example of separating the quality or value of things from their substantial existence. We treasure bits of paper, metal, and plastic as if by magic they in themselves held the savor of fine wine, the rarity of a precious gem, or the security of a home and real estate. Money is not a simple illusion, but the by-product of a linguistic practice based on a perceptual distortion of reality.

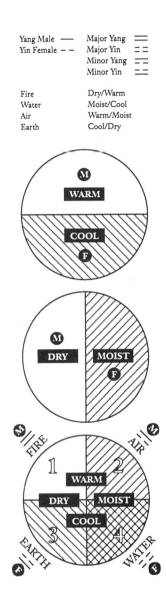

FIGURE 167
The four elements and the four qualities form a graphic quadrature of the circle and correspond to the fourfold yin and yang division of ancient Chinese philosophy.

323

The Aborigines' inability to separate qualities from physical or living entities indicates not a conceptual deficiency but rather an integrated vision of all levels of reality. Body and mind, subject and object, the physical world and the metaphysical Dreaming are the inseparable aspects of each totality.

PERCEPTION, LANGUAGE, AND TOTEM

For decades Edward de Bono has been at the vanguard of the study of thought patterns. His innovative books on lateral thinking have initiated a new approach to education: the direct teaching of thinking practices. These ideas have stirred interest in governments, universities, and major corporations worldwide. In his latest work, *I Am Right, You Are Wrong*, he claims that a renaissance of thought and language patterns must occur if humankind is to avoid self-destruction. He proposes turning away from the rigid, crude logic of traditional Western thinking in favor of developing a thought process based on perception. Recent developments in the understanding of self-organizing systems, as well as new ideas from information theory, have shed light on how the neural processes of the brain perform the activity of perception.[12] De Bono argues that the rock-hard, "table-top logic" of traditional thinking methods bears no resemblance to the way the brain naturally processes sensory information and transforms it into perception. The disjunction between organic brain processes and our present methods of thinking creates tension that undermines the health of our organism and our environment. We must, argues de Bono, develop thought patterns that reflect the nature of perception; our present methods have cut us off from the reality of both our inner and outer worlds and have sealed us into modes of conceptualization and action that are incapable of solving the problems that face humanity.

Argument, reason, and rigid logic are thinking habits, acquired from ancient Greece, that matured to form the basis of the fifteenth-century European Renaissance. They have proved to be excellent in the technical arena, but they have never been effective in dealing decisively and constructively with disease, moral collapse, warfare, and environmental demise. Argument (the contentious opposition of fixed positions), critical thinking, unilinear logic, dualistic opposition, mechanical causality, systematic formal proof, and a belief in absolute resolution and finalities—all these characteristics are fundamental to our religious, political, legal, and scientific thought. These characteristics predispose Western thinking to negativity and a defensive/aggressive mode. We have, in effect, developed in our language and thought a "word war game" characterized by confrontation, conflict, and competition. An argued victory takes precedence over exploration, constructivity, innovation, discernment—in other words, over creative thought.

De Bono has developed what he considers a new model of thinking based on the direct activity of perception. Perception operates in nerve networks like a feature of a self-organizing biological system. Incoming information falls on the mind like rainfall on a virgin landscape, organizing itself into streams and rivulets of temporarily stable patterns. These patterns can subsequently flow into new sequences and patterns. The perceptual mode of thinking encourages the mind to form multiple-branching flow patterns; the sensory information is not molded by fixed linguistic concepts, generalities, and logic. Perceptual thought patterns follow the natural behavior of neural networks; our present mode only recapitulates words and concepts provided by a preestablished cultural framework.[13]

This summary clearly links de Bono's perceptual thinking with Aboriginal totemic logic. Aboriginal society provides a structure for both body and mind to exist in just such fluid patterned formations. The multiple branching of Aboriginal totemic logic allows connections and insights to emerge that are useful for immediate perceived circumstances. Many of the characteristics that de Bono claims are of primary importance for the thought patterns of the future have been, in essence, fully embodied in Aboriginal life for at least 100,000 years. It seems that the cycle of the mind is returning to its origin.

Not only is the method of establishing relationships in Aboriginal logic expansive and multidimensional, but Aboriginal languages are in a state of continual change and transformation. In part, this is due to the fact that immediately following a death, all clan members are forbidden to pronounce the name of the deceased. To speak the name of the dead is an infraction that is punished severely. The effects of this custom on language development is discussed here, and the spiritual reasons for it are covered in Part Four.

The Aborigines derive people's names from plants or animals or their parts, for example, "long yam" or "possum paw." The taboo against speaking the name of the dead means that objects that shared the name must also be changed, so that new names had to be found for possums and yams.[14] In some cases, appellations that sounded like the deceased's name were also changed. Therefore, Aborigines became accustomed to an ever-shifting vocabulary. In addition to this type of mutability, each Aborigine possesses many different language forms. For example, there is a completely different language for retelling Dreamtime stories to children. At each initiation men receive not only new songs, dances, and

stories but a new linguistic mode for expressing that knowledge. If estimates of Aboriginal population at the time of colonization are correct (approximately 250,000 to 2 million people), then their nearly 300 distinctly different languages, each with two or three distinct dialects, amount to an incredible linguistic diversity.[15] Each linguistic variation was closely related to the particular geography of a region. Each Aboriginal language also maintained its own particular gesture language, as complex and effective as the spoken form.[16]

In contrast to this extraordinary linguistic diversity and mutability, our language is based on the goal of establishing a fixed, constructed meaning for each word. Each word is intended to be an enclosed entity, like a "toy block with an unchanging color and shape."[17] These characteristics of language generate thought patterns that seek absolutes, ideals, and sharply defined, exclusive categories. The science of communication has revealed that exact meaning cannot be communicated solely through words; it depends on many variables associated with the act of speaking. We gather understanding from perceptions of subtle body language and the minute changes in articulating muscles and voice resonance caused by emotional intonation. All of these subtle factors are indispensable to the communication of meaning—words alone do not possess the full power to communicate. Our emphasis on singular fixed definitions and logical processes is a direct result of our overreliance on the written word. Our language has lost what the Aboriginal communication processes have not: a sense that accurate and profound meaning must be "circumstance-dependent," that is to say, responsive to immediate perceptions of an ever-changing reality.

The fixity in thought and logic mirrors a fixity in our external environment. We have forged an illusory permanence through agriculture, architecture, concrete roads, and pathways. This equally shapes our psychology: our life-long names and identity, unvarying life roles, and fixed, limited family and vocational associates. Agriculture can be called an "argument with nature"; it is the foundation of our world of fixed position. Controlled production squares off against free-ranging patterns of natural growth. We have furrowed the neurons of the brain to adhere to fixed semantic and linguistic patterns. Language has become as real as, or more real than, the living world and cuts us off from the very habitat it is intended to describe.

There is no greater cultural division than that which exists between indigenous people and agrarian colonialists. This cultural divide is even reflected in deep physiological changes in the human brain. Microscopic examination of feline brain tissue shows that feral cats have networks of neural pathways that simply don't develop in their urban domestic counterparts.[18] Agriculture has led to extinctions in the earth's biosphere as well as in our brain and conscious awareness.

De Bono claims that written language, which developed hand in hand with agriculture, is a "museum of ignorance"—words and concepts have frozen intelligence and inquiry, creating a false permanence that is incapable of dealing with an ever-changing reality. Our fixed inner and outer worlds mutually support and incestuously feed on each other, disfiguring mind and nature alike. A transformation of our world view requires that we completely change our concept of language from a fixed, consistent, absolute structure to a mutable, spontaneous communion between beings in a living place and moment.

Spirit is movement; it is the invisible animator and motivator of all growth and change. It is the urge to extend, encompass, transform, and become. Because of the fixity we have created in our mental and physical existence, the Western tradition has needed the fantasy that the spirit, in order to be free, must be independent of the prison of the body— disassociated from, or transcendent of, the physical world. By maintaining self and society alive within expanding, flowing forms and processes, the Aborigines have no need to fantasize spiritual freedom based on transcendence. To the contrary, the Aborigines conceive of spirit as the constant lusting consort of the physical world.

Aboriginal cosmology diverges from de Bono's ideas at the point where he claims that systems analysis, information theory, computer simulations, and the neural analysis of the brain will provide the models from which we can "design" a language and thought pattern for the future. In the Aboriginal vision, only the living species and forms of the earth, in all their diversity, can provide the animated metaphors by which consciousness can maintain a flowing continuity between the self, the world, and their metaphysical source.

CHAPTER 19

TOTEM AND ANIMISM

A PERSON'S TOTEM designations are surrounded by food and sexual taboos that signal another, more subtle level of connectedness. The most prominent taboo is the prohibition against eating the flesh and blood of one's totem animal. This infraction is considered to be as serious as incest or cannibalism.[2] To understand the psychic knowledge underlying these taboos, it is important to trace totemism back to its origin in the Dreamtime stories of creation.

During the creative preformative Dreamtime, each animal species had not yet taken on an independent embodied shape. They were more like the subjective traits, expressive qualities, or personality characteristics of the proto-human ancestral beings. The life force of the Ancestors was exceptionally potent because each one combined both human and animal characteristics and could change back and forth between the two forms. The ample life force of the Dreamtime beings was necessary in the original forming of the earthly environment. As the physical manifestation took shape, however, the excessive power of the Ancestors became destructive, causing constant conflict, bloodshed, and confusion.[3] At the completion of the Dreaming, the Ancestors disappeared into the earth as potencies and, at the same time, permanently separated their human and animal powers. Humans, animals, and all natural species, therefore, owe their existence to the same spiritual beings. Each human genealogy traces to a Dreamtime Ancestor, as does a related species of animal. The spirit of that species remains in the blood of its animal forms and in that of its associate human kin.

The structure of Dreamtime cosmology is based on a subjective-objective reciprocal relationship between the natural world and the Dreamtime Ancestors. A similar relationship exists between animals and humans and is summarized in Figure 168.

1. The Aborigines believe that the source of creation is symbolized

---

Can I hurt your feelings without touching your body? What then do I hurt? . . . Are these same feelings capable of enjoyment? Are they warm? Are they active? The feelings or affections are the animals of the mind.[1]

JOHN WORCESTOR
commenting on the work of Emanuel Swedenborg's Correspondences of the Bible: The Animals.

FIGURE 168 →
The relationship of animals and humans in the Dreamtime creation.

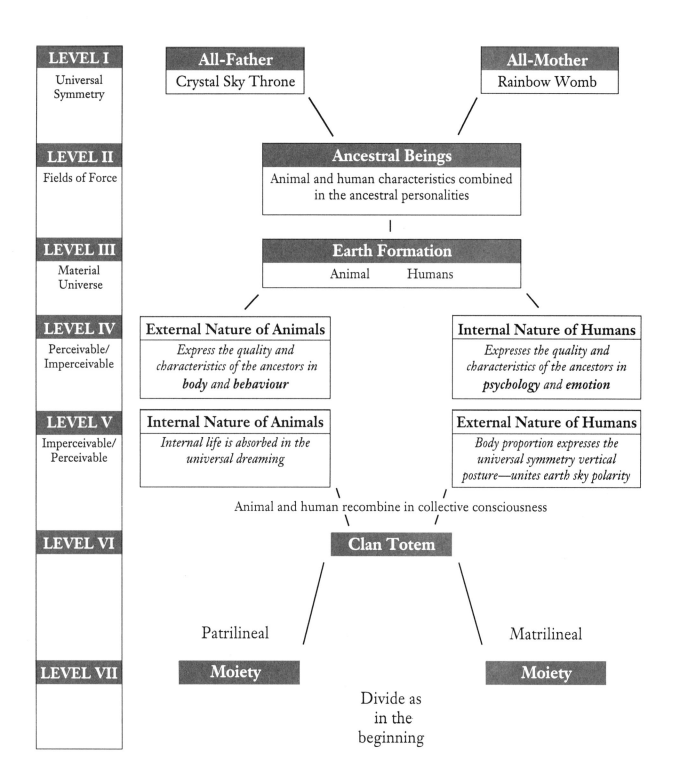

THE RELATIONSHIP OF ANIMALS
AND HUMANS IN THE DREAMTIME CREATION

LEVEL I
Universal Symmetry

LEVEL II
Fields of Force

LEVEL III
Material Universe

LEVEL IV
Perceivable/Imperceivable

LEVEL V
Imperceivable/Perceivable

LEVEL VI

LEVEL VII

All-Father
Crystal Sky Throne

All-Mother
Rainbow Womb

Ancestral Beings
Animal and human characteristics combined in the ancestral personalities

Earth Formation
Animal   Humans

External Nature of Animals
*Express the quality and characteristics of the ancestors in **body** and **behaviour***

Internal Nature of Humans
*Expresses the quality and characteristics of the ancestors in **psychology** and **emotion***

Internal Nature of Animals
Internal life is absorbed in the universal dreaming

External Nature of Humans
Body proportion expresses the universal symmetry vertical posture—unites earth sky polarity

Animal and human recombine in collective consciousness

Clan Totem

Patrilineal

Matrilineal

Moiety

Moiety

Divide as
in the
beginning

by a quartz crystal with an internal fracture that causes a rainbow spectrum to appear within it. This sort of quartz was referred to as the crystal throne of the sky; the clear stone itself was called the All-Father, the internal rainbow, the All-Mother. This Divine Couple is responsible for the entire creation, although all the other ancestral beings emerge from the belly of the All-Mother Rainbow Serpent as dreaming powers or, in scientific terms, universal field activities.

2. These numerous ancestral beings were disembodied psychic and physical qualities that together expressed the entire nature of the omnipotent All-Father and All-Mother.

3. During the Dreamtime, their interactions formed the earth, and as it ended their characteristics were embodied in both animals and humans.

4. These ancestral characteristics are reflected in the *external bodily forms and behavior* of animals and in the *psychology and emotions* of human beings.

5. The internal life of animals reflects the universal spirit or consciousness of the All-Father and All-Mother; the external human body, with its upright bilateral symmetry, expresses the same universal spiritual consciousness. Therefore, animals and humanity are an inverse representation of the metaphysical order that preceded the appearance of the physical world.

This inverse organization implies that humanity's internal psychological states and emotions are externally symbolized in the behaviors and bodily forms of animals. Hence, such metaphors as "brave as a lion," "delicate as a butterfly," "busy as a bee," and "free as a bird" appear in all languages throughout the world, bearing witness to the connection between human qualities and animal species. Psychologist Paul Shephard has suggested that Noah's ark is a symbol of humanity's collective unconscious. That dream researchers have found animals to be ubiquitous in the dreams of people throughout the world supports this theory.

> Each animal shows a characteristic quality or state of the mind, an instinct, an affect. Animals are to be studied as well as revered, because they are true manifestations of the hidden archetypal powers that lie behind the transformations of the human soul.[4]

The foundations of creation, the absolute universal symmetry referred to in the Aboriginal myth as the All-Mother/All-Father, are reflected in the uniform, enduring, instinctual nature of the inner life of animals. The same universality is projected in the external human form through the laws that govern the shape and arrangement of our bodies. These universal geometric proportions form a human canon, which most ancient cultures used as the ground plan for sacred temples dedicated to the source of creation (see Figure 169).

6. Humanity and the animals, therefore, are an internal and external reflection of each other. They are reunited in the collective psyche of the Aboriginal clan that carries the bloodlines of both animals and humans.

7. The clan repeats the entire structure of creation by its division into patrilineal and matrilineal moieties that reestablish the image of the All-Mother and All-Father. These moieties determine all marital or procreative partnerships in Aboriginal society.

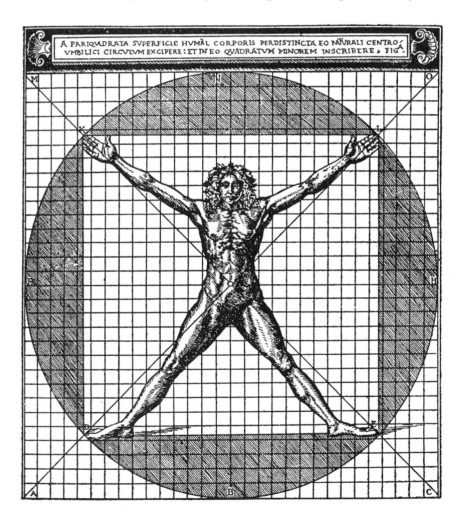

A PARIQVADRATA SVPERFICIE HVMAL CORPORIS PERDISTINCTA EO NATVRALI CENTRO, VMBILICI CIRCVLVM EXCIPERE: ET IN EO QVADRATVM MINOREM INSCRIBERE, FIG.

FIGURE 169
The Geometry of the Human Body. The human body is proportioned on a set of geometric ratios: 1 to π, 1 to the √2, 1 to the √3, and the golden mean 1 to ø. These ratios are found in the primary geometric forms: circle, square, equilateral triangle, and pentagon. They occur throughout all natural forms and growth processes as a governing principle beneath the shapes, sizes, and interrelationships of parts. These natural and anatomical geometric proportions were used as the basis for all art and architecture from ancient times to the European Renaissance.

In Aboriginal cosmology, the plant world does not descend directly from the Ancestors in the same way humans and animals do. Plants emerged later, from the potencies deposited during the formation of the earth. All human and animal species that ever have existed, or ever will exist, on earth have a continuous existence in the Dreaming. They manifest if their particular plant or other foods are put forth by the nourishing earth mother. The same view of creation is found in the ancient Indian Vedas: "A species will come into being only if its food exists. If the earth provides not its food, the species will exist but remain unmanifest."[5] In summary, humans and animals preexist in the Dreamtime as pure animistic energy and emerge simultaneously, while plants exist first as potencies in the earth during its formation, deposited by these animating forces, that physically manifest later after the completion of the Dreamtime. This ancient concept of the relationship between the three kingdoms affords a completely different view of nature and its recent crisis of species extinction, which is presently occurring at 400 times the natural rate. The plants of the earth are like Aboriginal message sticks: they call forth from the Dreaming various animal and human species. These species exist permanently in the Dreaming, but they manifest and disappear in specific combinations during particular eras as the earth's plants come forth to call them into existence. Human interference (i.e., agricultural propagation) with this plant-mediated dialogue between the earth and the Ancestral Dreaming disrupts not only the environment but the harmonic unfolding of creation.

A tribal man spent an entire evening unsuccessfully explaining to an anthropologist the totem relationship between humans and animals. The next day the anthropologist took a Polaroid photograph of the Aborigine and showed it to him. The Aborigine looked at the photograph and pointed to a small grazing kangaroo, saying, "In the same way this photograph is me, so is that kangaroo." He then walked off, content that he had finally made his ideas clear to the anthropologist.[6]

Animal and plant species are like the organs of a body: they are the vital components of the cosmic beings who dreamed the world into creation. The unique perceptual abilities of each species provide different facets to the cosmic dream while they animate the life of that dream in particular ways. The cosmic Ancestors existed both as unified beings and as multiplicities. Animals, humans, and plants also exist individually and collectively. In Aboriginal society human groups are reflections of the same species identities as animals or plants. *Individual animals participate in the spirit of only one species. Individual humans contain different proportional combinations of the spirit of a number of species.* Through an empathetic recognition of the collective identities we share with the creatures of the earth we participate in the Creative Beings of a higher reality. A spiritually realized Aborigine is capable of expressing divine human and animal characteristics. This is in stark contrast to the Western spiritual ideal of a silent, ascetic, meditating monk.

BLOOD AND SPIRIT IN HEREDITY

The Aborigines believe that an individual's strengths and imperfections are sustained by energies from the spirit of the species that makes up the totem identity. For the Aborigines, spirit is related to blood in the same way that a magnetic field is related to a lodestone. Blood carries channels of magnetlike resonance that make people the spiritual kin of the animals of their various totem identities. This resonance connects an individual to the energy flow from the spirit-field of a totem species. Eating the flesh and blood of that species is therefore akin to cannibalism; it interferes with the spiritual connection with that animal.

Dietary and marital totem taboo restrictions have beneficial environmental and social effects. These external benefits concur with the underlying metaphysical vision of the integration of man and nature.

Such beliefs are not exclusive to the Aborigines. Many world mythologies posit that the gods, or energetic beings, manifest their predominant characteristics as animals. The nature of these gods is defined by the animals and plants that are sacred to them. Some myths hypothesize a time when the gods manifest themselves as beings that are part animal and part human. This is especially evident in Egypt, where most members of the pantheon have this dual nature.

The Egyptian concept of the soul has many similarities to the totemic cosmology of the Dreamtime. Unlike Christian philosophy, in which the soul is the material possession of an individual, the Egyptians conceived of the soul as an aspect of a cosmological process. Like the Aborigines, the ancient Egyptians considered the perceivable world an incarnation or projection of similar realities that exist in a universal, spiritual sphere. For them, the human soul shares the threefold nature of the soul of the creating spirits: a universal soul, a natural soul of the species, and a unique individual soul. After death the soul of each person merges first with the spirit species of nature's soul before merging with its ancestral source in the Dreaming. The Egyptian term for the universal soul is *Akh*, a pure spirit power similar to the Dreamtime Ancestors. *Ba* is the animating spirit of the natural world that flows from the *Akh*, nourishing and animating the incarnate world. The physical body is called *Kha*, and associated with it is a field or layer of energy called the body's double, or *Ka*. This Ka, a shadow or phantom body, is multilay-

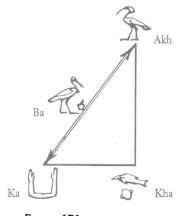

FIGURE 171
The triangular image of the soul in ancient Egypt.

← **FIGURE 170**
Some of the Egyptian Pantheon of animal-headed Neters: Anubis, Hathor, Khnum, Montu, and Horus.

TOTEM AND ANIMISM

ered; it receives the animating energy carried by the Ba from the pure spirit (or Dreamtime beings) and transmutes it into an energy form usable for the maintenance of the physical body.[7]

Between the most spiritual state (the Dreamtime) and the most physical state (the substance and energy of the embodied world) are elements that participate in both. On the invisible psychic level this interacting function is the animating Ba, or soul. On the physical level it is blood that communicates between the Dreaming and the perceivable world. Just as the body "drinks" the nourishing energy of the blood to maintain itself, so too the blood "drinks" subtle energies from the spirit world in order to maintain the nourishing communication between them.[8]

The Christian reverence for the body and blood of Christ, a concept borrowed from earlier Dionysian rites, also shows a mystical relationship between blood and spirit. The ancient Romans believed that each person had an angel or daimon within, which came down through family bloodlines like a celestial spark. They imagined this inherited spark or seed in the blood as a guide or a guardian angel, a messenger from a higher world that was halfway between the human and the divine. In a man this spirit was referred to as his genius, and in a woman, her juno.[9]

Similar ideas concerning the powers of blood have been expressed more recently by artists and scientists. D. H. Lawrence said in this regard, "Man is a creature that thinks with his blood. The heart dwelling in a sea of blood that flows through the body always in two inverse tides is where chiefly lies what man calls thought." The scientist Norbert Wiener, the inventor of cybernetics, stated, "Messages which cause conditional or associate learning are carried by the slow but pervasive influences of the bloodstream. The blood carries in it substances which alter nervous action directly or indirectly."[10]

All shamanistic and indigenous cultures, as well as many mystical traditions, acknowledge that blood has a psychic or spiritual aspect or vibration that is capable of transferring potencies, emanations, or characteristics from one being to another or from one generation to another. The idea of transmission of spiritual energy through generations also exists in modern religions, which have altered the more ancient idea of spiritual heredity into an abstraction such as karma or soul. The Aboriginal world view differs from these religions in its belief that every spiritual quality, no matter how subtle, has an objective form—in this case, blood.

Before the advent of modern genetic theory, blood was almost universally considered to be the carrier of hereditary characteristics. The Aborigines believed that blood carries a magnetic spiritual essence through the generations and forms spiritual connections between humans and earthly locations, species, and metaphysical sources. This belief does not necessarily conflict with the idea that genetic material transmits information that dictates physical characteristics. Spiritual transmission through the blood may simply parallel genetic heredity. There may be more than one mode of hereditary transference. Modern biology is developing a field theory to explain the heredity of morphic characteristics. This new theory suggests that the origin of characteristics lies in a higher energetic or spiritual source that, through resonance, imprints its image on the physical world.

THE PSYCHIC ENERGY OF BLOOD

In many occult traditions that preserve elements of tribal and ancient Egyptian knowledge, such as European alchemy, the subtle or spiritual energetic aspect of blood is believed to increase in potency with its dilution. Recent scientific research into highly dilute solutions verifies that reducing a substance to a minute quantity, such as a single atom, intensifies the need and capacity of that atom to bond with others and to imprint its own energetic qualities on the surrounding shell of different molecules.[11]

In tune with this line of thought, in 1976 a council of Aboriginal tribal elders proclaimed that all Australians with even the smallest amount of Aboriginal blood could consider themselves part of the Aboriginal people. Because the male colonists raped Aboriginal women and hid their sexual liaisons with them, there are many "white" Australians with traces of Aboriginal blood who either hide it or are unaware of it. Some Aborigines believe that, as their racial blood becomes increasingly diluted in the engulfing ocean of white blood, the spiritual essence of Aboriginal blood will increase in potency and cause the consciousness of the Aboriginal race to reemerge.[12]

When the last of the Tasmanian tribal Aborigines were told that they were to be exiled to an island reservation, they replied in resignation, "We will surely die on that island, but sometime in the future we will pop up again as white men."[13]

> To those who did not invent gunpowder nor the compass,
> who neither harnessed steam nor electricity,
> who explored neither the oceans nor the sky,
> . . . but surrendered to the nature of things, deeply moved,
> . . . truly the firstborn of this world,
> To those who shall survive in shoots of grass![14]

335

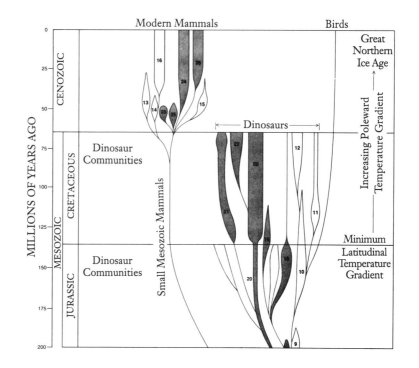

FIGURE 172
This fascimile of an early human based upon skulls may well reflect the qualities and characteristics of several animal species other than African primates.

FIGURE 173
The various species of animals, reptiles, and birds emerge and populate in a pattern that resembles a flowering or leafing. In Aboriginal myth the source of this flowering is the Dreaming, rather than the unverified theory of intermediary species proposed by Darwin. (After Scientific American)

FIGURE 174 ➝
The opposite of totemism. Humans often reflect animal characteristics in both physical and behavioral traits. In Aboriginal cosmology, one enters through initiation into the spirit of the species of the numerous animals that make up a person's totem. To be dominated by the power of one species would be considered a reversal, or a degeneration of totemism. (From an eighteenth-century French engraving)

DESCENT FROM TOTEM ANCESTORS

Recently, paleontologists have developed diagrams based on fossil remains for reconstructing the origins of various species both through the ages and in relation to each other. Viewed simply as patterns, these diagrams have a flowing structure, like that of leaves or flowers emerging from a stem. These patterns are in tune with the Aboriginal Dreamtime cosmology of the descent and increase of species from the spiritual source. They seem to have little to do with the linear logic of Darwinian theory, even less when we consider that these stemlike paths of descent are supposed to represent intermediate species, many of which have never been found.

I have seen artists' renderings based on skulls that are thought to represent the intermediate species between humans and higher primates. These depictions are more reminiscent of lions or wolves than they are of monkeys. Perhaps these skulls reflect a time when humans more physically reflected their totem lineages. In the totemic world view, individuals who excessively exhibit characteristics or impulses of animals and take on their physical features are regressing to the conflictual phase of creation, when human and animal traits were embodied in one being. This has been called reverse totemism, and it was graphically depicted by the eighteenth-century artist Le Brun.

Our culture, insensitive to the spiritual impact of animals and plants on us, has disproportionately absorbed characteristics such as gluttony, docility, and aggressiveness from the domesticated condition of our most exploited animal species—pigs, sheep, and cattle. As Bruce Chatwin points out, we have prepared for ourselves an urban world that reflects the corralled conditions to which we have subjected these animals. He says, "Within our city states the masses are to be corralled, milked, penned in, saved from fearful enemies from outside and, if need be, in time, lined up for slaughter. The city is a sheep fold superimposed on the garden of nature."[15]

An Aborigine grows in life by increasing and expanding the multiplicity of his or her identity rather than limiting, specifying, or reducing it. Within the restrained order and harmony of the natural world, humanity expands its own nature by absorbing the power and spirit of plants and animals. Humanity has the wondrous potential, through collective and individual forms of initiation, to integrate and express the essence of all the forces, energies, and species that are involved in creation.

These ideas are not intended to be rock-hard theories in the traditional mode of Western thinking. Rather, they are an attempt to apply a wider, more analogic process that gives equal credibility in interpreting information to the totemic thought patterns of tribal people and to the models provided by modern research. I hope that the widening of associations can be helpful in releasing us from the locked-in, singular, scientific definitions concerning human origins and our relationship to the natural world. It is obvious that our present mode of thought is leading humanity along an irreversible and dangerous course.

> Only human beings have come to a point where they no longer know why they exist. They don't use their brains and they have forgotten the secret knowledge of their bodies, their senses, or their dreams. They don't use the knowledge the spirit has put into every one of them; they are not even aware of this, and so they stumble along blindly on the road to nowhere—a paved highway which they themselves bulldoze and make smooth so that they can get faster to the big, empty hole which they'll find at the end, waiting to swallow them up. It's a quick comfortable superhighway, but I know where it leads to. I've seen it. I've been there in my vision and it makes me shudder to think about it.[16]

Aboriginal rock painting from the Kakadu region of Northern Australia.

PART FOUR

DEATH

AND THE INITIATIONS

OF HIGH DEGREE

INTRODUCTION

A TREE TRUNK GROWS by adding concentric rings of new wood. The Aborigines envision the pattern of human development like this, as a continuum of the expansion of being, with each successive phase a circle outside a circle. The circle of kinship relationships present at birth expands through initiations to an awareness of the sphere of totemic interconnectedness of human identity, the animal powers, earthly locations, and the great Ancestors. Life itself is but an embryo preparing for the final birth, the extension of being into the realm of the dead. Funeral ceremonies are, therefore, the last in the series of initiatic rites of rebirth.

The most direct avenue to discovering people's understanding of life is to study their response to death. If a culture views the afterlife as basically similar to life on earth, then it probably has a high regard for and connection to physical existence. This is true of the Australian Aborigines, who could not conceive of heaven as more beautiful or wondrous than life on earth. If, on the other hand, the afterlife is seen as an otherworldly, transcendental paradise, this usually means that earthly life for this culture is marked by struggle and conflict. If a culture philosophically denies, ignores, or intellectually rationalizes death and the afterlife, it probably also conducts its life on earth solely through the mind.

In the Aboriginal tradition, death, burial, and afterlife are rich in meaning and metaphysical interpretation. Aborigines use a wide variety of burial practices, including all of those known to have been used in other parts of the world, as well as varieties not practiced anywhere else. Although these rites vary, all Australian Aborigines share many fundamental ideas about death and its relationship to life.

← *FIGURE 176*
A bark painting of an episode from a fishing adventure between two great Ancestors.

341

CHAPTER 20

DEATH—EXPANDING INTO
THE DREAMING

THE DREAMTIME MYTHS from all parts of Australia confirm that death is an unavoidable experience of life. Death is the final crisis in a succession of initiatory rebirths that constitute the very nature of life. All Aboriginal stories relate that during the Dreamtime something might have been done to completely change the all-powerful, irreversible nature of death, but the fatal step was taken by some ancestral being and set the precedent for all time.[1] Each tribal group has a Dreamtime story that depicts the moment when death was introduced into creation. The story from the Flinders Range in South Australia portrays two invertebrate species; the presence of such characters designates it as a story from a very early stage of the Dreaming. One creature is a spider, *Adambara*. The other, a furry yellow caterpillar called *Artapudapuda*, burrows into decomposing wood underneath the bark of eucalyptus (*wida*) trees. This species of caterpillar gives off a strong odor of decomposition and resembles rotten grass in color and texture, which is what *Artapudapuda* means. It often attacks spiders.

Adambara and Artapudapuda sat together and had a talk. They were sorting out what should happen when people became so sick that they died. They went away to think about it for a while, then they came back together again to make a decision.

Artapudapuda said when a tribal person died, his body should stay in the grave and rot, and only his spirit should rise, after three days.

Adambara said no, that is not what he wanted. When a tribal person died, he said, he should be wrapped up in a web with a trap door, and the door closed and left for three days. During this time there would be a healing process, and at the end of the three days, he would come out, just as a butterfly comes out of a cocoon. This is what Adambara wanted for humans.

Artapudapuda won the argument, and the two insects went their separate ways. After a while Artapudapuda realized that his relations were dying and he wasn't seeing them again. He was getting really upset about it. He was ashamed of the decision he had made, and hid himself under the bark of a wida *tree.*

Adambara, on the other hand, knew he had tried his best for tribal people and was not ashamed. He stayed out in the open. This is why even today Artapudapuda is always found hiding under the bark of a wida *tree, whereas Adambara is always out where he can be seen.*[2]

DEATH—UNNATURAL
YET INEVITABLE

The first and most fundamental concept of death in the Aboriginal tradition is the doctrine of three worlds, the unborn, the living and the dying, and the Land of the Dead, discussed in relationship to male initiation in Chapter 11. *Each individual spirit passes through these three domains only once.* After death, it is the profound responsibility of the living to ensure that the spiritual component of the dead person is separated from this world and can proceed to the next.[3] There is no rebirth for the individual spirit aspect of consciousness. The Aborigines believe, as do Native Americans, that the notion of reincarnation is based on two factors: (1) the obsession with the illusion of individuality extends into the belief that the ego survives death and remains intact in the afterlife; (2) such cultures have lost the knowledge of burial practices that assist the spiritual energy of the deceased to separate from the earthly sphere, and so the spiritual atmosphere is polluted with fragmented, disembodied energies of the dead. Fragments of spirit from the dead can interact with the living, sometimes inhabiting, shadowing, or controlling conscious behavior and destiny. People may mistakenly refer to these influences as remembrances of past lives or "channelling." The Aborigines say that the earthly atmosphere is now saturated with dead spirits and that this pollution of the spiritual atmosphere parallels the physical pollution of the biosphere—both of which contribute to the self-destructive course of our civilization.[4]

The notions of reincarnation, past lives, and karma have recently swept into the popular imagination of many Western societies. The source of these concepts is for the most part Hinduism and some branches of Buddhism. Few Westerners realize that before the eleventh century, the doctrine of reincarnation was not a part of Indian Hindu philosophy. Much of the literature and drama of the period scorn the belief in rebirth

343

DEATH—EXPANDING
INTO THE DREAMING

and past lives as a childish fantasy. Many of the Eastern state religions went on to adopt the doctrine, but many esoteric traditions refuted it.

The second universally held Aboriginal belief about death is that at the moment of death, the spiritual component of the individual splits into three distinct parts.[5] The first aspect of spirit is the totemic center of being, or the *totemic soul.* This soul is related to the sources of the life of the body: the earthly location of birth and the spirit of the animal and plant species to which the person's bloodlines are connected and from which he or she has derived nourishment throughout life. After death, the totemic soul essence, once incorporated in the psychic and physical makeup of the person, is returned in ceremonial ritual to the spirits of nature, to the animals, plants, rocks, water, sunlight, fire, trees, and wind that have contributed their life and substance to the person's bodily existence. The realm of the unborn is the domain of the totemic soul of each of earth's forms and species. Returning spiritual energy to the animating forces of the totemic species reciprocates the debt to all those living things that were sacrificed for the sake of humans. In other words, they give back spiritual animation to that which has physically animated our bodily existence. In this exchange, the spiritual development of the tribal person contributes to the deepening spiritual unfolding of the entirety of the natural world.

The second aspect of an individual's spirit force that is released at death resonates with the great Creative Ancestors of the Dreamtime and can be called the *ancestral soul.* The domain of the unchanging metaphysical archetypes, the Dreamtime Ancestors, is the Land of the Dead, which is in the sky. The aspect of the deceased's soul that emanates from the Ancestors journeys to the constellations in a particular region of the sky. Each region of the starry heavens has not only a pictorial constellation (usually an animal) but also a particular pattern of invisible energy. These patterns are symbolized in the geometric clan designs painted on the abdomen of the corpse during burial rites. The same clan design was painted on the person at the time of his or her first initiation.[6] At the person's initiation and at death the celebrants chant, "May from here your spirit reach to the stomach of the sky."

The energy of the celestial field resonates with the geometry of the painted design and acts as a guide for the spirit in its journey to the heavens. Throughout life, the successive initiations encourage a person to identify his or her character and destiny increasingly with the primary patterns of the mythic creative beings. In this way the individual soul gradually merges with the archetypal ground of creation. The higher the initiation, the more an individual lives in the awareness of this Dreamtime reality and the stronger the ancestral soul will be at the time of death.

The third aspect of the human soul is referred to by the Aborigines as

FIGURE 177
At the time of initiation, as well as immediately following death, a person's clan totem design is painted on the abdomen, extending from the heart down to about four inches below the navel. The painted pattern carries a vibrational affinity to a particular region in the sky where the ancestral source of that totem clan is said to reside. This resonance assists the soul of the deceased in reaching its ancestral destination after death.

the Trickster.[7] It is the spiritual source of the individualized ego and can be characterized as the *ego soul*. This spirit force is bound to locality; to relationships with wives, husbands, and kin relatives; and to material things such as tools and items of apparel. It is the spirit force that bonds us to the finite and the particular and to the responsibilities, relationships, and pleasures of our individual existence. At the time of death the Trickster or ego soul is the most dangerous to deal with. It resents death, because this change of status removes contact from the material or local world in which it functions. It may get stuck in this world, so to speak, after the other aspects of the soul have departed.

The ego soul works throughout its life to plant the possibilities of a sort of earthly immortality. It often forms an attachment to the psyche of a wife, husband, or other relative, so that after death the relative is unable to break the emotional dependency. Sometimes the sorrow, grief, and wailing that a wife performs for her deceased husband fail to expunge the memory and connection that the ego soul has made with her consciousness. In such cases, the living relative accepts that the Trickster spirit of the deceased has made a permanent place in her psyche and wears a relic such as the skull, an armbone, or a finger of the deceased so that this spirit will take on a positive external influence in her life.[8] The ego soul jealously covets the pleasures of the living and, if precautions are not taken, may interfere with people's sexuality and other forms of self-fulfillment by distracting attention from the immediate physical moment. In a sense, the Aboriginal concept of ego soul is related to the trickster figure in Greek mythology, Hermes. Hermes is the archetypal force that makes the temporal world appear to be the eternal. We all have had the experience of Hermes, when a transitory thing or event appears to be all-important, or a fleeting disguise appears to be reality.[9]

Artists in our society are often positively imbued with a type of Hermes or trickster spirit. Through paintings, sculpture, architecture, books, or films, the artist implants designs for an earthly immortality. The very presence of a work of art acts like a relic, perpetuating the memory and force of the deceased artist. Eventually, however, this trickster soul fades and its traces in earth and memory disintegrate. Every soul ultimately must proceed to find true immortality in identifying itself with the enduring energy emanating from the celestial realms of the Dreamtime Ancestors.

These three aspects of the soul in Aboriginal ritual can be related to the three aspects of the soul in Egyptian religion: the Ba, the Ka, and the Akh. The totem soul, the ego soul, and the ancestral soul form a psychic trinity that is concrescent with the cosmic trinity of the unborn, the living and the dying, and the dead, as well as with the trinity of earthly order—species, place, and clan.

FIGURE 178
A selection of mortuary skulls, with their totemic dreamings, from the Anthropological Research Museum, University of Western Australia at Perth, Western Australia. The spouse of the deceased wears the skull slung over the shoulder until weathering obliterates the designs. Then the spirit is said to be finally at rest.

TOTEM SOUL	EGO SOUL	ANCESTRAL SOUL
BA	KA	AKH
Unborn	Living/ Dying	Dead
Animal Species	Place	Clan

FIGURE 179
The correspondences between the three aspects of the soul and the threefold division of the cosmos and the natural world.

Death and the Divine Marriage

The world monotheistic religions, in combination with materialistic philosophy and rationalistic science, have created a devastating conceptual and linguistic separation between the realms of the spirit and mind and between the levels of mind and body. Our survival as a race may depend on the marriage of Psyche and Soma, or what some mythologies call the Divine Marriage. The psychic, psychological, and physical processes of consciousness must be reintegrated. Motivated by a sense of great urgency, psychologist Carl Jung and the renowned atomic physicist Wolfgang Pauli explored the possible link between the profound developments emerging in Western psychology and the revolutionary concepts of quantum physics. The field of research they initiated, in which mind and matter are considered as a unity, now stands on the forefront of theoretical scientific philosophy.[10]

Over 100,000 years ago the Aboriginal world view had already achieved this integrated goal. Every aspect of their daily life expressed a sense of fusion between all the levels of consciousness. Aboriginal way of life provides powerful images and insights to assist in the dreaming of a future world order.

Figure 180 illustrates the progress made thus far in establishing the conceptual integration of mind and matter. These ideas provide a framework in which to evaluate Aboriginal psychic and magical practices that are based on the integration of mind and matter. Aboriginal burial proceedings particularly emphasize their belief that life results from a marriage of psychic components and bodily forms; at death these two require a diligent process of separation.

In Figure 180, matter and mind are represented as two overlapping circles. The central portion common to both, a vagina-shaped "visica," can be designated as the area of confrontation and reflection between (A¹), the tangible visible world, and (A), conscious perception and sensory cognitive awareness. The solid black line dividing them in half indicates the distinct independent appearance of mind and matter on this level of dualized awareness. By means of this duality we experience the world as a separation between subject and object, between observer and observed.

Both matter and mind are associated with increasingly subtle layers of organization and activity, represented by the three visicas nested around the center. The first layer beneath the conscious awareness function of mind is (B), the personal unconscious. Freud called this layer of the unconscious mind the id. It consists of psychological configurations formed from repressed personal experiences, traumas, desires, and unacknowledged drives and complexes. The content of the personal unconscious is hidden from the conscious mind, unrecognized and unexpressed. The inhibitions and obsessions imposed on the unconscious act to fix the potential of the individual's personality and character. The layer directly opposite, (B¹), beneath that of tangible matter, is the atomic structure of the substantial world. This causal level of material organization determines the external characteristics of substances and defines the limits of chemical interaction with other substances. The relationship of a substance to its molecular structure is therefore similar to the relationship of the external personality to the personal unconscious. They are like two sides of the same coin, one an inverse reflection of the other. The altering, breaking down, or recombination of molecular bonds allows substance to undergo material transformations, just as the breaking down of unconscious complexes allows the individual to go through transformations in conscious development. The parallel functions of these two levels of mind and matter may help explain why the molecular structure of some psychoactive drugs and plant extracts has a perfect chemical fit with the neurological structures of the brain, altering the conditions of the personal unconscious to bring about changes

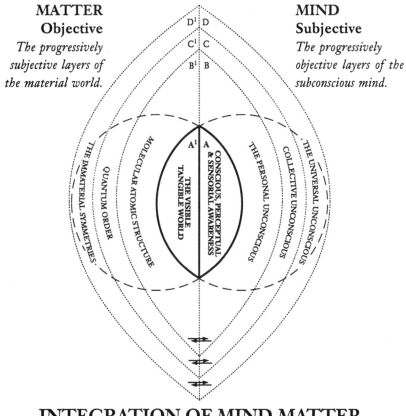

MATTER
Objective

*The progressively
subjective layers of
the material world.*

MIND
Subjective

*The progressively
objective layers of the
subconscious mind.*

FIGURE 180
*The integration of mind
and matter.*

INTEGRATION OF MIND MATTER

347

in conscious awareness. Psychosomatic phenomena may also be explained in terms of a mind-matter relationship on this level.

The striking similarities on the next interrelated level of matter and mind, the quantum level (C^1) with the collective unconscious (C), prompted the collaborative research of Pauli and Jung. Physicists have always maintained that atomic structure is a purely objective approach to the study of matter, whereas psychologists considered the personal unconscious a highly subjective description of mind. A revolution in both sciences occurred when quantum physics accepted subjective influences in the subtle levels of matter (C^1), and psychology uncovered universal or collective principles underlying subjective awareness (C). This layer of consciousness has been named the collective unconscious.

The subjective personal unconscious and its complexes and shadows are underscored by mythic and symbolic forms present in the collective unconscious of societies. Unlike the personal unconscious, the collective unconscious comes out of a great psychic continuum and is maintained by a dynamic flow of fundamental principles. Jung called these creative principles "Archetypes," whose powers and laws are eternal and beyond all individual conception. Similarly, at the quantum level the local static laws of matter are superseded by a dynamic interchange of fields, forces, and energy levels that rhythmically merge and recede from a universal continuum. The objectivity of these quantum levels is conceived as inseparable from the subjective forces of the observing mind, which can influence the energy expression of the subatomic particles of these fields. Acknowledging the interrelationship of mind and matter in this subtle realm of quantum energy and collective unconscious provides a ground for explaining psychic phenomena and is useful for describing some of the many Aboriginal methods of sorcery.

It seems that as psychologists progressed into the subjectivity of mind, they uncovered increasingly objective levels of dynamic structure, and as physicists progressed into the objective nature of matter, they encountered increasingly subjective subtleties and powers.[11] Western scientific theory is dissolving the boundaries between mind and matter and seeing them as emerging from the same universal continuum, each an internal and external reflection of the other. It is a world picture not unlike that which the Aborigines see in the eternal Dreamtime.

Surrounding the newly united fields of quantum physics and the collective unconscious are two more layers of being. Physicists describe a realm of pure immaterial symmetries and ethereal geometric patterns that guides the interactions and fluctuations of the quantum fields (D^1). In psychology, beyond the collective unconscious lies a domain referred to as the universal unconscious (D), which contains pure unimaginable potentials of identity, polarity, repetition, and reflection. In both physics and psychology, these prematerial, preformative patterns exist beyond the representational power of both matter and mind. The Aborigines also have a concept similar to these immaterial symmetries and potentialities. In traditional Aboriginal society this concept could not even be whispered between tribal members without fear of reprisal from the elders. It was the highest metaphysical duality: the All-Father/All-Mother. Its place of existence was the sky, and it is characterized by an invisible geometric lattice, like that of a quartz crystal or the recently discovered crystalline clarity of pure water.[12]

> Somewhere there must be primordial forms whose images are like ideals. If we could only see them we could understand the nature of existence and the connection between mind and matter.[13]

In the spheres of mind and matter, the more subtle layers do not manifest themselves directly. For example, the subatomic particles are not perceivable in the material world; their existence is known only by their tracks or imprints left in cloud chambers. Nor do the universal archetypes themselves appear, they only leave traces and imprints in dreams, clothed in attributes and identities familiar to the subject. This is the same attitude with which the Aborigines view the topography of the earth, as imprints left by an imperceivably higher order of creation. The Ancestors, while being the origin, also maintain and interrelate all the emergent qualities, identities, and variations throughout time.

Thus far, our ability to integrate spiritual and physical realities remains only a theory or belief system beyond the reach of our everyday existence. In contrast, every detail of Aboriginal daily life reflects and acknowledges a multidimensional sense of reality, and death is seen as a shift of the center of consciousness from the physical body to other levels in the increasingly subtle continuum between substance and consciousness.

PASSAGE INTO DEATH'S DREAMING

In death, as in other aspects of life, the Aborigines concentrate their attention on the interaction between the visible and the invisible, the Dreamtime reality and the external world. We consider dying to be a relatively short period just prior to death. In contrast, the Aborigines consider dying to be a constant complementary process to life, both in a biological sense and in the sense of death through initiation. Following

349

physical death, the most significant stage of dying begins: the spirit dies away from the earthly atmosphere in a process that can take months, even years.

Although Aboriginal burial rites are long and elaborate and the disposal of the corpse is complex, the ritual always focuses on the spiritual ramifications of death, not physical disposal or preservation. The primary goal of all Aboriginal funeral rites is to safeguard the well-being of the living. The correct funeral procedures and rituals are valued primarily for their benefit to the living.[14]

The older, initiated men of wisdom carefully observe each initiatic crisis that the young men and women of their clan pass through. They recognize which of the three elements of an initiate's soul is most engaged in confronting and accepting the various transitions of life. From this information, the men of high degree ascertain which is the most appropriate burial procedure to adopt for that person upon death.

Because the Aborigines vary their burial procedure according to the spiritual development of the deceased, anthropologists have been unable to make generalities about these practices, even within the same tribe or clan. A single tribe may practice methods as various as interment in the ground, exposure on tree platforms or rocks, cremation, mummification, dessication or dehydration in funerary huts, removal of organs, coffin burials in hollow trees, exhumation and reburial, ritual burial cannibalism, and various combinations of the above.[15] The experience of the afterlife is in many ways dependent on the person's spiritual development at the time of death—not in a moralistic sense of whether the person was "good" or "bad," but in terms of developing a resonance with the subtle structure of the cosmos through inner growth. Although Western society propounds the exalted value of the individual, our burial practices are relatively uniform, with superficial variations determined by a person's wealth rather than spiritual development.

When asked to describe existence in the ancestral or celestial realm, Aboriginal tribal people say, like Native Americans, "It is an unending, unchanging version of the gathering-hunting life which we have lived on earth . . . except the game is more plentiful."[16] I believe these statements express the certainty that the *afterlife cannot be anything but a reflection of the quality of consciousness and the state of being implicit in the life form each of us develops in our lives on earth.*

This is an acceptable or even agreeable vision of eternity for tribal people, who live in a natural world that is a primordial garden and in a society of kinship in which all emotions, whether dark, painful, or joyous, are shared and ritually expressed. The quality of life in our modern world, if it were cast into the dimensions of eternal afterlife, would become a frightful nightmare: for many, mass starvation, poverty, oppression, and suffering; for others, isolation, greed, and materialistic saturation—mind alienated from body, spirituality alienated from sexuality, science and knowledge alienated from a sense of the living world. Such an afterlife would be eternal hell.

Because our beings are habitually split apart as members of a Western society, in death our souls will lack a cohesive center and will disperse without retaining consciousness of their formation on earth. According to Aboriginal philosophy, the unreciprocated suffering of our era will not, therefore, be experienced by most people in the sense of an eternal personal suffering. The blind suffering of the world's masses today will echo like universal ritual suffering in the eternal Dreaming, calling forth from the universal creators the reciprocal energies needed to redress the imbalance of our present cycle.

After an Aborigine dies, the news is quickly communicated to all the clan groups, no matter how distant, in which kin members are living. The messengers approach distant groups and display the collection of clan totemic designs with which the deceased was affiliated. The displays alert people in the camp of their kin relationship and their responsibilities toward the dead person. The messengers may also sing songs that hint at the person's identity, but they never reveal the name.[17]

The name of the dead person may not be spoken by clan members or kin members for years after the death. All tools and personal effects are removed, burned, or buried with the deceased. The campsite where the person died is deserted by the group, and the exact place of death is examined by tribal elders or men of high degree, and then marked and completely deserted for years. The site of the deceased's birth and conception are also avoided for months, even years, after death. The taboo against pronouncing the name of the dead is strictly observed because it is believed that the vibratory pattern of the person's name can act as a hook or anchor to which the spiritual energy of the deceased can attach itself and thereby remain on earth. The name of the animal, plant, or land feature from which the person's name is derived must also be changed. Often words that rhyme or sound like the deceased's name are changed as well.[18]

The death of even one tribal member radically alters the fabric of kinship society and many of the hunting and ritual activities for the entire clan. These transformations in life patterns are reinforced by the changes in language and vocabulary. At the time of death, the ego soul of the deceased is believed to be greatly distressed by its separation from the living, and a concerted effort by the entire clan is necessary to return the spirit to its home of origin. The hours of intense mourning and wailing externalize the emotion of grief and pour forth a river of energy intended to carry both the ego soul and the ancestral soul toward their

351

FIGURE 181
During mourning ceremonies,
women challenge one another
to fight and cut their heads as
part of the intense public
rituals of anguish and sorrow.

vibratory home in the sky. The totemic soul is ritually returned by the men of high degree to the spirits of the natural species.

As in ancient Egyptian and other traditions, the Aboriginal journey to the other world is imagined in a sacred bark or spirit canoe with a mythic ferryman at its helm. The spirit canoe sets out across the sea to the island of the dead. An Aboriginal funeral song speaks of this long journey:

> The sail at the mast head dips from side to side,
> As the boat comes up from the south . . .
> The sail unfurled at the mast head flaps in the wind,
> It stands upright and flaps, as the boat goes on.
> The wind tosses the sail, up on the mast,
> And the mast head moves, dipping from side to side.
> The sail on the mast flaps, dancing, and 'talks' in the wind. . . .[19]

The only sails used by traditional Aborigines were large pieces of tree bark fastened together on a pole. The image of a sail in this song may have been adopted by the Aborigines from passing European ships, which they associated with the coming of death.

In many world myths the helmsman is an important archetypal figure at the beginning of the journey toward death. In the Aboriginal myth he is always abusive; he beats men and rapes or demands coitus with women.[20] The beating or rape by the helmsman symbolizes the severe assault and trauma that the consciousness undergoes in its initial separation from the body. These episodes are ritually replicated in initiatic circumcision and defloration.

In the nonhierarchal Aboriginal society, the helmsman is the first figure since childhood on whom the Aboriginal person is totally dependent. In our modern world, the helmsman is the archetypal image of leadership: the father, the king, the president, the captain who mans the rudder and steers the course of family or society for all. The title "Great Helmsman" has been popularly applied to some of the most tyrannical world leaders, including Mao Ze-Dong and Saddam Hussein. It is perhaps relevant that this archetypal character appears only once in Aboriginal Dreamtime myths, manning the boat heading for the Land of the Dead.

The Aboriginal coastal tribes all have offshore islands, and many inland tribes depict an imaginary one, that they consider the first destination of the deceased. Here, after a series of purification rites, they return to that condition in life when they were at their peak of development in

FIGURE 182
As in Aboriginal belief, many mythologies have an image of an obstinate and cruel helmsman who ferries the newly deceased souls across the first river to the realm of the dead.

physical strength, beauty, and intelligence. These islands of the dead are jumping-off points for the celestial journeys to the farthest reaches of the universe.

The clan members gather at the campsite of their dead kin and ritually grieve and wound themselves with increased intensity as the night falls and the number of mourners grows. The emotion of grief must be fully released, since any sorrow withheld in the psyche would also form a link to which the deceased spirit might cling. As clan members arrive from distant locations, the funeral ceremony divides the tribe along kinship lines, as in the circumcision rites, into active and passive mourners. As the night of wailing begins to subside, nonfamily male active mourners carry the body away from the camping area and dig a rectangular hole about three feet deep, lining it with leafy bushes and small logs. The body is placed inside after its hair is removed; very often, one arm is tied behind the back to discourage the spirit from going off to hunt or gather food. The body is interred in a fetal position.[21] There are many variations at this stage; some include building raised huts with fires underneath for dehydration that prepares the body for mummification.[22]

After the grave is closed and before the burial party departs, a man of high degree makes pronouncements to the spirit of the deceased: "Don't look back again at your wife and don't think about your children. Keep away from the camp and don't follow us. You have to go the other way now to your own water hole in the sky."[23] All remaining belongings and funerary decorations are then burned, and all depart. People stay well away from the place of death and burial until the time comes for reburial, which is usually between six months and two or three years.

The widow or close relatives cut all their hair off and may continue gashing their skulls to produce bleeding for weeks to come. Skull gashing as a mourning practice was apparently practiced worldwide; there are warnings in the Old Testament encouraging mourners to stop the practice of "head shaving and skull gashing." Close relatives, especially women, may also observe long periods of silence.[24]

Months or even years after the event, when it is determined that the soul of the dead has inhabited the earth long enough, the surviving wife or husband gathers together a group of kin to assist in the reburial process. En route to the grave the group members carry out a ritual in which they sing and perform many dances related to the Dreamtime stories of mourning. These dances can continue for several days and nights at a campsite near the grave. The day after the rites are completed, the widow or husband heads for the gravesite with a party of 10 or more mourners. The group always contains a man of high degree, a tribal doctor or shaman. As they draw near, the spouse sings out to warn the spirit of their presence. The spirit answers in the form of a bird call. The widow or widower then approaches with the shaman, who has the power to see any remaining spiritual entity of the dead and the capacity to absorb these spirits in his own body so that they will not cause any harm.[25]

Wailing and crying, the members of the burial party exhume the skeleton. They remove and clean the bones and then rub them over their bodies to absorb the last purified essence of the deceased into their own lives. The widow or widower does the same with the skull.[26] These practices emphasize the deep respect for any residue of spiritual force the deceased may have brought into the world. As with the material things of the earth, nothing is wasted or neglected. Every emotion, feeling, and sensitivity is embraced and amplified. The physical body grows in beauty as it acquires marks of emotional crises fully lived and fully experienced.

If sorcery was considered to have contributed to the death, at this time the shaman closely examines and scrutinizes the gravesite, the bones, and the lock of the deceased's hair that the widow or widower has kept for this moment in the hope of identifying the person responsible for the death. Sometimes the shaman uses a bird who has absorbed the higher or innate intelligence of the deceased to help him locate the sorcerer. Aborigines claim that frequently, at this sort of investigation, one of the many small birds who have nested in the vicinity of the grave lights upon the shoulder of a clan member, thereby identifying him as the killer. Should this identification take place, revenge is exacted, and the reciprocity between the living and dead regains its balance.[27]

In Aboriginal religion, birds play a significant role in much of the movement of spirits at the time of death, often absorbing the disembodied energy of the deceased and transporting it to farther realms. International societies dedicated to the protection and observation of birds, such as the Audubon Society, have a predominantly elderly membership. I believe that the elderly may become fascinated with the study of bird life as part of an unconscious realization that they must become familiar with bird species in preparation for their own spiritual departure.

DEATH AND SORCERY

Death from old age or a wound is considered natural by Aborigines, but death due to disease or an accident is never natural.[28] The introduction of death in the Dreamtime was circumstantial, a result of the excesses of the creative beings, but not part of the eternal ground of existence. Death exists in the world as do other Dreamtime events, as a psychic vibratory potency. As such it can be manipulated, focused, and projected with psychic knowledge and techniques.

Once one is able, like the initiated Aborigines, to tap the powers of the unconscious mind and its ability to influence and regulate matter, it becomes clear that there are states of consciousness in which the body is potentially immortal. The Aborigines believe that conscious or unconscious psychic forces always play a role in the occurrence of death. Each of us, often unconsciously, projects hostile and negative formations toward others, even our most loved ones, that can contribute to or result in that person's ill health or death.[29] In Aboriginal society sometimes the party who actually inflicted a fatal wound or injury to another is not blamed for the death but is considered only an agent for someone

FIGURE 183
Bone-pointing, Central Australia. This is one of the most frequently employed methods of sorcery.

else who psychically projected negativity to the victim through sorcery. This psychic projector is sought for punishment and revenge.[30]

One of the most potent forms of death-delivering sorcery is bone-pointing. Bone-pointing seems to involve the use of a subtle energy similar to magnetism. In the Aboriginal world view, physical energies always reflect psychic or dreaming powers; psychic sensitivity can be considered the subjective or inner nature of tangible magnetic-field activity.

The bone-pointing practice has three principal elements. The first is the bone itself; the bones of birds are considered the most effective, although human or kangaroo bones can be used. Sometimes this bone can be treated with blood; the most powerful sorcery uses the blood of a dead person or the intended victim. The next component is some sort of string, the most potent being a strand of the victim's hair wound around either the pointing bone itself or the sorcerer's finger as he points the bone. Some sort of receptacle, held on the bone by the string, is also needed. This can be a lump of either wax or clay.

Depending on the particular rite and on the particular powers held by the man of high degree, or shaman, the bone can act either as a projecting agent, which projects the lump of clay or wax into the victim's blood and infects or pollutes it, or as a magnet, which draws out energy from the victim's blood so that it moves invisibly into the bone along the connecting string and is deposited in the receptacle. When the shaman has completed the drawing-out procedure it is said that he has the "soul of the victim's blood" contained in the receptacle, which he oftens buries in the earth for several months. This marks the period of the victim's illness, characterized by fever and other symptoms. When the receptacle is finally disinterred, the sorcerer holds the victim's life in his hands. During prescribed chanting known only to the shaman, heating up the receptacle with fire would cause the victim's fever to worsen, burning the receptacle would kill him outright, and washing out the contents would cure him immediately.[31] Many modern, "rational" white Australians who have either witnessed incidences of or heard stories about Aboriginal sorcery are firm believers in its effectiveness.

CHAPTER 21

DEATH—THE PREPARED JOURNEY

I N THE *PHAEDO* Plato said that to die is to be initiated. Recent studies of near-death and out-of-body experiences, parapsychological research into remote viewing and telepathy, and a growing understanding of sacred texts concerning death, such as the Tibetan and Egyptian books of the dead and myths from shamanistic cultures, all provide a means for understanding the relationship of spirit and body and the complex process of separating these two at death. All of these sources state that one of the most important functions of society is to prepare individual members, through initiation, for the experience of death. Preparing for the death experience is as reasonable as learning how to swim before going out in a boat and plunging into the ocean. Without the journey to death being mapped and understood, human life becomes isolated on earth. Each person confronts mortality as if it were a fearsome emptiness, a state of nonbeing, often glossed over with childlike images of ultimate pleasure or punishment.

Aboriginal men plunge deep into the near-death experience, not only through long periods of fasting and sensory deprivation but also by undergoing devastating ordeals such as long exposure to the blistering sun or lying motionless while stinging insects are sprinkled over them. Just prior to and following the European invasion, in some tribes the near-death rituals in the name of Baiame, the All-Father, were so severe that many Aboriginal men actually died as a result of them.[1] This intrusion of physical death into the process of initiatic death symbolically foreshadowed the colonialist genocide that followed.

In many Eastern religions that accept the importance of a science of death and afterlife, the question remains, what value or meaning can the eternal afterlife have if we do not have an individual awareness of it? In other words, what, if any, is the relationship between the awareness we gain in life and our awareness in death? Figure 180, illustrating the relationship of mind and matter, helps to answer this question in the light of Aboriginal cosmology.

In Aboriginal terms, at death one leaves the *yuti*, the perceivable world in which mind and matter are separate and delineated, and enters the shimmering realm of the Dreaming, where bodies in their vibratory forms merge and correspond through a structural resonance that is the innate meaning of things. The personal unconscious (B), like the vibratory atomic world, is the level of awareness where animals exist most of the time. Research has shown that animal perception responds not so much to visible forms as to molecular vibration; thereby, animals are sensitive to forces that are invisible and intangible to us. Animals live, for the most part, in the Dreaming.

The movement into death is similar to the process of moving into sleep or trance, the difference being that the center of being or awareness shifts through the personal unconscious or the energetic realm of vibratory appearances (B), to the boundless activity of the quantum continuum (C), otherwise called the collective unconscious or the Ancestral realm. *Death, in the Aboriginal view, is not a termination or a dislocation from this world to another; rather, it is a shift of the center of one's consciousness to invisible, subjective layers that are substrate to, and involved within, the natural world of mind and matter.*

For the Aborigines the highest goal of initiation is to create a condition in which, for a time after death, the spirit can move at will between all three realms. This spiritual integration after death is possible for the Aborigines because during life, the mind, body, and spirit are cultivated to remain integrated, that is, all in one piece and in one place, *ngurra*. Throughout life the power of empathy is intensely cultivated so that the Aboriginal psyche, while centered in place, is permeable by the psyche and being of all of nature's forms and creatures. After death this same all-permeating force of being becomes the dominant tone of individual consciousness, allowing it to share in the being of the diverse creatures of nature and in the freedom of the boundless ancestral beings from which the world arose.

Some Aboriginal burial methods resemble those of ancient Egypt. On the Torres Strait Islands and among tribes in northern Australia, the corpse undergoes an elaborate dehydration and mummification process similar to those used in ancient Egypt.[2] The burial coffin (in the Aboriginal tradition, a large hollow log) is prepared with a small opening so that the soul can, for a period, come and go from its bodily home, just as the Egyptians provided an opening in the tomb for the Ka to leave and reenter.[3] In Egypt, mummification served the purpose of preserving the corpse indefinitely so that the spirit would have a home to which it could return. In the Australian tradition, although the mummy technically can remain intact for a long period of time, it is disposed of after several

FIGURE 185
*Erection of grave posts.
Melville Island, Northern
Australia, 1912. These grave
posts, though unique to the
Tiwi people of the northern
territory, resemble the hollow
log burials in other parts of
Australia. The burial customs
of most societies, throughout
the world, convey the body to
only one of the four primary
elements; earth, air, fire, or
water, whereas the consecutive
ceremonies of aboriginal
funeral rites often include
burial in the earth as well as
an exposure to air, fire, and
water.*

years so that the spirit, after having had this phase of coming and going, will be completely free to leave for the Land of the Dead.[4]

In most Aboriginal traditional burials, however, the deceased does not require a mummy to retain temporary resonance with the earth. *Ngurra*, or earthly place, together with the totemic spirits of nature, are sufficiently infused in the Aborigine's being during life to retain resonance for a phase during the afterlife.

Unlike the elite priests and pharaohs of Egypt, initiated Aboriginal men and women constitute a large proportion of traditional Aboriginal society. For a period of time after death, most Aboriginal men and women appear in the dreams, visions, and ceremonies of the living. Their being may flow into animals, flowers, water, clouds, and mountains, thereby absorbing the experience of the entire universal creation before entering forever into the Dreamtime.

DEATH AND MEDITATION

Meditation techniques in many Eastern religions differ significantly from the Aboriginal or shamanistic approach to spirit and afterlife. The meditational way attempts to disengage the spirit gradually through sustained disciplines throughout life, so that the center of being increases its identification with the spirit component. This identification is forged by restraining the ego so that it becomes a silent observer of mental and metabolic activities. The way of meditation, in effect, works to separate the ego and its subtle field from the physical workings of mind and body.[5] In contrast, the Aboriginal way ecstatically expands the pain-pleasure confines of the physical body and deepens the mind's external perception and its unconscious depths.

Meditation and singular, silent concentration gather a field of force in the subtle envelope of the individual being, creating a spiritual core distinct from the physical nature. The goal of meditation is to enhance the field of the individual or ego soul so that it acquires full independence from the physical body before death. Through constant exercise the spirit body of the individual ego soul is built up and transposed into a universal ego. As the meditative practice matures, the individual becomes capable of living simultaneously in life and the afterlife.[6] The advanced meditator achieves identity with the two extremes of existence, the undifferentiated universal continuum and the spirit of the encapsulated individual world. After death this ability to live simultaneously in the individual and the universal is said to be retained.

In the Aboriginal initiatic path, the ego soul or Trickster, is a minor, often irksome factor in the dying process and the achievement of universal awareness. The Aboriginal initiation strove for an integrated expansion of the entirety of being throughout life, so that in death one would identify with all the levels of creation and with the ancestral field from which it emerged.

In spite of these great differences, there are similarities in the meditational and Aboriginal approach to initiation. During life, the principal force of death plays a prominent role in releasing the spirit. In both traditions death is represented by inhibition of the life processes. Both initiatic paths, in different ways, involve activities that counteract the movement of life energy. In meditation these are inactivity, isolation, stillness, sexual and sensory denial, fasting, and food prohibitions. In shamanism the reversal of life energy is accomplished through wounding and bloodletting and through controlling and mastering the body's autonomic reaction to pain and exhaustion. It is also accomplished through ritual, ecstatic trance, and practices that have a poisonous "death" potential, including using hallucinogens.

The life-taking, life-restraining, life-reducing death tendencies employed in the initiatic process are characteristics of the Universal Masculine. The archetypal male power represents, on every level, the principle of death that enables or promotes rebirth. In Aboriginal belief, immediately after death (as well as after initiatic "death") the deceased is assisted by his or her biological father or grandfather, who acts as the first spirit guide in the dangerous passage out of bodily life.[7] The spirit of the biological mother, which plays such a nourishing and positive role in life, is considered a dangerous negative force at the time of death. In its pure form the Universal Mother, the unifying integrating force, opposes all processes of separate and individualized manifestation. For this reason, at puberty the child is emphatically separated from the mother so that his or her separate identity is secured. Initiation symbolizes the dynamic of the entire universe: the all-powerful, all-containing darkness of the cosmic Mother-Womb is the life ground of the entire creation. The separating, specifying power of the Universal Male spermatic force accomplishes individual, speciated life by bringing a temporary death to the Universal Oneness.

The ancient philosophies say that good hides behind evil, evil hides behind good. In death the positive qualities in life become negative and inhibitive. In the continuous cycles of rebirth that shape our existence, the positive-negative polarities reverse, just as they do in the earth's magnetic field.

The unrelenting absolute eternal ground beyond all differentiation, which many meditational philosophies seek as a goal of spiritual life, is for the Aborigines as well as the ancient Egyptians to be avoided—it means an end to participation in the continually unfolding cycles of creation. Meditational philosophies speak of one's spirit being absorbed into the uncreative eternity, just as "pure water blends with pure water and will, henceforth, never more separate in eternity."[8] This goal of some meditative religions is nihilistic and abhorrent to the creation-loving, adventurous soul of the Aboriginal Dreaming.

Eastern meditative asceticism and Western productive materialism both result from the polarization of humanity's spiritual vision. As Carl Jung has pointed out, they are like the left and right hand of the same body, each fulfilling and complementing the other. In recent years, the attraction between them has manifested in the numbers of educated, privileged Westerners who assume orange robes and begging bowls and enter severe monastic practices, while the Eastern swamis and yogis purchase Mercedes and establish corporate organizations and institutions. The ancient shamanistic religious practices are the body or central core of the left and right arms of materialism and asceticism, integrating the two extremes and including all the intermediate levels of nature and consciousness.

In modern society men have lost their role as initiators and disseminators of the positive, purposeful powers of death in the world of the living. The uninitiated males who control our society know nothing of the spiritual processes and journeys from the realms of the unborn to the

363

living to the dead. In this ignorance, modern men have lost their raison d'être.

In Western civilization men have attempted to transfer their knowledge and mastery of the journey of death to analysis and control of the physical world. Through mechanistic science, medicine, and the manipulation of nature and society they have attempted, like tricksters, to make physical death seem somehow controllable or avoidable. By denying the spiritual reality and necessity of death, we learn to consider death as a threat to be escaped personally through courage or caution, perhaps someday to be permanently removed through technological advancement. When we deny death's inevitable role in our lives, it saturates our sense of being as a threat to life.

The threat of death is quite different from the reality of death. The constant threat of death and the illusion that we can be victorious over it form the hallmark of modern warfare, business, and sports. These activities have replaced the true basis of male knowledge. Lost is the initiation process that allows men an internal experience of the journey from life to the realm of the dead. Loss of the knowledge of dying is at the marrow of our present dilemma as a race. The deterrents that modern male society has built—its industrial economy and war machine—cannot deter what they are meant to. The human species has impaled itself on the horns of a mad dilemma: "We must be willing to destroy ourselves in order to escape destruction."[9]

The crises that confront our society can never be understood or rectified without knowing and integrating the three realms of existence. We cannot know or understand how to exist in life unless we know how we exist in death. This world only has meaning to the degree that Death and the Unborn have meaning. The three worlds exist in an inseparable relationship. To deny or distort the purpose and meaning of one is to deny the same for all.

CHAPTER 22

WISE WOMEN AND MEN OF HIGH DEGREE

The Black Swans

When Wurrunna returned to his tribe after one of his walkabouts he brought with him some weapons never before seen by men. These, he said, were made in a country where there were only women, and they had given them to him in exchange for his opossum-skin rug, saying, "Go, bring us more rugs, and we will give you more weapons."

The tribes were delighted with the weapons, and agreed to go as far as the women's country with him on his next expedition to Oobi Oobi, the sacred mountain, taking rugs for purpose of ceremonial exchange.

Wurrunna, when they started, warned his companions that there were unknown dangers on that plain, for he was sure the women were spirits. They had told him there was no death in their country, nor was there any night; the sun shone always.

He said, "When the dark rolls away from our country it does not go into theirs, which is where Yhi, our sun, being a woman, goes to rest. The dark just rolls itself under the earth until it is time to come back there. We shall do well to smoke ourselves before we go out of the darkness on to that plain."

Wurrunna arranged that he would go round to the other side of the plain and make another fire to smoke them directly they came away, so that no evil would cling to them and be carried back to their tribe. And in case they were staying too long, he had a plan for warning them to leave.

He would take his two brothers with him. By his magic, for he was a great *wirinun*, or clever man, he could turn them into two large water birds. As there were no birds on the lake they would quickly be noticed. As soon as he had the smoke fire ready he would send his brothers swimming opposite the women's camp. Seeing them, the women would in their wonder forget the men, who were to go onto the plain and get what they wanted.

He told every man to take an animal with him, and, should the women interfere, to let the animal go. There were no animals on the plain, and the

365

FIGURE 186
Black swans are a species unique to Australia and were not seen by European observers until Australian colonization. However, they appeared in many ancient myths and fairy tales all over the world prior to their actual sighting.

women's attention would be taken off again. Then the men must hasten to make their escape back into the darkness, where these women of the country that was always light would fear to follow them.

Each man found an animal, and then started. Among them they had opossums, native cats, flying squirrels, various kinds of rats, and such.

When they reached where the darkness was rolled up on the edge of the plain they camped. Wurrunna and his two brothers sped through the scrub, skirting the plain until they reached the far side.

The Wurrunna lit a fire, produced a large gubbera, *or crystal stone, from inside himself, and, turning to his two brothers, crooned a sort of sing-song over them.*

Soon they cried "Biboh! Biboh!" changing as they did so into large, pure white birds, which the Daens call Baiamul, the swans.

The men on the other side of the plain, having lit their fire, were smoking themselves in it.

The women saw the smoke curling up towards their plain and ran toward it, armed with spears, crying "Wi-bulloo! Wi-bulloo!"

One of them gave a cry of surprise, the others looked round, and there on the lake they saw swimming two huge white birds. The smoke was forgotten; they ran toward the new wonders, while the men rushed to the deserted camp for weapons.

The women saw them, and turning from the swans, came angrily toward them.

Then each man let go the animal he had. Far and wide on the plain went opossums, bandicoots, bukkandis, and others. Shrieking after them went the women. The men dropped the opossum rugs and loaded themselves with weapons, then started toward Wurrunna's smoke signal, now curling up in a spiral column.

Having caught one of the animals, the women remembered the men, whom they saw leaving their camps laden with weapons.

Screeching with anger, they started after them, but too late. The men passed into the darkness, where they smoked all evil of the plain from them in Wurrunna's fire.

On the women came, until they saw smoke, then cried again, "Wi-bulloo! Wi-bulloo!" They feared a fire as much as they feared the dark, both unknown in their country.

Failing to get their weapons, they turned again to where the strange white birds had been. But they had gone.

The women were so angry that they began to quarrel, and from words they got to blows. Their blood flowed fast, and freely stained the whole of the western sky, where their country is. Ever since, when the tribes see a red sunset they say, "Look at the blood of the Wi-bulloos; they must be fighting again."

The men returned to their own country with their weapons, and Wurrunna travelled on alone toward the sacred mountain, which was to the northeast of Wi-bulloo land.

He forgot all about his brothers, though they flew after him, crying, "Biboh! Biboh!" to attract his attention, that he might change them back to men.

But heedlessly on went Wurrunna, up the stone steps cut in the sacred mountain for the coming of Baiame to earth.

The swans, tired of flying, stayed on a small lagoon at the foot of the mountain. As the eaglehawks, the messengers of the spirits, were flying to deliver a spirit's message, they saw in their own lagoon two strange white birds.

In their rage they swooped down, drove their huge claws into the swans, and flew far away from the sacred mountain, over plains and over mountain ranges, away to the south.

Every now and then, in savage rage, they stopped to pluck out a handful of feathers, white as ash of gidya wood. These feathers fluttered down the sides of the mountains, lodging in between the rocks, blood dripping beside them.

On flew the eaglehawks until they came to a large lagoon near to the big salt water. At one end of the lagoon were rocks; on these they dropped the swans, then swooped down themselves, and savagely started to pluck out the few feathers the birds had left. But just as they were tearing out the last ones on the wings, they recollected that they had not delivered the message of the spirits, so, fearing their anger, the eaglehawks left the swans and flew back to their own country.

The poor Baiamul brothers crouched together, almost featherless, bleeding, cold, and miserable. They felt they were dying, far away from the tribe.

Suddenly, softly fell on them a shower of feathers, which covered their shivering bodies. Gaining warmth, they looked about them. High on the trees overhead they saw hundreds of mountain crows, such as they had sometimes seen on the plains country, and had believed to be a warning of evil.

The crows called to them, "The eaglehawks are our enemies, too. We saw you left by them to die. We said it should not be so. On the breeze we sent some of our feathers to warm you and make you strong to fly back to your friends, and laugh at the eaglehawks."

The black feathers covered the swans all but on their wings, where a few white ones had been left. Also the down under the black feathers was white. The red blood on their beaks stayed on there forever.

The white swan feathers that the eaglehawks had plucked out when crossing the mountains took root where they fell, and sprang up as soft white flowers which you call flannel flowers.

Baiamul, the swans, flew back over the camp of their tribe. Wurrunna heard their cry, "Biboh! Biboh!" and knew it was the voice of his brothers, though, looking up, he saw not white birds, but black ones, with red bills.

Sorrowful as he was at their sad cry, Wurrunna had no power to change them back to men. His power as a wirinun *had been taken from him for daring to go, before his time, to Baiame's sky camp.*[1]

SLEEPING IN A FIRE

IN THE EARLY 1920s, Bill Harney was stationed as a ranger with the Australian government near Uluru (Ayer's Rock), the huge sacred monolithic rock formation in central Australia. Harney was an uneducated but very perceptive boy from an outback farm who, while in service at Uluru, married a part-Aboriginal woman, learned her dialect, and became deeply involved with the Aboriginal people. One of his many extraordinary reports about tribal people is particularly significant for understanding how Aborigines developed their spiritual and physical life in concert.

Harney was once given government blankets to be distributed to surrounding tribes. The scorching daytime heat of the Australian desert is transformed at night to severe subfreezing temperatures. In spite of this, the Aborigines at first refused Harney's blankets and continued to sleep, naked on the earth, in the open, using only a small fire to warm them just long enough to fall asleep. Harney also noted that once asleep, the natives would sometimes roll over on top of the hot coals without awakening and without incurring any burns.[2]

These stories of tribal Aborigines call to mind traditions of Hindu and Tibetan yoga. There are numerous cases of naked yogis in the Himalayas who enter trancelike states of consciousness in which they generate body heat adequate to withstand freezing temperatures. These disciplines also permitted yogis to prevent their bodies from bleeding or suffering burns by gaining control over the unconscious or autonomic neural centers and functions of the body.

Since Harney's time in the Australian outback, much clinical research into such phenomena has authenticated them. They are associated with the production of unusual brain wave activity (in the delta or theta range) similar to that produced in deep sleep, trance, or deep meditation. In addition to clinical tests with yogis and clairvoyants, research in hypnosis has proved that ordinary people can be induced, through suggestion, to states in which their bodies reproduce some of the extraordinary feats of the yogis. If the suggestion has been previously implanted in a hypnotized person's unconscious that a candle flame will not burn, the flame can be held close to the skin without producing a burn response.[3] Many ordinary people in Hawaii and California have been involved in group hypnotic sessions where, after being given the suggestion that they could walk over hot coals without injury, they do so.

According to the accounts of Harney, A. P. Elkin, Ronald Rose, and many other observers, Aboriginal men, women, and children often demonstrate psychophysical feats like those associated with hypnotic states or advanced stages of yoga. Almost all Aboriginal people have been reported to have some psychophysical power. For example, when an Aborigine is overcome with a sense of anxiety, he or she very often sits alone in a meditative state and waits for a twitch or tremor in a part of the body. Each part of an Aborigine's body is associated with a kin relative and a geographic location. When a body part twitches, the person touchs the agitated region and visualizes what is happening to that relative or at that place.[4] Time and time again, these Aboriginal practices have been observed by anthropologists to be accurate and effective. All Aborigines, including children, use dreams and dream images as mes-

FIGURE 187

Medicine man demonstrating technique of sucking and massaging a patient to withdraw the effects of evil magic. East Alligator River, Northern Australia, 1912. The capacity to heal by sucking is said to have been learned from the lizard totem, whose throat expands to swallow the large eggs of other creatures. Of his ability to heal a tribal doctor remarked, "My psychic power is strong enough to cause others to believe in themselves." If a patient is deemed fatally ill, the doctor will face him or her to the west, induce a hypnotic trance, and give a repeated suggestion that the "Ancestors are calling." This often causes a peaceful semi-conscious death by suggestion.

sages to guide their lives. All use visualization and concentration techniques, sometimes in association with sorcery methods, to achieve their desires. They also seem familiar with psychophysical healing techniques. When an Aboriginal man is suffering from a headache he may place around his forehead a hair belt made from his wife's hair, which she has worn around her head or waist. A few moments of silent concentration while wearing his wife's hair belt removes the headache. Very often the headache was caused by the same wife![5]

Throughout Aboriginal society there are advanced initiations for those with greater capacities for spiritual growth. In some cases these initiations, accompanied by rigorous disciplines such as food restrictions, purification rites, and extensive memorizing of songs, dances, and stories, can lead to achieving the title of a man of high degree. The Aborigines refer to these tribal doctors as the "clever men."[6] Recently, anthropologists have found that Aboriginal women also have secret higher initiations that early Western observers did not have access to because they were all men. Aborigines believe that women more naturally possess the psychic and intuitional powers men strive for through initiation. Aboriginal doctors often con-

sult older "wise women." Once again in Aboriginal social structure, men perform formal roles in which women hold informal powers.

The eminent anthropologist and author A. P. Elkin concentrated his early field work, beginning in 1927, on a continental survey of the mystic traditions of the Aboriginal men of high degree. From his own observations, native informants, and a great many discussions and interviews with tribal people, he gathered compelling and astonishing examples of the rites, practices, and powers associated with the advanced psychic specialization of the Aborigines. The Aboriginal doctors demonstrated or were reported to perform clairvoyant, telepathic, and trance or hypnotic practices; remote viewing; thought transference; psychic healing (nonsurgical removal of objects from the body); levitation (fast striding above the ground); journeys to other worlds; communication with spirit familiars and with the dead; sorcery and psychic projection (for both healing and killing); and multiple appearances (appearing at one place while actually being at another).

These powers, which were attained and increased through a lifetime of discipline, served a function in the community at large. Wise women and men of high degree held responsibility for the health and healing of the entire clan. They were also the psychologists of the society, dealing not only with physical ills but emotional and psychological traumas. They were indispensable to the maintenance of social justice, since crime was often detected and punishment enacted partly through psychic means. Their clairvoyance was useful in settling disputes of all kinds through their great capacity for evaluating the character and motives of those involved in conflict. Reciprocation, reprisal, and revenge for any infraction of the Dreamtime Laws were the only means used by the Aborigines to restore coherence and balance to the social group.[7] In effect, the powers inherent in the unconscious, psychic levels of the minds of the highly initiated served as the governing moral and social authority.

In spite of the importance of advanced psychic capabilities in the functioning of Aboriginal society, these powers were not placed at the spiritual pinnacle of the entire culture. Psychic skills were not revered any more than those of hunting, dancing, or boomerang making. The exclusive pedestal on which we place priests, scientists, and yogis is antithetical to the balanced Aboriginal world view.

Ancient Egypt is another example of a culture in which psychic or unconscious mind processes served as the highest authority in a social order. The initiate-king or pharaoh achieved and maintained secular power through continual initiatic and psychic development. The pyramids of ancient Egypt are considered by many to have been centers for psychic or out-of-the-body journeys and other initiatic rites performed by the reigning pharaoh.[8]

371

In the 1930s, while Elkin was absorbed in research into the Aboriginal tradition, W. Y. Evens-Wentz was the first Westerner to unearth the mystic and psychic traditions of Tibet. Elkin came across an article by Evens-Wentz and was stunned by the exact parallels between Tibetan and Indian yoga practices and those of the Australian Aborigines.

> There the great Yogi, possessed of clairvoyant vision is said to be able to observe the physiological processes of his own body. He requires no mechanical devices in order to traverse air or water or land, for he tells us that he can quit his gross physical body and visit any part of the earth or pass beyond the stratosphere to other worlds with a speed greater than light. As a result of his discipline and training, he can acquire fleetness of foot, lightness of body and immunity to harm by fire. He can become immune also to severe cold, the result of practising the Yoga of Psychic Heat. This includes concentration and visualization of fire at the meeting point of the nerves at the psychic centre. The latter is situated four fingers below the navel. It is "the hidden abode" of the sleeping Goddess Kundalini, the personification of the Serpent Power, of the latent mystic fire-force of the body.[9]

FIGURE 188
The serpent is a universal symbol of pure energy and invisible force. For this reason, the symbol is always ambivalent, bisexual, and multivalent in meaning.

Elkin realized that the Aboriginal tradition probably predated those of India and Tibet by 50,000 or 60,000 years. Long before such ideas existed in India, the Aboriginal men of high degree had consciously concentrated on the same body center (four fingers below the navel), where they said the cord of the great Rainbow Serpent (kundalini) lay coiled. Through the same center the Aborigines also drew body heat from the "rainbow fires" that helped them endure cold. The Aborigines spoke of projecting psychic powers from these centers that were unhindered by time or space—powers that could bring healing life, death, and knowledge, or transfer thoughts. When this power was raised up and projected from the forehead the Aborigines referred to it as the "strong eye," through which they could view distant worlds or penetrate the surface of matter to the worlds within.[10]

The presence of initiatic sacred tradition in societies so disparate in history and geographic location as Egypt, Tibet, India, and Australia may find a logical explanation in prehistorical research. Prior to all the great early agricultural-based societies of India and the East, there existed in the same regions timeless, indigenous gathering and hunting societies. As the earth's magnetic energy slowly diminished and the dance of creation in this cycle began to turn toward twilight, the psychic potencies of the Dreaming in both humanity and the earth declined. The diminishing of the life force resulted in deep doubt, uncertainty, and separation between humans and earth, like a garden at nightfall when the clarity of green plants, black earth, and azure sky sinks into dark, barely discernible forms, cold and threatening. Agriculture was one of the great collective reactions to this loss of vision and alienation.

In Egypt and India, the spirituality of the older indigenous peoples was recorded, formalized, and retained within the secret traditions of the temples, like a seed of hope through which the initiated could return to the First Day. The source of the temple traditions of Egypt and India were almost certainly the shamanistic cultures of the tribal peoples who preceded them. The source of the much older Aboriginal tradition is the Dreamtime itself.

The change from hunter-gatherer to pastoralist provoked great changes in the deepest layers of consciousness in both men and women. Men no longer had the roles of ecstatic trance-dancer; the wild, wandering, highly sensitized and perceptive hunter; and the mystic absorbed in the power of animal dreaming. A man became instead the guardian of the tedious cycles of controlled cultivation, the builder of complex stagnant settlements, the soldier/defender of fixed boundaries and territories, the deceitful profiteer of material possessions and exchanges, and the ruler of subjugated flocks, both human and animal.

For women the change was equally radical. No longer could they embody all the forms of the Universal Feminine: the ravished virgin, the ritual prostitute, the all-loving mother, the healing and nourishing wife, the laughing storyteller, the naked dancer, the wandering, silent, old wise woman. The Universal Feminine primarily took the form of the earth-mother hag, whom men tormented and exploited to maintain their authority over her natural power and propensity to give life and nourish.

During a conversation with an Aboriginal elder I came to see clearly the effect of the loss of hunting and gathering on the deeper workings of the human psyche. The old man explained that in the trance vision one can see a "web of intersecting threads" on which the scenes of the tangible world as well as dreams and visions are hung. "Inner fears," he said, "break that glimpse of an invisible webwork, leaving only a world of isolated things." He thought for a while and added, "Some of the young Aboriginal men today talk and act very smart, they no longer have the vision, 'cause they have the same fear inside as white fellas. That's because they can't go off in the bush and feed themselves like I do. I know where all the roots and berries and fruits are. Anyone who does not know how to find food and feed himself is always frightened inside like a little child who has lost his mother and with that fear the vision of the spirit world departs."[11]

Crystals and Initiations of High Degree

The supernormal, supersensory powers of Aboriginal wise women and men of high degree, by their own accounts, comes directly from initiations administered by the ancestral sky heroes themselves and by the totemic spirits. Those who have gone through these initiations alone, in a deep trance that makes them lose their personal identities and confront manifestations of the ancestral powers, are held in the highest regard. A. P. Elkin compiled descriptions of Aboriginal initiations from diverse clans and distant tribes and found, beneath the innumerable variations, underlying universal themes. The most common was the implanting of a resonant substance in the body.

> Amongst the Deiri, near Lake Eyre, a spirit makes an incision in the postulant's abdomen and inserts a spirit-snake, his future "familiar." He also visits the sky by means of a hair-cord. In the neighbouring Piladapa tribe, a spirit drives a "pointing-stick" into the back of the postulant's head, but the latter recovers, and receives power and quartz from the spirit. Included in this power is that of extracting a person's "inside." . . .
>
> In western South Australia, the postulant is put in a waterhole, where a mythical snake swallows him, but later ejects him in the form of a baby on to a supposedly unknown place. After a long search, he is found by the doctors, and is restored to man's size by being sung in the midst of a circle of fires. After a period of seclusion and converse with spirits, he is red-ochred and treated as a corpse. Then the head doctor ritually breaks his neck, wrists and other joints by marking them with a magic stone (australite). Into each mark or cut, and also into his stomach, the doctor inserts *mabain* life-giving shell, after which the postulant is "sung" and revives, now full of power. . . .
>
> The description of the operation in the Mandjindja tribe, Warburton Ranges, Western Australia, adds the detail, that two totemic spirits or heroes "kill" the postulant, cut him open from his neck to his groin, take out all his "insides" and insert magical substances (*mabain*). They also take out his shoulder and thigh bones and insert *mabain*, before drying and putting them back. They treat frontal bone in the same way, and also cut round the ankles and stuff *mabain* into those parts. . . .
>
> In the Wiradjeri and neighbouring tribes of western New South Wales, crystals extracted from their own bodies are pressed and scored and "jerked" into the postulant's body. He is also given crystals in his food and drink. In addition, a hole is pierced in his tongue.[12]

Throughout Australia one of the most consistent themes in Aboriginal initiation is the insertion into the body of quartz crystals, or *mabain*.

This procedure symbolizes the transformation of consciousness from physical to psychic levels. The Aborigines seek quartz crystals with internal fractures that produce vivid rainbow light refractions. These fractures signal that the stone resonates powerfully with the primordial energies of the Rainbow Serpent.

In recent years, the science of crystallography has gained new insights into the chemical and physical properties of crystalline substances. Computers and telecommunication technology employ the crystal's amazing capacity for focusing, storing, transducing, transmitting, and amplifying all kinds of energy radiation.

> The crystal is the arch manipulator of radiation in the realm of matter. When a beam of light passes through a crystal, it is bent in ways characteristic to that particular crystal. . . .
>
> Crystals have unique properties. When pressure is applied to some, an electric current is set in motion; others convert heat to electricity, or electricity into fluorescence or phosphorescence. Crystals can also be made to act as oscillators, initiating and controlling a wide spectrum of radiation.[13]

Wherever the body requires rapid, smooth transmission of energy, as in the organs of perception, tissue assumes a discernable crystalline form.

> The rhodopsin molecules in the cone and rod cells of the retina, for example, are assembled in sparkling, transparent crystal-like plates; and the microstructure of muscle fibres—only recently unravelled—consists of inter-contracting molecules in an epitome of crystalline precision.[14]

In Aboriginal initiation, inserting crystals into the body symbolizes that the obduracy of matter can be transformed into an all-seeing, all-hearing, all-perceiving conduit of cosmic energy.

The role that crystals play in resonating and transmitting energy between ourselves and the surrounding cosmos offers the possibility of completely revising our scientific and spiritual understanding.

> Semiconductivity occurs naturally in inorganic crystals such as silicon, changing their structure so that each time a current passes through, it does so more easily—making such crystals, in effect, very lifelike; more responsive to their environment. And if the arrangement of proteins in our nerves gives us possession of such conductors, it could also give us greater awareness of subtle environmental patterns such as the fields produced by underground water. It could, in addition, give us access to signals on very low frequencies—the sort that travel round the globe with little attenuation—and provide information about the currents

The inner sanctuaries of the Egyptian Temple followed the anatomical plan of the position and location of the principal organs in the human brain (left). In the final initiations of the Pharaonic King, the wall that corresponds with the ethmoid bone (center, 18) was ceremonially broken through, thereby forming a direct entrance to the chamber containing the olfactory bulb (17). Experiments with altered states of consciousness have shown that heightened visionary states are accompanied by acute olfactory sensitivity, in which a person's capacity to perceive odors increases to that of animals. The Egyptian texts describe this state as becoming aware of the "odor of the Gods." An Aboriginal initiation describes a similar shattering of the ethmoid bone to permit entrance to the inner chambers of the brain or enable the initiate to reach heightened states of consciousness. The verification for the Aboriginal shaman that this initiation has occurred is a hole left in his tongue (right), made by an invisible lance hurled through the back of his head. The ethmoid bone also contains a cluster of crystalline protein, which is acutely sensitive to geomagnetic fields.

and fields produced by other organisms. It is admittedly tenuous, but all at once there is at least a prospect of coming to terms with phenomena such as dowsing, telepathy, and auras.[15]

Scientists have been investigating how the body receives information from the environment without being consciously aware of it. They have found, for example, that crystalline substances in the cells and glands are tuned to the most subtle oscillations of the earth's geomagnetic field as well as the magnetic fields that surround all living things. These biomagnetic fields extend into space from our bodies, carrying wave patterns that reflect what is happening inside our brains and organs.[16] For perhaps 100,000 years, the medicine men of Australia have professed the power of consciousness to perceive these energies: with the strong eye they can look into another person's mind, see the workings of the body, and perceive the energy fields associated with the sick and the dying or the guilty and the innocent. In short, this enhanced vision can view the spiritual condition of all things—living, dead, and unborn.

Dr. Robin Baker at the University of Manchester, England, has located a cluster of cells containing magnetite in the posterior wall of the ethmoid sinus, high up at the back of the nasal passage just in front of the pituitary gland. This "magnetic organ" functions with exquisite sensitivity, like the internal compass of a bird, providing an exact sense of direction based on the earth's magnetic field. The pineal gland, which stands directly behind the posterior wall of the nasal passage, is also tuned to the earth's geomagnetic field and senses the daily fluctuations in this field. This gland is sensitive to any energy changes due to increases or drops in radiant energy in the earth's magnetic field, such as those caused by lightning or solar radiation.[17] The magnetic potential of the earth is highly responsive to these sky-born radiations. The pineal gland uses the information from earth's magnetism in timing the daily secretion of the brain's most powerful hormones, which it produces in great quantities. These hormones include melatonin, serotonin, and dopamine, all of which regulate the state and level of the brain's conscious awareness.[18]

Higher Aboriginal initiation involves a procedure that may symbolically relate to these earth-tuned sensory processes in the pineal and nasal passages. The advanced initiate is said to be drawn into a cave where a most powerful ancestral being died and left his potency. Inside the cave the initiate is said to be killed by the ancestor, who drives a spear through the back of his skull, down through the center of the head so that the spear breaks through the nasal passage and penetrates the center of his tongue.[19] Anatomically, this spear would pierce the pineal region and break the ethmoid bone. When the initiate emerges, he must demon-

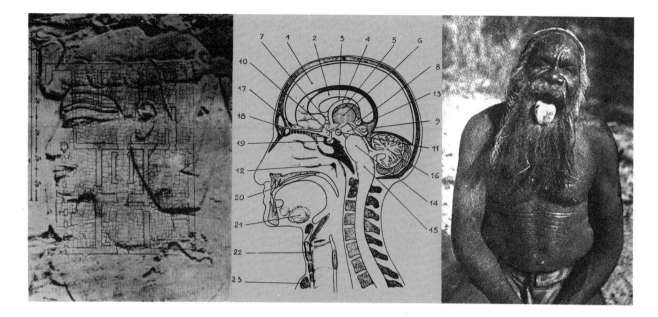

strate the evidence of his ordeal by displaying a hole in his tongue, into which he then inserts a crystal. This event is said to symbolize that the initiate has "broken through" to a very high degree of enlightenment.

The ancient Egyptians used a similar initiatic symbol. R. A. Schwaller de Lubicz projected an anatomically precise image of a human skull on the inner sanctuaries of the temple of Luxor, where the highest initiations of the young king were supposed to have occurred. The final stage of enlightenment was symbolized by a ritual in which the wall corresponding to the ethmoid bone, which separates the nasal passage from the pineal gland, was forcibly broken down, allowing the king to enter the mysteries of the inner sanctuary (the pineal and pituitary glands) directly through the broken passageway.[20]

The Dreaming Body

Robert Becker, the leading researcher in bioelectricity and biomagnetism, has developed a theory based on the presence of earth-tuned magnetic crystals in living cells. He postulates the existence of two separate nervous systems in the body. The first is the conventionally recognized central nervous system. This system, as he describes it, functions similarly to an AC-driven (alternating current) digital computer.

> In both the computer and the brain, the basic signal is a digital one, a single pulse. The information is coded by the number of pulses per unit of time. . . . Our senses smell, taste, hearing,

Wise Women and Men
of High Degree

sight, and touch work by means of this type of pulse. The digital computer on my desk works in the same way. This digital system works extremely fast and it can transmit large amounts of information as digital "bits" of data.[21]

In addition to the central nervous system, Becker postulates the existence of another entire nervous system. This one seems to flow from the perineural cells, which generate not AC but DC (direct current). Its existence was first deduced from observation of the field of direct current that all creatures generate as part of the healing process. Investigation into this second nervous system has just begun, but already it is clear that its functions are closely tied to the pineal gland and the minute magnetite crystals in organs and cells. The perineural nervous system communicates information gathered by the pineal gland from environmental fields to the entire body.[22]

The function of this DC perineural nervous system, or deep neural system, can be compared to an analog computer transmission. Analog computers are older than the digital systems and do not operate on single pulsations per unit of time. Instead, information is coded by the strength of the current and the direction of its flow. This system is much slower than digital systems, but it is extremely precise and varied in content because it is based on the subtle variations in intensity of wave frequencies.

> If we combine all of the above observations, we can only conclude that a more primitive, analog data-transmission and control system still exists in the body, located in the perineural cells and transmitting information by means of the flow of a semiconducting DC electrical current. This system appears to have been the original data-transmission and control system present in the earliest living organisms. It senses injury and controls repair, and it may serve as the morphogenetic field itself. It controls the activity of body cells by producing specific DC electrical environments in their vicinity. It also appears to be the primary system in the brain, controlling the actions of neurons in their generation and receipt of nerve impulses. In this fashion it regulates our level of consciousness and appears to be related to decision-making processes.[23]

Becker believes that the discovery of this second nervous system in the human organism constitutes the most important revolution in biological science. It provides us with a new understanding of the way all living creatures are interrelated with the life of the earth.

Parallels abound between the functions of the analog neural system and the descriptions of Dreamtime states of perception. The perineural cells of the analog system surround and envelop all the nerve fibers in the brain and spinal cord, as well as the myriad branches of nerves that terminate in the skin surface. All nerve fibers are submerged in perineural cells, like raisins in a pudding. These perineural cells protect and nourish the nerve fibers as a placenta nourishes a fetus. Perineural cells are constructed like a crystalline lattice and transmit energy like semiconductors; the electrical potentials move through the crystalline lattice in an undulating wave over an entire field. This phenomenon recalls the description of the Dreamtime Creators as fields or wavelike continuums, each field carrying a particular energy potential or psychic activity or quality. The field moves through the crystalline structure so that each position in the field gathers a slightly different voltage power, a different current strength, and a different flow or current direction. All these subtle variations in the field are a code for large amounts of information, each with a potency for describing form or energy experience.

The word *field* applied to energy recalls its original meaning, a feature of the landscape.[24] The image of an undulating energy field, with each position or region having a particular potential within an integrated flowing movement, is precisely the way Aborigines visualize their mythic landscape. It is as if the Aborigines perceived the landscape in its pure

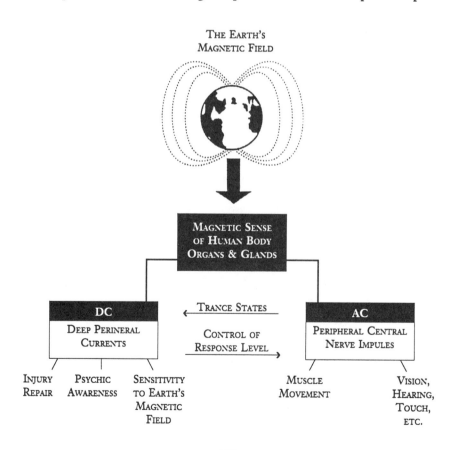

THE EARTH'S
MAGNETIC FIELD

MAGNETIC SENSE
OF HUMAN BODY
ORGANS & GLANDS

TRANCE STATES

CONTROL OF
RESPONSE LEVEL

DC
DEEP PERINEURAL
CURRENTS

AC
PERIPHERAL CENTRAL
NERVE IMPULSES

INJURY
REPAIR

PSYCHIC
AWARENESS

SENSITIVITY
TO EARTH'S
MAGNETIC
FIELD

MUSCLE
MOVEMENT

VISION,
HEARING,
TOUCH,
ETC.

FIGURE 192
The relationship of a dual nervous system to the earth's magnetic field. In effect, we as a culture have failed to develop an entire neural network and therefore perceive the world through only half of our natural capacities.

379

energetic state. Aboriginal paintings, based on pointillist dots and energetic cross-hatched fields, suggest this. The geometric, cross-hatched designs of early Aboriginal bark paintings were codes of information through which an Aborigine could visualize a specific topography, the animal species related to that land area, and the clans belonging to that land. In later bark paintings, the Aborigines added animals and figurative events for the benefit of European viewers who were unable to visualize anything from the energetic patterns alone.[25]

Our every perception provides information not only about external stimuli but also about our body's instruments of perception. The linear time and separative forms of the external world reflect the functioning of the central nervous system, just as the visionary, integrated, flowing patterns of the Dreamtime reflect the all-encompassing perineural analog nervous system.

Steps into the Dreaming

From all indications, the Aborigines developed the central and deep neural systems with equal intensity. Their life in the *yuti* (perceivable world) is one of intense observation of the specific detail of every aspect of nature. An even greater proportion of daily life is spent in song, dance, and chant and in other ecstatic ceremonies that activate the deep neural system, which echoes with the voice of the Dreaming. As with dreaming, this hypnogogic, ecstatic state is always present in the body. Rhythmic rituals help to activate brain chemistry so that our conscious awareness is released from the domination of the central nervous system. Once freed from the confines of external perception, the perceptive power is actually elevated. Hyperesthesia, or intensified sense awareness, is the first stage in the return to Dreamtime consciousness.

In 1922, naturalist Eugene Marais became aware of "hypnotic hyperesthesia" while working with African natives.

> He tested the effect of hypnosis on the sense of smell by getting twenty people each to handle a different object before placing it on a tray. The tray was then presented to another subject, this time a twenty-one-year-old girl, also hypnotised. The girl, blindfolded, took out one object after another and by smelling the object and the hands of the different people, handed each object back to the person who had handled it first, without a mistake.[26]

The second stage of Dreamtime awareness is marked by a state of perception called *synesthesia*, the mingling of the senses. Clinically, syn-

← *FIGURE 193*
Aranda man. Tempe Downs Station, MacDonnell Ranges, Central Australia, 1894. The plucking of hair from the forehead of initiated men symbolizes the elevation and intensification of their inner vision.

esthesia is defined as a condition in which the sense perceptions become scrambled in the neural networks. For example, a particular color can actually trigger a particular sound in the audio perception of a synesthetic person, or a particular taste can trigger a color response or even the sensation of a sharp or round object in the mouth. Extreme synesthesia has been recognized in a number of great poets, including Arthur Rimbaud, Vladimir Nabokov, and Marcel Proust. To some extent, however, *all* poetic analogy depends on a cross-reference from one sense perception to another.[27] Rainer Maria Rilke often spun off synesthetic phrases:

> My eyes already touch the sunny hill
> going far ahead of the road I have begun.[28]

Aborigines frequently make synesthetic statements. In conversation with photographer Donald Thompson, a tribal man described his entrance into a vision. He said it began by his listening intensely to the sound of a humming bee. He reproduced the sound on the didjereedoo (long wooden flute) so that the bee's body appeared from the flute sound in its Dreaming form. The flute player then dissolved his own body so that it became the humming sound of the bee, thereby entering the bee's body and flying off inside him.[29] Our perception of the tangible world depends on the distinct separation of the five sensory levels. The synesthetic experience, which occurs in the deep neural system, marks our entrance into the blending, merging world of the Dreamtime.

The Aboriginal flute player was aided in his "flight of the bumblebee" journey of consciousness by the rigorous breathing needed to blow the didjereedoo. Many similar descriptions have been reported from drug-induced psychedelic experiences. There is some evidence that the Australian Aborigines, like most indigenous tribal cultures, use plant substances, along with breathing, dance, rhythmic motion, and hypnogogic suggestion, to achieve altered states of consciousness, but for the most part this aspect of their tradition has been kept secret. The large-scale psychedelic experimentation that exploded in the West during the 1960s was a germinal source for many of the worldwide changes and movements that are with us today: changes in art forms, environmental awareness, sexual attitudes, spiritual involvement, and advance in philosophic, cognitive, and linguistic studies. The awkward brush of our culture with the Dreamtime experience 30 years ago ignited change on many different levels. The depth and quality of psychedelic experience is, to some degree, shaped by the consciousness that undergoes it. In general, Western mental, linguistic, and social processes are so literal, rigid, and externalized that, for Westerners, the psychedelic experience has often led to schizophrenia and fanaticism. Aboriginal society allows shamanistic and psychedelic experiences to blend with, enhance, and uphold the full expression of life.

Research is beginning to show that, rather than being an abnormality, synesthesia underscores all memory processes. The capacity for recall often depends on *eidetic images*, in which the mind blends together sensory image associations, such as a particular sound or word, with a particular image or object. The mixing together of sensory perception "lowers the threshold level of all senses and widens the reducing valve, thus exposing the mind to larger more memory enriched concerns."[30] A richer synesthetic capacity often means a stronger, richer memory. Oral traditions that require extraordinary memory always employ synesthetic imagery.

One universally important revelation that anyone can experience in the blending of sensory perception that occurs in a synesthetic state is this: there is no *single* thing. Nothing exists in this world isolated from everything else. Each object, each process, is more than it appears to be. Everything experienced in the perceivable world (*yuti*) implies, or quivers with, dense connotations of the Dreaming. Beneath the separate appearances of *yuti* is the expanding riddle of resonating images deposited by the Dreamtime Beings, in whom all are reflectively interconnected.

The perceivable world is a magic symbol tuning our sense of reality to another world more powerful, more awesome, more wonderful than we have allowed ourselves to believe. The network of correspondences that flood our vision as the sense perceptions merge is not a neural malfunction, a psychic illusion, or a device of poetry and romanticism. It is the experience of a crucial, long-ignored mode of intelligence, founded in a deep neural physiological base and essential to the full manifestation of our conscious being.

Hyperesthesia and synesthesia occur readily in hypnotic or trancelike states. Under hypnotism a man can be told that there is a brick wall in front of him and he will see a wall whether it is there or not. He will also find it impossible to walk past or through the line where the imaginary wall stands. A similar process is at work in our daily use of language. Words and word meanings slip into our subconscious like hypnotic suggestions, remaining there as images of the world around us. This process can also be associated with the internal dreaming body, or perineural nervous system: words and language enter the deep nervous system, there to be transformed synesthetically into images. These images then form our view of reality, often fixating into internalized belief systems. Our experience of what we subsequently perceive as reality is shaped by these internalized images or beliefs. We usually perceive only those things that correspond with our inwardly held image of reality. Like hypnotic suggestion, unconsciously absorbed word images allow us to see things that are not there and keep us from seeing what is there.

> Now each of us, from infancy onwards, is subjected to a complex set of suggestions from our social environment, which in effect teaches us how to perceive the world. We may from time to time, especially in early childhood, have experiences that do not conform to this cultural norm—but we eventually "correct" these perceptions and cease experiencing the anomalies, through the power of the socializing process. And so each of us is literally *hypnotized* from infancy to perceive the world the way people in our culture perceive it.[31]

Our society does not consciously cultivate or utilize the hypnotic trance or dreamlike states of awareness. We are unfamiliar with our deep neural system in which the images and forms of our world are created and projected. We have become cut off from an entire aspect of our being. Those deeper aspects are gifts from our Creative Ancestors, and they provide a means of entry into the worlds of the Dreamtime. Not only are we cut off from the wisdom of these worlds, we have also become victims of the unconscious and destructive aspects of these powers. Government, politics, media, and commercial interests feed on the universal suggestibility of the human unconscious. We see as realities the images that our culture implants in our uninhabited dreaming nature. We are manipulated like pawns by those who project false, illusory words, meanings, and images. Our governmental and religious institutions are founded on much the same processes of mass-induced suggestion used by infamous mind-control cults. We work and pray, spend and steal, live and die for empty words that have created false realities within us. Just before the 1991 Gulf War, a journalist reported that he found Iraq to be an entire country in a state similar to that of the Jonestown cult.[32] A murderous little gangster had hypnotized an entire population through propaganda, so that they saw him as a godlike hero.

American politicians continue to mouth slogans such as "The New Frontier," "A New World Order," or "Peace and Justice for All." Mainstream Americans continue to wave flags, vote in increasingly choiceless elections, raise children, and take out mortgages. The slogans blind them to the fact that the urban infrastructure is crumbling, the agricultural base of the society is eroding, the financial structure is debt-ridden, and the educational system is increasingly ineffective. Injustice and immorality are rife, and disease epidemics, drug addiction, homelessness, malnutrition, and overpopulation constantly increase.

Spelling means to construct words from alphabetic letter sounds. *Spelling* also means to cast destructive shadows over someone's consciousness. Words can and do cast spells. Because we are so trapped in our rational mind, we are unaware of the deep levels of our being in which unborn images are brought to life through word sounds—"In the beginning was the Word." We have lost the inner vision by which we might observe the role language plays in giving birth to our perceived world. As a result, language, particularly that which is broadcast by mass media, functions like a sorcerer's spell, hypnotizing us into a fraudulent, ungrounded sense of reality.

Toward the end of his life, Carl Jung became very pessimistic because he clearly saw that human society was ignoring the unconscious aspects of mind and attempting to run the world through totally rational constructs. At the same time, society was (and still is) plagued by repressed, unconscious forces that are triggered and exploited by hypnoticlike suggestion:

> This always happens when consciousness takes on too many unconscious contents upon itself. . . . It is incapable of learning from the past, it is incapable of understanding contemporary events, and incapable of drawing conclusions about the future. It is hypnotised by itself and therefore cannot be argued with. It inevitably dooms itself to calamities that might strike it dead.[33]

All of human society has fallen to such deplorable levels because, as the Aborigines say, "white men have lost their Dreaming." The Aboriginal Dreaming is tuned to receiving suggestions, images, and potencies directly from the pervading, pulsating voice of the earth and the prevailing echoes of the Creative Ancestors in the heavens. Hypnosis proves that even in modern man the degeneration of this hidden power of consciousness is not organic. The potential of the Dreamtime is still alive within us, both physically and psychologically, and holds the promise of an astonishing awareness that stretches beyond the bounds of our five senses. No objective can be of greater significance for human survival than the recovery of the Dreaming. The Aboriginal way of life and the Aboriginal revelation hold the seeds for the rebirth of the Dreamtime in humanity.

385

CHAPTER 23

PRESERVING THE SEED

DEATH HAS BEEN DESCRIBED as the ultimate healing crisis. Humanity is in the midst of such an experience. No matter what form it may take—whether it is a total apocalyptic destruction of the physical existence of our race or a near-death experience in which the collective organism mobilizes the feverish force of the illness to survive in part—in both cases the result is rebirth.

At the outset of any healing crisis, there are two considerations. The illness must be correctly diagnosed, or the cure will not be effective and any pain during the crisis will be of little future value in a recurrence. The infirm person must also discover and hold an image of his or her most potent healthy form as a guide for all cells and metabolic processes during the healing. Both the diagnosis and the image of wholeness need to be visualized and projected from within the consciousness of the ill, as well as through the external eyes of the healer. The spirit of Aboriginal culture provides eyes through which we may view, as if from the outside, our deteriorated and purulent condition. Only when viewed from both within and without can the affliction be fully recognized and surpassed.

I believe that the most important priority of the environmental and revisionist movements throughout the world should be to establish areas of land in which indigenous peoples can practice traditional gathering and hunting lifestyles. The worldwide issue of land rights for tribal people could be transformed into the goal of establishing centers for the rebirth of the "seed" cultures of humanity. The universal and symbolic content of indigenous language forms, perceptual modes and ceremonies, metaphysics, healing, and cosmology could become centers of learning for a vision of humanity reintegrated with nature. The present elaborate plans and designs for the future—green politics, environmental government, bioregionalism, sustainable development, renewable resource–based economies, alternative environmental technologies—all remain empty external forms unless accompanied by a deep concurrent linguistic, neural, psychophysical, and spiritual transformation at the very core of our being.

Australia, with its vast uninhabited areas of land and the living presence of the oldest indigenous culture yearning for its renaissance, is one of the most plausible regions for this worldwide process to begin. Land rights for Aborigines is more than a political and economic question. It is a question of preserving the seed within which rests the chances for human survival during the closing and opening of an enormous cycle. The Australian government's total lack of vision is viciously symptomatic of governments all over the world: instead of recognizing the cultural treasure of the Aboriginal people, it continually thwarts their efforts for land rights in a charade attempt to belatedly launch an "industrial revolution" in Australia.

As I write this, over 500 oil wells in Kuwait are spewing flames more than 500 feet high into our already dying atmosphere, burning like candles at a final requiem for our civilization. It is no longer feasible to seriously consider plans for reforming the existing structure of our societies. It is either vain or infantile for us to fail to acknowledge that the crisis descending on us is one of a cycle that includes the entirety of nature, the living, the dead, and the unborn. The dream of rebirth must step beyond the boundaries of nations, governments, and other existing structures and move toward a world process that includes an understanding of the purpose and necessity of death in the cycles of universal rebirth. For death to be able to grant the gift of rebirth, we must see through its fearful mask and recognize it as initiation.

This dreaming has already begun in a rudimentary form. The struggle to protect wilderness areas wherever they exist in the world is a high priority, and not simply to preserve potentially useful gene pools. The animating spiritual force that sustains life is manifested in nature's wild plants and animals. Without wilderness, the spiritual forces depart and life is doomed. The most spiritless religions, philosophies, and societies have arisen in long-established desert regions, such as the Middle East, or in urban centers such as London, Paris, Rome, or New York, where the spirit-force of nature is most diminished.

From the salvation of the wilderness, the list of emerging world concerns mounts, each reflecting the need of a return to the Dreaming: efforts to preserve and renew native species of plants and animals along with an absorption in, and preservation of, indigenous cultures; the yearning of individuals to live outside the boundaries of architecture and urban settlements; the emerging commitment to health and disciplines that integrate mind and body; disassociation of the naked body from sinfulness and immodesty to experience its natural strength and beauty; the spiritualization of sexuality so that its metaphysical meaning is re-

vealed; the ritualization and freer expression of emotion, along with the understanding of emotion's empathetic powers to bond people to one another; the humanization of child-rearing practices; regaining earth worship and nature rites; the empowerment of the Universal Feminine's role in society and the living world; the rediscovery of energy medicine, herbal healing, and the subtle, energetic sources of disease; the inner stirring of the sense of the tribal and the spirit of kinship; the acknowledgment of the God-like intelligence in animals and plants; a renewed awareness of the all-prevailing powers and intelligence of the unconscious mind. These and many more trends are emerging. They are the early echoes of the voices of the First Day.

As we, individually and collectively, descend into the crisis of an initiatic death, perhaps the resonance of a vision from deep within a dying world will touch the chords of the ancestral forces that hold the universe in balance. Perhaps they will reciprocate with flowing fields to carry forth the inevitable rebirth of the human spirit.

Adambarra, the web-spinning Dreamtime spider, spoke of a creation in which death, decline, and decay were not the inevitable result of the great cycles of time. The spider envisioned a world where rebirth could occur almost immediately, as a butterfly comes out of a cocoon. The ancient Egyptians symbolized this dream with the image of a lotus flower that gives birth to the next cycle of flowering directly out of its own center. In other words, the seed does not become engulfed and plunge

FIGURE 194
The lotus in both Egypt and India symbolizes the union of the four elements; earth, air, fire, and water. The roots are in the earth, it grows in and by means of water, its leaves are nourished by air, and it blooms through the power of the sun's fire. The lotus is therefore the perfection of the fourfold order of the natural world. The growth of a new flower directly from the earth-bound original (infloresent proliferation) may be interpreted as a symbol of transcendence as found in Indian philosophy: a spiritual emergence of a higher world directly from our physical manifestation. It may also be interpreted, as in Egypt, as the exaltation of the essence quality of the lotus. In the Aboriginal view the lotus may symbolize the physical world and the Dreaming, held together so that each constantly reflects the other.

into the depths of decay before being reborn. The lotus blooming out of the center of the previous flower is an image in which the flowering, fruiting, and seeding are an integrated trinity, simultaneously occurring one within the other. During the performance of the initiation of death, Aboriginal men of high degree eat only seed cakes made from the ground seeds of lotus flowers, perhaps to evoke the metaphysical principle symbolized by this plant. The butterfly from the cocoon, the flower born from the flower—these images share the same relationship as an attracting field to a magnet, a genetic imprint to an organic process of growth. They are all metaphoric images of the relationship of the Dreamtime to the world creation.

These images do not depict creation through evolution; they evoke the simultaneous presence of the primal division, that of the unconscious and the conscious. The Western tradition has precipitated a split in the Divine Couple. We observe and follow the externalized portion of consciousness, a cycle of birth, growth, and decline, as if it were not held in the embrace of an invisible lover. This partial vision is our entire reality. But the power and presence of the seed endures throughout the successive phases of growth. The plant never grows outside or beyond the seed's Dreaming. Our consciousness can be cultivated, as was the Aborigines', so that we can live simultaneously and continually in that enduring power as well as the external world. From our externalized point of view, earthly life and the universe may appear to contain innovation, change, sequential growth, even evolution. In the Dreaming vision there are no new energy, matter, or events in the universe; all has existed from the beginning somewhere in the deep dreaming of the Creative Ancestors. Therefore, all living is reliving. Every action, every substance, every phase has already been accomplished in the Dreamtime and exists either as a temporary actuality or an enduring potential of this world.

Viewed from the perspective of Aboriginal cosmology, our theories of evolution are muddled with unacknowledged contradictions. Biological science (including the new morphic field theory) emphasizes the role of relentless change—nature dominated by an open process in which chance mutations and adaptations lead to survival or extinction. Physics, on the other hand, emphasizes regularity, with eternal fixed mathematical or probabilistic laws. It is as if life and matter exist as two different worlds without the difference being recognized or defined.[1]

In comparison, the Aboriginal world view admits and clearly defines two utterly different and equally real worlds: the *yuti*, the always-changing and adapting realm of perceivable nature, symbolized by the lotus flower rooted in the mud of the physical and the waters of the subconscious. The second lotus rising from within the earthly flower is

FIGURE 195
Aboriginal cosmology allows us to conceive of a creation without a need to hypothesize a physical evolution nor a spiritual transcendence. A creation fully present, embodied, and magical in the union of its physical and metaphysical dimensions.

PRESERVING THE SEED

FIGURE 196
The Mimi spirit with a
serpent symbolizes the power of
Eros in association with the
primal forces of the earth.

the Dreaming, the enduring changeless and timeless precedent. For the Aborigines there need be no evolutionary scenario, such as the lower flower transforming or disappearing into the upper, as is pictured in various ways by idealistic and transcendental philosophies and religions. Nor is there the image of evolution as a purely physical and chemical biological mechanism exposed to endless permutations and chance. The Aborigines replace all these elaborate images of evolution with a few simple phrases: "The Dreaming is the Law. . . . It is not our idea. . . . It is a big law. . . . We must, while on earth, sit down next to that Law as do all creatures and as all dead people have done before us."[2]

The goal of Aboriginal culture is to conduct life so that the two lotus flowers, the Dreaming and the natural world, exist simultaneously, each the image of the other. The adaptability of nature exists for the purpose of maintaining the image of the Dream in creative ways. Through ritual culture, the most recent experiences of the living can remain continuous with those of its enduring origins: flower from flower, dream within dream.

For the Aborigines, our ideas of an open-ended, endlessly mutating and changing world order result from the scrambled, desperate illusion of our ungrounded mentality. One need only be aware of the intricate interwoven fabric of the body, mind, and spirit of nature to know that any change or innovation is already contained and integrated in a fully realized wholeness. Nothing is left to chance or probability in the wondrous woven web of creation. As the Aborigines say, "The life of the universe is a one-possibility thing."[3]

ENDNOTES

CHAPTER 1

1. Sun Bear, with Wabun Wind, *Black Dawn, Bright Day*, 51.
2. Rupert Sheldrake, *The Rebirth of Nature*, 28–40.
3. Robert M. Augros and George Stanciu, *The New Biology*, 231.
4. Personal communication, Prof. Richard Moore, State University of New York, Plattsburgh, New York, May 1991.
5. Sheldrake, 113.
6. Among the works that discuss similarities between genetics and the *I Ching* are Jean Marolleau, *La Galaxie, The Yin-Yang Universe* (Paris: Robert Dumas Editeur, 1975), and Martin Schonberger, *The I Ching and the Genetic Code* (New York: ASI Publishers, 1979).
7. Sheldrake, 116.
8. Ibid., 117.
9. Augros and Stanciu, 89–129.
10. David M. Raup, "Conflicts between Darwin and Paleontology," *Bulletin of the Field Museum of Natural History* 50 (January 1979): 22–29.
11. Augros and Stanciu, 158–161.
12. Ibid., 159
13. Ibid., 160.
14. Jeremy Rifkin, *Algeny*, 86.
15. John Gribbin and Jeremy Cherfas, *The Monkey Puzzle*, 16.
16. Ibid., 247.
17. Ibid., 258.
18. Ibid., 271.
19. "Uncovering Early Life in Australia," *Time* (March 30, 1987).
20. Burnum Burnum, *A Traveller's Guide to Aboriginal Australia* (Sydney: Angus & Robertson, 1988), 17.
21. Carleton Coon as cited in Joseph Campbell, *The Historical Atlas of World Mythology, Vol. 1: The Way of the Animal Powers*, Part 1, 29.
22. G. Singh, N. D. Opdyke, and J. M. Bowler, *Journal of the Geological Society of Australia* 28 (4, 1981): 435–452 .
23. "Quantum—Tracking the Dreamtime." ABC Documentary (Sydney: Ian Finley, producer, 1990).
24. Campbell, *Vol.1*, Part 1, 10.
25. Ibid., 33.
26. Augros and Stanciu, 184–186.
27. A. P. Elkin, *The Australian Aborigines* (Sydney: Angus & Robertson, 1954).
28. Carleton Coon as cited in Joseph Campbell, *The Historical Atlas of World Mythology, Vol. 1: The Way of the Animal Powers*, Part 1, 42.
29. Lyall Watson, *Beyond Supernature*, 44.
30. Owen Barfield, *Speakers Meaning* (Hertfordshire, U.K.: Rudolf Steiner Press), 95.
31. Personal communication, Prof. Richard Moore, May 1991.
32. "Coming Out Show." Women's affairs program. ABC Radio (Sydney, 1990).
33. Personal communication, Prof. Richard Moore, May 1991.
34. John Robbins, *Diet for a New America* (Santa Cruz, Calif.: Earth Save, 1990).
35. Ibid., 34.

CHAPTER 2

1. "The Spear and the Stone." Television Documentary by Rhys Jones. (Canberra: Australian Institute of Aboriginal Studies, producer, 1983).
2. Nancy D. Munn, "The Transformation of Subjects into Objects in Walbiri and Pitjandtjartjara Myths," 59.
3. Ibid., 62.
4. Ibid., 61.
5. Conversations with Brian Syron, Aboriginal teacher and director, 1987.
6. Conversations with Willie Whitefeather, Native American teacher and healer, March 1991.
7. "Blackout." ABC Documentary Series (Aboriginal Production Unit, 1990).
8. James Lovelock, *The Ages of Gaia*, 218.

CHAPTER 3

1. K. Langloh Parker, *Australian Legendary Tales* (Sydney: Angus &Robertson, 1974), 4.
2. Kenneth Maddock, *The Australian Aborigines* (Harmondsworth, U.K.: Penguin, 1974), 35.
3. Richard Heinberg, *Memories and Visions of Paradise*, 64.
4. Conversations with Bobby McLeod, teacher of self-healing, singer, and political activist, 1988.

CHAPTER 4

1. K. Langloh Parker, *Australian Legendary Tales* (Sydney: Angus & Robertson, 1974), 205.
2. Andrew Bard Schmookler, *The Parable of the Tribes*, 47.

3. Ibid., 44.
4. Ibid., 79.
5. Rupert Sheldrake, *The Rebirth of Nature*, 16.
6. Schmookler, 46.
7. Sheldrake, 20–21.
8. Josephine Flood, *Archaeology of the Dreamtime*, 40–44.
9. Schmookler, 29.
10. Jared Diamond, "The Worst Mistake in the History of the Human Race," *Discover* (May 1987): 64–66.
11. Ibid.
12. Flood, 219–234.
13. "Uncovering Early Life in Australia," *Time* (March 30, 1990).
14. Ian Donaldson and Tamsin Donaldson, eds., *Seeing the First Australians*, 74.
15. "The World's Water," *Time* (November 11, 1990).
16. Ibid.
17. Ibid.
18. Schmookler, 135.
19. Robert Tonkinson, *The Mardudjara Aborigines*, 34.
20. "Open 24 Hours a Day," *Time* (November 25, 1991).
21. Flood, 74.
22. M. J. Meggitt, *Desert People* (Sydney; Angus & Robertson, 1986), 31-33.
23. Tonkinson, 31.
24. Edward de Bono, *I Am Right. You Are Wrong*, 19.
25. Jamake Highwater, ed., *The Primal Mind*, 39.

CHAPTER 5

1. Quoted in Andrew Bard Schmookler, *The Parable of the Tribes*, 210.
2. K. Langloh Parker, *Australian Legendary Tales* (Sydney: Angus & Robertson, 1974), 9–10.
3. Quoted in Jean W. Sedlar, *India and the Greek World*, 42–49.
4. Richard Heinberg, *Memories and Visions of Paradise*.
5. Ian Donaldson and Tamsin Donaldson, eds., *Seeing the First Australians*, 35.
6. Ibid., 43–44.
7. Heinberg, 210.
8. Sedlar, 46.
9. Betty J. Dobbs, *The Foundations of Newton's Alchemy* (Cambridge: Cambridge University Press, 1976), 105–111.
10. Julia Clark, *The Aboriginal People of Tasmania*, 32.
11. Ibid.
12. Donaldson and Donaldson, 21–34.
13. Clark, 9.
14. Ibid., 22.
15. Ibid., 23.
16. Ibid., 19.
17. Donaldson and Donaldson, 56–58.
18. "Recent Rhys Jones Finds in Southwest Tasmania." ABC Radio Documentary (1990).
19. Donaldson and Donaldson, 41–42.
20. Ibid.
21. Josephine Flood, *Archaeology of the Dreamtime*, 30–33.
22. Alain Daniélou, *While the Gods Play*, 191–199.

23. Flood, 124–125.
24. Ibid., 112.

CHAPTER 6

1. Jennifer Isaacs, *Australian Dreaming*, 49.
2. Personal communications from Bobby McLeod, teacher of self-healing, singer, and political activist, 1988–89.
3. *Indjuwanydjuwa*, interpreted from a cave painting in Kakadu National Park, Northern Territory (Petaluma, Calif.: Pomegranate Calendars and Books, 1989).
4. R. S. Dietz and J. Holden, "The Breakup of Pangaea," in J. T. Wilson, ed., *Continents Adrift and Continents Aground* (San Francisco, W. H. Freeman, 1976), 130–133.
5. Ibid., 142.
6. Christopher Hill, *Energy, Matter, and Form*, 242–243.
7. Guy Murchie, *The Seven Mysteries of Life*, 391–393.
8. Robert O. Becker, *Cross Currents*, 179.
9. Louise B. Young, *Earth's Aura*.
10. Becker, 182.
11. Ibid., 180.
12. Ibid., 178–179.
13. Ibid., 184.
14. Personal communications with Lucie Lamy concerning the unpublished notes and diagrams of R. A. Schwaller de Lubicz, 1950–1955.
15. José Arguelles, *The Mayan Factor*, 83–107.
16. Albert Roy Davis and Walter C. Rawls, *Magnetism and Its Effects on the Living System*, 6–7.
17. Terence K. McKenna and Dennis J. McKenna, *The Invisible Landscape*, 115.
18. Victor Beasley, *Your Electro-Vibratory Body*, 16.
19. Ibid., 75.
20. Ibid.
21. Ibid., 76.
22. Davis and Rawls, 118.
23. Paul Deveraux, John Steele, and David Kubrin, *Earthmind*, 72–73.
24. Fred Hoyle, *The Intelligent Universe*, 254.
25. Isaac Asimov, *Understanding Physics*, 145.
26. Ibid., 144.
27. Personal communications, Bobby McLeod, 1987.
28. Isaacs, 239–240.
29. Ibid.
30. D. P. Faith, "Search for the Thylacine's Sister," *Australian Natural History* 23 (7, Summer 1990–91): 547.
31. Beasley, 16.
32. R. M. Berndt and C. H. Berndt, *The World of the First Australians*, 171–172.
33. Andrija Puharich, *Uri* (New York: Anchor Doubleday, 1974), 116.
34. Berndt and Berndt, 271–272.
35. Deveraux, Steele, and Kubrin, 76–77.
36. H. Ling Roth, *The Aborigines of Tasmania*, 97–98.
37. Robert K. Temple, *The Sirius Mystery*, 158–174.
38. Fred Hoyle, *Frontiers of Astronomy* (London: Heinemann, 1963), 211-12.
39. Lyndall Ryan, *The Aboriginal Tasmanians*, 11–14.

40. Ibid., 32–39.
41. James Wyly, *The Phallic Quest*.
42. Personal communication from Dr. C. A. Champaclow, Indian physicist.
43. John Michell, *The New View Over Atlantis*.
44. Bruce Chatwin, *Songlines*, 14.
45. Michell.
46. Quoted in Beasley, 91.
47. Robin Baker, *The Mystery of Migration*, 27.
48. Rupert Sheldrake, *The Rebirth of Nature*, 132–134.
49. Millay, 1986, as quoted by Ralph Metzner, "Resonance as Metaphor and Metaphor as Resonance." *Revision* 10 (1, 1987).
50. Deveraux, Steele, and Kubrin, 82.
51. Joseph Campbell, *The Historical Atlas of World Mythology, Vol. 1: The Way of the Animal Powers*, Part 2, 137.
52. Ibid., 145.
53. Ibid.
54. Deveraux, Steele, and Kubrin, 66.

CHAPTER 7
1. Kenneth Maddock, "World Creative Powers," in Charlesworth, Morphy, Bell, and Maddock, eds., *Religion in Aboriginal Australia*, 85–86.
2. Jennifer Isaacs, *Australian Dreaming*, 62.
3. R. M. Berndt and C. H. Berndt, *The World of the First Australians*, 438.
4. Isaacs, 67.
5. Lucie Lamy, *Egyptian Mysteries*, 82.
6. Ibid.
7. Isaacs, 62–65.
8. Judith Ryan, *Spirit in Land: Bark Paintings from Arnhem Land* (Melbourne: National Gallery of Victoria, 1990), 83.
9. *Encyclopedia Britannica*, 11th ed., vol. 2 (Cambridge, 1910), 954–956.
10. Big Bill Neidjie, *Kakadu Man: An Aboriginal Life Calendar* (Petaluma, Calif.: Pomegranate Calendars and Books, 1986).
11. David Ash and Peter Hewitt, *Science of the Gods*, as reviewed in *Cereologist* (London: John Mitchell, 1990.
12. Andrew Bard Schmookler, *The Parable of the Tribes*, 64–65.
13. Robert Tonkinson, *The Mardudjara Aborigines*, 106.
14. Peter Kolosimo, *Timeless Earth*, 85–90.
15. Robert O. Becker, *Cross Currents*, 248.
16. John Ott, *Health and Life*, 17–18.
17. Benjamin Lee Whorf, *Language, Thought, and Reality* (Cambridge, Mass.: MIT Press, 1956), 150–152.
18. Joachim-Ernst Berendt, *Nada Brahma*, 45.
19. Joseph Campbell, *The Historical Atlas of World Mythology, Vol. 1: The Way of the Animal Powers*, Part 2, The Great Hunt, 147–156.
20. Kolosimo, 65–87.
21. Ibid.
22. Martin Bernal, *Black Athena*, 9.

CHAPTER 8
1. Clive Turnbull, *Black War*.
2. Jacqueline Decter (with the Nicholas Roerich Museum, New York), *Nicholas Roerich: The Life and Art of a Russian Master*, 52.

3. D. H. Lawrence, quoted in an interview with Marion Woodman in *East West Journal*, Boston, June 1991.
4. Josephine Flood, *Archaeology of the Dreamtime*, 238–239.
5. Peter Mason, "Blood, War, and Iron." ABC Radio Documentary (Sydney, 1989).
6. Ibid.
7. Ange-Pierre Leca, *The Cult of the Immortal*, 37.
8. Joseph Campbell, *The Historical Atlas of World Mythology, Vol. 1: The Way of the Animal Powers*, Part 1, 41–44.
9. "The Visit of a Black African to the Inuit People of Greenland." ABC Television Documentary (Sydney, 1990).
10. Article on Mohawk uprising in Canada, *Time* (December 1990).
11. Benjamin Lee Whorf, *Language, Thought, and Reality* (Cambridge, Mass.: MIT Press, 1956), 244.
12. Campbell, 42.
13. R. A. Schwaller de Lubicz, *The Egyptian Miracle*.
14. Marija Gimbutas, *The Language of the Goddess*.
15. Jack Weatherford, *Indian Givers* (New York: Crown, 1988), 175–216.
16. "The Sweet Things in Life." ABC Radio Documentary (Sydney, 1990).
17. Weatherford, 197–216.
18. Ibid., 133–150.
19. Alain Daniélou, *The Four Aims of Life* (Rochester, Vt.: Inner Traditions International (manuscript in preparation).
20. Martin Bernal, *Black Athena*.
21. Marilyn McCully, ed., *A Picasso Anthology*.
22. Remy de Gourmont, *A Virgin Heart*.
23. Robert Johnson, "Dionysius," *The Caroline Jones Show*. ABC Radio (Sydney, 1990).
24. "The New New Age," *Time* (June 1987).
25. James Lovelock, *The Ages of Gaia*, 144–145.
26. "James Lovelock." ABC Television Documentary (Sydney, 1990).

CHAPTER 9
1. R. M. Berndt and C. H. Berndt, *The World of the First Australians*, 62.
2. H. Ling Roth, *The Aborigines of Tasmania*, 56.
3. Ibid., 57.
4. Berndt and Berndt, 62–63.
5. Ibid., 150.
6. Ibid., 153.
7. Robert Tonkinson, *The Mardudjara Aborigines*, 61.
8. Conversations with government guide to Ayers Rock, Central Australia, August 1987.
9. Kenneth Maddock, "World Creative Powers," in Charlesworth, Morphy, Bell, and Maddock, eds., *Religion in Aboriginal Australia*, 37.
10. Lucie Lamy, *Egyptian Mysteries*, 27.
11. Burnum Burnum, *Burnum Burnum's Aboriginal Australia*, 78.
12. Tonkinson, 62.
13. Berndt and Berndt, 153–156.
14. Ibid.
15. Vivienne Rae Ellis, *Trucanini—Queen or Traitor?*, 145–152.
16. Fred Myers, *Pintupi Country, Pintupi Self*, 130–131.

17. Berndt and Berndt, 161–162.
18. Ron Vanderwal, ed., *The Aboriginal Photographs of Baldwin Spencer*, 101–102.
19. Berndt and Berndt, 158–159.
20. Ibid.
21. Phillip Greven, Jr., *Spare the Child: The Religious Roots of Punishment and Psychological Abuse* (New York, Alfred A. Knopf, Inc., 1991), as reviewed in *Publishers Weekly* (January 4, 1991).
22. Tonkinson, 65.
23. Myers, 107–108.
24. Sylvia Brinton Perera, *The Scapegoat Complex* (Toronto: Inner City Books, 1988), 23–27.
25. Morris Berman, *The Reenchantment of the World*, 192–193.
26. Tonkinson, 64–67.
27. Ibid.
28. Berndt and Berndt, 164–165.
29. Ibid.
30. Ibid.
31. "Interview with Northern Territory Policeman." ABC Radio (Sydney, 1990).
32. "Death—The Prepared Journey," *Time* (October 20, 1989).
33. Louis-Claude de Saint-Martin, *Tableau naturel—des rapports qui existent entre Dieu, l'homme, et l'universe*, 151.
34. Berndt and Berndt, 164–165.
35. Claude Levi-Strauss, *The Savage Mind*, 31–32.
36. Tonkinson, 60–67.

CHAPTER 10

1. Personal communications from Bobby McLeod, teacher of self-healing, singer, and political activist, 1988–1989.
2. Robert Bly, *Iron John*.
3. Ibid., 36.
4. Ibid., 22.
5. The description of the puberty ritual on the next pages is drawn from Robert Tonkinson, *The Mardudjara Aborigines*, 67–80.
6. Diane Bell, *Daughters of the Dreaming*, 224–225.
7. L. R. Hiatt, "Swallowing and Regurgitating in Aboriginal Myths and Rituals," in Charlesworth, Morphy, Bell, and Maddock, eds., *Religion in Aboriginal Australia*, 31–56.
8. Kenneth Maddock, *The Australian Aborigines*, 166–169.
9. Claude Levi-Strauss, *The Savage Mind*, 73.
10. Marion Woodman, *Addiction to Perfection*, 19.
11. Ronald Rose, *Living Magic*, 97.
12. R. M. Berndt and C. H. Berndt, *The World of the First Australians*, 173–176.
13. Ibid.,175.
14. Barbara Walker, *The Woman's Encyclopedia of Myths and Secrets*, 146–147.
15. Resit Ergener, *Anatolia: Land of Mother Goddess*, 123.
16. Robert Lawlor, "Origins and End of the Male Dominant World Order," in John Matthews, ed., *Choir of Gods* (London: Harper & Collins, 1991).
17. Ron Vanderwal, ed., *The Aboriginal Photographs of Baldwin Spencer*, 92.
18. Walker, 133.

19. James Wyly, *The Phallic Quest*.
20. Zecharia Sitchin, *The Wars of Gods and Men*, 12–13.
21. Bell, 207–226.
22. Ibid., 207.
20. Tonkinson.
24. Berndt and Berndt, 91–101.
25. Berndt and Berndt, 406–407.
26. The description of the female initiation rituals is based on Berndt and Berndt, 180–187.
27. Bill Harney, *To Ayer's Rock and Beyond*, 98.
28. In Stephen Larsen, *The Mythic Imagination*, 234.

CHAPTER 11

1. R. M. Berndt, *Three Faces of Love: Traditional Aboriginal Song Poetry* (Melbourne: Thomas Nelson, 1976).
2. W. H. Edwards, *An Introduction to Aboriginal Societies*, 47.
3. Diane Bell, *Daughter of the Dreaming*, 52.
4. Robert Tonkinson, *The Mardudjara Aborigines*, 120.
5. Berndt and Berndt, *The World of the First Australians*, 202–204.
6. Bell, 193–194.
7. Kenneth Maddock, *The Australian Aborigines*, 57–59.
8. Tonkinson, 33.
9. Bell, 182.
10. Tonkinson, 80.
11. Berndt and Berndt.
12. Anthony Easthope, *What's a Man Gotta Do?*, 126.
13. Berndt and Berndt, 200.
14. Ibid., 91–101.
15. Ibid., 180–187.
16. Diane Bell, "Love Ritual," in Charlesworth, Morphy, Bell, and Maddock, eds., *Religion in Aboriginal Australia*, 358–359.
17. Robert A. Johnson, *She*.
18. Robert Tonkinson, 33.
19. Barbara Walker, *The Woman's Encyclopedia of Myths and Secrets*, 585–587.
20. Ibid.
21. Berndt and Berndt, 204.
22. Ibid., 319.
23. Christopher Hill and Phil Allen, eds., *Energy, Matter, and Form*.
24. Berndt and Berndt, 205.
25. Hans Peter Duerr, *Dreamtime*.
26. Walker, 544.
27. Berndt, 11–35; Chapter 1, Songs 2, 6, 8, 12, 14.
28. Tonkinson, 120.
29. Berndt and Berndt, 205.

CHAPTER 12

1. *Sydney Morning Herald*, Letters to the Editor, 12 October 1990.
2. Ernest Weekly, *An Etymological Dictionary of Modern English, Vol. 1, A–K* (Toronto, Dover, 1967), 516, 756.
3. Alain Daniélou, *The Gods of India*,181.
4. Jean W. Sedlar, *India and the Greek World*, 22–25.
5. Alan Watts, *The Book*, 8.

6. Fred Myers, *Pintupi Country, Pintupi Self*, 54.
7. Ibid., 55.
8. Ibid.
9. "Uluru," ABC Television Documentary (Sydney, 1989).
10. Personal communications, Bobby McLeod, teacher of self-healing, singer, and political activist, 1988.
11. Quoted in James Cowan, *Mysteries of the Dreaming*, 102.
12. Dorothy Turnbridge, *Flinders Range Dreaming*, xxxv.
13. Bill Harney, *To Ayer's Rock and Beyond*, 104.
14. Hermann Grassman, *Rig-Veda* (Leipzig, 1876), stanzas 7 and 12.
15. Personal communication, Bobby McLeod, teacher of self-healing, singer, and political activist, 1987–1988.

CHAPTER 13
1. Claude Levi-Strauss, *The Savage Mind*.
2. See the works of K. Maddock, R. M. and C. H. Berndt, D. Bell, and others to fathom the subtlety and complexity of detail within the Aboriginal kinship system.
3. W. H. Edwards, *An Introduction to Aboriginal Societies*, 46–47.
4. Kenneth Maddock, *The Australian Aborigines*, 12.
5. R. M. Berndt and C. H. Berndt, *The World of the First Australians*, 80–81.
6. Robert Tonkinson, *The Mardudjara Aborigines*, 48–49.
7. Ibid.
8. Fred Myers, *Pintupi Country, Pintupi Self*, 103–126.
9. Ibid.
10. Ibid.
11. Ibid.
12. Conversations with Brian Syron, Aboriginal teacher and director, 1988.
13. Myers, 109–112.
14. Berndt and Berndt.
15. Myers, 103–126.
16. Ibid.
17. Ron Vanderwal, ed., *The Aboriginal Photographs of Baldwin Spencer*, 94.
18. Myers, 103–126.
19. Ibid., 113.
20. Tonkinson, 43.
21. Marie-Louise von Franz, *Number and Time*, 1974.
22. Tonkinson.
23. Myers.
24. Tonkinson, 123.
25. Ibid., 125.
26. Ibid.
27. Myers, 171.
28. Tonkinson, 28.
29. Berndt and Berndt, 357–358.
30. Ibid.
31. Tonkinson, 116–128.
32. Ibid.
33. Ibid., 119.
34. S. Karpeles, *Dhammapada*, 4.
35. S. S. Jhunjhunwala, *The Gita*.
36. Tonkinson, 119.

CHAPTER 14
1. Dorothy Turnbridge, *Flinders Range Dreaming*.
2. Fred Myers, *Pintupi Country, Pintupi Self*, 47–48.
3. Ibid., 48.
4. Wendy D. O'Flaherty, *Dreams, Illusions, and Other Realities* (Chicago: University of Chicago Press, 1984), 17.
5. Myers, 47–48.
6. Ibid., 48.
7. Ibid.
8. Hans Peter Duerr, *Dreamtime*, 76–83.
9. Ronald Rose, *Living Magic*, 214.
10. David Peat, *Synchronicity*, 141–142.
11. Marie-Louise von Franz, *Number and Time*, 18–19.
12. Ralph Metzner, "Gaia's Alchemy: Ruin and Renewal of the Elements," *Revision Magazine* (Winter/Spring 1987).
13. Peat, 47–48.
14. E. Wigner and M. Eigen, *Laws of the Game* (New York: Harper Colophon Books, 1983), 141.
15. Charles Hampden-Turner, *Maps of the Mind*, 76–77.
16. Peat, 141–142.
17. Daniel Goleman, *Vital Lies, Simple Truths*.
18. Bernie Neville, *Educating Psyche*, 138.
19. Myers, 107.
20. Ibid.
21. James Cowan, *Mysteries of the Dreaming*, 87.

CHAPTER 15
1. K. Langloh Parker, *Australian Legendary Tales* (Sydney: Angus & Robertson, 1974), 159.
2. R. M. Berndt and C. H. Berndt, *The World of the First Australians*, 35–40.
3. W. H. Edwards, *An Introduction to Aboriginal Societies*, 19–20.
4. Clive Turnbull, *Black War: The Extermination of the Tasmanian Aborigines* (Sydney: Lansdowne Press, 1965), 149.
5. Kenneth Maddock, *The Australian Aborigines*, 21–44.
6. Fred Myers, *Pintupi Country, Pintupi Self*, 71–102.
7. Ron Vanderwal, ed., *The Aboriginal Photographs of Baldwin Spencer*, 159–160.
8. Berndt and Berndt, 231–240.
9. Claude Levi-Strauss, *The Savage Mind*, 172–175.

CHAPTER 16
1. Susan Lerner, "The Australian Aborigines—Contemporary Art from a Recent Exhibition." *Journal of Pacific Asia Museum* (Pasadena, Calif., 1989), 110–141.
2. Ibid., 116.
3. Ibid., 117.
4. Ibid., 119.
5. Robert Layton, "Naturalism and Cultural Relativity in Art," in *Form in Indigenous Art*, Peter J. Ucko, ed. (Canberra: Australian Institute of Aboriginal Studies, 1977), 33–34 .
6. Ibid., 41.
7. Ibid., 42–43.

8. Judith Ryan, *Spirit in Land: Bark Paintings from Arnhem Land* (Melbourne: National Gallery, 1991), 115.
9. Lyall Watson, *Beyond Supernature*, 58.
10. Ibid., 60.
11. Robert O. Becker and Gary Selden, *The Body Electric* (New York: Morrow, 1985), 18–19.
12. Guy Murchie, *The Seven Mysteries of Life* (Boston: Houghton Mifflin Co., 1978), 236–238.
13. Henry Munn, "The Mushrooms of Language," in Michael Harner, ed., *Hallucinogens and Shamanism*, 110–111.

CHAPTER 17
1. R. M. Berndt and C. H. Berndt, *The World of the First Australians*, 395.
2. Ibid., 108.
3. Ron Vanderwal, Ed., *The Aboriginal Photographs of Baldwin Spencer*, 164.
4. Sri Aurobindo, *Hymns to the Mystic Fire* (Pondicherry, India: Sri Aurobindo Ashram, 1951), 247.
5. H. Ling Roth, *The Aborigines of Tasmania*, 41.
6. Sir E. A. Wallace Budge, *The Egyptian Religion*, 123.
7. Jamake Highwater, *The Primal Mind*, 62.
8. Berndt and Berndt, 112.
9. Jim Nollman, *Animal Dreaming* (New York: Bantam, 1988), 32, and conversations with Uncle Bul, an Aboriginal tribal elder from Nowra, New South Wales, 1988.
10. Robert M. Augros and George Stanciu, *The New Biology*, 46–47.
11. Ron Cowen, "Animal Heal Thyself," *Science News* (November 1990).
12. Kathy A. Fackelmann, "Self-Sacrifice Is for the Birds," *Science News*, (June 1989).
13. Augros and Stanciu, 77.
14. Ibid., 51.
15. Nancy M. Williams and Eugene S. Hunn, eds., *Resource Managers: North American and Australian Hunter-Gatherers*, 114.
16. Fay Cole, *Women's Role in Aboriginal Society*, 36–46.
17. Ibid., 72.
18. Williams and Hunn, 86–87.
19. Ibid., 91.
20. Berndt and Berndt, 110–111.
21. Williams and Hunn, 49–53.
22. Ibid., 45–47.
23. Hans Peter Duerr, *Dreamtime*, 71–75.
24. Berndt and Berndt, 112.
25. Robert Tonkinson, *The Mardudjara Aborigines*, 34.

CHAPTER 18
1. K. Langloh Parker, *Australian Legendary Tales* (Sydney: Angus & Robertson, 1974), 36.
2. Claude Levi-Strauss, *The Savage Mind*.
3. Ibid., 129.
4. As quoted in Robert M. DeGraaff, *The Book of the Toad* (Rochester, Vt.: Park Street Press, 1991), 79–80.
5. Ibid., 79.
6. Ibid., 80.
7. Ibid., 22–23.

8. Marie-Louise von Franz, *Number and Time*, 70.
9. Nader Ardalan and Abol Ghassem Bakhtiar, *The Sense of Unity* (Chicago: University of Chicago Press), 47.
10. C. G. von Brandenstein, "Identical Principles behind Australian Totemism and Empedoclean Philosophy," in *Australian Aboriginal Concepts*, L. R. Hiatt, ed. (Canberra: Australian Institute for Aboriginal Studies, 1978), 134–144.
11. Ibid., 143.
12. Edward de Bono, *I Am Right. You Are Wrong*, 145–227.
13. Ibid., 10–11.
14. Robert Tonkinson, *The Mardudjara Aborigines*, 85.
15. Barry J. Blake, *Australian Aboriginal Languages*.
16. Ron Vanderwal, ed., *The Aboriginal Photographs of Baldwin Spencer*.
17. De Bono, 225.
18. *Brain Mind Bulletin* (February 1978).

CHAPTER 19
1. Quoted in Stephen Larsen, *The Mythic Imagination*, 157.
2. Claude Levi-Strauss, *The Savage Mind*, 257–258.
3. R. M. Berndt and C. H. Berndt, *The World of the First Australians*, 231–240.
4. Larsen, 157.
5. Sri Aurobindo, *Hymns to the Mystic Fire* (Pondicherry, India: All India Press, 1951), 173.
6. Hans Peter Duerr, *Dreamtime*, 290 and notes 71–75.
7. Lucie Lamy, *Egyptian Mysteries*, 26–27.
8. Isha Schwaller de Lubicz, *Her-Bak: Egyptian Initiate*, 356–357.
9. Robert Bly, *Iron John*, 213–219.
10. Robert Lawlor and Keith Critchlow, *Lindisfarne Letter*, 90–91.
11. Robert O. Becker, *Cross Currents*, 123.
12. Personal communication from Dr. Grant Lambert, biochemist and healer using Aboriginal methods.
13. H. Ling Roth, *The Aborigines of Tasmania*, 136.
14. Holger Kalweit, *Dreamtime and Inner Space*, 251.
15. Bruce Chatwin, *Songlines*, 14.
16. Kalweit, xvi.

CHAPTER 20
1. R. M. Berndt and C. H. Berndt, *The World of the First Australians*, 471.
2. Dorothy Turnbridge, *Flinders Range Dreaming*, 3–6.
3. Robert Tonkinson, *The Mardudjara Aborigines*, 83.
4. Fred Myers, *Pintupi Country, Pintupi Self*.
5. Berndt and Berndt, 483.
6. From the unpublished field notes of Donald Thompson, an Australian photographer.
7. Berndt and Berndt, 483.

8. Ibid.
9. Karl Kerenyo, *Hermes*.
10. Marie-Louise von Franz, *Number and Time*, 35–56.
11. David F. Peat, *Synchronicity*.
12. K. Langloh Parker, *Australian Legendary Tales*, (Sydney: Angus & Robertson, 1974), 205.
13. Holger Kalweit, *Dreamtime and Inner Space*, 193.
14. Berndt and Berndt, 476–479.
15. Ibid., 459–470.
16. Kalweit, 37.
17. Tonkinson, 84–85.
18. Ibid.
19. Berndt and Berndt, 471.
20. Ibid., 470.
21. Ibid., 462.
22. Ibid.
23. Tonkinson, 83–87.
24. E. Bendann, *Death Customs: An Analytical Study of Burial Rites* (New York, Alfred A. Knopf, 1930), 91. "That haircutting must have been a vogue amongst the Israelites is seen in God's injunction to his children to the effect that they must not disfigure themselves in mourning: 'Ye shall not cut yourselves nor make any baldness between your eyes for the dead' (Deut. 14:1)."
25. Tonkinson, 85.
26. Ibid., 85–86.
27. Berndt and Berndt, 460–461.
28. Ibid., 461.
29. von Franz, 278–283.
30. Berndt and Berndt, 473–474.
31. Ibid., 321.

CHAPTER 21

1. Joseph Campbell, *The Historical Atlas of World Mythology, Vol. 1: The Way of the Animal Powers*, Part 2, p. 171.
2. R. M. Berndt and C. H. Berndt, *The World of the First Australians*, 460–461.
3. Lucie Lamy, *Egyptian Mysteries*, 24.
4. Berndt and Berndt, 461.
5. Marie-Louise von Franz, *Number and Time*, 278–283.
6. Ibid.
7. Berndt and Berndt, 476..
8. von Franz, 278–283.
9. Barbara Walker, *The Crone*, 166.

CHAPTER 22

1. K. Langloh Parker, *Australian Legendary Tales*, (Sydney: Angus & Robertson, 1974), 121.
2. Bill Harney, *To Ayer's Rock and Beyond*, 69–71.
3. Nigel Calder, *The Mind of Man* (New York: Viking Press, 1970), 78–79.
4. Harney, 69–71.
5. Ron Vanderwal, ed., *The Aboriginal Photographs of Baldwin Spencer*, 86.
6. A. P. Elkin, *Aboriginal Men of High Degree*.
7. Ibid.
8. William R. Fix, *Star Maps*.
9. Elkin, 58–59.
10. Ibid., 59.
11. Conversations with Bobby McLeod and Uncle Bul, 1988.
12. Elkin, 20–21.
13. Frank Avray Wilson, *Crystal and Cosmos*, 80.
14. Ibid., 81.
15. Lyall Watson, *Beyond Supernature*, 96.
16. Robert O. Becker, *Cross Currents*, 70.
17. Ibid., 75.
18. Ibid., 76.
19. Joseph Campbell, *The Historical Atlas of World Mythology, Vol. 1: The Way of the Animal Powers*, Part 2, 171.
20. R. A. Schwaller de Lubicz, *The Temple in Man*, 102–103.
21. Becker, 59.
22. Ibid., 65.
23. Ibid., 63.
24. Rupert Sheldrake, *The Rebirth of Nature*, 146.
25. Judith Ryan, *Spirit in Land: Bark Paintings from Arnhem Land* (Melbourne: National Gallery of Victoria, 1991), 4, 104.
26. Watson, 160–161.
76. J. Page, "Roses Are Red; E-Flat Is Too," *Hippocrate* (September/October 1987).
28. As quoted in Robert Bly, *Iron John*, 49.
29. From the unpublished field notes of Donald Thompson.
30. Watson, 90–91.
31. Willis Harman, *Global Mind Change*, 18–21.
32. *Time* (January, 1991).
33. James Wyly, *The Phallic Quest*, 116.

CHAPTER 23

1. Rupert Sheldrake, *The Presence of the Past*, 18–38.
2. Fred Myers, *Pintupi Country, Pintupi Self*, 53.
3. Ibid.

BIBLIOGRAPHY

PHYSICAL SCIENCE

Asimov, Isaac. *Understanding Physics: Light, Magnetism and Electricity*. New York: Signet Science Books, 1966.

Augros, Robert M., & Stanciu, George. *The New Biology*. London & Boston: New Science Library, 1988.

Baker, Robert. *The Mystery of Migration*. London and Sydney: McDonald, 1980.

Beasley, Victor. *Your Electro-Vibratory Body*. Boulder Creek, Ca.: University of the Trees, 1978.

Becker, Robert O. *Cross Currents: The Perils of Electropollution*. Los Angeles: Jeremy P. Tarcher, 1990.

Davis, Albert Roy, and Rawls, Walter C. *Magnetism and Its Effects on the Living System*. Smithtown, N.Y.: Exposition Press, 1974.

Deveraux, Paul; Steele, John; and Kubrin, David. *Earthmind*. New York: Harper & Row, 1989.

Eigen, M., and Winkler, R. *Laws of the Game*. New York: Harper Colophon Books, 1983.

Gribbon, John, and Cherfas, Jeremy. *The Monkey Puzzle*. London: Bodley Head Ltd., 1982.

Hampden-Turner, Charles. *Maps of the Mind*. New York: Macmillan Publishing Co., Inc., 1981.

Hill, Christopher, and Phil Allen, Eds. *Energy, Matter and Form*. Boulder Creek, Ca.: University of the Trees Press, 1979.

Hoyle, Fred. *The Intelligent Universe*. London: Michael Joseph, 1983.

Lovelock, James. *The Ages of Gaia*. New York and London: W. W. Norton & Co., 1988.

Murchie, Guy. *The Seven Mysteries of Life*. Boston: Houghton Mifflin Co. 1978.

Ott, John N. *Health and Life*. New York: Pocket Books, 1976.

Peat, David F. *Synchronicity: The Bridge Between Matter and Mind*. New York: Bantam Books, 1988.

Rifkin, Jeremy. *Algeny*. New York: The Viking Press, 1983.

Sheldrake, Rupert. *The Presence of the Past*. New York: Times Books, 1988.

Sheldrake, Rupert. *The Rebirth of Nature*. London: Century Books, 1990.

Wilson, J. T. *Continents Adrift and Continents Aground*, Scientific America series. San Francisco: W. H. Freeman & Co., 1976.

Young, Louise B. *Earth's Aura*. New York: Avon Books, 1977.

HISTORY, PHILOSOPHY, AND PSYCHOLOGY

Arguelles, Jose. *The Mayan Factor: Path Beyond Technology*. Santa Fe, N. Mex.: Bear & Co., 1987.

Barfield, Owen. *Saving the Appearances: A Study in Idolatry*. New York and London, Harvest/HBJ Books, 1965.

Berendt, Joachim-Ernst. *Nada Brahma: The World Is Sound*. Rochester, Vt.: Destiny Books, 1987.

Berman, Morris. *The Reenchantment of the World*. New York: Bantam Books, 1988.

Bernal, Martin. *Black Athena*. New Brunswick, N. J.: Rutgers University Press, 1987.

Bly, Robert. *Iron John: A Book About Men*. Reading, Mass.: Addison-Wesley Publishing Company Inc., 1990.

Brinton Perera, Sylvia. *The Scapegoat Complex*. Toronto: Inner City Books, 1988.

Budge, Sir E. A. Wallace. *The Egyptian Religion*. London, Routledge & Kegan Paul, 1972.

Burnum, Burnum. *Burnum Burnum's Aboriginal Australia: A Traveller's Guide*. Sydney: Angus & Robertson, 1988.

Campbell, Joseph. *The Historical Atlas of World Mythology, Vol.1: The Way of the Animal Powers*. Part 1. Mythologies of the Primitive Hunters and Gatherers. New York: Harper & Row, 1988.

Campbell, Joseph. *The Historical Atlas of World Mythology, Vol.1: The Way of the Animal Powers*. Part 2. The Great Hunt. San Francisco: Harper & Row, 1987.

Chatwin, Bruce. *Songlines*. London: Jonathan Cape, 1987.

Cowan, James. *Mysteries of the Dreaming*. Dorset, UK: Prism Press, 1989.

Daniélou, Alain. *The Four Aims of Life*. Rochester, Vt.: Inner Traditions International (manuscript in preparation for publication).

Daniélou, Alain. *The Gods of India: Hindu Polytheism*. New York: Inner Traditions International, 1985.

Daniélou, Alain. *While the Gods Play*. Rochester, Vt.: Inner Traditions International, 1987.

De Bono, Edward. *I Am Right. You Are Wrong*. London: Viking, 1990.

Decter, Jacqueline (with the Nicholas Roerich Museum). *Nicholas Roerich: The Life and Art of a Russian Master*. Rochester, Vt.: Park Street Press, 1989.

De Gourmont, Remy. *A Virgin Heart*. New York: Modern Library, 1927.

de Saint-Martin, Louis-Claude. *Tableau Naturel: Des Rapports Qui Existent Entre Dieu, L'Homme Et L'Univers*. Paris: Robert Duman Editeur, 1974.

Duerr, Hans Peter. *Dreamtime: Concerning the Boundary Between Wilderness and Civilization*. New York and London: Basil Blackwell, 1985.

Easthope, Anthony. *What's a Man Gotta Do?* London: Paladin Grafton Books, 1986.

Ergener, Resit. *Anatolia: Land of Mother Goddess*. Turkey: Hitit Publications Ltd., 1988.

Fix, William R. *Star Maps*. London: Jonathan James Books, 1979.

Ghalioungui, Paul. *Magic and Medical Science in Ancient Egypt*. London: Hodder & Stoughton Ltd., 1963.

Gimbutas, Marija. *The Language of the Goddess*. San Francisco: Harper & Row, 1989.

Goleman, Daniel. *Vital Lies, Simple Truths*. New York: Simon & Schuster, 1985.

Harman, Willis. *Global Mind Change*. Indianapolis, Ind.: Knowledge Systems, 1988.

Heinberg, Richard. *Memories and Visions of Paradise*. Los Angeles: Jeremy P. Tarcher, 1989.

Highwater, Jamake. *The Primal Mind*. New York: Meridian Books, 1981.

Jhunjunnwala, S. S. *The Gita*. Pondicherry, India: Auro Publications, 1974.

Johnson, Robert A. *She*. San Francisco: Harper & Row, 1981.

Kalweit, Holger. *Dreamtime and Inner Space: The World of the Shaman*. Boston and London, Shambhala, 1988.

Karpeles, Mme. S. *Dhammapada*. Pondicherry, India: All India Book, 1983.

Kerenyo, Karl. *Hermes: Guide of Souls*. Dallas, Tex.: Spring Publications, 1987.

Kolosimo, Peter. *Timeless Earth*. London: The Garnstone Press, 1968.

Lamy, Lucie. *Egyptian Mysteries*. London: Thames & Hudson, 1981.

Larsen, Stephen. *The Mythic Imagination*. New York: Bantam Books, 1990.

Lawlor, Robert. *Earth Honoring: The New Male Sexuality*. Rochester, Vt.: Park Street Press, 1989; Australia: Millenium Books, 1990.

Lawlor, Robert. "Origin and End of Male Dominant World Order." In: John Matthews, Ed. *Choir of Gods*. London: Harper & Collins, 1991.

Lawlor, Robert. *Sacred Geometry: Its Philosophy and Practice*. London: Thames and Hudson, 1987.

Lawlor, Robert, and Critchlow, Keith. *Lindisfarne Letter: Geometry and Architecture*. Great Barrington, Mass.: Lindisfarne Press, 1980.

Layton, Robert. "Naturalism and Cultural Relativity in Art." In: Peter J. Ucko, Ed. *Form in Indigenous Art*. Canberra: Australia Institute of Aboriginal Studies, 1977.

Leca, Ange-Pierre. *The Cult of the Immortal*. London: Souvenir Press, 1980.

Levi-Strauss, Claude. *The Savage Mind*. Chicago: University of Chicago Press, 1970.

McCully, Marilyn, Ed. *A Picasso Anthology: Documents, Criticisms, Reminiscences*. London: The Arts Council of Great Britain, 1981.

McKenna, Terence K., and McKenna, Dennis J. *The Invisible Landscape*. New York: Seabury Press, 1975.

Michell, John. *The New View Over Atlantis*. San Francisco: Harper & Row, 1983.

Munn, Henry. "The Mushrooms of Language." In: Michael Harner, Ed. *Hallucinogens and Shamanism*. London: Oxford Street Press, 1973.

Neville, Bernie. *Educating Psyche*. Melbourne: Collins Dove, 1989.

Nollman, Jim. *Animal Dreaming*. Toronto and New York: Bantam Books, 1988.

Redgrove, Peter. *The Black Goddess and the Unseen Real*. New York: Grove Press, 1987.

Schmookler, Andrew Bard. *The Parable of the Tribes*. Boston: Houghton Mifflin, 1986.

Schwaller de Lubicz, Isha. *Her-Bak: Egyptian Initiate*. Rochester, Vt.: Inner Traditions International, 1978.

Schwaller de Lubicz, R. A. *The Egyptian Miracle*. Rochester, Vt.: Inner Traditions International, 1983.

Schwaller de Lubicz, R. A. *The Temple in Man*. Rochester, Vt.: Inner Traditions International, 1981.

Sedlar, Jean W. *India and The Greek World*. Lanham, Md.: Rowman & Littlefield, 1980.

Sitchin, Zecharia. *The Wars of Gods and Men*. New York: Avon Books, 1985.

Sri Aurobindo. *Hymns to the Mystic Fire*. Pondicherry, India: Sri Aurobindo Ashram, 1951.

Sun Bear, with Wabun Wind. *Black Dawn, Bright Day*. Spokane, Wash.: Bear Tribe Publishing, 1990.

Temple, Robert K. *The Sirius Mystery*. Rochester, Vt.: Destiny Books, 1987.

Turnbull, Clive. *Black War: The Extermination of the Tasmanian Aborigines*. Sydney: Lansdowne Press, 1965.

von Daniken, Erich. *According to the Evidence*. London: Souvenir Press, 1977.

von Franz, Marie-Louise. *Number and Time*. Evanston, Ill.: Northwestern University Press, 1974.

Walker, Barbara. *The Crone*. San Francisco: Harper & Row, 1988.

Walker, Barbara. *The Woman's Encyclopedia of Myths and Secrets*. San Francisco: Harper & Row, 1983.

Watson, Lyall. *Beyond Supernature*. New York: Bantam Books, 1987.

Watts, Alan. *The Book*. New York: Vintage, 1972.

Weatherford, Jack. *Indian Givers*. New York: Crown Publishers Inc., 1988.

Whorf, Benjamin Lee. *Language, Thought and Reality*. Cambridge, Mass.: M.I.T. Press, 1956.

Wilson, Frank Avray. *Crystal and Cosmos*. London: Coventure Ltd., 1977.

Woodman, Marion. *Addiction to Perfection*. Toronto: Inner City Books, 1982.

Wyly, James. *The Phallic Quest*. Toronto, Inner City Books, 1989.

AUSTRALIAN ANTHROPOLOGY

Bell, Diane. *Daughters of the Dreaming*. Melbourne, Australia: McPhee Gribble Publishers in association with George Allen & Unwin Australia Pty. Ltd., 1988.

Berndt, Ronald M., and Berndt, Catherine H. *The World of the First Australians*. Canberra: Aboriginal Studies Press, 1988.

Blake, Barry J. *Australian Aboriginal Languages*. London and Sydney: Angus & Robertson, 1981.

Charlesworth, M; Morphy, H; Bell, D; and Maddock, K.; Eds. *Religion in Aboriginal Australia*. St. Lucia, Queensland: University of Queensland Press, 1984.

Clark, Julia. *The Aboriginal People of Tasmania*. Tasmania: Tasmanian Museum and Art Gallery, 1986.

Cole, Fay. *Women's Role in Aboriginal Society*. Canberra: Australian Institute of Aboriginal Studies, 1986.

Donaldson, Ian, and Donaldson, Tamsin. *Seeing the First Australians*. Sydney, London and Boston: George Allen & Unwin, 1985.

Edwards, W. H. *An Introduction to Aboriginal Societies*. Wentworth Falls, Australia: Social Science Press, 1988.

Elkin, A. P. *Aboriginal Men of High Degree*. St. Lucia, Queensland: University of Queensland Press, 1980.

Ellis, Vivienne Rae. *Trucanini—Queen or Traitor?* Canberra: Australian Institute of Aboriginal Studies, 1981.

Flood, Josephine. *Archeology of the Dreamtime*. Sydney and London: William Collins, 1983.

Harney, Bill. *To Ayers Rock and Beyond*. Victoria, Australia: Ian Drakeford Publishing, 1988.

Hiatt, L. R. *Australian Aboriginal Concepts*. Canberra: Australian Institute of Aboriginal Studies, 1978.

Isaacs, Jennifer. *Australian Dreaming: 40,000 Years of Aboriginal History*. Sydney and London: Lansdowne Press, 1980.

Isaacs, Jennifer. *Bushfood*. Sydney: Weldon, 1987.

Maddock, Kenneth. *The Australian Aborigines*. London: Penguin Books, 1974.

Munn, Nancy D. "The Transformation of Subjects Into Objects in Walbiri and Pitjantjatjara Myths." In: M. Charlesworth, H. Morphy, D. Bell and K. Maddock, Eds. *Religion in Aboriginal Australia: An Anthology*. St. Lucia, Queensland: University of Queensland Press, 1984.

Myers, Fred. *Pintupi Country, Pintupi Self*. Washington, D.C., and London: Smithsonian Institution Press, 1986.

Parbury, Nigel, Ed. *Survival: A History of Aboriginal Life in New South Wales*. Sydney: Ministry of Aboriginal Affairs, 1986.

Parker, K. Langloh. *Australian Legendary Tales: Folklore of the Noongahburrahs as Told to the Piccaninnies*. (Collected by Mrs. K. Langloh Parker. Introduction by Andrew Lang.) London: David Nutt/Melbourne: Melville, Mullen and Slade, 1896.

Parker, K. Langloh. *Australian Legendary Tales*. (Collected from various tribes by Mrs. K. Langloh Parker.) Selected and edited by H. Drake-Brockman. Sydney: Angus & Robertson, 1974.

Parker, K. Langloh. *The Euahlayi Tribe: A Study of Aboriginal Life in Australia*. (Introduction by Andrew Lang). London: Constable, 1905.

Parker, K. Langloh. *More Australian Legendary Tales*. (Collected from various tribes by Mrs. K. Langloh Parker.) London: David Nutt/Melbourne: Melville, Mullen and Slade, 1898.

Parker, K. Langloh. *The Walkabout of Wur-run-nah*. Compiled by Catherine Stow (Mrs. K. Langloh Parker). Adelaide: Hassell, 1918.

Parker, K. Langloh. *Woggheeguy: Australian Aboriginal Legends*. Collected by Catherine Stow (Mrs. K. Langloh Parker). Illustrated by Nora Heysen. Adelaide: Preece, 1930.

Rose, Ronald. *Living Magic*. New York: Rand McNally, 1956.

Roth, H. Ling. *The Aborigines of Tasmania*. Hobart, Tasmania: The Fulton Book Series, 1970.

Ryan, Lyndall. *The Aboriginal Tasmanians*. St. Lucia, Queensland: University of Queensland Press, 1982.

Tonkinson, Robert. *The Mardudjara Aborigines: Living the Dream in Australia's Desert*. New York: Holt, Rinehart & Winston, 1978.

Turnbridge, Dorothy. *Flinders Range Dreaming*. Canberra: Aboriginal Studies Press, 1988.

Vanderwal, Ron, Ed. *The Aboriginal Photographs of Baldwin Spencer*. Victoria: Viking O'Neil Penguin Books, Australia Ltd., 1987.

Williams, Nancy M., and Hunn Eugene S., Eds. *Resource Managers: North American and Australian Hunter-Gatherers*. Canberra: Australian Institute of Aboriginal Studies, 1982.

ILLUSTRATION CREDITS

In all cases the publisher has made every effort to contact and get permission from the artists and appropriate institutions for the images and photographs in this book. Nevertheless, if omissions or errors have occurred, we encourage you to contact Inner Traditions International.

In addition to the specific credits listed below, this book has motifs and elements from various tribal groups decorating the margins, the table of contents, and the ending of each chapter.

Cover, Figure 1, *Namangwarri—Salt Water Crocodile*, 1988, by Jimmy Njiminjuma. Kunwinjku; Maningrida, central Arnhem Land, N.T. Earth pigments on eucalyptus bark, 99 x 48. Photo by Jennifer Steele. Reproduced courtesy of The Australia Gallery, New York.

Endpaper design based on *Lorrgon ceremony*, c. 1965, by Yirawala.

Title page motif based on *Kawirrin*, 1984, by Jock Mosquito Jubarlji.

Page xiv, Figure 2, from the journal of the voyage of Captain Cook, a collection of engravings, courtesy of Jonathan Cohen. Photo by Ken Burris.

Page xv, Figure 3, *Bush Tucker Dreaming*, 1988, by Sonda Turner Nampijinpa. Pintupi; Papunya, Western Desert, N.T. Acrylic on canvas. Courtesy of The Australia Gallery, New York; reproduced with permission of the Aboriginal Artists Agency, North Sydney, Australia.

Quarter title motif based on *Painting*, c. 1974, by Declan Apuatimi.

Page xviii, Figure 4, from the Baldwin Spencer Photographic Collection. Photograph courtesy of the Museum of Victoria Council, Melbourne, Australia.

Page 2, Figure 5, illustration by Ray Rue.

Page 3, Figure 6, from the Baldwin Spencer Photographic Collection. Photograph courtesy of the Museum of Victoria Council, Melbourne, Australia.

Page 4, Figure 7, illustration by Ray Rue.

Page 5, Figure 8, from the Baldwin Spencer Photographic Collection. Photograph courtesy of the Museum of Victoria Council, Melbourne, Australia.

Pages 6 & 7, Figure 9, from the Baldwin Spencer Photographic Collection. Photograph courtesy of the Museum of Victoria Council, Melbourne, Australia.

Page 8, Figure 10, detail of a photograph from the Baldwin Spencer Photographic Collection. Photograph courtesy of the Museum of Victoria Council, Melbourne, Australia.

Page 10, Figure 11, photograph by Ehud C. Sperling

Page 12, Figure 12, *Wandjina*, artist unknown, Kimberly, W.A., photo by Jennifer Steele. Reproduced with permission of Aboriginal Artists Agency, North Sydney, Australia.

Page 14, Figure 13, photograph courtesy of Peter Carrigan, Australian News and Information Photographic Library, Australian Consulate General, New York.

Page 15, Figure 14, photograph courtesy of Peter Carrigan, Australian News and Information Photographic Library, Australian Consulate General, New York.

Page 16, Figure 15, illustration by Ray Rue.

Page 24, Figure 16, *Survival*, illustration by John Hickey, courtesy of NW Ayer Inc., New York, © NW Ayer Inc. 1989.

Page 25, Figure 17, illustration by Randi Jinkins.

Page 25, Figure 18, illustration by Bonnie Atwater.

Page 26, Figure 19, illustration by Randi Jinkins.

Page 27, Figure 20, Neg. No. 2A9531, courtesy of the Department of Library Services, American Museum of Natural History, New York.

Page 28, Figure 21, map by Alex Wallach and Virginia Scott.

Page 29, Figure 22, Neg. No. 333504, photo by R. A. Gould, courtesy of the Department of Library Services, American Museum of Natural History, New York.

Pages 30 & 31, Figure 23, illustration by Bonnie Atwater after an illustration from *The New Biology*, by Robert Augros and George Stanciu.

Page 31, Figure 24, illustration by Randi Jinkins.

Page 32, Figure 25, illustration by Randi Jinkins.

Page 35, Figure 26, illustration by Ray Rue.

Page 35, Figure 27, illustration from *The Aboriginal People of Tasmania* by Julia Clark, © 1986, Tasmanian Museum and Art Gallery, Tasmania.

Page 37, Figure 28, Neg. No. 332926, photo by R. A. Gould, courtesy of the Department of Library Services, American Museum of Natural History, New York.

Page 38, Figure 29, illustration by Randi Jinkins.

Page 39, Figure 30, *Rainbow Snake Borlung*, by Bargudubu, Arnhem Land, N.T. Ochre on bark. Reproduced with permission of Aboriginal Artists Agency, North Sydney, Australia.

Page 40, Figure 31, photograph by H. Frauca, courtesy of Peter Carrigan, Australian News and Information Photographic Library, Australian Consulate General, New York.

Page 45, Figure 32, photograph courtesy of Peter Carrigan, Australian News and Information Photographic Library, Australian Consulate General, New York.

Page 46, Figure 33, *Kangaroo Dreaming*, 1988, by Hiliary Tjapaltjarri. Papunya, Western Desert, N.T. Courtesy of The Australia Gallery, New York; reproduced with permission of the Aboriginal Artists Agency, North Sydney, Australia.

Pages 48 & 49, Figure 34, illustration by Bonnie Atwater after carvings of the Dreamtime history of the honey ants.

Pages 52 & 53, Figure 35, Neg. No. 298402, courtesy of the Department of Library Services, American Museum of Natural History, New York.

Page 60, Figure 36, from the Baldwin Spencer Photographic Collection. Photograph courtesy of the Museum of Victoria Council, Melbourne, Australia.

Page 62, Figure 37, Neg. No. 334013, photo by Kota, courtesy of the Department of Library Services, American Museum of Natural History, New York.

Page 63, Figure 38, from the Baldwin Spencer Photographic Collection. Photograph courtesy of the Museum of Victoria Council, Melbourne, Australia.

Page 64, Figure 39, from the Baldwin Spencer Photographic Collection. Photograph courtesy of the Museum of Victoria Council, Melbourne, Australia.

Page 66, Figure 40, illustration by Bonnie Atwater.

Page 72, Figure 41, from the journal of the voyage of Captain Cook, a collection of engravings, courtesy of Jonathan Cohen. Photo by David Garten.

Page 73, Figure 42, from the journal of the voyage of Captain Cook, a collection of engravings, courtesy of Jonathan Cohen. Photo by David Garten.

Page 75, Figure 43, Neg. No. 298397, courtesy of the Department of Library Services, American Museum of Natural History, New York.

Page 76, Figure 44, illustration by Ray Rue.

Page 77, Figure 45, illustration from *The Aboriginal People of Tasmania* by Julia Clark, © 1986, Tasmanian Museum and Art Gallery, Tasmania.

Page 78, Figure 46, Neg. No. 324829, photo by J. W. Beattie, courtesy of the Department of Library Services, American Museum of Natural History, New York.

Page 79, Figure 47, illustrations from *The Aboriginal People of Tasmania* by Julia Clark, © 1986, Tasmanian Museum and Art Gallery.

Page 80, Figure 48, from the journal of the voyage of Captain Cook, a collection of engravings, courtesy of Jonathan Cohen. Photo by David Garten.

Page 81, Figure 49, from the Baldwin Spencer Photographic Collection. Photograph courtesy of the Museum of Victoria Council, Melbourne, Australia.

Page 82, Figure 50, map by Alex Wallach and Virginia Scott.

Page 82, Figure 51, illustration by Ray Rue.

Page 84, Figure 52, illustration by Bonnie Atwater.

Page 85, Figure 53, illustration from *The Aboriginal People of Tasmania* by Julia Clark, © 1986, Tasmanian Museum and Art Gallery, Tasmania.

Page 92, Figure 54, illustrations by Bonnie Atwater.

Page 93, Figure 55, map by Alex Wallach and Virginia Scott.

Page 94, Figure 56, illustration by Bonnie Atwater.

Page 95, Figure 57, illustration by Bonnie Atwater.

Page 95, Figure 58, illustration by Randi Jinkins.

Page 96, Figure 59, illustration by Bonnie Atwater.

Page 97, Figure 60, illustration by Robert Yerks.

Page 97, Figure 61, illustration by Bonnie Atwater.

Page 100, Figure 62, illustration by Virginia Scott.

Page 102, Figure 63, illustration by Ray Rue.

Page 103, Figure 64, illustration by Bonnie Atwater.

Page 104, Figure 65, illustration by Randi Jinkins.

Page 104, Figure 66, Figure 53, illustration from *The Aboriginal People of Tasmania* by Julia Clark, © 1986, Tasmanian Museum and Art Gallery, Tasmania.

Page 105, Figure 67, illustration by Penny Slinger from *Sexual Secrets*, by Nik Douglas and Penny Slinger, Destiny Books, Rochester, Vermont. © 1979, Nik Douglas and Penny Slinger.

Page 106, Figure 68, illustration by Bonnie Atwater.

Page 108, Figure 69, courtesy of the Department of Library Services, American Museum of Natural History, New York.

Page 109, Figure 70, illustration by Robert Yerks.

Page 110, Figure 71, Neg. No. 330835, photo by A. P. Elkin, courtesy of the Department of Library Services, American Museum of Natural History, New York.

Page 111, Figure 72, Neg. No. 128402, courtesy of the Department of Library Services, American Museum of Natural History, New York.

Page 112, Figure 73, *Giant Rainbow Serpent*, 1985, by John Mawundjal. Gunwinggu; Oenpelli, Arnhem Land, N.T. Ochres on bark. Courtesy of The Australia Gallery, New York; reproduced with permission of the Aboriginal Artists Agency, North Sydney, Australia.

Page 115, Figure 74, illustration by Ray Rue with Randi Jinkins and Virginia Scott.

Page 116, Figure 75, illustration from *Sacred Science*, by R. A. Schwaller de Lubicz, © 1982, Inner Traditions International, Rochester, Vermont.

Page 117, Figure 76, illustration by Lucie Lamy.

Page 118, Figure 77, *Yawk Yawk—Female Freshwater Spirit*, 1988, by John Dalna Dalna, Kunwinjku Language, Nangalord Outstation, via Maningrida, Central Arnhem Land, N.T. Courtesy of The Australia Gallery, New York; reproduced with permission of Maningrida Arts & Crafts, Winnellie, N.T. Australia.

Page 120, Figure 78, from the Baldwin Spencer Photographic Collection. Photograph courtesy of the Museum of Victoria Council, Melbourne, Australia.

Page 121, Figure 79, illustration by Bonnie Atwater.

Page 122, Figure 80, *40,000 Years Awakening*, four-panel mural, oil on canvas, by Terry Shewring, Fora Centre, Redfern, N.S.W., Australia.

Page 124, Figure 81, illustration by Ray Rue.

Page 126, Figure 82, map by Alex Wallach and Virginia Scott.

Page 126, Figure 83, map by Alex Wallach and Virginia Scott.

Page 128, Figure 84, *Fire Dreaming at Tarkulnga*, 1988, by George Tjapaltjarri. Courtesy of The Australia Gallery, New York; reproduced with permission of the Aboriginal Artists Agency, North Sydney, Australia.

Page 131, Figure 85, map by Alex Wallach and Virginia Scott.

Page 136, Figure 86, illustration by Bonnie Atwater.

Page 138, Figure 87, *Human Forefathers*, 1911, tempera on canvas, by Nicholas Roerich from *Nicholas Roerich: The Life and Art of a Russian Master*, by Jaqueline Decter with the Nicholas Roerich Museum, © 1989, Park Street Press, Rochester, Vermont.

Page 145, Figure 88, illustration by Virginia Scott.

Page 150, Figure 89, from the Baldwin Spencer Photographic Collection. Photograph courtesy of the Museum of Victoria Council, Melbourne, Australia.

Page 152, Figure 90, photograph by Philip Quirk, courtesy of Wildlight Photo Agency, New South Wales, Australia.

Page 157, Figure 91, illustration by Ray Rue.

Page 161, Figure 92, photograph by Peter Solness, courtesy of Wildlight Photo Agency, New South Wales, Australia.

Page 163, Figure 93, from the Baldwin Spencer Photographic Collection. Photograph courtesy of the Museum of Victoria Council, Melbourne, Australia.

Page 164, Figure 94, photograph by Carolyn Johns, courtesy of Wildlight Photo Agency, New South Wales, Australia.

Page 165, Figure 95, illustration by Ray Rue.

Page 167, Figure 96, from the Baldwin Spencer Photographic Collection. Photograph courtesy of the Museum of Victoria Council, Melbourne, Australia.

Page 174, Figure 97, photograph by Philip Quirk, courtesy of Wildlight Photo Agency, New South Wales, Australia.

Page 175, Figure 98, from the Baldwin Spencer Photographic Collection. Photograph courtesy of the Museum of Victoria Council, Melbourne, Australia.

Page 178, Figure 99, illustration by Randi Jinkins.

Page 179, Figure 100, illustration by Bonnie Atwater.

Page 180, Figure 101, from the Baldwin Spencer Photographic Collection. Photograph courtesy of the Museum of Victoria Council, Melbourne, Australia.

Page 181, Figure 102, Neg. No. 2A9536, courtesy of the Department of Library Services, American Museum of Natural History, New York.

Page 182, Figure 103, from the Baldwin Spencer Photographic Collection. Photograph courtesy of the Museum of Victoria Council, Melbourne, Australia.

Page 187, Figure 104, Neg. No. 298404, courtesy of the Department of Library Services, American Museum of Natural History, New York.

Page 188, Figure 105, from the Baldwin Spencer Photographic Collection. Photograph courtesy of the Museum of Victoria Council, Melbourne, Australia.

Page 191, Figure 106, illustration by Bonnie Atwater after an illustration from *The Mardudjara Aborigines*, by Robert Tonkinson.

Page 196, Figure 107, from the Baldwin Spencer Photographic Collection. Photograph courtesy of the Museum of Victoria Council, Melbourne, Australia.

Page 197, Figure 108, from the Baldwin Spencer Photographic Collection. Photograph courtesy of the Museum of Victoria Council, Melbourne, Australia.

Page 199, Figure 109, Neg. No. 2A9511, courtesy of the Department of Library Services, American Museum of Natural History, New York.

Page 203, Figure 110, illustration by Ray Rue.

Page 204, Figure 111, illustration by Ray Rue.

Page 207, Figure 112, illustration by Ray Rue.

Page 210, Figure 113, photograph courtesy of the Aboriginal Arts Board, Australian Consulate General, New York.

Page 211, Figure 114, illustration by Randi Jinkins.

Page 212, Figure 115, illustration by Bonnie Atwater after an illustration from *The Australian Aborigines*, by Kenneth Maddock.

Page 214, Figure 116, illustration by Ray Rue.

Page 217, Figure 117, from the Baldwin Spencer Photographic Collection. Photograph courtesy of the Museum of Victoria Council, Melbourne, Australia.

Page 218, Figure 118, illustration by Ray Rue.

Pages 222 & 223, Figure 119, *Nawalberd & his Four Wives*, 1988, by Dick Ngulei Ngulei Muru Muru, courtesy of Kate Flynn.

Page 225, Figure 120, photograph courtesy of Peter Carrigan, Australian News and Information Photographic Library, Australian Consulate General, New York.

Page 227, Figure 121, Neg. No. 333471, courtesy of the Department of Library Services, American Museum of Natural History, New York.

Pages 238 & 239, Figure 122, from the Baldwin Spencer Photographic Collection. Photograph courtesy of the Museum of Victoria Council, Melbourne, Australia.

Page 245, Figure 123, illustration by Randi Jinkins.

Page 248, Figure 124, illustration by Harish Johari

from *Tools for Tantra*, by Harish Johari, © 1986, Destiny Books, Rochester, Vermont.

Page 249, Figure 125, photograph by Mike Brown, courtesy of Peter Carrigan, Australian News and Information Photographic Library, Australian Consulate General, New York.

Page 250, Figure 126, from the Baldwin Spencer Photographic Collection. Photograph courtesy of the Museum of Victoria Council, Melbourne, Australia.

Pages 254 & 255, Figure 127, courtesy of The Australia Gallery, New York.

Page 256, Figure 128, illustration by Ray Rue.

Page 257, Figure 129, Neg. No. 334011, photo by Kota, courtesy of the Department of Library Services, American Museum of Natural History, New York.

Pages 258 & 259, Figure 130, from the Baldwin Spencer Photographic Collection. Photograph courtesy of the Museum of Victoria Council, Melbourne, Australia.

Page 261, Figure 131, illustration by Bonnie Atwater after a photograph by Alex Ozolins, courtesy of Peter Carrigan, Australian News and Information Photographic Library, Australian Consulate General, New York.

Page 262, Figure 132, illustration by Ray Rue.

Page 265, Figure 133, photograph courtesy of Peter Carrigan, Australian News and Information Photographic Library, Australian Consulate General, New York.

Page 269, Figure 134, illustration by Bonnie Atwater.

Page 270, Figure 135, illustration by Randi Jinkins.

Page 271, Figure 136, illustration by Robert Yerks.

Page 276, Figure 137, *Sacred Kingfish Totem*, 1987, by Baluka Maymura. Natural ochres on wood carving. Courtesy of The Australia Gallery, New York.

Page 281, Figure 138, photograph by Alex Ozolins, courtesy of Peter Carrigan, Australian News and Information Photographic Library, Australian Consulate General, New York.

Page 282, Figure 139, Neg. No. 2A9282, photo by A. P. Elkin, courtesy of the Department of Library Services, American Museum of Natural History, New York.

Page 283, Figure 140, from the Baldwin Spencer Photographic Collection. Photograph courtesy of the Museum of Victoria Council, Melbourne, Australia.

Page 286, Figure 141, *Rainbow Serpent and Witchetty Grub Dreaming*, 1988, by Mary Dixon Nungurrayi. Warlpiri; Mt. Leibig. Acrylic on canvas. Courtesy of The Australia Gallery, New York; reproduced with permission of the Aboriginal Artists Agency, North Sydney, Australia.

Page 287, Figure 142, illustration by Ray Rue.

Page 288, Figure 143, Neg. No. 2A9528, courtesy of the Department of Library Services, American Museum of Natural History, New York.

Page 290, Figure 144, Didgeridoos, from *Aboriginal Art*, by Frank Norton, © 1975, The Art Gallery of Western Australia.

Page 291, Figure 145, photograph by Alex Ozolins, courtesy of Peter Carrigan, Australian News and Information Photographic Library, Australian Consulate General, New York.

Page 292, Figure 146, illustration from *Rebel in the Soul*, by Bika Reed, © 1978, Inner Traditions International, Rochester, Vermont.

Page 294, Figure 147, photograph courtesy of Peter Carrigan, Australian News and Information Photographic Library, Australian Consulate General, New York.

Page 295, Figure 148, illustration by Ray Rue.

Page 295, Figure 149, illustration by Bonnie Atwater.

Page 296, Figure 150, photograph courtesy of Peter Carrigan, Australian News and Information Photographic Library, Australian Consulate General, New York.

Page 297, Figure 151, illustration by Ray Rue.

Page 300, Figure 152, from the Baldwin Spencer Photographic Collection. Photograph courtesy of the Museum of Victoria Council, Melbourne, Australia.

Page 301, Figure 153, from the Baldwin Spencer Photographic Collection. Photograph courtesy of the Museum of Victoria Council, Melbourne, Australia.

Page 303, Figure 154, photograph by Oliver Strewe, courtesy of Wildlight Photo Agency, New South Wales, Australia.

Page 304, Figure 155, illustration by Ray Rue.

Page 305, Figure 156, illustration by Ray Rue.

Pages 306 & 307, Figure 157, based on a photograph by Alex Ozolins, courtesy of Peter Carrigan, Australian News and Information Photographic Library, Australian Consulate General, New York.

Page 308, Figure 158, illustration by Ray Rue.

Page 309, Figure 159, illustration by Ray Rue.

Page 311, Figure 160, illustration by Ray Rue.

Page 318, Figure 161, illustration of *Bufo marinus*, by Terence Shortt, from *The Book of the Toad* by Robert M. De Graaff, © 1991, Park Street Press, Rochester, Vermont.

Page 319, Figure 162, Neg. No. 128397, courtesy of the Department of Library Services, American Museum of Natural History, New York.

Page 320, Figure 163, Neg. No. 128398, courtesy of the Department of Library Services, American Museum of Natural History, New York.

Page 320, Figure 164, illustration by Robert Yerks.

Page 321, Figure 165, illustration by Randi Jinkins.

Page 321, Figure 166, illustration by Randi Jinkins.

Page 323, Figure 167, illustration by Robert Yerks.

Page 329, Figure 168, illustration by Robert Yerks.

Page 331, Figure 169, illustration from Cesariano's Edition of Vitruvius.

Page 332, Figure 170, illustration by Lucie Lamy from *Her-Bak: Egyptian Initiate*, by Isha Schwaller de Lubicz, © 1978, Inner Traditions International, Rochester, Vermont.

Page 333, Figure 171, illustration by Lucie Lamy.

Page 336, Figure 172, courtesy of the Department

of Library Services, American Museum of Natural History, New York.

Page 336, Figure 173, illustration by Virginia Scott after *Scientific American*.

Page 337, Figure 174, from an eighteenth-century engraving by Le Brun.

Page 338, Figure 175, photograph by Philip Quirk, courtesy of Wildlight Photo Agency, New South Wales, Australia.

Page 340, Figure 176, Aboriginal bark painting, photograph courtesy of Peter Carrigan, Australian News and Information Photographic Library, Australian Consulate General, New York.

Page 344, Figure 177, illustration by Ray Rue.

Page 345, Figure 178, photograph by Mike Brown, courtesy of Peter Carrigan, Australian News and Information Photographic Library, Australian Consulate General, New York.

Page 345, Figure 179, illustration by Randi Jinkins.

Page 347, Figure 180, illustration by Robert Yerks.

Page 352, Figure 181, from the Baldwin Spencer Photographic Collection. Photograph courtesy of the Museum of Victoria Council, Melbourne, Australia.

Page 353, Figure 182, illustration by Albert Dürer from Dante's *Inferno*.

Page 356, Figure 183, Neg. No. 330823, courtesy of the Department of Library Services, American Museum of Natural History, New York.

Page 359, Figure 184, Neg. No. 2A9525, courtesy of the Department of Library Services, American Museum of Natural History, New York.

Page 361, Figure 185, from the Baldwin Spencer Photographic Collection. Photograph courtesy of the Museum of Victoria Council, Melbourne, Australia.

Page 366, Figure 186, photograph courtesy of Peter Carrigan, Australian News and Information Photographic Library, Australian Consulate General, New York.

Page 370, Figure 187, from the Baldwin Spencer Photographic Collection. Photograph courtesy of the Museum of Victoria Council, Melbourne, Australia.

Page 372, Figure 188, illustration by Penny Slinger, based on a Gujarat miniature painting of the late seventeenth century, from *Sexual Secrets*, by Nik Douglas and Penny Slinger, Destiny Books, Rochester, Vermont. © 1979, Nik Douglas and Penny Slinger.

Page 377, Figure 189, illustration from *Temple in Man*, by R. A. Schwaller de Lubicz, © 1977, Inner Traditions International, Rochester, Vermont.

Page 377, Figure 190, illustration from *Temple in Man*, by R. A. Schwaller de Lubicz, © 1977, Inner Traditions International, Rochester, Vermont.

Page 377, Figure 191, Neg. No. 128401, courtesy of the Department of Library Services, American Museum of Natural History, New York.

Page 379, Figure 192, illustration by Randi Jinkins.

Page 380, Figure 193, from the Baldwin Spencer Photographic Collection. Photograph courtesy of the Museum of Victoria Council, Melbourne, Australia.

Page 388, Figure 194, illustration from *Sacred Science*, by R. A. Schwaller de Lubicz, © 1982, Inner Traditions International, Rochester, Vermont.

Page 389, Figure 195, illustration from Museum of Paris Bulletin, from *Sacred Science*, by R. A. Schwaller de Lubicz, © 1982, Inner Traditions International, Rochester, Vermont.

Page 390, Figure 196, *Mimi & Snake*, by Nyiminyuma, Arnhem Land, N.T. Ochre on bark. Reproduced with permission of the Aboriginal Artists Agency, North Sydney, Australia.

INDEX

Aborigines
    Australian attitudes toward, 2–3
    communication habits of, 166
    cosmology of, 45–47, 71, 76,
        87, 100, 109–111, 121–122,
        328–333, 336
    culture as primary activity, 65
    directional sense of, 105–106
    and environment, 3–4, 74
    integrated life of, 151, 251,
        346–349
    land rights and, 138–139
    metaphysical concepts of,
        235–241
    psychophysical powers of,
        369–373
    racial characteristics of, 30
    skin color beliefs of, 158
    Tasmanian, see Tasmania
    thought processes of, 267–271,
        314–317, 319–323, 325–327
    world view of, 1, 14–18, 26–27
    vs. empiricism, 33–34
African-American culture, 143
African genesis theory, 25–26
Agriculture, 5–6, 55–57, 140, 147,
    163
    vs. hunting-gathering, 59–65,
        124–125, 133, 311–312
    rejection by Aborigines, 59–61
    and warfare, 55, 144
Akh, 333, 345
Alchemy, medieval, 234
Al-Ghazzali, 321
Ancestors, Dreamtime, 14–15, 45,
    87, 114–115, 236, 291, 307,
    328–333
Animals, see also Totemism
    in conception of child, 161–162
    in Dreaming, 15–17
Animism, 328–333, see also
    Totemism
Anpu, 305
Antarctica, atmospheric hole in,
    149
Anubis, 332–333
Archaic consciousness, 6–8, 69
Archetype(s)
    fourfold patterns in, 32
    marsupials as, 30

Architecture, 61, 140, 228
Arguelles, José, 97
Aristobolus, 71
Aristotle, 34
Arjuna, 259
Art, 285–299, see also Bark
        paintings, Rock carvings,
        Rock paintings, X-ray
        paintings
Ash, David, 123
Augros, Robert M., 23, 24
Australia
    attitude toward aborigines in, 2–3
    author's experiences in, 10–11
    colonization of, 51, 137, 172
Australian genesis theory, 25–20,
    85–86
Avoidance, in kinship system, 226,
    244–245
Ayer's Rock, 160–161, 368

Ba, 333–334, 345
Bacon, Francis, 19, 58
Baker, Robin, 376
Bands, 282–283
Bark paintings, 381
    Ancestors fishing, 340
    facing x-ray kangaroos figures,
        281
    Fire Dreaming, 128
    Giant Rainbow Serpent, 112
    goanna track, 296
    grouper fish and shark, 291
    Kangaroo Dreaming, 46
    Mimi & Snake, 390
    Namangawarri—Salt Water
        Crocodile, front cover
    Nawalberd & his Four Wives,
        222–223
    Rainbow Snake Borlung, 39
    Wandjina, 12
    Yawk Yawk—Female Freshwater
        Spirit, 118
Barnwell, F. H., 105
Barung, Albert, 8
Bateson, Gregory, 42–43
Becker, Robert, 94, 129,
    377–378
Bell, Diane, 200
Bellamy, David, 84

Bergier, 132
Bernal, Martin, 132
Berndt, Catherine, 309
Berndt, Ronald, 201, 209, 311
Bestowal, 212–215
Betrothal, 194, 212–213
Beyond Supernature (Watson), 292
Bhagavad Gita, 259
Birth, see Childbirth
Biomagnetism, 377–381, see also
    Magnetism
Blood, 141, 334–335
    in Aboriginal ritual, 102–103,
        186–187, 194, 254
    and earth magnetism, 100–105
    and Rainbow Serpent, 115
Blood relatives, 211–212
Bly, Robert, 181–182, 187
Body decoration, 187–188,
    203–205, 287–288, 344
Body scarring, 198, 199, 207
Book of the Dead (Egyptian), 305
Bone-pointing, 356–357
Boundaries, 274–275, 279
Brown, F. A., 105
Buddha, Guatama, 233
Buddhism, 69, 258–259, 343–344
    individuality in, 232, 233–234
Burial, 354–355, 360–361
Bush, George, 147

Campbell, Joseph, 74, 132, 189
Canaanites, 197
Capitalism, 59
Chatwin, Bruce, 337
Cherfas, 25
Cherubino, Fra, 221
Child(ren)
    bodily functions of, 169
    care of, 165–166, 176–177, 247
    discipline of, 169–170
    emotional expression by,
        170–172
    role in Aboriginal society, 163
    sexuality of, 173–176
Child abuse, in West, 170, 173
Childbirth, 156–159
Christ, 19, 208
Christianity, 19–20, 57–58, 64,
    69, 191, 195, 209, 211, 264

ethical principles in, 323
individuality in, 232, 233–234
monogamy, 220
soul in, 333, 334
Churchward, James, 127
Circumcision, 190–192, 212
Circumpolar cults, 132
Civilization
  and continental drift, 96
  shadow side of, 140–142
Clans, 280
Clothing, 61, 83, 140
Cold, Tasmanian Aborigines and,
  83–84
Coleridge, Samuel Taylor, 148
Colonization, 54–59, 145–146
  of Australia, 51, 137, 172
  characteristics of, 54–55
  and indigenous peoples, 62,
  143
  of Tasmania, 79, 85
Compassion, importance of,
  246–248
Conflict, 55
  ritualization of, 253–258
Conquest, vs. colonization, 54
Consciousness, 36–40, 59, 71
Continental drift, 92–93, 96
Cook, Captain James, xiv, 83, 70,
  247
Coon, Carleton, 28, 30
Copernicus, Nicholas, 19
Consciousness, in Aboriginal
  culture, 41–43
Corroborree, 248
Creation
  and Dreamtime, 45–50, 123,
  328–333
  initiatic rituals of, 107–108
Creation story, 120
  Aboriginal, 14–18, 26–27,
  36–41, 45–50
  Darwinian, 18–20
  Egyptian, 48, 116–117
Crystals, 40–41, 374–378
Culture, 144
  African-American, 143
  and Aborigines, 65, 84–85,
  138–139
  modes of, 142–144
  northern vs. southern,
  129–130
Cyclic activity
  of earth, 91–94
  of seeds, 135–137, 138–139

Dance, 47–48, 280–282, *See also*
  Ecstatic ritual
Darwin, Charles, 18, 19
Darwinism, 4, 18–22, 26, 67, 76,
  317, *see also* Neo-Darwinism
da Vinci, Leonardo, 76
Davis, Albert Roy, 99
Dead, realm of, 179, 240
Death, 178, 341–345, 349–355
  grieving in, 249–251
  and sorcery, 355–357

Death and rebirth, in initiation,
  185–186
de Bono, Edward, 324–325, 327
Defloration, 205
de Gourmont, Remy, 148
Democracy, 147
Descartes, René, 19, 22, 34, 307
Diamond, Jared, 60, 68
Dionysian rites, 192, 334
Disputes, settlement of,
  253–258
Divorce, 224–225
DNA, 21, 22, 25–26
Dot paintings, 285, 381
  Bush Tucker Dreaming, xv
  Fire Dreaming, 128
  Kangaroo Dreaming, 46
  *Rainbow Serpent and Witchetty
  Grub Dreaming*, 286
Dravidians, compared with
  Tasmanians, 120–122
Dreaming, 1–2
  and creation, 45–50, 123
  and death, 349–355
  and magnetism, 101–102
  vs. physical world, 266–272
  and world future, 386–391
Dreamtime, 14–18, 33, 36–41,
  264–265, 328–333
  and earth cycles, 96
  landscape in, 42–43, 236–237,
  261–263
  rebirth of, 385
Dreamtime Ancestors, *see*
  Ancestors
Dreamtime consciousness,
  381–385
Dreamtime Law, 49, 77, 86, 257,
  260
Dreamtime legends
  black swans, 365–368
  Chicken Hawk steals fire,
  300–302
  colonization predicted, 51
  courtship, 219
  death, 342–343
  frog heralds, 313–314
  Goola-willeel, the topknot
  pigeon, 278–279
  how the sun was made, 44–45
  landscape formation, 261–263
  quartz tools, 35–36
  Rainbow Serpent, 113–114,
  119–120
  Southern Cross, 68–69
  Sun Mother, 88
  trickster and girl, 202–203

Earth, *see also* Mother Earth
  ecstatic ritual and, 106–109
  as living organism, 89–94
  magnetism of, *see*
  Geomagnetism
  rhythms of, 90–94, 96
  and sexuality, 209–210, 229
Ecstatic ritual, 106–109, 117,
  304, 381, *see also* Dance

Egypt, 86, 96, 104, 228, 371
  creation myth of, 48, 116–117
  religion in, 74–75, 305, 333, 376
Electromagnetic pollution,
  129–130
Eliot, T. S., 9
Elkin, A. P., 369, 371, 374
Emotional expression, 170–172,
  244–246, 248–249
Empiricism, vs. Aboriginal
  culture, 33–34
Energy, and revelation, 71
Energy fields, 46, 379–380
Engels, Friedrich, 146
Environment, 9
  aborigines and, 3–4, 65, 90
  destruction of, 34, 38–40,
  62–64, 149–151, 241
  restoration of, 312, 386–387
Eroticism, *see* Sexuality
Evens-Wentz, W. Y., 372
Evolution, 18–23
  earth magnetism and, 94–95
  genetic, 21–22
  patterned activity in, 32
Existence, three realms of, 179,
  180–184, 240
Extrasensory powers, 221–224

"Fall" from paradise, in Golden
  Age myths, 71–72
Feather-foot attacks, 255–256
Female initiation, 202–207, 212
Fertility
  Aboriginal concepts of,
  162–163
  Rainbow Serpent and, 119
Fertility ritual, 226
Fire
  in childbirth, 156–157
  in hunting, 311
  Tasmanian Aborigines and,
  80–81, 86
Fire ceremony, 226–227
First Day, 74, 77, 122
Fish, scale, Tasmanian
  Aborigines and, 79–80
Food-gathering practices,
  308–311
Fourfoldness, as archetype,
  31–32
Franklin, Benjamin, 146
Freud, Sigmund, 148, 346
Frobenius, 29, 91

Gaia concept, 90, 150–151
Genesis theories, African vs.
  Australian, 25–30
Geomagnetism, 93, 94–100,
  97–106, 125, 127–120
  and Rainbow Serpent, 119
  reversals in, 131–134
Geomancy, 104–105
Gilbert, William, 106
Glaciation cycles, 92–93
Gnosticism, 57, 195, 233
God, 56

Golden Age, 69–77, 139
  hunter-gatherers and, 71–72
  and Tasmanian Aborigines, 77
Gondwanaland, 93, 127
Gorbachev, Mikhail, 147
Grief, 249–251, 351–352

Hammurabi, 198
Harney, Bill, 368–369
Harvalik, Zaboj, 100
Hathor, 117–118, 305, 332–333
Heredity, 333–335
Hermes, 345
Heroic myth, journey in, 189
Hesiod, 69
Hewitt, Peter, 123
Highwater, Jamake, 306
Hinduism, 69, 75–76, 230,
    258–259, 264, 343–344, 369
  and glaciation cycles, 92
Hitler, Adolf, 170
Horus, 332–333
Hoyle, Fred, 24, 103
Humans, in Dreaming, 15–17
Hunting-gathering, 8–9, 48,
    55–56, 59–61, 142–143, 146,
    386, 302–307, 315
  vs. agriculture, 59–65,
    124–125, 133, 311–312
  psychic effect of loss, 373
Hussein, Saddam, 200, 353, 384
Hyperesthesia, 381

I Am Right, You Are Wrong (de
    Bono), 324
Ice age(s), 83–84, 92–93
I Ching, 21–22
Imagery, 285–299
Increase rites, male, 180, 194
India
  author's experiences in, 9–10
  creation myth of, 48
  Tantric Sadhus in, 77
Indigenous peoples, 89, 105–106,
    314–315
  colonization and, 62, 143,
    147–149
  Dravidian compared with
    Tasmanian, 120–122
  and integrated perception,
    133
Individuality, in Western
    civilization, 232–235
Initiatic death, 358–360
Iniatic wound, 197
Initiation, 178–179, 207–208, see
    also Female initiation, Male
    initiation
  advanced, 194–200, 236–237,
    370–371
  death as, 349–350, 358–360,
    362–363
Iron, 100–105, 141
Iron John (Bly), 181–182, 187
Isaacs, Jennifer, 88
Islam, 206, 211, 234
  ethical principles of, 323

Italian Renaissance, 58

Jainism, 233
Jefferies, Thomas, 70–71
Jefferson, Thomas, 146
Joking, in kinship system, 244–245
Jones, Rhys, 61
Judaism, 55–57, 69, 233
Judeo-Christian tradition, 55–59,
    206
Jung, Carl, 1, 74, 104, 148, 346,
    348, 365, 385
Jungian psychology, 148, 264,
    272, 273

Ka, 333, 345, 360
Kali, 76
Kangeroo, as maternal role
    model, 164–165
Kepler, Johannes, 19
Kinship systems, 242–244
  avoidance in, 226
  behavior patterns in, 244–246
  and death, 351–355
  and food, 309–310
  instruction of child in,
    166–167, 173
  and marriage, 211–215, 219
  and psychophysical powers,
    369–370
  reciprocity and, 251–253
Kha, 333
Khnum, 332–333
Koch, Robert, 293
Kolosimo, Peter, 132
Krishna, 259
Kundalini, 372

Ladder mentality, in Darwinism,
    18–19
Land
  in Dreaming, 15–17, 42–43
  and marriage, 220
  and sexuality, 220
Language, 22, 267–268, 315
Lawlor, Robert, 9–11, 126–127,
    411–412
Lawrence, D. H., 139, 334
Levi-Strauss, Claude, 242, 314
Ley lines, 104–105
Life, biological, and earth
    magnetism, 97–98, 105, 125
Living and dying, realm of, 179,
    240
Lotus symbolism, 388–389
"Love magic," 222
Lovelock, James, 150–151

Maddock, Kenneth, 113
Magnetism, 93, 94–109, see also
    Biomagnetism
Male initiation, 179–202
  advanced, 194–200, 236–237
  women's role in, 185–186, 190,
    193, 200–202
  responsibility for spirit child, 160
Mann, Felix, 317–318

Mao Ze-Dong, 353
Marais, Eugene, 381
Marriage, 215–221
  and extramarital affairs,
    221–224, 229–231
  and kinship system, 211–215
  and land, 220
Marsupials, 30, 165, 280
Marx, Karl, 146
Mary, Virgin, 220
Masculine energy, and realms of
    existence, 179–184
Mayan cosmology, 97
Meditation, 361–362
Men
  art of, 286–287
  food-gathering practices of,
    309–310
  of high degree, 354, 371
  and marriage, 215–221
Menstruation, 205, 206, 213
Metallurgy, 140–141
Michell, John, 104
Mimi spirits, 222–223, 390
Mind
  and earth magnetism, 97–98,
    105
  vs. matter, 346–349
Mind-body relationship, 224
Moieties, 283–284
Monogamy, serial, 216–219
Monsoon ritual, 226, 228–229
Montu, 332–333
Morrison, Jim, 89
Mother Earth, 56
Mu, lost world of, 127
Munn, Henry, 297–298
Music, 290–291, see also
    Songlines, Songs
Mutations, 22–26, 95
Myers, Fred, 244
Mysticism, Aboriginal vs.
    Western, 321–324
Myth(s)
  historical importance of, 127
  serpent Dreaming, 115–119

Nabokov, Vladimir, 382
Natural selection theory, 18, 23,
    55
Neidjie, Bill, 122, 237
Neo-Darwinism, 22–23, 25, 34
New Age, 149
Newcomb, W., 55
Newton, Isaac, 19, 34, 76
North Pole, 94, 96–99, 120
Nut, 305

Objective, vs. subjective, in
    Aboriginal culture, 36–41,
    383
Oenpelli, Gunwinggu, 114
Old Melanesia, 28
Osiris, 228, 305

Paradise, in Aboriginal culture, 74
Paraviti, 230

Parkman, Francis, 54
Pauli, Wolfgang, 346, 346
Pauwels, 132
Penis-holding rite, 260
Persinger, Michael, 106–107
Phaedo (Plato), 385
Phosphenes, 295–299
Place, identity conferred by, 235–238
Plato, 358
Plutarch, 103
Polygamy, male, 216–219
Projection, 272–274
Prostitution, ritual, 230
Protestant Reformation, 58
Proust, Marcel, 382
Psyche
  integration with nature, 293
  shadow in, 148
  and songlines, 125–127
Puberty, *see* Female initiation, Male initiation

Raup, David, 23
Rainbow Serpent, 113–114, 115–120, 181, 375
Rawls, Walter C., 99
Reciprocity, 48–49, 251–258, 282–283, 302
Red ochre, 101–103, 141, 187
  and Rainbow Serpent, 115
Retaliation ceremony, 206
Revelation, 71
Revenge, clan, 255–256
Rhythm, of earth, 90–94
Rimbaud, Arthur, 148, 382
Ritual sexuality, 225–231
Rock carvings, Tasmanian, 84–85
Rock paintings, 40, 110, 210, 265, 294, 338
  spirits, 265
  turtle totem, 294
Roerich, Nicholas, 138, 139
Rose, Ronald, 369
Rousseau, Jean-Jacques, 79, 146
Rules of Marriage (Fra Cherubino), 221

Satni, 162
Savage Mind, The (Levi-Strauss), 314
Schmookler, Andrew Bard, 124
Schwaller de Lubicz, R. A., 96, 135, 377
Scientific revolution, 58–59
Seed power, 6–8, 21–22, 36, 135–137, 389
  and childbirth, 154
  and culture, 144–146, 148
Serpent, *see also* Rainbow Serpent
  in Egypt, 116–117
Sexuality
  childhood, 173–176
  and creation, 47–48
  and environment, 209–210, 220, 229
  extramarital, 221–225

ritual, 225–231
  in Western society, 176
  of women, 215
Shadow, human, 139–140, 148–149
Shamanism, 117, 132, 148, 192, 298
Sheldrake, Rupert, 19, 57
Shephard, Paul, 330
Shiva, 230
Shivite rites, 192, 228
Singh, Gurdip, 28
Sixties' culture, 89
Skin relatives, 211–212
Sleep, and Dreaming, 50
Social groupings, 279–284
Society, image and, 287–289
Songs, erotic, 223–224
Songlines, 48, 104–105, 236, 274–275
  and psyche, 125–127
Sorcery, 355–357
Soul, 344–345
  in Egyptian religion, 333
South Pole, 94, 96–99, 119, 120
Space, 41–43, 238–241
Spencer, Baldwin, 283–284, 303
Sperm child, 159–163
Spirit, 333, 344–345, 360
Spirit child, 159–163
Stanciu, George, 23, 24
Stichin, Zechaniah, 132
Subincision, 194–197, 260
Subjective, vs. objective, in Aboriginal culture, 36–41
Sufism, 321, 234
Swedenborg, Emanuel, 328
Symbolism, sacred, 289–292
Synchronic logic, 316–319
Synesthesia, 180–181, 381–384
Syron, Brian, 1–5

Tagore, Rabindranath, 64
Tantricism, 77
Taoism, 31
Tasmania
  aborigines in, 1–2, 4–5, 28, 66, 72–73, 77–87, 104, 120–122, 137
  author's experience in, 11, 127
Thigh, wounding of, 197–198
Thomas (apostle), 208
Thompson, Donald, 382
Tibetan tantricism, 234
Tibetan yoga, 369
Time, 37, 238–241
Tonkinson, Robert, 258, 259
Toad, 317–318
Tools, Tasmanian Aborigines and, 79
Totemism, 279–284, 302–307
  and advanced initiation, 374
  and animism, 328–333
  and thought processes, 314–320, 325–327
Tracking, 174–175
Trance, in initiation, 184, 192

Transformation
  in Dreamtime, 15
  and sacred art, 289–295
Transition, rites of, 178–179
Tribes, 279–280
Trickster, 345, 362
Truganini, 166
Truth, vs. Dreamtime, 266–268
Turnbull, Clive, 137

Uffen, R. J., 94
Unborn, realm of, 179, 240
Unconscious, 41–43, 384
Universal Feminine, 179, 181, 195, 373
Universal Masculine, 179, 195, 362

Van Allen belt, 109–110, 127
von Brandenstein, C. G., 321

Walker, Barbara, 195
Warfare
  agriculture and, 55, 144
  metals industry and, 141
Washington, George, 146
Watson, Lyall, 100, 292–293
Western civilization, 55–59, 154–155
  animals in, 336–337
  children in, 171–172, 173
  death in, 364
  heroism in, 272–273
  and indigenous peoples, 62, 147–149
  individuality in, 232–235
  marriage in, 221
  men in, 181–182, 185
  sexuality in, 175
Whorf, Benjamin, 130
Wiener, Norbert, 334
Wife lending, 229–230
Wigner, Eugene, 269
White, Leslie, 60
Whitefeather, Willy, 40–41
Wilson, Allan, 26
Wood-based culture, 91–92, 124
Women
  art of, 285–286
  food-gathering practices of, 308–309
  in male initiation, 185–186, 190, 193, 200–202
  and marriage, 215–221
  sexuality of, 215
  widowed, 250, 354
Worcester, John, 328
Written language, 61, 141

X–ray paintings, 261, 281, 306–307

Yahweh, 56
Yin/yang categories, vs. Aboriginal mysticism, 321–322

Zealots, 195
Zeus, 56
Zoroastrianism, 69

ABOUT THE AUTHOR

Robert Lawlor has lived in Australia for the past 13 years. His educational background includes a BSc from the State University of New York and an MFA from the Pratt Institute in New York.

Robert's youthful artistic talents were fostered by devoted working-class parents. He studied in New York's Greenwich village in the 1960s while painting and teaching. While he was still in his early twenties, his abstract work received recognition in several museum shows and was featured in *Life* magazine. His boyhood dream of becoming an artist turned into a nightmare when he and another artist were injured by toxic fumes while mixing chemicals for a polyurethane sculpture exhibition.

Disillusioned, he gave up his art and a teaching position at the Pratt Institute, and embarked on a lonely odyssey to the East. For months he traveled, accompanied by a donkey and disguised as a peasant for safety, through the remote parts of the Ural mountains in the south of Turkey. During this time he fasted on brown rice to eliminate the urethane toxins.

With an Indian friend, Robert hitchhiked through Syria, Iraq, and the Bedouin desert regions in southern Jordan. He was one of the first people in 1965 to arrive at the experimental community of Auroville in Pondicherry, South India, and in 1968 was one of the first to develop a settlement in this utopian "new age" international city. Here, for six years, he worked on reforestation of the desert, experimental architecture, and the production of fresh water algae as a new protein source. During this entire time he lived among the Tamil villagers, in thatched huts with no electricity or running water, traveling only by bicycle and bullock cart. Through close contact with the Tamils he was exposed to their ancient language and customs, which maintain some remnants of pre-Vedic matriarchal society. This Auroville-inspired combination of drawing from ancient sources, and dreaming of a new transformed world, molded all his future work.

Since his experience in India, Robert has followed his intuition and interests. Through the work of French Egyptologist R. A. Schwaller de Lubicz, he became interested in the history of ideas, particularly Pythagorean geometry. He then studied French and mathematics to work on the translations of this controversial European philosopher. This period involved him in several published translations of R. A. Schwaller de Lubicz's work, including *The Temple in Man* in 1977. Robert's first book, *Sacred Geometry*, was published in London by Thames and Hudson in 1980.

While living in France and London he also worked on the translations of Alain Daniélou, a leading Indian historian and musicologist. Robert then moved to Australia but continued to return to the United States for three or four months each year for five years to lecture at the Lindisfarne Association in Colorado and New York. With Keith Critchlow, he developed a curriculum for a school of sacred architecture based on ancient geometry, music, and cosmology. At this time they co-authored *Homage to Pythagoras* and *Geometry and Architecture*, published by Lindisfarne Press. Robert's articles also appeared in *Parabola* and *Corona*. During these years he continued to live in Tasmania, Australia, first in the foothills of its vast wilderness region and then on an island off the Tasmanian coast. For many years he grew most of his own food and used only alternative power sources.

In Robert's last book, *Earth Honoring: The New Male Sexuality*, published by Inner Traditions International, he drew on the sexual practices and myths of tribal, earth-honoring cultures to gain a perspective on the necessary deep transformation of the understanding and expression of male sexual energy. His essay on matriarchy/patriarchy, "Male Power on Earth—The Beginning and End of the Male Dominant World Order," is included in the book *Choirs of the God*, published by Mandala in 1991. Recently he has lectured at the Open Center in New York and Interface in Boston.

While living in Sydney in 1987, Robert was asked to write a documentary film script on the healing of alcoholism among the Australian Aborigines by tribal methods. The film script was based on the life experiences of Aboriginal musician and activist Bobby McLeod, with whom Robert worked closely. Much of Robert's past interaction with village people and analogical thinking already resonated with the Aboriginal culture, and from this dialogue his research and immersion into the oldest spiritual tradition on earth, that of the Australian Aborigines, began.

COLOPHON

The text mechanicals for *Voices of the First Day* were produced on the Inner Traditions in-house Macintosh typesetting system, which is composed of a Macintosh IIcx with double-page monitor and double syquest driver, a IIci with double-page color monitor and single syquest driver, an SE superdrive with double-page monitor, a Microtek MSF-300GS image scanner, and a Newgen Turbo PS/400 laser printer. All the artwork for the book was scanned into the Pagemaker files for use either as position only photographs for final cropping and sizing by the printer or as final line illustrations suitable for reproduction. All of the charts and diagrams were created on the Macintosh either in-house or by Robert Yerks of Marketing Arts in Waitsfield, Vermont.

This computerized production represents the collective efforts of Inner Traditions staff members Bonnie Atwater, Leslie Carlson, Sherwood Herben, Randi Jinkins, Jeanie Levitan, Virginia Scott, and Charlotte Tyler.

The cover and text for *Voices of the First Day* were designed by Frank Olinsky and Pat Gorman of Manhattan Design. The text is 11/14 Janson with Lithos display type and Orchard Inline initial caps.

This first edition was printed on 60# Finch Vanilla at Semline, Inc., in Westwood, Massachusetts. The cover was printed on Crystin™ Cream Suede cover stock in four-color process with spot varnish and matt film lamination by New England Book Components in Hingham, Massachusetts. The color separations were done by Pre-Press Company in Whitman, Massachusetts.

Chief Editor: Ehud C. Sperling
Managing Editor: Leslie Colket
Project Manager/Production Editor: Jeanie Levitan
Editor: Cornelia Bland Wright
Project Development: Estella Arias, Deborah Graham
Art Directors: Ehud C. Sperling, Estella Arias
Cover and Text Design: Manhattan Design
Interior Design and Layout: Bonnie Atwater
Typesetter: Randi Jinkins
Keyboarding: Joanna Lambert, Charlotte Tyler
Production Managers: Leslie Carlson, Sherwood Herben, Sean Konecky
Copyeditors/Proofreaders: Anna Congdon, Dana Goss, Joan Kocsis
Artist Renderings: Ray Rue
Computer Illustrations: Bonnie Atwater, Randi Jinkins, Robert Yerks
Maps: Alex Wallach and Virginia Scott
Photo Research: Joanna Lambert, Estella Arias, Ehud C. Sperling